A KINGDOM OF
THEIR OWN

A KINGDOM OF THEIR OWN

The Family Karzai and the Afghan Disaster

JOSHUA PARTLOW

Alfred A. Knopf   New York   2016

Library of Congress Cataloging-in-Publication Data
Names: Partlow, Joshua, author.
Title: A kingdom of their own : the family Karzai and the Afghan disaster /
Joshua Partlow.
Description: New York : Knopf, 2016.
Identifiers: LCCN 2016007281 | ISBN 9780307962645 (hardback) |
ISBN 9780307962652 (ebook)
Subjects: LCSH: Afghan War, 2001– | Afghanistan—Foreign relations—
United States. |
United States—Foreign relations—Afghanistan. | Karzai, Hamid, 1957– |
BISAC: HISTORY / Middle East / General. | POLITICAL SCIENCE /
International Relations / General.
Classification: LCC DS371.412 .P37 2016 | DDC 958.104/71—dc23 LC
record available at http://lccn.loc.gov/2016007281

Jacket photograph by Christoph Bangert / laif / Redux
Jacket design by Stephanie Ross

To Javed, Asad, and Habib

Contents

A KINGDOM OF
THEIR OWN

A RESCUE FROM DEMONS

THE VILLAGE OF KARZ sits amid grape fields in the low river valleys southeast of Kandahar, one of the last weak patches of green before the land empties into miles of flat desert browns. You can get there by the one paved road that runs down from Kandahar, a scorched outpost on the old Asian trade and conquest routes. Most of the people who live in Karz are sheepherders or peasant farmers. They irrigate their fields from generator-powered wells and dry their green grapes into raisins in mud structures perforated to let the hot wind blow through. The other business is brickmaking, and from where I stood at the entrance to the village I could see black smoke drifting sideways from the towering sand-colored kilns, adding another layer of haze to the dusty air. One thing that distinguished Karz from the countless identical mud-hut villages across southern Afghanistan was that it happened to be the ancestral home of the family of the then Afghan president, Hamid Karzai, the place from which they had taken their name. That was why I was standing exposed on that lonely country road, a foreigner sweating through his unconvincing Afghan costume of billowy brown blouse and matching pants, on the morning the president's favorite brother would be buried.

An Afghan army Humvee had parked crosswise in the road, blocking my approach. In case anyone wanted to slip past, Afghan snipers wearing wraparound shades stood on the rooftops of the roadside shops, muttering into their earpieces. On my way out of Kandahar City, I had seen American soldiers idling in their mine-resistant armored vehicles at various intersections, their Apache helicopters running slow loops overhead. They would be staying away from the ceremony this morning, in a distant cordon, and I began to think I would miss it, too. The day before,

July 12, 2011, I had left my house in Kabul, where I worked as a reporter for *The Washington Post*, and rushed to the airport when I'd learned that Ahmed Wali Karzai had been shot to death inside his home by one of his closest lieutenants. To me, he was one of the war's mythical figures, a short, scowling, anxious man who had, everyone took for granted, amassed more power and fortune than anyone else across Afghanistan's south, at the center of America's war against the Taliban. How he'd made that fortune and exercised that power was one of the mysteries that none of his American allies could fully explain. Everyone had theories: the CIA payroll, the opium trade, a private security army, a healthy cut of the logistical billions needed to house and feed and arm the tens of thousands of U.S. soldiers and Marines in outposts across the south. You could find among American soldiers and civilians those who considered him our country's best friend or its worst enemy, the only man preventing a Taliban takeover or the reason America was losing the war.

President Hamid Karzai was even more of a puzzle. He was the pacifist commander in chief for the duration of the longest war in the history of the United States. On the spectrum of Afghan politics, he held liberal, pro-Western beliefs but had become the scourge of America. He was the ascetic in a family of millionaires; the workaholic head of an ineffective government; a profane lover of poetry with a weeping heart and tactical mind and twitchy left eye. He was constantly sick. He had ridden a miraculous wave of luck and circumstance into the presidential palace after holding only one government job, a one-year stint a decade earlier as deputy foreign minister that had ended with his arrest, torture, and escape into exile. He was not brave in battle, like Afghanistan's other bearded and berobed leaders. He commanded no militia following and had grown up in Kandahar leafing through *Time* magazine, playing Ping-Pong on the dining room table, and riding a horse named Almond Blossom.

In the family of seven sons and one daughter from two mothers, the half brothers Hamid and Ahmed Wali had been particularly close. During Hamid's post–September 11 return to Afghanistan, Ahmed Wali devoted himself to the logistics of fomenting the Pashtun uprising against the Taliban and helped the CIA set up its operations in Kandahar. Throughout Hamid's presidency, Ahmed Wali had been the enforcer of his political agenda in southern Afghanistan. They talked on the phone nearly every day. Ahmed Wali worked to undercut tribal rivals to keep their Pashtun tribe, the Popalzai, dominant and well funded. He helped the other siblings realize their outlandish dreams, smoothing the road for elder brother Mahmood Karzai to build a giant gated city in the Kandahar desert, while blocking challengers within the family who burned to steal his mantle as Kandahar's reigning don. Ahmed Wali put his elder brother Shah Wali, a shy engineer, to work for him after he couldn't find a job he wanted in the palace. For years, while other siblings sought their daily comforts in Maryland or Dubai, Ahmed Wali grappled every day in the death match of Kandahar politics. And in his sudden absence, nobody knew what to expect.

Out on the road to Karz, I felt a throb of energy, thinking about this prospect. Work as a journalist, even in war zones, often numbs into routine. Foot patrols, tea with governors, round-table briefings, village council meetings. PowerPoint slides, press releases, bar charts, death tolls. The war got explained and narrated and re-created, and you often felt absent from whatever forces were animating it. Your vantage point was always obscured. You were always racing toward something you had just missed, arriving just as men were hosing down the blood and sweeping up the glass. Bombings in Kabul roused us from our desks and beds. We would meet at the scene to jot down the particulars—red Corolla, severed head—and chat about parties. Who even read bombing stories anymore? Kabul City Center. The Finest supermarket. Bakhtar guesthouse. Serena Hotel. Kabul National Military Hospital. ISAF front gate. Indian embassy. Ariana Circle. Microrayon 4. Jalalabad Road. Lebanese Taverna. The British Council. I used to be surprised by how quickly the vendors set up shop and put out their wares after their market was shredded by explosives, or their neighbors, friends, or coworkers killed. After some time in Kabul, the question seemed naïve. For Afghans, and for those of us involved in this late stage of the war, bombings had become both as routine and as unpredictable as a clap of thunder: attacks as natural disasters—an unfortunate run of climate.

There was always a strong element of mindlessness to this deadly weather. We were accustomed to bombings, yes. But we were also accustomed to ignorance, to the acceptance that these crimes would not be solved, these dramas and plots would not be unraveled, or ever explained. We would never really know whether a certain explosion was the result of the meticulous planning of Mullah Omar, the Taliban's one-eyed leader, or a heroin trafficker or Pakistani intelligence or a scorned lover or a thirteen-year-old boy who got nervous and blew himself up two blocks before his intended target, one he didn't even know why he'd been sent to bomb. It was easy to speculate and, for those who didn't have to, even easier not to. The Afghanistan I experienced was all aftermath and poorly informed interpretation.

What interested me in the Karzais, why I was trying to get to Karz, was the hope that traveling in their world would offer some chance, however slim, at explanation. If anyone understood Afghanistan's motives, if anyone knew its causes and effects, I imagined it might be them. They seemed to offer something to hold on to even if that thing wasn't hope or good faith. I wanted some relief from misunderstanding. That Wednesday morning in Karz felt promising if only because I was there early, waiting for whatever would come down the road.

What came down the road was a group of men carrying bamboo broomsticks, then a man pushing a wheelbarrow, a guy toting a shovel, and four policemen in mismatched shoes and white cruise-ship captain's hats. I wondered if maybe I was, once again, too late. Then a procession of men, twenty abreast and filling the road, came into view. They wore turbans and blazers and sandals and wristwatches that glinted in the sunlight, row after unsmiling row. The procession swept by and through us and we fell in among them, following the surging crowd through the village until we came to a grove of eucalyptus trees ringed by a white metal fence topped with arrow-shaped spikes that surrounded the Karzai family cemetery. We entered through the gate.

Across the cemetery grounds, dozens of humble headstones marked the graves of lesser Karzais. In the center stood a small, open-air domed mausoleum, an inner sanctum reserved for family royalty. The president's father, Abdul Ahad Karzai, a former parliament member and leader of the Popalzais, was buried here, as was his grandfather, another tribal *khan*, Khair Mohammad. That morning, men from the village had used picks and shovels to pierce its marble floor and dig the grave where Ahmed Wali lay in the dirt under a white sheet.

The crowd surged around the open grave. Shouting and jostling, mourners pushed toward it six and seven men deep. Among them were many Popalzais who lived in the area and surrounding villages. There were also dignitaries who had flown in from Kabul the night before. I recognized cabinet ministers, army generals, and provincial governors, sweating in their suits and uniforms. People were wailing and crying. Security guards in black bulletproof vests with curly cords tucked behind their ears tried in vain to keep control, screaming and shoving people back from the lip. The sound of rotor blades rose above the din, and a

U.S. military Black Hawk helicopter touched down in a plume of dust. The president had arrived.

Hamid Karzai, looking wan, pushed through the tangle of bodies and stood at the edge of the grave. He wore a simple white tunic and a dark vest. He looked down into the hole and said nothing. I could see he was crying. For a second the scene seemed to freeze, bodies teetering over the pit, all eyes trained on him.

Then he dropped into the grave. He knelt to kiss his murdered brother, and the crowd closed in over him, breaking like water through a dam. People enveloped him in a tangle of interlocking limbs. He stayed down there, out of sight under the bodies, for what seemed like minutes, amid the keening moan of the crowd. Then the bodies parted and he rose from the ground, hoisted up and out of the grave by the men around him. He walked quickly through them, out through the cemetery gate to his waiting convoy, and drove off without saying a word.

A group of men lowered a concrete slab over the corpse and shoveled in dirt. When they had filled the grave, they pressed in two saplings, one at either end, and tied them together with pink ribbon. Almost everyone had dispersed by the time it was done.

Ahmed Wali's funeral took place in the middle of Hamid Karzai's second and last full term, nearly ten years after he moved into the palace in Kabul. The thirty-three thousand additional troops that President Obama had sent to Afghanistan, pushing the total American commitment to more than one hundred thousand, would begin withdrawing in the next few months. The headline battles—in the small town of Marja, in Helmand Province, the offensive to retake the Taliban birthplace in Kandahar—had ended inconclusively. The first became known by General Stanley McChrystal's evocative phrase: "a bleeding ulcer." The initial enthusiasm of the second had faded into a stalemate punctuated by embarrassment when nearly five hundred Taliban fighters burrowed out of Kandahar's main prison through an underground tunnel. The month of Ahmed Wali's burial, there were more than three thousand Taliban attacks across the country.

During the five years I lived in or was visiting Afghanistan, over the course of that second term, 2009 to 2014, the Taliban were largely nameless, faceless adversaries. No one could say for certain much about Mullah Omar—where he lived, how he spent his time, whether he actively led and guided his troops or whether he was merely a rallying symbol. Hundreds of news stories about the war quoted Zabiullah Mujahid, the Taliban spokesman, about the day's events. But the Afghan reporters who made those phone calls—in the Pashto language—heard several different voices over the years all claiming to be that singular Mujahid. I went to a briefing at U.S. military headquarters once about the Taliban propaganda machinery—their mobile radio transmissions, their inflated claims of destruction of the infidel cowards—by the "strategic communications" team from the U.S.-led coalition, known as the International Security Assistance Force (ISAF), and was told there were more than a dozen Zabiullahs. For the Americans, the Taliban movement was never about the individual. It was about the sporadic, anonymous waves of violence, never overwhelming but never ceasing, coming in small ambushes, hit-and-run attacks and assassinations, across farmlands, deserts, and mountains, much of it far away and out of sight.

In the inability to stop or even greatly alter this insurgency, the fixation for many American soldiers and diplomats fell on those Afghans they could manipulate, including our supposed allies in government, the Karzai family. For the U.S. military commanders and diplomats in Kabul, Hamid's failings, and the wider problems represented by his family— corruption, warlordism, a disregard for democratic institutions—became a parallel but equally intense preoccupation. So it was not so much the combat that defined, for me, the war in Afghanistan, but these political struggles: to remake an ancient tribal society into a modern democratic country, to constrain the very people the United States endowed with immense power and money, to relate and find common ground in a culture with deeply different customs and beliefs than those of the American soldiers fighting on its behalf. The Karzais stood at the center of all these struggles, and in their personal rivalries and political lives I found a way to understand the war and why we could not win it.

The president and his brothers began as symbols of a new Afghanistan: moderate, educated, fluent in East and West—the antithesis of the brutish and backward Taliban regime, which blew up Buddha statues and banned kids from flying kites. Most of them had spent the bulk of their adult lives in America and had come back to Afghanistan to help rebuild it into the peaceful country they remembered from childhood. Hamid Karzai was celebrated around the world as a unifier and peacemaker. But by the time of Ahmed Wali's burial, the Karzai name had become shorthand for corruption, greed, and a bewildering rage at America. His family had descended into deadly feuds and scrambles for money that Ahmed Wali's death would intensify. President Karzai's relations with U.S. diplomats and soldiers amounted to little but distrust and traded insults. On his next trip to Kandahar, Hamid Karzai, with tears in his eyes, would tell villagers that Americans were "demons," adding, "Let's pray for God to rescue us" from them.

Hamid Karzai standing above the grave of his half brother Ahmed Wali Karzai on the day of his burial, July 13, 2011, in the family cemetery in Karz

2

ANY PATH WILL LEAD YOU THERE

THREE DAYS BEFORE Afghan voters would go to the polls to elect a new president, Timothy Carney sent a worried note to U.S. ambassador Karl Eikenberry. The subject line read, "Fraud Marker for Karzai."

Carney had spent his diplomatic career navigating far-off conflicts and despotic regimes: in Saigon during the Tet offensive, Phnom Penh during the Khmer Rouge era, Port-au-Prince during the American invasion, two tours in Iraq. He hunted big game; he wore a boater. In a crisis, he felt at ease. His old State Department colleague Richard Holbrooke had called on him for one more run: fly to Kabul to oversee what had become the most important political test of the Afghan war, the election in which Hamid Karzai was running for a second term.

Karzai became Afghanistan's leader three months after September 11, and for a few years he was held up as an exceptional statesman. He had corralled a coalition of ethnic rivals and kept them from warring with each other. He'd created a government out of mostly nothing, planted democratic seeds in a country where dynasty or brute force had normally prevailed. He was an eager partner in whatever designs American officials had on his country, the suave and modern face of a backward nation. None of that had been enough to halt his steadily slipping authority. By the summer of 2009, the Taliban's fighters were running a parallel government that ruled rural villages and towns across the Pashtun provinces in the south and east. In the months prior, suicide attackers had detonated car bombs outside American military bases in Kabul, laid siege to the Justice Ministry building, and fired rockets at the U.S. embassy. American soldiers were dying at a rate of nearly two per day, higher than in any month in the eight previous years of fighting. "I won't say that things are all on the right track," General David McKiernan had noted six months earlier, just before he was ousted from command in Kabul. "So the idea that it might get worse before it gets better is certainly a possibility."

In his first election, in 2004, Karzai had run without any serious challenger and with the full support of the United States, but the shine had long since worn off. His Afghan opponents, energized by his perceived weakness and growing alienation from the United States, campaigned with relentless attacks against his family and administration. His most prominent adversary, Abdullah Abdullah, who had once been Karzai's foreign minister, was barnstorming the country in creaky Russian helicopters, presenting himself as a pan-ethnic savior-in-waiting, a distinction, in earlier days, that Karzai had claimed for himself. Over American protest, Karzai had made the desperate decision to welcome back two of the country's most loathed warlords. He had chosen as his running mate Mohammad Qasim Fahim, the pug-faced battle-ax of the Northern Alliance, to win ethnic Tajik support, and he'd cajoled Abdul Rashid Dostum, a drunk plunderer most famous for baking Taliban prisoners alive in a shipping container, into returning from Turkey and helping him win the Uzbek vote. Even more worrying for those around him, Karzai no longer had America at his back. President Obama had cut the avuncular link that Karzai had established with President Bush. The White House wanted a new approach to this failing war, and coddling a man increasingly considered an ungrateful and ineffectual tribal chieftain was not how it intended to find one. American officials believed that Karzai tolerated flagrant government corruption and had failed to extend his administration very far beyond the walls of his palace. "On all fronts," a senior American official declared not long after Obama took office, "Hamid Karzai has plateaued as a leader."

As election day approached, American diplomats and spies were hearing that Karzai's supporters were preparing to keep him in power by any means. Candidates, local election officials, and informants were reporting back to the American embassy a range of voting scams in the works. Carney wrote to Ambassador Eikenberry on the afternoon of August 17: "We have information about wholesale fraud planned in Kandahar," where Ahmed Wali Karzai ran the province. The next day Eikenberry was to meet President Karzai to discuss the vote. The situation could be so bad, Carney predicted, that a large-scale quarantine of ballots might be required, "with possible voiding of ballots of Pashtun areas," which could drop Karzai below the 50 percent threshold needed to win in the first round of voting. Such a dirty election, Carney wrote, "could force a second round. It would weaken Karzai domestically. It would be horrendous internationally, and risk continuation in the coalition from a number of key allies. It would require a strong response from us."

The Obama administration was not well positioned for a strong response. Nine months earlier, the president had been sworn in to office on promises to end the Iraq war and train the country's attention on this one. That spring, fewer than forty thousand American troops were deployed to Afghanistan, about a third of those stationed in Iraq. Years of American military neglect and a reenergized insurgency, its leaders based safely across the border in Pakistan, had overwhelmed Afghanistan's young and ill-trained army and police force. The incoming commander, General Stanley McChrystal, would describe, in his initial assessment that summer, a war being lost—"a resilient and growing insurgency," "a crisis of confidence among Afghans" about the U.S. mission and Karzai's government, and an overall situation that was, in his understatement, "deteriorating." The Taliban had developed a full complement of guerrilla tactics—buried bombs, lobbed rockets, trip-wire mines, ambushes, potshots, pressure-plate IEDs, car bombs, suicide vests—and at nearly six hundred attacks per week, the pace of violence was faster than ever before.

In response, the tenor of the American mission had changed. Men with heavyweight reputations assumed jobs across the battlefield. Karl Eikenberry, an earnest and determined former three-star general who had already served two military tours in Kabul, had begun a hiring spree that would triple the size of the embassy. Holbrooke, a diplomatic star since Vietnam, had created a rump bureau within the State Department to plan the war effort and was in constant circulation with his entourage between Kabul, Islamabad, and the capitals of Europe. Two months before the election, McChrystal, a gaunt and ascetic former black ops commander famous for his one-meal-a-day regimen and innovations on the art of killing, had taken over as battlefield commander. Overseeing all of it from U.S. Central Command in Tampa was the celebrity general David Petraeus. There was a sense of momentum, even excitement, and a curious optimism, which years of evidence to the contrary had not dispelled, that a foreign ground war against Islamic militants could be won if only the proper "resources" were brought to bear. "It was night and day," said a staffer in the U.S. embassy in Kabul who lived through the transition. "You had all of the sort of military might, intel might, diplomatic might literally grinding like an old fire truck off of Iraq and onto

Afghanistan. There was a mentality of: the grown-ups have arrived. Time to knock all this shit off."

Within three weeks of moving into the Oval Office, Obama had ordered seventeen thousand more troops to Afghanistan, and less than a year later he would up that by another thirty-three thousand. The U.S. embassy, in a collection of mustard-colored concrete office buildings and white metal trailers, would bring in hundreds of staffers, becoming the country's largest diplomatic mission, with a budget exceeding $4 billion per year, or more than four times Afghanistan's domestic revenue. In the months before the election, despite trouble all around, the cables the U.S. embassy sent home brimmed with the can-do spirit of the moment: "The government and the public here have welcomed the United States' new strategic purpose: strengthen security, build access to justice and broader governance capacity at both the national and local levels, and develop the economy."

With the stakes in the war growing so rapidly, Carney wasn't the only one worried about the consequences of a fraudulent election. Afghanistan's defense minister, Abdul Rahim Wardak, had told Americans that if the elections fail, they should "not waste any more blood or treasure here." From his makeshift office in the election team trailer, he typed out his e-mail to Eikenberry, urging him to warn Karzai, once again, to play fair.

"Wholesale electoral fraud risks the very partnership we are embarked on," Carney wrote. "I believe you should tell him we have good information on attempts by his supporters to engage in fraud with ballot boxes. If this happens, it will be detected and the consequences are incalculable."

Each morning, Hamid Karzai awoke in his second-floor bedroom in Palace Number 2, his residence within the presidential complex in downtown Kabul, where he lived with his wife, Zeenat Quraishi, a gynecologist, and their young son, Mirwais. The house had been built in the 1960s for one of the sons of the last king, Zahir Shah, and was a rather bland, unlavish two-story building with no central air-conditioning. On normal mornings, Karzai dressed in a simple, collarless tunic, white, gray, or black, buttoned at the neck and falling to his knees, over matching billowy pants, and a dark vest or blazer. Much had been made of his more ceremonial wardrobe, used for speeches, meetings with dignitaries, and travels abroad, since he had become president.

When thrust into the world's spotlight, he had debated with his aides what type of image to portray to his rural, undereducated citizenry. Afghans were then largely unfamiliar with telephones, television, and the Internet, a nation of illiterate peasant farmers in mud huts emerging from a regime where they had been forced to give up music, movies, raising pigeons, and flying kites, where the women could not work outside the home and the men had to grow beards, where adultery or unfaithfulness or any number of sins against the Islamic dictates established by the Taliban could be punished by severed hands, rifle execution, or public stoning. Hamid Karzai wanted a new image for a new day, different from the kohl-eyed and flower-decorated flowing locks of the defeated mullah leaders, something for each of the many warring tribes and ethnic groups that made up Afghanistan. He adopted the peaked lamb's-wool cap of the Tajiks and the iridescent green-and-blue striped cape of the Uzbeks. Among Pashtuns, he often added a turban. His costumes left a startling impression. "He looked like he'd just come off the Serengeti," one Washington staffer recalled about the first time he saw Karzai move through the halls of Congress. "I expected to see lions and tigers walking behind him." Early on, Karzai had considered a more sober, business-suit attire, befitting his position as a leader in the modern world. But after the designer Tom Ford described him as "the chicest man on the planet," his costume was set. He wanted to be seen, above all, as a man of his country. He once told an American visitor, "I'm the Tom, Dick, and Harry of Afghanistan."

In the morning, Karzai would step out of the steel-plated front door of his residence, his personal bodyguards following closely behind, and onto his circular gravel driveway, where he strode around a small fishpond for exercise in the evenings, and make the short walk to his office in the Gul Khana, or Flower House. The presidential palace, known as the Arg (the name means "citadel") was a collection of aged stone buildings and quiet gardens behind ramparts and turrets designed by British architects 130 years earlier to withstand the types of assaults that the country's rulers were always enduring. The moat that had once surrounded the castle walls had disappeared, and razor wire and gun emplacements had replaced the cannon mounts for protection, but many of the old structures remained inside. More than one thousand people worked within the grounds—cooks, gardeners, tea boys, clerks, advisers, accountants, doctors, a palace poet—and another thousand were devoted to guarding it. There were stately houses for visitors and great ceremonial halls, separate stone buildings for the National Security Council, for the office of administrative affairs, for the Presidential Protection Service guards. There were cafeterias, a mosque, a Victorian mansion, and grounds lit by wrought-iron lanterns at night. Karzai's office faced a wide plaza of stone slabs interspersed with fountains, lawns, tall firs. For all the elaborate fortifications, the entrance to his office building was a simple screen door, a guard posted on either side, epaulets on their shoulders. It had two levels, with white columns running along the second-floor balcony. To the left of the lobby, a multicolored marble-floored solarium offered views of the grounds, and ahead, a wide, red-carpeted stairway led up to the dark wood of the cabinet meeting room, at one end, and his office, at the other.

The palace had, by virtue of its exotic history and its great contrast from the loud, congested, dusty potholed chaos outside its walls—a perpetual gridlock of begging children, armor-plated convoys, crutch-wielding amputees, Toyota Corollas, and donkey carts—a hidden, somewhat magical allure. Its courtyard was wide, green, calm, with tailored lawns. Dark-suited aides strolled the footpaths in quiet council, heads bent, thumbing their prayer beads. The presidential guards stood at attention wearing earpieces with cords diving into their collars. On some afternoons, you could see waiters flapping out white tablecloths for a lunch under the trees. Karzai considered the palace a showcase of his country's wonders. Karzai kept several antelope, once owned by Mul-

Afghan interim president Hamid Karzai is an animal lover.
At his home in Kabul, he keeps several pet antelope that formerly
belonged to the Taliban leader, Mullah Omar. July 11, 2003

lah Omar, as pets in his backyard. Karzai housed goats and kittens in his residence and kept a coat hanger, made from the horn of a Marco Polo sheep, in his office. At the entrance to the Gul Khana, Karzai posted a Sikh man wearing a *dastar*, to highlight Afghanistan's ethnic diversity. As part of the palace welcoming committee, Karzai also employed a giant, a seven-foot-tall Afghan man who palace staff chose to believe was the tallest man in the world. He had been found by Norwegian soldiers on patrol in Faryab Province and brought to Kabul, where his job, in his own words, was to "walk around the palace and be tall." The giant napped on the floor, because the Afghans could not find a bed to fit him. General McChrystal once bought him two pairs of size 17 shoes, earning his gratitude to America. There were also, apparently, three midgets wandering around, and though I never saw them, one former British ambassador insisted they lived in a tree.

Years of stalemate guerrilla war had won Karzai the reputation as a weak leader. To outsiders, he was the tinfoil-crowned "mayor of Kabul," the ungrateful puppet imprisoned within his own palace walls, swiping from his cage at the many foreign hands that fed him. This was never quite the case. It was true he couldn't claim to have quelled the insurgency or established a humming civil service. Even in Kabul, the most modern, developed city in the country, only a third of the roughly five million residents received electricity, and that only sporadically; one in ten residents had access to the city's water supply.

And yet Karzai had considerable powers at his disposal. The position of president, atop the highly centralized government designed in part by the United States, came with considerable authority, and the courts and the squabbling parliament had not matured enough to check his authority. He ruled, essentially, by decree. Each day his aides brought him dozens of orders to sign: military promotions, execution orders, land transfers, medals of honor. His edicts could free convicted murderers or sentence men to death. He could shut down companies, impose new taxes. He established special commissions to investigate American air strikes and special courts to rule on financial scandals. He traded government sinecures for political support. He ordered money to be given to the families of bombing victims, declared national days of mourning, convened emergency sessions of parliament. He proclaimed that female newscasters must wear head scarves, that hunting with falcons was illegal, that Afghan hounds were a national treasure and could not be removed from the country. He decided, to the dismay of some of his more business-minded brothers, that the weekend would be Thursday and Friday.

His decrees created new penalties for rape and child marriage; they established commercial laws about arbitration, corporations, partnerships, mediation. He mandated that schools be built for nomads in all thirty-four provinces. He appointed all of the provincial governors and the district governors below them, the members of the human rights commission. He created a multimillion-dollar discretionary fund for governors and allowed them to form their own militias. He had personal authority over much of the nation's budget, according to his former intelligence chief, and could choose which villages received foreign aid. He micromanaged a country of thirty million people. It was a job he enjoyed and felt destined to continue.

Even so, he'd run a lackluster campaign. He had acted as if he were above the fray, the foreordained leader of Afghanistan, the father of a great Pashtun nation. He had skipped the candidates' debates and attended his first one in a Kabul auditorium just four days before the election, where he said Afghanistan had been totally lost and "I saved it." He released a seven-page platform that was filled with bland pabulum and priorities such as "peace and tranquility." Just three months before the election, his campaign headquarters in a rented three-story home near the U.S. embassy had the "feel and resources of a sleepy mayoral election-level campaign office in the U.S.," as one American visitor described it. Karzai had stayed mostly inside the palace, leaving the work of rounding up votes from tribal and religious leaders to his family.

In Kandahar, his half brother Ahmed Wali had been meeting southern Afghanistan's tribal strongmen on a daily basis and promising favors in return for their support. Rival candidates said Ahmed Wali warned them against even campaigning there, with ominous suggestions that it would lead to violence. Two young Karzai nephews had arranged for pro-Karzai Pashto text messages to be sent en masse to cell phones in Kandahar. In Kabul, his elder brother Mahmood Karzai had opened a parallel campaign headquarters and held fund-raisers for his business cronies, including the shareholders of one of his companies, Kabul Bank.

Despite the growing insurgency and his own limited efforts, Karzai was still the favorite to win. Polls showed him ahead, although with less than a 50 percent majority. These polls reflected the surprising conclusions that most Afghans, across ethnic groups, felt Karzai was doing a good job. The violence and government corruption that so preoccupied American officials apparently did not seem, when compared to the brutalities of recent Afghan civil wars, particularly grave to many of its citizens. During Karzai's tenure, daily life for many citizens, particularly in the cities, had improved. Under the Taliban, Afghans would have to drive to Pakistan to make a phone call. Now many had cell phones, Internet access, and television with an *American Idol* knockoff show, *Afghan Star.* The time of rival commanders strafing Kabul with rocket fire during the early 1990s civil war was not yet forgotten; the bullet-pocked buildings around Kabul still showed those scars. But now roads were being paved, new businesses opening; jobs could be found in private security, logistics, shipping—the whole wartime profiteering bonanza.

Those low expectations, plus the work of his family, seemed to be about all Karzai had going for him. I stood with a man in a roadside gravel lot outside the eastern city of Jalalabad as he pointed to the spot where his three cousins had died in a suicide car bomb. He lived with his four children in a mud home without electricity and was praying for a president who could bring peace and security. He would be voting, again, for Karzai. "We don't have any alternative," the man told me. "We are afraid of what the other candidates might do."

For all his faults, Karzai was widely recognized as a master of tactical maneuvering and political games. He didn't take vacations or have many hobbies. Outsmarting his rivals, keeping both his enemies and his loyal aides off balance, was his daily passion. One small example took place before the election. On February 28, 2009, Karzai issued a decree establishing the date of the vote. By that time he had already agreed publicly that the election should be held in late August. But his surprise decree, announcing that the vote should be held "in accordance with the constitution," meant, without saying it directly, that the election should occur within two months, before his first full term ended, in May. It was a timeline that nearly everyone, not least the U.S. government, considered impossible.

The new American troops Obama had ordered up, in part to secure the elections, would not arrive in Afghanistan until summer. The Afghan government had to hire 165,000 election workers and secure some seven thousand polling centers. These staffers needed to find three thousand donkeys to haul ballot boxes in from remote mountains. And even if the donkeys could be procured, the snows in those mountains would not have melted enough by then to be passable.

But Karzai's decree was, it turned out, just a parry against his rivals in the Northern Alliance (then known as the United Front). They had been insisting that Karzai step down at the end of his term and establish a caretaker government if the election was to be held anytime after May. Even his first vice president, Ahmad Zia Massoud, had defected and was openly criticizing him. Karzai had no intention of allowing an interim government to take over for any period of time. And he knew that it would be even harder for his rivals to win on short notice. To place a Tajik candidate in a palace ruled for most of the country's modern history by a Pashtun was a long shot even under the best circumstances.

Almost instantly, his rivals abandoned their position that an August election would be unconstitutional and began arguing in favor of Karzai's earlier platform. Four days after Karzai's decree, the date went back to August 20, as Karzai had wanted all along. His gambit had exposed the opposition as solely interested in inflicting political damage, all while affirming the constitution. The U.S. embassy marveled at Karzai's maneuvers, writing that the opposition "seriously underestimated Karzai's skill as a political strategist and have fallen behind in their efforts to remove him from power."

"As messy and convoluted as this has been so far," a diplomat cabled back to Washington, "it's likely to look tame in comparison to what comes next as the Afghans get into politicking in their national style."

It was a forty-one-way race among old and young, men and women, warlords and technocrats, those who lived in lavish fortress-castles and a guy who was working out of a roadside tent. There were clerics, widows, and an erstwhile Taliban commander with the nom de guerre Mullah Rocketi, for his prowess with missiles. The candidates traveled by helicopter, in armed convoys, in cargo planes supplied by the U.S. military. A retired Air Force colonel campaigned on a bicycle.

The official American policy vis-à-vis the election, as outlined in cable after cable, was to be impartial. But none of the Afghans believed it, and the American diplomats weren't helping themselves make the point. The U.S. embassy was buying commercial airline tickets to fly Karzai's opponents to campaign events and also allowing candidates to use its airplanes. Two months before the vote, Ambassador Eikenberry spoke at televised press conferences alongside Abdullah, the most prominent challenger; Ashraf Ghani, a former finance minister; and other opposition candidates, prompting Karzai's foreign minister to call him to complain. The effect of his appearances was not subtle. At one of them, Eikenberry told the country why he was meeting the candidates: "We would like to know what their views are on poor governance, because we know that poor governance leads to insecurity." The election, he said, "is a chance for the people of Afghanistan to give the government a report card for its performance over the last five years."

Holbrooke, Obama's special representative to the region, held Karzai in even lower regard and had disparaged him to other Afghan politicians for years. Abdullah remembered talking with Holbrooke at a conference in Bali about Karzai's bizarre behavior. Holbrooke, then chairman of the Asia Society, had recently visited the western Afghan city of Herat to check up on one of his pet projects, the restoration of the ancient minarets tilting in neglect downtown. In his meeting with Karzai afterward, Holbrooke told Abdullah, the president had lied to him about the state of the restoration, then shouted some orders into the phone, and ultimately got distracted by a bird outside his palace window. Holbrooke was not impressed with the performance. Holbrooke's "conclusion out of this was that Karzai was a person who was telling a lie before your eyes, and he knows that you know that he's lying, but still he lies," Abdullah recalled. Holbrooke had published an op-ed piece in *The Washington Post*—just months before he'd rejoined the government—that criticized Karzai's handling of the warlord Dostum, who had allegedly sodomized a neighbor with a bottle and then escaped to Turkey while Karzai failed to arrest him. "Excuses were made," Holbrooke wrote, "but none justified his open disregard for justice."

In the election run-up, Holbrooke was hardly more discreet, and he encouraged other candidates to challenge Karzai. Holbrooke felt Afghanistan needed a leader with a different set of skills, less a tribal peacemaker and more an executive who could run a bureaucracy. He joked to Abdullah, a famously dapper diplomat, about how nice it would be to have a president of Afghanistan "with a three-piece suit." Holbrooke talked to European diplomats about the possibility of giving Karzai a prominent position at a foreign university, or with the United Nations. In a meeting with Afghan and foreign election official monitors in Kabul, Holbrooke let slip "I hate that guy" when the topic of Karzai came up. In a mid-February meeting at Ambassador Eikenberry's residence, Holbrooke asked his fellow diplomats if they could live with Karzai for another five years. "Who would be the best candidate to replace Karzai?" he asked. He then suggested Haneef Atmar, the popular Pashtun interior minister. The United Nations envoy at the time, Kai Eide, later wrote that he took Holbrooke's comments as an "attempt to sideline Karzai." Holbrooke had also urged the parliamentarian Mirwais Yasini to join the race—a fact Yasini would mention to other American diplomats.

When I asked Yasini about this later, he said Holbrooke and others "didn't promise any financial support," but they gave the distinct impression they were not happy with Karzai. "And not only them, the whole world was giving that impression." Holbrooke's handpicked ally with the

*Ambassador Eikenberry, left, speaks with Ambassador
Richard Holbrooke on a flight from Marja back to the
Camp Leatherneck base on June 21, 2010.*

U.N. mission in Afghanistan, Peter Galbraith, was openly hostile to the
prospect of a second Karzai term. One of his advisers, Jane Marriott,
described to me their approach, in proper British understatement, as
"actively impartial." But it was far more than that. Even Defense Secretary Robert Gates would later write that Holbrooke had concluded that
Karzai "had to go."

Holbrooke had already had a legendary diplomatic career before taking on the Afghan war, from a young dynamo in Vietnam to the bullying
negotiator in Bosnia. He seemed to revel in his persona, and to believe
his own devotion to his ideas enough to justify them. But I'd seen him be
brusque and uncurious, even nod off in mid-conversation with an Afghan
governor. He didn't offer the deference that Afghan leaders seemed to
crave. His angling against President Karzai also veered into the wider
family. Before the vote, Holbrooke tried to persuade both Eikenberry
and McChrystal that Ahmed Wali Karzai should be dropped from the
payroll of the CIA, which had been his patron for the duration of the
war. What was left unsaid by Holbrooke was that casting out Ahmed
Wali would debilitate President Karzai in the Pashtun south. And even
though such proposals would die, Holbrooke's maneuvers would invari-
ably trickle back to the palace, where Karzai would dutifully catalog them
in his overflowing file of grievances.

"Would Holbrooke have found it a much better scenario if Karzai lost the election?" one of Holbrooke's advisers said. "Absolutely." Just two months before the vote, Secretary of State Hillary Clinton sent a cable to Kabul with a message that seemed to vastly misinterpret the political climate. Addressing diplomats there, she wrote, "despite your best efforts, there remains an Afghan and international perception that the U.S. and most of the international community are supporting Karzai's candidacy. Unless Afghans find not only our words but our deeds credible, they will vote for the candidate they think will win and we support. We need to do everything we can to rebalance a playing field increasingly viewed as tilted towards Karzai."

Since Karzai's first election in 2004, when the United States had essentially functioned as his campaign manager, and when his victory had been hailed by Vice President Dick Cheney as a major moment "in the history of human freedom," the playing field had tilted, if anything, steeply away from him. As early as the spring of 2007, European officials had proposed to Karzai that he promote himself out of his job—to a ceremonial position as head of state or king and let a prime minister assume the real work of governing. In battles with American officials, Karzai was already a scarred veteran. They had fought over what to do about Pakistan—Karzai thought the U.S. military should pursue al-Qaeda and the Taliban there, rather than in Afghanistan. The United States needed to send Pakistan an ultimatum to stop "using Islamic radicalism as an instrument of policy," Karzai had told Obama, then a senator, over lunch in Kabul in July 2008. "Softly, softly, won't work."

U.S. officials also disagreed on whom Karzai should appoint as governors—the American government believed some of them were drug traffickers. Eighteen months before the election, embassy staffers were describing the country's "endemic corruption and widespread frustration over the Karzai government's failure to meet expectations." Civilian casualties, private security mercenaries, air strikes, Afghan prisoners in U.S.-run jails—all the political battles to come had already, to one degree or another, been fought. "He had raised objections to nighttime raids on houses, men going into women's quarters, the use of dogs, the random international feeling that it [the U.S.-led military coalition] could arrest anybody they thought should be arrested, regardless of whether they were a tribal chieftain," William Wood, the U.S. ambassador who preceded Eikenberry, told me. "He had a long list of recurring complaints, which I have to say we have not responded to very satisfactorily.

"Certainly I had failed in my primary assignment from the Bush administration, which was to develop a more workable relationship with Karzai," Wood said. "I like to think it deteriorated more slowly with me than it otherwise would have, but the relationship wasn't a good one." An American bombing in the village of Azizabad a year before the election killed nearly one hundred people, so infuriating Karzai that he wouldn't allow Wood to see him for fifteen days. "It was completely unprecedented," Wood said. "It was effectively the end of my ability to influence Karzai."

Now Hillary Clinton's orders were to push the anti-Karzai agenda even harder. Some within the embassy noticed that this could be problematic. Just two weeks after her memo, the embassy's political officer, Alan Yu, warned Eikenberry that he should tone down his public profile in the election. "You've already had meetings, including significant media coverage, with these candidates," Yu wrote. From now on, he suggested, meet them at your residence, and don't allow reporters in. "Continued high-profile media with these candidates risks shifting the story to defiance of Karzai instead of promoting U.S. policy of neither supporting nor opposing any legitimate candidate."

A month before the vote, Eikenberry wrote back to Washington that "Karzai clearly expected (or hoped) to receive the same U.S. support for his candidacy that he received in the 2004 election, and interprets our neutral stance in this election as evidence that the U.S. is 'against' him." Before that first election, the U.S. embassy, then led by Zalmay Khalilzad, would parade Karzai around the country to events where he could cut a ribbon on an American-funded school or clinic in order to demonstrate to villagers how much better off they were with Karzai in the palace. The embassy had little time for rival candidates. One American diplomat recalled struggling to arrange a meeting for another Afghan politician who wanted to explore running against Karzai. "I got stonewalled," the diplomat said. "The order to the political section was that the presidential candidate was Karzai and no one else. They were not to meet with others."

"Did we help him win the election?" Colonel David Lamm, who was the chief of staff for the U.S. military commander in Kabul at the time, asked me. "Yeah. You're damn right. He was our guy. And we wanted him to win. He was a very honorable guy. All of us thought highly of him."

Before the second election, Karzai's rivals could sense that the political winds had tacked sharply since the last go-round and aggressively courted U.S. support. The former World Bank official and Columbia University–

Hamid Karzai speaks to the press during an inauguration ceremony after winning his first presidential election, December 7, 2004.

educated finance minister, Ashraf Ghani, had taken on political operative James Carville as an adviser and was running as the data-driven pragmatic problem solver to Karzai's heart-on-his-sleeve haplessness. Abdullah's campaign mantra was all about "hope" and "change." Several opposition candidates flew to Washington for Obama's inauguration, while Karzai was left feeling slighted that he didn't get invited. When Obama had visited Afghanistan as a presidential candidate himself, he had stopped in to visit Karzai's old Kandahar rival Gul Agha Sherzai, then the governor of Nangarhar Province. Sherzai took that as a personal endorsement. As he mulled over whether to run for president, Sherzai told the local American diplomats stationed at the base in Nangarhar that he would challenge Karzai if he got a green light from the States. "A general can lose a battle and come back to win the war. A businessman can lose his money but earn it back. In politics, you get one chance. I would be surer of taking the chance if the U.S. supported me," Sherzai said. That support had been critical for Karzai earlier in the war, he noted. "You were like an eagle that flew out of the sky and landed on his forehead. After that everyone knew that this was who we needed to support. I am waiting for the eagle to land on my forehead."

The Obama administration's approach to handling Afghan politics worsened Karzai's sense of alienation. There had been periods of frequent personal contact between Bush and Karzai via videoconferencing that, Obama's representatives told Karzai, would become much less common. Obama might visit Afghanistan; he might not. There would be no coddling. The administration wanted to work around Karzai as much as possible, building up the provincial and district leaders, although two-thirds of the country's district governors didn't even have office buildings and all of them answered to Karzai. Eikenberry and Holbrooke, the chosen representatives of the U.S. government, would deliver the messages, not the president. The Afghans saw this distancing as odd, given the fact that Obama was about to invest vastly more time, money, and lives in the war. What American officials saw as a bureaucratic reordering was interpreted by the palace as a personal and intentional slight.

"President Karzai would not understand why he had to deal with an ambassador," Said Tayeb Jawad, who was Karzai's ambassador to Washington at the time, told me. Jawad began to notice real political consequences beyond hurt feelings. Lower-ranking diplomats on both sides had a harder time communicating informally, fewer chances to have coffee the day before a meeting and talk about what was coming up. "If you take away that operating level of the working relationship, every meeting turns into a surprise," Jawad said. "For Holbrooke, it was an issue of centralizing authority and making people go through him. He made that point many times: 'Those days are gone.'"

Karl Eikenberry's views on Karzai were more nuanced than Holbrooke's, but the Afghan leader was no less an obsession for him. Eikenberry had already spent as much or more time with Karzai than any American official. He had arrived during the first year of the war, a former Army Ranger risen to major general, in charge of building a new Afghan army from the scraps of civil war militias. He had returned to Kabul in 2005 for a second tour, spending eighteen months as the top U.S. military commander. He retired from the military as a three-star general to take his first civilian job as ambassador, but he did not seem particularly comfortable in the role. He was earnest, analytical, sober, a workhorse in gold-button blue blazers and sensible shoes. In public settings or surrounded by reporters, he came across as stilted, almost robotic. Asked even benign questions, he would compress his attention inward as he scrutinized each word before freeing it from his teeth. The awkwardness made him an easy target for mockery by his staff. And lots of his subordinates resented his exacting demands. I had seen him stop a visiting State Department staffer outside an embassy elevator to grill him about his itinerary back to Washington, upset that he had not chosen cheaper flights to save taxpayer money. He had barred a female diplomat from a meeting at the palace because he felt her pants revealed too much ankle and might be offensive to Afghans. After a riotous embassy Mardi Gras party that ended with smashed liquor bottles and the deputy Turkish ambassador peeing on the wall of the chancery, he banned parties for months.

But Eikenberry thought as deeply about the problem of Afghanistan and his personal responsibilities to it as anyone I met there. Before the war started, he'd given the place very little thought. He had originally been a China expert, with a master's in East Asian studies from Harvard and course work toward a PhD at Stanford. He had studied in Hong Kong, spoke Mandarin well enough to receive an interpreter's certification, had married a Chinese-born woman, Ching, and wrote papers for military journals with titles like "The Imjin War" and "The Campaigns of Cao Cao." It wasn't surprising that after a decade in Afghanistan, he knew the country well. By the end of his tenure as ambassador, he'd visited every one of the country's provinces. He'd escaped mortar rounds in Nurestan, rockets in Wardak, and a grenade that landed within a hundred yards of him at a peace conference in Kabul. He seemed to hold genuine affection for Afghanistan. During his travels in the country, he would stop teachers, street vendors, and peasant farmers to query them about their thoughts and criticisms about their government, their views on the American presence, their aspirations.

He had analyzed U.S. failures in Afghanistan and could quickly summarize a decade of the war's politics, much of which he witnessed firsthand. In the early years, when the mission was to kill the Taliban and al-Qaeda, the U.S. government had allied itself with brutal warlords and their militias. Attention drifted away toward Iraq in the middle period. In the later years, U.S. troops surged back in without knowing exactly what they were supposed to accomplish. He did not avoid blaming himself. "Look," he told a group of diplomats and soldiers in Kandahar one day, "I served here in 2002, and I remember standing in front of a group of soldiers and occasionally civilians and saying, 'Okay. Our job here is to get another first down. We're not going to win this on our watch. But get another first down on your year.' And I came back in 2005, and I recall saying, 'Get another first down.' And then I got back here in 2009 as the ambassador, and I started to say to groups, 'Get another first down.' And I realized, you know, where's the goal line?

"And that *Alice in Wonderland* quote: If you don't know where you're going, any path will lead you there."

As Eikenberry puzzled over Afghanistan, more often than not Hamid Karzai was the central riddle. The Karzai he first met was giddy, ebullient, naïvely idealistic. When he heard an idea, he liked it. Eikenberry remembers having to help persuade Karzai not to approve a United Nations war crimes special rapporteur to investigate the various Afghan warlords' sordid pasts, because such an investigation could wipe out half his government. In one meeting, as the U.N.'s representative, Lakhdar Brahimi, outlined the risks with this approach, Karzai got wide-eyed, childlike. Really? Brahimi named a governor who could be accused of war crimes, and Karzai replied, "He's a very big thief, but he's not a war criminal." Karzai seemed to feel as if his very presence in the palace was proof that everything was surmountable. "Don't be distressed," he said. "We're such a good team." Karzai told Brahimi, "Your Excellency, you are always worried about problems, and I like that about you. You see a big hole in the ground and point it out, and I jump over it."

The early Karzai wasn't yet burdened with the drudgery of building government institutions or the tragedies inherent in losing a guerrilla war. Heads of state from around the world would visit him in his palace, and they would sit as equals. To the Americans, Karzai would reminisce fondly about visiting his brothers in Maryland, about how he liked Starbucks coffee and country music. He found Thanksgiving a splendid holiday and believed that if they could just find some way to export Afghan pomegranates en masse, they would make a fine complement. He was prone to such grand pronouncements. "We want very soon to stand on our own feet, to become a donor country, rather than a recipient country," he said two months after moving in to the palace. During one meeting with governors from Georgia, Kansas, and Mississippi, Karzai told them that Afghanistan before his presidency had been a "sad black-and-white movie." It was now a film of "color and hopefulness."

That was before thousands of other such meetings, before hundreds of congressional delegations, presidential visits, NATO conferences, United Nations resolutions, years of arguments and demands and negotiations, strategic assessments, pilot programs, policy reviews and re-reviews. Everything had been tried and then tried again. Karzai had heard from representatives of dozens of countries on how to rule Afghanistan. He'd been lectured on military operations from twelve ISAF commanders from seven different countries. He'd received the American president's messages from five U.S. ambassadors. So many times, he had been ignored. Karzai did not have any authority over which roads American Humvees drove on, onto which homes F-16 fighter jets dropped their missiles, over whose farmland Predator drones spied. By the time Eikenberry moved in to the embassy, Karzai had become someone Eikenberry saw as "a pure survivalist."

Karzai used to talk about his support for democracy or the need to decentralize authority in soaring terms, without yet having experienced the sacrifices this entailed. Eikenberry now felt that Karzai had no interest in working to strengthen parliament, the courts, the army and police—nothing except the office of the president. Karzai had once said the Afghan people were all that mattered and he was no fan of governments. Eikenberry remembered the time Karzai came back from a trip to China saying how well the country was doing without holding elections.

Before the election, Eikenberry was meeting with Karzai several times a week, and growing ever more worried about what he was hearing. He felt Karzai did not accept his responsibilities to America for the support he received, that he had little interest in building democratic institutions or a strong Afghan military. Karzai kept repeating in those meetings that the United States was not speaking clearly to Afghanistan about its intentions, and that the clarity of purpose America had once had after September 11 was now lost. He was suspicious that the United States simply wanted a weak Afghanistan so as to have a free hand to pursue its larger goals in neighboring Pakistan and Iran. He felt that the United States had failed by giving too much authority to cautious NATO allies in southern Afghanistan, and that it had not protected the country's tribal leaders from assassinations by insurgents. Karzai spoke openly of the notion that America was secretly allied with Iran to support his rival Abdullah. At a meeting in front of Karzai's national security aides, as well as General Stanley McChrystal, Karzai mentioned that America was against him. Eikenberry denied it and said "there was no overt or covert U.S. program to support any presidential candidate," he wrote in a summary of the meeting. "I then asked Karzai if he took me at my word on this issue. Karzai, perhaps not wanting to back down in front of his advisors, said that he did not."

Eikenberry was seeing flashes of two different Karzais. "The first is of a paranoid and weak individual unfamiliar with the basics of nation building and overly self-conscious that his time in the spotlight of glowing reviews from the international community has passed," Eikenberry wrote to Washington just over a month before the vote. "The other is that of an ever-shrewd politician who sees himself as a nationalist hero who can save the country from being divided by the decentralization-focused agenda of Abdullah, other political rivals, neighboring countries, and the U.S. In order to recalibrate our relationship with Karzai, we must deal with and challenge both of these personalities."

Eikenberry believed that Karzai was too thin-skinned but that he reflected the legitimate grievances of the Afghans about the mistakes made and aggravations caused by the foreign troops—"a vessel for his people's anger," as Eikenberry put it—and that the problems in the relationship would need to be dealt with if he prevailed in the election. "I will begin a frank, collaborative (and perhaps, at times, confrontational) dialogue with Karzai," Eikenberry wrote back to his superiors in Washington. "No alternative approach is now evident."

In Karzai's mind, the bottom line for America was a bit different.

"They wanted me out by all means," he told me.

Ten days before Obama's inauguration, his vice president–elect, Senator Joe Biden, and Republican senator Lindsey Graham, a reserve colonel who had worked as an Army lawyer, had dinner with Karzai at the presidential palace. It was an encounter that has been rehashed at length in the journalism of the war. Bob Woodward writes several pages of dialogue about the evening in his book *Obama's Wars*. In some ways it was a typical encounter: talking points flying past each other, self-serving statements, frustration. Biden came with a message that Karzai needed to clean up his government and deliver services to the people and that he wouldn't have the type of chummy relationship or easy access to Obama that he had enjoyed with Bush. Biden alluded to the drug-trafficking allegations against Ahmed Wali, in front of Karzai's ministers. Karzai started getting defensive and said the only important issue was civilian casualties. Biden wanted Karzai to save his criticism for private meetings, not bash the United States in public. Karzai said he had a duty to speak up, that Afghans had lost faith in America's war plan. Biden said they didn't need to send any soldiers if Karzai didn't want America's help. Karzai said no one cared about Afghanistan. Biden chucked down his napkin.

This type of pressure tended to backfire. The Afghans present, even those with little sympathy for Karzai, found it offensive. They saw Biden as not just impolite but condescending. "He was talking as if he were negotiating with some wild mountain people who knew nothing. He was showing a lot of disrespect," Amrullah Saleh, Karzai's intelligence chief at the time, told me. "Biden's way of conducting that talk was not diplomatic. It shattered the image of American grandness. Slamming a cup.

It's over. This is not Hollywood. These are negotiations. It's real life. It's not a movie. He was not professional. Whatever he wanted to convey, he couldn't convey it. He just expressed his anger. Karzai's reaction was very decent. Very brave. Very courageous. He kept his composure. He was much higher than Biden. Much higher.

"Even if you read books about the British going to the Mughal court three hundred years ago," Saleh went on, "they would present gifts, they would start by compliments, talk about nature, enjoy a little food, and then be very gradual. But three hundred years later someone comes to your court, regardless of how powerful he is, and acts this way? At the end of the day, we are all human beings and we have pride. Your [American] pride is your economy. It's your military. It's your wonderful land. It's your technological advances. It's your universities. But don't forget, our pride is our history, our religion, our country. So simply because we are poor, we should not be degraded in every meeting. And unfortunately in that particular meeting, the guy was looking at the American pride only, and we were like, What?"

Karzai enjoyed ceremony. That characteristic was hard to miss. Everything he does has a certain flourish. When you meet him, he doesn't walk over to greet you but strides. He grips your hand with fervor. His eyes actually seem to twinkle. It struck me that what he liked most about being president was that it afforded so many opportunities to act grandly, to display gravitas. Every day at his palace he would have audiences, delegations of dozens of villagers from around the country coming to him with personal appeals for his help: the need for a school; a relative wrongly imprisoned; a dispute over property. In this way, the presidency of Afghanistan was a hybrid role—part modern head of state, part Pashtun tribal leader. Karzai embraced this aspect of his job. These gatherings gave him ground-level intelligence about how people felt about the war, but they also gave him the chance to preside. His voice had the timbre of oration even in conversation. He enjoyed riding the momentum of a sentence, indulging long, repetitive riffs and musings. He often ignored speeches written for him and improvised his remarks. "When I prepared talking points, he would disregard them totally," Javed Ludin, a former Karzai spokesman and chief of staff, told me. "He had a flair for media."

In one of our interviews in his office, apropos of nothing, Karzai started discussing climate change. "Really abusing Mother Earth," he said, "in terrible, terrible ways. I don't think the earth can cope with all the wrongdoing." He asked me where I was from. "Seattle? Oh, Northwest. Nice place. It's rising? The temperatures rising there as well? Too much smoke. Too much pollution. Too much mining activity, perhaps. Too much everything, huh? Too much cement around, too much asphalt around. Too many planes around. Too many cars around. Tremendous wastage of water. *Tremendous* wastage of water. I have tremendous difficulty at home telling everybody to use water, you know, miserly. They don't understand. Even electricity they don't understand. They keep switching the lights on, and I go and turn them off. They turn them on. I turn them off. They don't know. We will learn in a terribly costly way for the next generation."

Karzai wanted to be a great man, to have his views respected. Being embarrassed in front of his cabinet ministers by the U.S. vice president–elect was an affront to his sense of stature, a diminishing in the eyes of his peers. For all his eloquence in English and his worldly experience, people who met with him regularly felt that Karzai didn't understand American politics that well. When he read a critical article in the U.S. press, he assumed it was essentially a public memo from the government, written by a reporter carrying out U.S. policy. "He does not understand Washington, our politics, our open system, where everybody runs their mouth all the time," Ronald Neumann, a former U.S. ambassador to Kabul, told me. "The public criticism, Biden and the rest, this is inconceivable to an Afghan. That you would criticize a friend publicly like this, unless you intended to weaken them."

This type of meeting set the tone for the relationship going into the most important phase of the war. Whatever interests the Afghan and U.S. governments might have had in common were strained through this filter of distrust and wounded pride. By this time, everyone knew everyone else so well. This had been going on for so long. These personal feuds began to feel like the only fight that mattered. "As soon as the Democrats won the election, they started treating President Karzai's government not as a partner but as a client," said Mohammed Amin Farhang, a cabinet minister in that government for seven years.

When I asked him about the dinner, Karzai remembered how Senator Graham had raised the issue of Afghan prisoners and said that the U.S. military would soon be taking in far more detainees. Karzai told him the Soviets had done the same thing and he would not allow it.

"You are one man," Graham told him. "How can you stop us?"

In this exchange, Karzai said, he saw the "essence" of Obama's government.

"They were there to give us a message," he told me. "A threatening message.

"The U.S. government was trying to silence me. That's what they keep telling me during these meetings. Not to go public on issues. And I remained committed to speaking publicly," he said. "Corruption was there. True, sure. But they didn't raise it because corruption was there. They raised it as a pressure tactic. And we knew that. So the main purpose all along of the pressure was to turn me silent on issues that we raised and were very important to us.

"It was actually funny," Karzai said. "It amused me, you know, to hear that. Because the United States had troops here, had an engagement here, wanted a relationship with Afghanistan. And then to say that the contacts would not be as frequent didn't go with the reality of the situation.

"So it was . . . I don't know how to describe it. It sounded empty.

"I think they were trying again to use all that as a pressure tactic. They thought it mattered to us. It doesn't matter for us in the sense of a person to person. But it does matter at the level of government to government. When you have such strong engagement on the ground with troops and people dying. You need to be in contact, frequently, to sort out issues, to clear up things. To me it sounded a bit naïve, that one would threaten loss of contact. Well, who loses? We don't lose."

Foreign countries had just paid $488 million for the election, the United States contributing $263 million of that total. The Afghan government's share was $1.5 million. More than ten thousand people on fifty-one different election observation teams from around the world were on the ground to monitor the polls; drones peered down from the skies. The official watchdog organization, the Electoral Complaints Commission, led by foreigners, had a staff of 220 people deployed around the country. The goal was to open more polling stations and have more people vote than in the previous election, in 2004, all while having more eyes on those polls to ensure that the election was carried out fairly.

It didn't turn out that way. Only about 4.5 million Afghans voted, out of the more than 15 million who registered—half the turnout of Karzai's win five years earlier. The Taliban launched more than four hundred attacks that day, the most of any day in the war. At least thirty people died. More than seven hundred of the polling centers failed to open. After all but the first hours of voting, when eager American and European officials declared the election a relative success—"I want to congratulate the Afghanistan people on carrying out this historic election," Obama said from the South Lawn the day after the vote—Americans in Kabul and everyone else quickly realized that by any measure, the election had been a disaster.

The fraud that Tim Carney had worried about in his e-mail to Ambassador Eikenberry began to materialize in a bewildering diversity of methods and schemes. There were people who voted more than once, those who voted on behalf of others, whole sheaves of six hundred ballots with the same exact vote in the same exact pen. "Ghost" polling centers that never opened racked up votes. In voting rooms that opened, gunmen forced people to fill out ballots, or police took them home and checked the boxes themselves. Some voting booths were blown up or set on fire. The retrospective reports on the election showed the fraud had been conducted with such abandon, and so free from any worry about detection or consequence, that it suggested the whole democratic experiment was for show.

"Massive, unbridled, unsophisticated, blatant and untrammelled" was how Carney described the fraud in a Democracy International report eight months after the vote. Ten votes in the box became one hundred on the results sheet, the extra zero added later, in different handwriting. Losing candidates showed up in election offices carrying cardboard boxes full of shredded votes they'd purportedly been denied. At least fifteen candidates reported that election staff members at tally centers were requesting seven dollars per vote. "Top-off voting," where election staffers marked the leftover ballots for their preferred candidates, was common. In the Panjshir Valley, candidates got identical results in three separate voting stations: 427, 427, 427 for one candidate and 10, 10, 10 for another. Supporters of both leading candidates took part. A week after the election, I went up to the northern city of Mazar-e-Sharif, an Abdullah stronghold, and talked to a depressed election official slumped in a jail cell, bruises on his face and blood speckling his scarf, who told me he'd been arrested and beaten after protesting that police were shutting down booths because people were voting for Karzai. "I am in pain," he said.

When asked about the voting fraud long afterward, Americans involved in the election said they believed that palace staffers, Karzai supporters, election officials, and police officers all helped orchestrate a Karzai victory. But they were less sure about whether Karzai ordered that to happen or even knew the details of the trickery. "Did Karzai call in his team and say, 'Cheat your way into a first-round success?' I don't think so," Eikenberry said. "Did Karzai design a team with an intent that was known, to do what has to be done? Absolutely." Carney saw it the same way: "We have absolutely unimpeachable information that palace officials were deeply involved in ballot stuffing." Karzai's defense was to flail, accusing foreigners, including a European general, of a ridiculous plot of stuffing ballot boxes themselves.

At markets in Kandahar, voter registration cards were being sold in bundles of three hundred. In station after station, hundreds of pages of identical ballots showed Karzai winning 100 percent of the vote. "The counting of the ballots was unobserved," one U.S. military commander told me. U.S. military intelligence officers in Kandahar reported to their Kabul headquarters that there were more votes for President Karzai across the south than there were voters and that Ahmed Wali had had a "major hand in that." Abdul Raziq, the young border police commander and Karzai ally, stored ballot boxes overnight inside his own home. In his domain, Karzai won 8,341 votes. Abdullah got 4.

The other candidates had already dismissed the election as hopelessly flawed. The parliament member Mirwais Yasini called it the "end of democracy." Abdullah Abdullah was holding press conferences in his garden nearly every day with new accusations of ballot-box stuffing.

"They ripped ballots out and stuffed them in. You could see they just marked them all in the same hand. It was such an amateurish, idiotic attempt, so incredibly, childishly transparent" was how one Canadian adviser in Kandahar described it. A video aired on Afghan television showed men and women sitting on the floor calmly doctoring votes, folding and stamping ballots. One of them told the camera that "the same stuffing was taking place in all districts" and that it was "fun to do."

It took weeks before the scope of the fraud came clearly into view. On election night, the U.S. embassy cabled home that "no reliable early returns exist." And yet by the next morning, Richard Holbrooke seemed to have come to his own conclusion about the results. Before heading to the palace to see Karzai, Holbrooke met with the U.N. envoy Kai Eide, along with Eikenberry and other members of the American election team. As Eide wrote in his memoir, "Holbrooke's main point was that Karzai needed to be prevented from declaring victory. We should now insist on the need for a second round to clear the air after all the irregularities." Eide wondered how they could ask Karzai to do this if the votes had not yet been counted, and he urged Holbrooke not to raise this with the president. "You have to understand," Eide told him, "that Karzai sees you as someone who wants to get rid of him."

When Holbrooke arrived at the palace, he ignored that advice and made it clear that he felt that Karzai had not won more than 50 percent of the vote and that a runoff would be necessary. In Karzai's recollection of that lunch meeting, Holbrooke told him that "the election must go to the second round."

"The vote had not even properly begun to be counted by then. Not even counted. Not even begun the counting," Karzai told me. "I said we should wait for the results. He said, 'No, the results are ready, we should go to the second round.'"

Others present in the palace that day have similar memories of the exchange. The president's spokesman, Waheed Omar, recalled Holbrooke telling Karzai that "there was a need for the second round. The president said, 'How do you know? We barely voted. And the ballot boxes are not even in the provincial centers yet, most of them are still locked in the voting stations. How do you know it's going to go to the second round?'" Holbrooke, as Omar remembered it, said the United States knew of election fraud that would make the vote illegitimate in the minds of the Afghan people and the international community. "In the president's mind, the Americans did not want to replace him, they wanted to wound him, they wanted to delegitimize him in a way that he would not stand in their way as a strong president with opinions of his own, as a president who could drive his own agenda and push his agenda against that of the Americans," Omar said. "That's the way he took it." Karzai told me the same thing. At that moment, he said, he knew the Americans "were working on trying to have an election in which, if they could not defeat me, they would leave me as illegitimate."

For their part, Karzai and his team were just as quick to jump to conclusions about the outcome. Within one day, his campaign manager was telling reporters that Karzai had won by more than 50 percent and a runoff would not be necessary; within four days, his finance minister announced that the president's margin was 68 percent of the vote. But as more than three thousand complaints about fraud poured in from across the country, it became clear that a recount of some fashion would be necessary. The Electoral Complaints Commission (ECC) went into triage mode, and decided that only the most blatant cases would be scrutinized. Weeks passed in arguments over what happened in far-off voting booths and how to arrive at some approximation of a true result. In those weeks, the fraud seemed to harden American officials' feelings against Karzai. Palace officials hunkered down, insisting that everyone was out to wrest power from them.

The country's official arbiter of the voting, the Independent Election Commission, found that Karzai had won 54.6 percent of the vote, but the organization was widely believed to be biased in Karzai's favor. American officials tended to trust the ECC, which would audit and recount the votes. It had a majority of foreign members and was led by a Canadian. The Americans saw the ECC as made up of objective, rigorous experts who hewed closely to the facts. The palace saw the ECC as more foreigners plotting against Karzai. This type of Afghan vs. foreigner division deepened the longer the confusion dragged on, particularly as Karzai's camp made it clear that they might not accept the results of the recount if it pushed them below 50 percent.

When that came to pass—the ECC found that of the 3 million votes for Hamid Karzai, at least 800,000 were fraudulent and would be wiped away, costing him his majority—it set up a showdown over whether Karzai would accept the conclusions of his own government's institutions, however imperfect, or throw out the rules and steer Afghanistan toward some place where the rules no longer applied.

Karl Eikenberry had spent days insisting to angry Afghan officials that Holbrooke and the State Department had not rigged the recount to swipe a victory from Karzai, nor had they been planning for a runoff the whole time. Now he faced the task of convincing them, and Karzai, that they should accept that very fate. The White House sent Senator John Kerry, chairman of the Foreign Relations Committee, to help argue the point, instead of Holbrooke.

Given how the first round had gone, American diplomats were in fact dreading an encore, risking soldiers' lives and millions of dollars more to organize another potential sham vote. Eikenberry sensed reluctance from Secretary of State Hillary Clinton when talking about it with her on the phone. But he saw this as a defining moment for the Afghan government. If they could accept the rulings made by their own institutions, even if politically painful for the incumbent, it would add ballast to the shaky young democracy and elevate Karzai, making it clear that he wasn't just some third-world thug. It would show that Afghanistan could be the type of country that Eikenberry, and the rest of the Americans, hoped it could be.

Karzai simply refused, convinced that he had won by a majority in the first round. In McChrystal's memoir, he described Karzai's attitude toward Eikenberry as "rage." Karzai shouted, argued, rationalized, schemed. He warned that a second round would lead to brutal ethnic violence. To persuade him otherwise, Eikenberry knew, he needed Afghans to make the argument to Karzai; he would never listen to Americans.

Eikenberry and the embassy political team fanned out to its various Afghan contacts: the governors, ministers, warlords, and technocrats, as well as the sympathetic diaspora Afghans with McMansions in suburban Virginia and the Islamist clerics who preached about the evils of American occupation in their Friday sermons. Eikenberry's subordinates went out to meet with the old lions of Afghan politics, men whose lives were one long, bloody struggle for power—Mohammad Qasim Fahim, the vice president; Ismail Khan, the ruler, in effect, of western Afghanistan; Abdul Rasul Sayyaf, a former ally of Osama bin Laden's—to try to convince them to accept the ruling of an electoral commission composed of a majority of foreigners: that enough votes for Karzai were fraudulent that he had not actually won a majority. If Karzai unilaterally declared himself the winner, Eikenberry believed, in addition to weakening Afghanistan it would energize all of Karzai's enemies, from the opposition groups to the Taliban, and it would put his government in open opposition to the United States, just as tens of thousands more troops were on their way to fight on his behalf. They needed to find some way to make Karzai blink. The message from his diplomats in those meetings, as Eikenberry remembered it, was that Karzai "was driving toward a cliff. And he may run over that cliff. The question is, Are you going over the cliff with him? Or are you going to try to dissuade him?"

One night, Eikenberry and his deputy, Frank Ricciardone, were invited by the minister of public health to meet in his office next to the embassy. Most of the employees had left for the day. They followed the minister down a darkened hall into a large conference room they had not visited before. Eikenberry was startled by what he saw. Around a vast table sat dozens of Pashtun government leaders and elders in turbans and robes, a group of men who formed the core of Karzai's political support and afforded him his authority with their fellow tribesmen. At the head of the table, in a white turban and large square spectacles, sat Sibghatullah Mojaddedi, the ailing former president of Afghanistan, who had been Karzai's boss when he was a lowly political water boy living in exile in Pakistan.

Karzai's whole public image had been crafted as an appeal for Afghans to transcend ethnicity. The brutality of the civil war that had followed the Soviet departure, with so much killing of Pashtuns, Hazaras, Tajiks, and Uzbeks, had been a black period for him; it was what had forced him to flee the country as a young man, what he would do anything as president to avoid. And yet many would argue over the years that Karzai saw himself, above all, as the leader of the Pashtuns. Of the two main branches of the Pashtuns, an ethnic group comprising tens of millions of people and hundreds of tribes that straddled both Afghanistan and Pakistan, the Karzais were Durranis, those who had founded modern Afghanistan and, since the eighteenth century, had often ruled it. Karzai's father had been the leader of the Popalzai tribe until he was killed, in 1999, and then that mantle passed to Hamid. Hamid's style of politics was often likened to that of a tribal leader rather than a modern bureaucrat: sitting with audiences of any social standing, hearing their grievances, seeking compromise, conciliation.

American officials in Kabul, when frustrated or enraged at Karzai, which was often, would dismiss him as just another backward tribesman, "a spoiled Durrani princeling," as one top U.S. political adviser described him. Leaders of the minority ethnic groups, like the Tajiks and Hazaras, would accuse Karzai of manipulating a pro-Pashtun agenda that slowly was stripping them of the power they had amassed early in the war. "At least in the deep recesses of his mind," General Dan McNeill, the top military commander during two tours in Afghanistan, told me, "he considers himself the father figure of all Pashtuns, *all Pashtuns*, both sides of the border. Of that I'm absolutely convinced."

The assembly of Pashtun leaders facing Eikenberry, then, were as influential with and important to Karzai as any group of Afghans. And they felt as adamantly as Karzai did that he had won the election with a clear majority. They argued to Eikenberry that forcing a second round on the nation would mean more chaos and uncertainty; avoiding it would spare a lot of bloodshed.

"Ambassador, you don't have to do this," one Pashtun minister told him. "You have options. This election can be decided in President Karzai's favor."

Eikenberry had known many of these men for years. He'd walked bazaars and drunk lukewarm green teas with them. He'd listened to them drone on about the same tired slights: that America had abandoned them after the Soviets left, then given their country back only to ruin it with meddling. He was tired of and frustrated by their whining. He slammed his fist on the table.

Do you think we have American soldiers here risking their lives to secure this election so that you can make a mockery of it?

There was so much massive corruption, he said, so much flaunting of any sense of rules or fairness, that the country needed a second round. They needed to clean their hands of this farce. All of them, Eikenberry said, had lived through the civil war of the early 1990s, when tens of thousands died in the streets of Kabul, when ethnic groups slaughtered one another, when crossing town meant running a gauntlet of militia front lines of war-shattered rubble.

"There were no rules. It was the jungle," Eikenberry said. "Now you are returning to the jungle. What we are talking about is rules. The rules aren't perfect. But if you don't follow them, you're going back to the jungle. This is your chance."

The meeting ended after two hours. It was late, and Eikenberry was exhausted. The room emptied out, and he rose to leave. Mojaddedi, the former president, a man Eikenberry knew well, raised a hand.

"My son," he said. "Come back."

It was just the two of them. Mojaddedi put his hand on Eikenberry's knee. He said that because he represented the United States, he could have any outcome to this election he wanted. Eikenberry, with his earnest North Carolina–bred patriotism, really believed that representing the United States meant standing for certain values—in this case, respect for a fair democratic process. And he told Mojaddedi that.

"So what you are saying is there has to be a second round?"

"That is exactly what I'm saying."

Mojaddedi smiled. He patted Eikenberry's knee.

"Okay. There will be a second round."

When the Pashtuns met later at the palace with Karzai, their message was simple: you can either have the majority of the vote from the first round, or you can have the United States of America.

The palace press conference had been delayed for hours. The reporters, trapped inside the palace meeting hall, had been stripped of their cell phones. Outside, walking among the rose gardens, President Karzai and Senator John Kerry were nearing the end of their twenty-hour marathon negotiation, meant to be the culmination of the effort by Americans and Afghans alike to get Karzai to agree to the second round. It was two months after the vote had taken place. Karzai had finally agreed, and the announcement was scheduled for one p.m. The press was called in.

Ambassadors and other dignitaries went to the palace to be in attendance for the news. But Karzai was still resisting and was refusing to show up.

As they walked around the grounds and visited the palace mosque, Karzai was still convinced that he had been cheated out of a legitimate win. Kerry felt that Karzai needed to put the interests of the country and its institutions in front of his own. Kerry, who'd lost to George W. Bush five years earlier, commiserated with Karzai about what political failure felt like. He told Karzai, as others had, that it would be difficult, if not impossible, for the United States and Afghanistan to work together if he refused a new election. These types of veiled threats and ultimatums were coming in from many sides. The United Nations representative, Kai Eide, urged Karzai to accept a second round, saying that otherwise he would resign. "This was probably the most difficult conversation I experienced with Karzai," he wrote later. "I was exhausted."

One of the things that most infuriated Karzai was enduring the public humiliation of having to submit to this foreign, and primarily American, arm-twisting. Having to concede that his votes had been rigged, that he was not the clear favorite of the Afghan people, was an epic loss of face. Karzai wanted some way to preserve his dignity and emerge from the election as a decisive winner. During their talks, Karzai asked Kerry for assurances that if he agreed to participate in a second election, it would actually take place. A decisive second-round win over Abdullah would vindicate him and legitimize the election. As his spokesman, Waheed Omar, remembered it, Karzai told Kerry: "Look, I'm going for the second round, I accept the second round, but can you guarantee that it will happen?" Kerry said, "I swear to the Bible and the Koran that there will be a second round."

When I asked Karzai about this later, he said the same thing. "Kerry swore on the Bible," Karzai said, "over there." He pointed to the chair in his office next to the fireplace. "He was sitting in that chair. Yes. He swore on the Bible."

Karzai finally appeared for the press conference at four-thirty p.m. Grim, tired, he stood at the podium flanked by Kerry, Eikenberry, and Kai Eide. British ambassador Mark Sedwill, who had been hoping to avoid participating in the bizarre public spectacle, got ordered by London otherwise and rushed over late to join the crowd. Lined up behind Karzai, the foreigners looked like the very thing he had accused them of being: puppet masters meddling in his sovereign government.

"Afghanistan's elections have unfortunately been defamed, and any results we got from the first round of elections would not have ensured legitimacy in the system," Karzai told those in the room. "Now, it may be in my personal interest if I now insist that I won the first-round elections, but the interests of the people of Afghanistan are more important. Therefore, we are now going to hold second-round elections."

The second round never happened.

After the press conference, Abdullah Abdullah, perhaps fearing an unwinnable vote or perhaps, as he said, convinced that the system was so rotten it could not be trusted, decided to drop out of the race. That left Karzai—damaged, discredited, feeling betrayed—a winner by default.

Ten weeks passed between the vote and the final announcement that the election was over. During that period, Karzai willfully disregarded the obvious and voluminous evidence that his supporters had tried to cheat him to victory, as Abdullah's supporters had also, to a lesser extent. His approach was self-serving, to say the least. But the United States acted with ugly hypocrisy, touting the rhetoric of democracy while scheming against the favored candidate. It managed to humiliate Karzai but not defeat him. That period transformed Karzai into the president he would become. The years preceding the election had been marked by a slow erosion of interaction, friendship, and trust between the American and Afghan governments that culminated in the collapse of relations during the months of the disputed vote. As Waheed Omar later described it, the election was "the wound that never healed."

After watching the final announcement at the palace, Kevin Brady, an embassy press officer, sent an e-mail to Tim Carney and the elections team.

"No second round, as you know by now. Articles 156 and 49 (?) cited as reasons, plus security, costs, and ony [*sic*] one candidate," he wrote. "Intl journalists here just shaking heads; afghans hungry for more q and a. Over."

3

SO MUCH IN LOVE

HAMID KARZAI TOOK UP RESIDENCE as Afghanistan's new leader on the chilly night of December 12, 2001, when he was twelve days shy of his forty-fourth birthday. He had long since gone bald, and his beard had flecks of gray, but he moved with youthful vigor. He had married two years earlier, at an unusually advanced age for an Afghan, but still had no children. Before the airplanes flew into the World Trade Center and the Pentagon, Karzai had had no inclination that he would soon be ruling a country he had not lived in for years. A relatively novice politician, Hamid had not distinguished himself in battle, as other, more venerated leaders had done. He was living in a salmon-pink house in an upscale suburb of Quetta, in western Pakistan, a critic of the Taliban and al-Qaeda, the hard-line Islamic groups that the Pakistani government supported and the Western world ignored. His father had been murdered, and he feared Pakistan would revoke his visa.

Karzai and his seven siblings were among the millions of diaspora Afghans scattered into exile by the Soviet invasion, the civil war, and the Taliban regime. They came from a prominent family distinguished not so much by their wealth as by their political and diplomatic posts, their leadership of the Popalzai tribe, and their favor under the former king Zahir Shah, who had ruled for forty years before being overthrown and exiled to a villa outside Rome. Their stature was comparable to that of other political families abroad, and in a region where violence and religious intransigence were celebrated, the Karzais were moderates, open to compromise. They wanted the return of the exiled king. They tried to interest the United States and other countries of the West in the brutalities of the Taliban regime. They wished for Afghanistan to rediscover the peaceful times they remembered from childhood.

But for most of them, the turmoil of Afghan politics, and the hope of returning to their country, had faded into the background of their daily lives. Since moving to the United States in the late 1960s, Hamid's elder brothers Mahmood and Qayum had established a network of successful Afghan restaurants in Baltimore, Boston, Chicago, and San Francisco. The family's lone sister, Fawzia Royan, along with her husband, managed one of their restaurants, the Helmand, not far from the Harvard campus. The oldest brother, Abdul Ahmed, had trained as a mechanical engineer and worked at BWI Airport, in Baltimore. The youngest brother, Abdul Wali, had earned his doctorate at Johns Hopkins University and taught biochemistry at SUNY Stony Brook, on Long Island. Several of the siblings had become American citizens, along with their children. They had spouses who sold insurance, worked in department stores. They were accustomed to their suburban lives.

Among the siblings, Hamid had stayed the most politically active during his exile years, but even he could not expect that in the condensed frenzy of three months, he would be transformed from an obscure exiled Afghan diplomat into the country's wartime head of state. This brief period has also been the most thoroughly documented of Karzai's public life. Books such as *The Only Thing Worth Dying For*, by Eric Blehm, and *A Man and a Motorcycle: How Hamid Karzai Came to Power*, by Bette Dam, have chronicled in minute detail Karzai's post–September 11 journey into Afghanistan. But in light of the years of attacks that followed, it's important to revisit that period, if just to remember that Karzai's success in those first days, and his very survival, was vouchsafed by the United States.

After the terrorist attacks, Jason Amerine, a thin, bearded, quietly intense thirty-year-old U.S. Special Forces captain from Honolulu, received his orders while at an Uzbek air base known as Karshi-Khanabad. The mission was both simple and grandiose: meet up with an Afghan rebel commander and topple the Taliban. Other CIA and Special Forces teams had been assigned to the rebels in northern Afghanistan, and air strikes had been pounding Taliban positions for a few weeks. But no one had yet tried to mobilize the Pashtuns in the south to take on their fellow tribesmen in the Taliban. Amerine's Special Forces A-team, Operational Detachment Alpha 574, consisted of himself and ten other people. The Afghan commander they would be meeting, he was told, was Abdul Haq, about whom Amerine knew nothing. The plan was "to link up with these bloodthirsty warlords and do what we can to work with them." Haq was a Pashtun who had earned his fame, and lost a foot, as a mujahedeen commander against the Soviets. He was charismatic, thrived in the spot-light, and cultivated the press; his nickname was "Hollywood Haq." As an offering to a fellow warrior, Amerine's team brought a large blade for Haq. A BFK, he called it: big fucking knife.

"It was just: 'Give us our warlord and we'll go.' "

Then suddenly Haq was dead, surrounded by the Taliban and uncer-emoniously murdered along with nineteen other people. So Amerine's team got assigned a new warlord equally unknown to him: Hamid Karzai. Then Amerine was told Karzai was dead. Then the news changed again: Karzai was alive, but in trouble. It turned out that Karzai at that moment was being airlifted out of Afghanistan by a team of Navy SEALs. Since September 11, Karzai had been in contact with CIA officers about his plans to spread the word among Pashtun tribes that the time had come to rise up against the Taliban. In early October 2001, Karzai, unarmed and with a CIA-donated satellite phone, had ridden a motorcycle into Afghanistan with three companions to foment rebellion. But his war party got surrounded in the mountains of Uruzgan. The Bush administration, afraid that another Pashtun opposition leader would be killed, like Haq, sent soldiers to rescue him. Karzai and Amerine ended up finally con-vening at a CIA safe house across the border in the Jacobabad district of Sindh Province, Pakistan, to prepare for another attempt. When Ame-rine met Karzai for the first time, on the morning of November 3, he knew he would not be giving this man a knife.

"He's not a warlord in any way. He came off as very intelligent, soft-spoken, almost scholarly," he said. "I thought, Okay, this is going to be very different than my initial assumptions."

Karzai had no military expertise. After leaving Afghanistan for col-lege in India, he had gravitated to Pakistan during the Soviet war in the early 1980s; there he taught English and got involved with Afghan rebel groups. Living first in the northern city of Peshawar, Karzai worked as a political adviser and spokesman for Sibghatullah Mojaddedi (who Eiken-berry would have a showdown with years later), the leader of the Afghan National Liberation Front (ANLF), one of the seven Afghan rebel fac-tions that relied on American money and weapons to fight the Soviets. Karzai got the position through the influence of his father, Abdul Ahad, who was also working with the group.

On the spectrum of these Afghan cold warriors, the ANLF was weak. It received a fraction of the CIA-funneled largesse that other, more radi-cal Islamist parties were given. Karzai nevertheless became well known in the foreign embassies in Pakistan and on the wider diplomatic circuit because he spoke fluent English and presented a modern, worldly image to foreigners, unlike many Afghan leaders, who looked as if they'd stepped with their sandals and robes out of biblical times. In his meetings with Western diplomats at the time, Karzai tended to wear blue blazers, ties, and slacks. In his spare hours, he could be found riding his bicycle or swimming laps in the Pearl Continental Hotel's swimming pool.

"What you have to remember about Hamid is, he was just a nice guy," said Larry Crandall, who was the USAID director in Pakistan in the mid-1980s and met with Karzai frequently. "And the way we thought of him then was as somebody you could always invite, if you had politicians in town, and we had them coming through all the time in Islamabad then. . . . We often had to bring Afghans to them, because they didn't always want to go down to Peshawar or Quetta. And Hamid was always available and he was articulate, somewhat knowledgeable, and presentable. He wouldn't say horrible egregious things in front of them like some of them would."

Karzai had worked for Mojaddedi essentially as a public relations officer, meeting with foreign journalists, writing speeches, translating, dining with diplomats. He coordinated humanitarian aid and helped with day-to-day logistics for his boss. He and his father were moderately important in the anti-Soviet resistance, and foreign visitors often sought them out to hear their views on the war across the border. Hamid, in particular, made a good impression on many of the foreigners he met at the time. The journalist Edward Girardet wrote of his "charming, salon demeanor." Steve Coll wrote in his book *Ghost Wars* that Karzai was a "born diplomat, rarely confrontational and always willing to gather in a circle and talk." Francesc Vendrell, a Spanish diplomat who was the United Nations envoy to Afghanistan before September 11, described him to me as "bubbling with ideas."

"Hamid Karzai represented for me all that was larger than life in the Afghan character," the journalist Robert D. Kaplan wrote in his book *Soldiers of God* about meeting the thirty-year-old Karzai. "He was tall and clean-shaven, with a long nose and big black eyes. His thin bald head gave him the look of an eagle. Wearing a sparkling white *shalwar kameez*, he affected the dignity, courtly manners, and high breeding for which the Popalzai are known throughout Afghanistan." Kaplan found Karzai's fluency with East and West beguiling, how he could sit on the floor speaking Pashto to a Kandahari relative with a copy of George Eliot's

The Mill on the Floss by his side. With his immaculate diction tinged with a British accent, he could play "foreign *wazir*" to Americans better than almost anyone, recalled Richard Smyth, a diplomat in the U.S. consulate in Peshawar in the early 1990s. There were, however, several more dominant Afghan strongmen. "The Karzais were known, but major players? Not really," Smyth recalled.

Although Hamid had been an early supporter of the Taliban movement, which had emerged in 1994 as a response to the predations of warlord militias, he gradually turned against its rulers, until he advocated for their overthrow. He became known among the Afghan diaspora as an astute politician and anti-Taliban advocate who lobbied for the return of the exiled king and the congregation of a traditional council, or *loya jirga*, to select a new government. He'd canvassed the State Department, hat in hand, begging for some type of help to drive out this regime. He had met with Ahmad Shah Massoud, the guerrilla commander of the Northern Alliance, which amounted to what little military opposition there was to the Taliban, and discussed plans for a "Southern Alliance" of Pashtuns to join the fight. Karzai had testified before the U.S. Senate Committee on Foreign Relations in July 2000 about the flourishing terrorist haven that his country had become. Before September 11, these types of appeals tended to fall on deaf ears. U.S. foreign policy was oriented elsewhere, and fixing such a war-torn, backward nation as Afghanistan was not high on anyone's to-do list.

Karzai had just come out of a meeting at the U.S. embassy in Islamabad when his brother Ahmed Wali phoned him with the news that an airplane had crashed into the World Trade Center. Hamid was on the way to his mosque to pray when Ahmed Wali called back about the second plane. Hamid would recall later that he felt certain from these first moments that al-Qaeda had been behind the attack and that they would change Afghanistan's fate forever. He heard his brother shouting joyously to the family guards. The brothers quickly assumed that al-Qaeda, working from Afghanistan, had planned the terrorist operation, and that the United States would be forced to respond. "The Taliban are finished," Ahmed Wali said.

By the time Jason Amerine arrived in Pakistan, Karzai had already been working with a CIA paramilitary team led by a man named Greg, who wore his brown hair swept back and had a thick handlebar mustache. Amerine's Special Forces team and Greg spent a few days in early November with Karzai in Pakistan, planning the logistics of their mission. Their goal was to capture Tarin Kowt, a town about seventy-five miles north of Kandahar in Uruzgan Province, where Karzai had tribal support, and spread their guerrilla movement out from there, with the ultimate goal of seizing Kandahar and the rest of the Pashtun south.

At the time, the Americans didn't know whether Karzai had popular support within Afghanistan, how a well-spoken exile politician would relate to poor Pashtun farmers. Amerine's superior, Colonel John Mulholland, commander of the 5th Special Forces Group, didn't want to approve the mission until Karzai could prove he had three hundred men under arms to accompany him. The CIA team was also hesitant to go and discussed flying a Predator drone over Afghanistan to essentially do a head count to confirm whether Karzai could rally enough fighters. There was a feeling the Northern Alliance would win the war on its own and there would be no need for a fight in the south. But Amerine worried that the Northern Alliance sweeping south could provoke further civil war, and he also risked losing Karzai, who was itching to get into Afghanistan. "Hamid was going to go in without anybody. He said, 'I need to go in. If you guys aren't going to go, I'm going to leave this area and do it myself.'"

Karzai told Amerine, "If I go in, three hundred men will arrive."

"Good enough for me," Amerine replied.

On November 14, 2001, five Black Hawk helicopters carrying the Special Forces and CIA teams, plus Karzai and his men, drifted down in single file into a darkened Afghan valley lit by four signal fires, raising a billow of dust as they descended. Karzai stepped onto the valley floor in gleaming white leather tennis shoes given to him by the CIA. Within three weeks, their war against the Taliban was largely over. In the interim, Amerine learned that Karzai had been right and tribesmen had flocked to him to offer their support, while the Taliban had melted away under the barrage of air strikes, targets that Amerine and Karzai often called in together. Tarin Kowt fell. Kandahar would soon follow. Taliban foot soldiers surrendered to Karzai. Residents tore down the white Taliban flags. During this period, Amerine remembers, Karzai seemed to hold no vengeance toward his enemies; anyone who surrendered was welcomed to end his fight peacefully. "He was happy to send everybody home," Amerine recalled. "Hundreds or thousands. If they surrendered to him, he sent them home. Their leader would come to him and he'd say okay, 'Welcome back.'"

When they had a moment to talk about anything beyond the immediate present, Karzai spoke of his dream of the *loya jirga*, not of any personal ambitions. "The best person for the job is not for me to decide," Karzai told Amerine. "That is for the Afghan people to consider. I want to see the people voting, as in the United States."

Karzai was not, at the time, the only or obvious choice to be the country's leader, even among his friends. The most famous Afghan battling the Taliban was Ahmad Shah Massoud, the tall, photogenic, French-speaking rebel commander and poet known as the Lion of Panjshir, after the name of the narrow river valley north of Kabul that he and his men had held against years of ferocious Soviet onslaughts. His fighters formed the bulk of the ground forces resisting the Taliban. But Massoud was killed two days before September 11, by al-Qaeda operatives posing as video journalists, with a bomb hidden in their camera. His death, along with the demise of the other strong Pashtun candidate, Abdul Haq, elevated Karzai's political stature by default. Even so, for the Afghan representatives who were convened by the United Nations in late November 2001 in Bonn, Germany, to form a new Afghan government Karzai still had competition.

The conference took place at the luxurious Grandhotel Petersberg, on a pine-forested hill from which guests could see boats cruising down the Rhine. The participants included four main anti-Taliban Afghan factions and was overseen by the American envoy, James Dobbins, and the U.N. representative, Lakhdar Brahimi, with observer delegations from several other countries. The conference began during Ramadan, the month when Muslims fast during daylight hours, and so the power-sharing discussions would reach their greatest intensity after the evening *iftar* meal and rage late into the night.

Karzai did not attend the conference, as he, Amerine, and the CIA team were still outside of Kandahar. Politically he was associated with the conference delegates known as the Rome Group, the collection of exiles loyal to the eighty-seven-year-old former king, Zahir Shah, who had ruled for forty years before his ouster in a coup d'état in 1973 and was still viewed by many Pashtuns as a symbol of traditional Afghan unity and more peaceful days. One of Karzai's elder brothers, Qayum, attended the conference as an adviser to the Rome Group delegation. The Taliban were not invited to the meeting, and they had no voice in the creation of the new government, an omission that Brahimi would later describe as Afghanistan's "original sin." The others in attendance were mostly Afghan exiles based in Pakistan, those with ties to Iran, and leaders of the predominant Northern Alliance.

During the Taliban's rule, the Northern Alliance had been the only real on-the-ground opposition. The alliance of Tajik, Uzbek, and Hazara rebels held shards of territory in northern Afghanistan, mostly in the mountains along the borders with Tajikistan and Uzbekistan, funded and armed with the help of Russia and Iran. Their dwindling fortunes changed dramatically on September 11. Coordinating with an American bombing campaign, the Northern Alliance broke through Taliban lines the following month. Their soldiers routed them in northern cities such as Mazar-e-Sharif and flooded into Kabul against the wishes of the Bush administration, which wanted to forge a plan for a new government before Northern Alliance forces seized ministries and barracks and took the country for themselves. They would clearly be getting a large share of government posts, but the Americans didn't want them to take everything. At the Bonn conference, Dobbins saw his primary mission as persuading the Northern Alliance leaders to "dissolve their administration and join other Taliban opponents in a more broadly based government."

The delegates were mainly in agreement that there should be an interim government for several months, followed by the *loya jirga*, to elect a transitional government for another period of time, while a new constitution could be written and, ultimately, democratic elections held for the first time in the country's modern history. The more immediate decisions were thornier: whether foreign troops should participate in peacekeeping in Kabul and who should be the leader of the new government. Some hard-line Northern Alliance members—including the front's leader, Burhanuddin Rabbani, the white-bearded former president, who promptly moved back into the palace in Kabul when the Taliban fled—demanded that any talks about new governments take place inside Afghanistan. They insisted that their own militiamen handle security in the capital, and they wanted their own representative in the palace. Others conceded that the best chance to avoid civil war was to have a Pashtun as the nominal face of the government.

As the conference opened, attendees heard welcoming remarks from the German foreign minister, Joschka Fischer, and from Afghan representatives. When Brahimi leaned into the microphone to speak, he added a surprise announcement: "Someone else would like to talk to us, from Afghanistan." A speaker that had been hanging from a wire in the center of the room above the tables crackled to life. The guests suddenly heard the congested voice of Hamid Karzai, sniffling through a cold, transmitted by his CIA-supplied satellite phone. At the moment, Karzai was sitting on a scrap of parachute on the floor of a mud hut in southern Afghanistan. He told the delegates to forget their differences and unite for the peace of the country.

"We are one nation, one culture; we are united and not divided," he said. "We all believe in Islam, but in an Islam of tolerance.

"This meeting is a path towards salvation," he added.

The brief address shocked many of the Afghans present. The very fact that Karzai was addressing the conference, a speech arranged by Brahimi and the American representatives, was an unsubtle signal of how American preferences were coalescing around him. "It went over terribly badly with the Afghans," recalled Francesc Vendrell. "It was quite obvious the international community had a plan."

Throughout the conference, the American team ended up playing a strong, arguably decisive role in Karzai becoming the new leader of Afghanistan. Some have claimed their support rose from old, clandestine links with the CIA dating back to Karzai's days on the diplomatic circuit in Pakistan. This may have helped to some degree, as he was known and generally liked, but so were many Afghan cold warriors. The more decisive factor seems to be that he was benign—both to the Americans and their rivals. Dobbins heard positive comments about Karzai from both the Northern Alliance and one of its enemies, Pakistan's intelligence service. Turkey didn't have a problem with him. The Iranians weren't opposed. The Russians spoke positively. During the conference, Dobbins spoke several times over the phone with Karzai. "He just indicated what he was doing in and around Kandahar," Dobbins recalled. "He was not campaigning for the job. He wasn't doing anything overt to push his own candidacy."

One of Karzai's ethnic rivals, the Northern Alliance's Abdullah Abdullah, lobbied for him. Abdullah knew Karzai from the early 1990s in Kabul, when Karzai worked as deputy foreign minister and Abdullah was a spokesman for the Ministry of Defense, in the newly formed mujahedeen government after the Soviet war. They became better acquainted a few years later, as comrades in the lonely pre–September 11 struggle to get the world to pay attention to the brutalities of the Taliban regime. They would meet in the Roman villa of the exiled king, at United Nations general assemblies, in the offices of the Heritage Foundation, on Capitol Hill, in foreign embassies, at academic conferences. They were cut from the same cloth: refined men who traveled among rough fighters but were not fighters themselves. They were diplomats, politicians, strategists, both educated, fluent in English. Abdullah was a foreign policy adviser to the guerrilla commander Ahmad Shah Massoud, and Karzai represented the moderate Pashtuns allied with the former king. They recognized in themselves a common vision. "I found his ideas democratic, progressive, very bright, way above an ethnic line," Abdullah told me years later.

Abdullah remembered a pre–September 11 dinner at the Rosslyn, Virginia, condo of Omar Samad, a friend who ran a radio station for diaspora Afghans. At the time, Karzai and Abdullah agreed about many things. They knew that after the Soviet withdrawal, the infighting between ethnic groups and political parties had led to terrible violence and a sense of lawlessness that had helped the Taliban movement gain momentum as a force to restore order. They agreed that Ahmad Shah Massoud's fighters, holed up in the Panjshir Valley north of Kabul, could not defeat the Taliban and that Pashtun tribes from the south needed to get more involved. "They realized there was a real problem," Samad said of the dinner meeting. "That armed resistance inside the country is absolutely essential, and how it should be expanded and should include more Pashtuns. We arrived at the point where we didn't see any solution to the Taliban other than Massoud and the king's people coming together." During the dinner, Abdullah appreciated Karzai's sense of nationalism and his arguments about transcending ethnic politics. "He was very charming," Abdullah remembered. "Very impressive."

He added, "It was naïve of me to judge someone for the destiny of a nation from these things, but these were the things that had impressed me."

There were other reasons why Abdullah advocated for Karzai at the Bonn conference, including Karzai's relative weakness (he had no militia to speak of) and his perceived malleability. Most important to Abdullah, Karzai was a Pashtun, and choosing someone from the majority ethnic group would avoid the perception among the rest of the world that "this was an ethnic war." He recognized that if the Northern Alliance tried to keep all the governing positions for itself, there would be no hope for a consensus among the other elements in opposition to the Taliban. As opposed to the king, Karzai was also relatively young. "To have these new ideas, and being exposed to the world, was important," Abdullah said. "And we knew also he had some link to the Americans. He had brothers there, family there."

"In 2001," Dobbins told me years later, "we wanted somebody who was a conciliator, somebody who would unify as much of the country as possible, somebody who would be regarded as broadly representative. We weren't looking for a tough executive who'd make hard decisions, antagonize elements of his constituency, imprison corrupt supporters. We were looking for quite the opposite."

Karzai, then, was a compromise candidate known for compromising, the favorite of no Afghan group—even his own—but the least objectionable, and least threatening, to all. The diplomats at the Bonn conference felt pressure to choose the government quickly, to fill the vacuum left by the departing Taliban and then get back to hunting al-Qaeda terrorists. There were no methodical deliberations at the conference; nor did the Americans have knowledge of the leadership qualities of all potential candidates.

After arranging for Karzai to speak at the conference, the Americans intervened on his behalf again when his own faction, the Rome Group, voted against him as its new leader. Many of these royalists felt he was too inexperienced to lead the nation. In a 9-to-2 vote, the delegation nominated Abdul Sattar Sirat, an Islamic scholar who had been justice minister decades earlier, under the king, and had more recently been teaching theology courses at a university in Saudi Arabia. Sirat had been a prodigy, the youngest member of the king's cabinet.

Hamid's elder brother Qayum was dismayed to find the family's presidential chances slipping away. He believed that Sirat had bought votes by promising cabinet seats. To his relief, the Americans preferred his brother for the role, and would not let him lose. Sirat did not meet the prevailing criteria of the moment: he had mixed Uzbek heritage, he had not been an important figure in the anti-Soviet jihad, and he was not on the ground fighting the Taliban in Afghanistan. As Dobbins wrote, "Nothing in his appearance or background conveyed charisma, popular appeal, or leadership skills, all of which the next Afghan leader would need." Dobbins, Brahimi, and their teams tried unsuccessfully to convince the other Afghan groups to veto Sirat. For one thing, the head of the Northern Alliance delegation, Yunus Qanooni, was related to Sirat by marriage. Sirat was also a leader of the Rome Group. Left with no choice, they resorted to demanding directly that Sirat step aside.

"That was the beginning of Americans intervening in Afghanistan's domestic affairs," said Mohammed Amin Farhang, another Rome Group member. Some of the other foreign representatives at the conference thought the Americans had overstepped. "What are we even doing here," Sirat told Brahimi in frustration. "It seems we have nothing to choose."

"Sirat has never forgiven the Americans," Vendrell said.

For all the rage, angst, and frustration that Karzai would cause American officials in the years to come, there is no one else to blame for his presence but themselves. The U.S. government paid him, armed him, protected him.

On the morning of December 5, 2001, the day the Bonn conference delegates agreed on the chairman of the interim administration of the new Afghan government, an American B-52 Stratofortress bomber circled forty thousand feet above the Afghan town of Shah Wali Kot. Karzai was in that town, nearing the end of his effort to liberate the Pashtun south from the Taliban. A high-level Taliban delegation was on its way across the desert to discuss with Karzai the end of hostilities. Just before nine a.m., the pilot of the B-52, confused about his target, dropped a two-thousand-pound JDAM bomb that killed some fifty men from Karzai's entourage and injured dozens more.

The bomb exploded as Karzai, a tan wool blanket around his shoulders, was in a room with his CIA team leader, Greg. It shattered the windows, and shards of glass slashed into Karzai's cheek and head. Thinking they were under attack, Greg dove on top of Karzai to protect him. Fifteen minutes after the explosion, Karzai's satellite phone rang.

"Congratulations, sir." It was Lyse Doucet, a BBC reporter calling from Bonn. "You have just been named the chairman of the interim government."

Hamid Karzai pulled up to the palace on December 12, 2001, in a convoy of SUVs driven by Americans. To get there, he had been flown by a U.S. military Chinook helicopter and then by C-130 cargo plane from Kandahar to Bagram Airfield, where the commander of the Northern Alliance forces, Mohammad Qasim Fahim, waited on the floodlit tarmac with two hundred of his soldiers. Bagram, an old Soviet base north of the capital, featured two intact buildings, a decrepit yellow control tower, and a small structure behind it with blown-out windows. When the cargo plane touched down, shortly after nine p.m., hundreds of Fahim's soldiers broke from their formation and ran toward the plane like kids freed for recess, waving their rifles and jostling for a glimpse of their new leader.

Karzai stepped out of the plane, into the chill mountain air, and looked at Fahim. Much had changed since their last run-in.

In 1993, Fahim had controlled Afghanistan's Soviet-created secret police. The decade-long Soviet conflict, the bloodiest Cold War battleground with the United States, killed nearly a million people, or about 6 percent of the nation's population, and drove five million more into exile in Pakistan, Iran, and elsewhere. But the horror of urban warfare reached its peak in the years that followed. After the Soviet Union's dissolution in 1991 and the fall, eleven weeks later, of their Afghan proxy, President Mohammad Najibullah, the front lines were drawn in the muddy blocks of the capital. Indiscriminate rocket barrages brought to Kabul a level of death and destruction these hardy survivors had not previously known. The commanders, who formed and betrayed alliances as casually as changing clothes, blocked medical and food supplies as residents perished by the thousands. Rival leaders President Burhanuddin Rabbani, the white-bearded Tajik, and Prime Minister Gulbuddin Hekmatyar, a harder-line Islamist, traded bombardments, with Hekmatyar retreating to a base south of Kabul, in Char Asiab.

Karzai at the time was deputy foreign minister, and for months he had navigated the dangerous roads between Kabul and Char Asiab in a vain attempt to mediate between Hekmatyar and Rabbani. The northerners suspected Hekmatyar of collusion with Pakistan's intelligence service in supporting Pashtun-led plots against them. In early 1994, Fahim apparently received information that Karzai himself was a Pakistani spy, and sent intelligence officers to Karzai's office in Kabul. Karzai was taken to a small, dingy interrogation room with a bare radiator, at the intelligence department. Over the course of several hours, two interrogators, including Muhammad Aref Sarwari, who would later lead Karzai's own intelligence service for a time, grilled Karzai about his connections to Pakistan and his ties to Hekmatyar. Fahim may well have been in the room. Some say that Karzai was tortured. Luckily for Karzai, rockets happened to be pummeling the city that day, and one of them smashed into the roof of the building where Karzai was imprisoned. "I saw that the roof was not there," Karzai said. "I saw that sunshine was coming in."

The commotion allowed him to escape. Reeling and bleeding, he ran home, changed his clothes, hailed a taxi, and fled the city, as well as the country.

Now, seven years later, the fact that the first person he met was Fahim said a lot about where he stood in his native country. A man's strength in Afghanistan was measured by the size of his militia. Karzai had shown up with none. He had come from Kandahar with his younger half brother Shah Wali, an aging uncle, and a few others. He had no weapons or bodyguards. Karzai and his small team immediately recognized the extreme vulnerability of their position. In his new political perch, he would be standing on the shoulders of his enemies. In order to survive, he became accustomed, quickly, to conceding to the demands of the more powerful Afghans.

"Where are your men?" Fahim asked him on that airstrip, in an exchange that Karzai would recount for years to demonstrate the trust he laid at the feet of an ethnic rival.

"You are my men," Karzai replied.

The convoy of SUVs whisked Karzai and his small entourage onto the rutted road that ran past the dark expanse of the Shomali Plain, past bomb craters, downed bridges, and derelict Soviet tanks. Karzai arrived in the darkened palace at midnight. The only guards were two Afghan men at the gate with rifles, plus a third man with a revolver, standing inside. All of them reported to the Northern Alliance, not to Karzai.

Karzai had been given a title, chairman of the Afghanistan Interim Authority, a position stipulated by the terms of the agreement at Bonn to last six months; eventually, as noted earlier, democratic elections could be held.

"I remember when he came in and we saw him first on TV after the Taliban were gone. We were so excited," recalled Waheed Omar, who had studied in Britain and would later join his government as spokesman. "I think most of the Afghans, the majority, the absolute majority of the Afghans in the country, when they saw him for the first time, and when they saw him speak for the first time, they were so much in love with him. And I was one of the people who was in love with him."

Although Karzai was propped up publicly by America, he had few domestic levers to pull. After the five years of Taliban rule, and the urban fighting of the civil war before that, the presidential palace was in abject disrepair. The eighty-three-acre grounds were wild and overgrown, with feral dogs wandering in untended gardens. Turrets on the perimeter walls had crumbled. Rooftops were battered, and bullet holes speckled the armored glass. Cockroaches skittered through the kitchen. The plumbing was broken, and the president's office smelled of sewage. That winter, a bitter chill suffused the rooms, with their vaulted halls and marble floors covered in worn and threadbare rugs. What water ran through the pipes was ice-cold. The power was often out.

The Arg had been built under Abdur Rahman, a king who wore knee-high leather boots and a fur hat. Construction on the palace had started after 1880, when British troops damaged the Bala Hissar, a fortress across town that had served as the palace, during the Second Anglo-Afghan War. For the king, referred to as the Iron Amir, this lack of lodgings insulted both his pride and his comfort. "Until the time that I built a new palace for myself, I lived in tents and in borrowed mud-houses belonging to my subjects," he wrote in a memoir.

The Iron Amir's palace included a complex of government offices and halls for public gatherings—gardens, as he wrote, nearly as large as the whole surrounding city of Kabul. All of it was enclosed by walls and a moat. The king's government kept twenty-four thousand horses, plus various camels and elephants, for dragging machinery and heavy guns. He employed footmen to deliver flowers to the various rooms, ushers to hand fruit to palace officials, water and tea boys, gardeners and barbers, draftsmen and sappers, a court astrologer, professional chess and backgammon players, a personal reader of bedtime stories, plus a man known as an *arz begi*, whose job was to loudly shout out any complaints that visitors might have. From his new palace, the Iron Amir expected anything but a middling future for his beloved country. All would be triumph or disaster. "There is no doubt that Afghanistan is a country that will either rise to be a very strong, famous kingdom, or will be swept altogether from the surface of the earth," he wrote. "The latter state of things would come about if the country came under the rule of an inexperienced and weak [king]. In this case the country would become divided, and the very name of the kingdom of Afghanistan would cease to exist."

The fate of all those who followed the Iron Amir, weak or strong, was one long, bloody scroll of violent death, often at the hands of a relative. In the twentieth century alone, leaders left the throne in the following ways: pistol shot to the head (Habibullah, 1919); forcibly deposed after eight days (Habibullah's younger brother Nasrullah, 1919); chased out of Kabul by cavalry (Habibullah's son Amanullah, 1929); airlifted out of Kabul by the Royal Air Force after three days (Habibullah's son Inayatullah, 1929); shot by firing squad (Bacha-e-Saqao, 1929); shot by a student attending an afternoon award ceremony in the palace garden (King Mohammed Nadir Shah, 1933); ousted while in Europe for an eye operation (King Zahir Shah, 1973); shot in a palace hallway (President Mohammed Daoud Khan, 1978); suffocated with a pillow (President Nur Mohammad Taraki, 1979); either shot while drinking a cocktail in the palace or slain by grenade fragments (Hafizullah Amin, 1979); forced out by Mikhail Gorbachev (Babrak Karmal, 1986); resigned after Soviet withdrawal then later tortured, castrated, shot, tied to a vehicle and dragged around the palace grounds by the Taliban, then hanged from a traffic police booth, with Pakistani rupees, American dollars, and cigarettes stuffed into his mouth and nostrils (Mohammad Najibullah, 1996).

The Taliban announced their arrival in Kabul with this last flourish of brutality. But the group kept its capital in the southern city of Kandahar, and those officials who occupied the Kabul palace imitated the ascetic lifestyle of their leader, Mullah Mohammed Omar. When meeting in the Arg, the mullahs would unroll mattresses and arrange pillows on the floor for their discussions. As Karzai's team explored the palace, they found a certain faded elegance in those first weeks, with its candle sconces on the walls, exposed ceiling beams, dark wood walls, and crystal chandeliers. The palace housed the national treasury, rooms filled with old maps and documents, and a famous collection of loot known as the Bactrian Hoard, a collection of more than twenty thousand items of gold, ivory, and gems.

Shah Wali Karzai, who'd joined his elder brother, lived for several months in the palace. The Taliban's handiwork was hard to miss. The pre-Taliban president, Burhanuddin Rabbani, had returned to the presidential residence and was showing no intention of leaving, so Hamid Karzai and Shah Wali slept in one of King Zahir Shah's old rooms. It was known as the Peacock Room, for the hundreds of birds that decorated its silk wallpaper. The Taliban had painted white blotches over each bird's head to hide such an indecent display. In a painting of a man with a cow, they'd scratched out the faces of both. Stone lions guarding the entrance of the palace had been decapitated. A large wooden boat, a gift for the monarchy, remained dry-docked inside the palace. Shah Wali noticed that the Taliban censors had somehow overlooked the cross on its prow. One day, Shah Wali got dispatched by his elder brother to buy two pickup trucks for the palace, so they wouldn't be stranded inside. "We looked everywhere," he said. "We couldn't find anything to buy."

To many of the exiled Afghans who had grown up in the monarchy's relative calm, the city they returned to in the winter of 2001 seemed unrecognizable. Bullet-pocked and rocket-strafed husks stood in place of once elegant homes and shops and universities. The boulevards were cratered, trees razed. Shops and restaurants were closed and empty. It was a town of wood smoke, wheelbarrows, donkey carts. It smelled of the open sewage that trickled into the gutters. On the streets, there seemed to be as many stray dogs as cars. On his first evening back in Kabul, Mohammed Amin Farhang, who would become commerce minister in Karzai's government, stayed at the Intercontinental Hotel, perched on a hill overlooking the capital. "I looked out my window and I saw very few lights in the entire city," he recalled. "On the streets, people had long beards. They had depressing faces. They were not smiling."

Said Tayeb Jawad, who quit his law practice in San Francisco to join Karzai as his spokesman, later becoming chief of staff, almost got attacked by a pack of stray dogs while walking home from the palace one night. "The city was full of them," he said. "Nobody was in the city."

The CIA was handing out millions of dollars in Rubbermaid plastic tubs to the regional warlords they had worked with to drive out the Taliban, but the Afghan government had hardly any money. On their way out of Kabul, the Taliban looted the vault of the Central Bank. The financial system was chaos; there were four different currencies in use throughout the country. Ryan Crocker, the veteran American diplomat appointed on January 2, 2002, as the embassy's first chargé d'affaires, spent one freezing January night—the glass had been blown out of the windows—huddled on a satellite phone, trying to get several million dollars unfrozen out of the Federal Reserve to give Karzai's government some seed money.

"We basically need billions of dollars," Karzai said that week.

The palace had no computers. The cell phone network had not been built, and the landline system had been destroyed. Press aides would travel by bicycle to deliver handwritten stories to the state news agency. In the frigid palace, note takers fumbled as they tried to write with gloves on. The earliest meetings of the cabinet were recorded on stationery left behind by the Taliban, with their emblem of two swords curled around a sprig of wheat, and the sun rising behind a Koran. Karzai's first inaugural speech was penned by the glow of a flashlight. When the cabinet convened, the twenty-six ministers, five vice presidents, and Karzai's staff sat in a ragtag collection of different types of seating. The security guards wore camouflage clothes and sandals.

"It was like Flintstone-istan," one aide said.

At the United States embassy just down the road, which had been closed since 1989, the arriving diplomats had walked into their own Cold War time capsule. The main chancery building had no heat, electricity, or water. "Pictures of Ronald Reagan and George Shultz adorned the walls. Warm beer and Coca-Cola sat in the refrigerator, and a half-empty bottle of Jack Daniel's stood on the bar in the basement," James Dobbins wrote in his memoir. The small State Department team was sleeping in an underground bunker heated by kerosene stoves, waiting in long lines each morning for the toilet, and sharing a single computer and telephone.

Couriers from the palace ran back and forth down the street delivering messages. In a vault they found a folded American flag and a note from Sergeant James M. Blake, one of the departing Marines from the earlier decade. "Take care of the flag. For those of us here it means a lot," the note read. "We Kabul Marines endured, as I am sure you will."

The United States made clear in those first months that it would not be pouring money into the Afghan government for major infrastructure improvements, though it was obvious that the war-ravaged country would benefit from some investment. Ambassador Robert Finn argued for ambitious infrastructure projects, such as rebuilding the country's major highway, the "ring road" that connected major cities, but the Bush administration refused. The United States donated $297 million to Afghanistan in 2002, about half of what Europe gave. "Nation building" for the Bush administration was a slur. Condoleezza Rice had written before the 2000 elections that the U.S. military "is not a civilian police force. It is not a political referee. And it is most certainly not designed to build a civilian society." Karzai, therefore, did not have at his disposal vast sums or patronage projects with which to buy off his enemies or win support for his government.

Four days after Karzai's arrival, on December 16, under an overcast sky, a small gathering convened to reopen the embassy. Dobbins stood at a podium in a tan trench coat. "We are here," he told the small crowd. "And we are here to stay."

Karzai's early months were a whirlwind of meetings with foreign visitors and local well-wishers. Wrapped in robes and blankets, Karzai met an unending stream of Afghan and foreign dignitaries. (The Northern Alliance would later scoff that Karzai would have frozen without its blankets.)

"Everything had to be done, and almost all of it had to be done by Karzai," Crocker said.

The smallest details were his responsibility. During one breakfast meeting, Karzai mentioned to Crocker that Afghanistan needed a flag. Neither the horizontally striped tricolor flag of the pre-Taliban Rabbani government—green, white, and black behind an emblem of crossed curving swords—nor the Taliban's spare white banner was acceptable. He asked Crocker what it should look like.

"Sir, that is well beyond my pay grade," Crocker remembers telling him.

Karzai thought that it should look something like the monarchical flag that flew during King Zahir Shah's reign, but not exactly. As Crocker watched, Karzai sketched out a design on a napkin.

To the governments of the West, Karzai touched down heaven-sent. He was urbane, peace-loving, eloquent in several tongues, amenable to modernity, democracy, rights for women, with none of the barefoot bizarreness of other Afghan longbeards, none of their outlandish rap sheets of baking, impaling, and raping their enemies. He enjoyed poetry, literature, strategic discussions of geopolitics. He had charm, charisma, a flair for the stage. He was lauded in dozens of articles in the American press for his "deft diplomatic and political touch," for his vision as a "courageous Afghan leader," for being "elegant and eloquent," "brave, even heroic," a "Western favorite," with "good intentions."

So much had to be built anew, but in those first months Karzai presented himself to foreign diplomats as calm and optimistic. He would hardly miss a chance to regale his visitors with his unabashed support for the American project in Afghanistan. "There was only admiration for the Americans," Javed Ludin, one of Karzai's first spokesmen, told me. "Simply in every conversation—for a time it became too repetitive—when he spoke to the Afghan people, in his office or outside, he would always talk about America." Karzai himself would recall this period as the "golden age" of his relations with the Americans.

Those who met him came away impressed with his energy and enthusiasm. "He was open. He was honest. And he was very keen to work with the international community," recalled John McColl, a British Army general who was the first commander of the International Security Assistance Force. "He was delighted that we would be there."

Karzai received delegations every day from around Afghanistan, many of them asking for foreign troops for their village or province. While the country was relatively secure at the time, they worried that new gangs or militias would fill the void left by the Taliban, and they believed that foreign troops could best keep them safe. Karzai supported this view and often begged visiting American officials to send more troops. McColl wanted to expand ISAF quickly and deploy to other major cities to secure the country and prevent a resurgence of the Taliban. Instead, the American footprint remained about the same for years. Graphs showing the U.S. troop presence are largely flat for the first several years of the war; the troop line wouldn't shoot up dramatically until after Obama's inauguration in 2009.

"I'm afraid the United States lead is critical in all these things," McColl said. "It shouldn't be the case, but I regret that it is. And at that stage, the American view was that American forces don't do nation building."

The most important job for the Kabul-based peacekeeping mission was to ensure that Karzai and his fledgling coalition government remained intact. Karzai knew he was a man surrounded. Most of the power the Bonn conference had allotted to the new Afghan government had gone to the Northern Alliance. The four most important ministries—defense, interior, intelligence, and foreign—were controlled by the Northern Alliance, and all by lieutenants of the slain Ahmad Shah Massoud. "They were dominating and no one else's views mattered," one of Karzai's aides said.

The commander Mohammad Fahim's fifteen thousand Northern Alliance militiamen had become the nation's military, and Karzai, even as commander in chief, did not have de facto control over them. For this reason, among others, Karzai had welcomed the arrival of ISAF to Kabul. These coalition troops could keep the peace in the capital, preventing power grabs by the Northern Alliance or any Taliban return, while American troops conducted their cave-bombing campaign against al-Qaeda Karzai constantly asked for more American troops to be deployed to more Afghan cities.

The palace staff was frightened of Fahim. He was brusque and bullying and would talk brashly about his power over Karzai. He sometimes sat in Karzai's chair in the palace office, even while Karzai was present. Fahim's office was outside the palace, and whenever he wanted to see Karzai, his convoy would breeze through the palace gates and deposit him directly outside Karzai's office. He acted like the warlord of Kabul.

During the *loya jirga*—the June 2002 conference stipulated by the Bonn meetings to select the transitional government—Afghans brokered deals for cabinet seats. Fahim had mentioned to a fellow Panjshiri that if Karzai's demands were unacceptable to the Northern Alliance, he could have one of his loyal guards in the palace kill Karzai. It was just Fahim's dark sense of humor, some of his friends believed, but the sentiment reflected the precarious nature of Karzai's hold on the government. At night, when Pashtun staffers left their offices and walked across the darkened palace grounds, Tajik guards would cock their guns from the shadows, "just to intimidate you," one staffer recalled.

"There were continuously threats," Jawad, the chief of staff, said. "There was always a threat of assassination of the president. . . . It was not coming from outside the palace, it was inside."

When the Americans started supplying cash to the palace, used to pay salaries and other expenses, Fahim's men demanded that Jawad give them a cut. He refused. One of Fahim's outraged guards told him, "You better give us this money or you won't be living the next day." Fahim was well known in the government for demanding that his men receive prompt payment. He would get infuriated if there were any interruptions. "I will cut you in pieces, like meat in a butcher shop," Fahim raged to bureaucrats in the Finance Ministry.

Karzai believed that four of his own bodyguards had been designated to kill him whenever Fahim gave the signal. He mentioned this several times to Robert Finn, the first American ambassador in Kabul during the war. "He knew he was in an uneasy situation," Finn told me. "This was a world in which people got killed all the time, and they deal with that, and live with that. That was one of the reasons why he kept them close to him, and didn't want to piss them off."

Karzai's desire to transcend ethnicity, to unite Afghans and move past the brutalities of the civil war, was also central to his political identity. He always opposed political parties, fearing that such factionalism could lead to more bloodshed. Once the spigots of American foreign aid began to ease open, one of the first priorities for Karzai and the United States was to rebuild the Kabul–Kandahar Highway, a three-hundred-mile portion of the ring road, initially built in the 1960s with American financing, that linked Afghanistan's two most important cities. At the start of the war, it could take two jarring days to traverse the potholed moonscape. "You were likely to get hit by bandits along the way," recalled James Bever, the head of the Kabul office of the U.S. Agency for International Development at the time. "You were likely to lose not your muffler but your entire axle, if the car wasn't washed out in a flood." For Karzai, the road represented a tangible demonstration of his goal for national unity, by physically connecting southern Pashtuns and northern Tajiks.

After the $500 million project was deemed completed, in December 2003, shrinking the journey between cities to six hours, Bever sat down with Karzai to plan the next phase of the road-building effort. Bever wanted to focus on cities in the south and east, where the Taliban insurgency was showing signs of life. Karzai picked up a pen and drew lines on a map in the country's north and west. Karzai insisted the roads should go to provinces such as Faryab and Badakshan, even the Panjshir Valley. "I wanted to focus more of our assistance effort where more of our troubles were," Bever recalled. "He said that was not sufficient. He said, This can't be just about the Pashtuns. We've got a country to build."

They also had a palace to build. Karzai's security guards would find people climbing over the walls—when they didn't just walk through the holes—to use the palace as their toilet. "A mess, an insecure mess. It was so horrible and so hard for us to secure," recalled Mohammad Latifi, one of Karzai's first bodyguards. "We had to go through so much to block these people. All the warlords, generals, saying, 'I'm going. You cannot block me.' It took a lot of hard work." The wiring in Karzai's home was so shoddy that part of the kitchen caught fire in 2003; the palace staff brought fire extinguishers from the National Security Council offices to douse the blaze. "Your house is not a security risk," an adviser told Karzai. "It's a fire risk."

Among the staff there were holdovers from earlier administrations and jobs that dated back to the monarchy: one position was that of *galam-e makhsus*, or "special pen," a man employed because of his lovely handwriting; his job was to write out decrees in calligraphy. Many of Karzai's new aides had little experience with either Afghanistan or government. Several of them were friends or acquaintances of the Karzai family who had returned from exile to pitch in. Some had degrees from universities in Europe or America, but others had survived during their exile years on whatever jobs they could find as immigrants. An early legal adviser had worked in the kitchen of Qayum's Baltimore restaurant. Another adviser would regularly complain that he could make more money pumping gas in San Diego than working for the president.

"You basically had ice cream dealers, car salesmen running policy in the palace," recalled one Karzai aide. "People had no credentials."

When it came time to train a new presidential guard force, one of the palace aides, Khaleeq Ahmad, supervised a round of tests for a group of one hundred young men brought in from a village in Uruzgan Province. Ahmad passed out pens and watched as the recruits stared helplessly at the quiz. Many got up and handed him blank pages. Others had made random scribbles or had written only their names. "I said, 'Hey, guys, one person passed, all the others failed. Can we keep this person?' They went and huddled and came back. 'Khaleeq Jan, he's our teacher in the village. If we give him to you, we won't have anybody to teach our children.'"

During one outdoor meeting between Karzai and the Iranian foreign minister, in a tree-shaded palace courtyard, a loud gunshot shattered the calm. Jawad, the chief of staff, ran off to find the source of the gunfire and discovered a guard on the ground gripping his bloody boot. He had shot himself in the foot.

Within seven months of moving into the palace, one of Karzai's vice presidents, Abdul Haji Qadir, a Pashtun from eastern Afghanistan, was shot and killed as he drove through Kabul. The assassination caused enough alarm that General Dan McNeill, the U.S. military commander at Bagram, got ordered by Defense Secretary Donald Rumsfeld to visit Karzai late one night to convince him to accept American bodyguards. McNeill felt it would be rude to meet inside Karzai's home, with his wife, Zeenat, present, so they sat in the yard on the warm July night. They talked about the threats to Karzai's life and America's responsibility to protect him. Karzai immediately refused McNeill's offer, which he found humiliating.

"He was adamant," McNeill recalled. "He said, 'I'll be perceived as less of a man. I'm a puppet of the United States of America.'"

McNeill prevailed after a couple hours, promising Karzai that the guards would be temporary and unobtrusive. The United States supplied Karzai with a close-protection detail of about fifty special operations troops, who were posted in Karzai's office and traveled with him everywhere he went. Not long afterward, Karzai went to Kandahar to attend the wedding of his brother Ahmed Wali. The new team of Delta Force security guards trailed him wearing tan vests, khakis, and wraparound shades.

It was the first time Karzai had returned to his hometown since becoming the country's leader. Kandaharis came out in enthusiastic greeting, thousands of them lining the streets to watch the president's motorcade.

"This was amazing," Karzai told me years later. "At that time I would move freely through the streets of Kandahar and other Afghan cities. I went in an open-roofed car. What is that called—a convertible?" In fact, it was a gray Lexus SUV with a sunroof, and Karzai sat in the back seat, behind a mustachioed driver with three-starred epaulets on his shoulders. As the convoy crept through town, Karzai stood up through the sunroof and waved at the cheering masses.

Karzai's main political rival, the new Kandahar governor Gul Agha Sherzai, had organized the visit, and the entourage stopped at the newly renovated governor's house before heading to the wedding. Karzai waved his left hand out the open window, his watch glinting in the sun.

A teenage boy walked up to Karzai's window as the car inched along. He wore a white skullcap and a tan *shalwar kameez*. He was smiling. The first two gunshots were fired at that moment, followed quickly by two more. A pause. Five. Six. Then firing everywhere.

"I had not heard that sound since Vietnam," wrote Peter Tomsen, a veteran American diplomat who was traveling with Karzai. "I jumped out of the car, as did several Delta commandos. The assassin stood outside Karzai's window, firing into his car as it inched forward. Sometime between his second and third round, the Delta Force squad went into action. A commando fired right through the front window of his vehicle."

At the sound of gunshots, Karzai hunched over in the back seat, sinking his head into his shoulders. The crowd scattered and ran. American bodyguards rattled off rounds, taking aim behind the open doors of trailing cars. A black sedan honked and rear-ended Karzai's vehicle, pushing it forward, out of the firing zone. A bullet had ripped into the driver's seat, tearing the tan fabric beneath the headrest. Another hit a window. An eighteen-year-old shopkeeper named Azimulah Khaksar who tried to stop the shooting was killed, as was the would-be assassin. Governor Sherzai, who was sitting next to Karzai, and the president's Delta Force commander were both grazed with bullets. Karzai was unharmed.

Afterward, Karzai spoke to a BBC reporter from inside the governor's compound, where he was collecting himself after the assassination attempt. He seemed unfazed by the chaos.

"I didn't even know who was firing where, so . . ." Karzai said. He shrugged and sort of smiled. He held yellow prayer beads in one hand. "I'm safe and sound."

"How do you feel now, a bit shaken?" the reporter asked him.

"No, I'm fine. I expect things like that to come across the way. I've been through it before."

After that warm September day in Kandahar, Karzai's helicopter would be shot at with rocket-propelled grenades, gunmen would ambush a dignitary-filled celebration marking the end of the Soviet war, and a group of Kabul University students and their professor would be arrested for plotting his assassination. "Nothing new for us," Karzai told me.

The shooter in Kandahar was named Abdul Rahman; he was of the same tribe, the Barakzais, as Governor Sherzai, and from neighboring Helmand Province. Speculation would always linger that Sherzai was somehow involved in the shooting, but when I asked, Karzai discounted the idea. He told me he had eventually tracked down the family of the shooter. "I sent a note to the parents that I have forgiven their son, that I'm sorry he's dead," Karzai said. He later paid for their pilgrimage to Mecca.

After the Kandahar assassination attempt, the chairman of the House

Afghan interim president Hamid Karzai in front of the pool outside his home on the grounds of the presidential palace, July 11, 2003

International Relations Committee, Henry J. Hyde, and ranking member Tom Lantos wrote a letter to Secretary of State Colin Powell and Defense Secretary Donald Rumsfeld about their "grave concern over the safety of Afghanistan President Hamid Karzai." They wanted an even larger private security force to guard the president.

"The stability of the Afghan Transitional Government is of paramount importance both to the security and diplomatic interests of the United States," they wrote. "The linchpin of that stability for the foreseeable future is the safety of President Karzai."

In those years, the odds were stacked against Karzai surviving, let alone succeeding, in his job. An American who worked for Lakhdar Brahimi recalled one trip, when they asked an old wizened villager what he thought of Karzai.

"Hamid is a good boy. He doesn't kill people. He doesn't sell drugs. He doesn't do any of those bad things." The man paused. "What makes you possibly think he could be president of Afghanistan?"

4

JUMP-STARTING A COUNTRY

Aino. Aino is a woman. She's very famous in Kandahar. Her tomb is here. You know the person who established Afghanistan, Ahmad Shah Durrani, the king? He came back from India. He had been in India to beat people up and get back the gold that was taken from him. The old ways, eh? Like the pirates. So he came to Afghanistan with a lot of gold. A lot of gold. He and his men stayed outside of Kandahar City to rest and clean themselves so they could see their families the next day. Well, one husband who was newly married, he couldn't wait. He left the camp and knocked on his wife's door. He said he just couldn't stay away, he had been gone so long, "Oh, I miss you so much. Could you open the door?" She stares at him and said: "Where is the king?" He says, "It's fine, everyone else will come tomorrow." She says "Go away. Don't come back without your king." So when he went back to camp, he was captured by the other soldiers, for being a deserter. He said, "Yes, I left, but I came back." He was taken to the king. And the king said, "Why did you escape?" He told the story and the king was not happy with him. So the king called the man's wife before him. He gave her a big piece of land. Land that had water. This land right here. Aino Mena. We named it after her. Because she's very popular. And she's buried here. You should thank me that I didn't name it after myself.

—Mahmood Karzai, July 13, 2011

THE SUMMER SUN WAS SETTING, and Mahmood Karzai was feeling expansive.

"You know where the most beautiful girls in the world are?" he asked me. "China. I swear. For some reason, nobody is overweight. It's amazing. And, you know, there are two reasons for that. First of all, they don't eat bread. And there's no dessert in China. Absolutely none. At the end of every meal, people eat one piece of watermelon. That's it."

Mahmood was driving me around in his Land Cruiser touring Aino Mena, the gated community in Kandahar that he had spent the past eight years building in the middle of a desert war zone. Everything was walled off from the chaos outside, the fertilizer bombs and gunmen on dirt bikes, and it felt wholly foreign to Afghanistan. The first thing I noticed about the place was the trees. The scorched city outside of rickshaws and dirt bikes and mud huts gave way to quiet rows of bushy eucalyptuses casting dappled shade on smoothly paved roads. These were California trees, their seeds hand-carried and planted by the thousands. Water gurgled in prodigal wetness inside Aino Mena. Kids splashed in the canals and danced under a cataract pouring from a car wash. The property was immense, and only about two thousand houses had so far been built on it, a fraction of what Mahmood intended. Much of the land was empty desert, running flat until it ended at some barren foothills in the distance. In the city outside, people fought and died over water; the reservoirs were silted up. But inside Aino Mena, in the empty land far from any of the houses, I once saw a line of seventeen water tankers pumping hoseloads of fresh water into the ground for a row of decorative saplings. On the medians of the split-lane highways, sunflowers and buttercups lazed their yellow heads. The grass on the soccer field was bright green.

"There's so many beautiful things around the world," Mahmood told me. "I'll show you something I copied from Rome. Let's see if you recognize it."

He turned the wheel, and we started down Fountain Street. As we passed houses, he mentioned that he'd installed polished granite countertops in the kitchens and bathrooms. "I've got very good furniture. All American standard. Very good stuff. People have not seen stuff like this. Once you show them the good life, they love it. That's how you change a society. Not by talk, but by practical steps. See, we've already changed the attitude of the people regarding design. They no longer design like Pakistanis."

We came upon a double-decker fountain in the middle of a traffic circle. Two young Afghan girls in flower-print shawls were sitting on the rim, watching the water splash down.

"This one was designed by architect Mahmood Karzai," he said proudly. "Do you know which one is this?"

I didn't.

"It's right in front of the Vatican." He laughed. "I brought a picture of it, and then they made it."

He went on: "This is the fountain road. This is our largest road. Part of it is commercial. You go shopping, you come and park here. You walk around, you enjoy yourself, and then you go home." He sped along the wide lane, ticking off the features of the brilliant future he imagined. "Fountain. Commercial. Fountain. Commercial. Then you have trees, every ten meters. Then we'll have Christmas lights on all these trees. You know, the white ones."

Mahmood slowed for a speed bump, painted with jaunty white and yellow stripes, something I'd never seen in Afghanistan, then sped up again. The road was wide and nearly empty and stretched out far into the desert. "A good road for racing," he noted. We passed over a canal and through a decorative white fencerow topped by potted plants and thirty-two glass lanterns, then drove out to a large lake in the middle of the property. From the sky, I was told, it resembled the map of Afghanistan. In the middle of the lake he planned to install five more fountains to wow the future crowds. Along the shore he would build a park where families could picnic under tented overhangs.

At the far end of the property, abutting the rocky foothills that rose from the desert, earthmovers were building a dam. The dam would create a reservoir for the project and another lake, where he planned to build a hotel at the water's edge. "This will be outside, the patio for the hotel," he said, pointing at a slope between two barren hills. "You'll be able to sit by the water and have a nice hamburger.

"Now, who would criticize something like this?" he asked. "You tell me."

Mahmood could be an amusing guy to be around. He was blustery, brash, buffoonish, full of outlandish plots and plans, a man who spoke without filter or seeming regard for the facts—Afghanistan's version of Donald Trump. The arrival of Hamid Karzai in the palace had transformed the fortunes of the entire family, and no one had benefited as handsomely as Mahmood had. He was perhaps the best example of one of the familiar archetypes of the war: the profiteering capitalist who saw the conflict as a fabulous economic opportunity.

As the insurgency picked up again, the Bush administration quickly shook off its aversion to nation building and resorted to trying to buy a better Afghanistan. A dirt-poor country where most people lived on a couple of dollars a day had become a petri dish for billion-dollar experiments in American foreign-aid spending—a way for the U.S. government to experiment in remaking Afghanistan in its own image. This type of opportunity brought all sorts of people out of the woodwork. Mahmood's kind could be found everywhere: private security contractors in khaki vented shirts and American-flag caps swinging open the heavy doors of their armored SUVs; shipping and logistics entrepreneurs sipping tea to a Muzak sound track of Enya's "Orinoco Flow" in the marble-floored café of Kabul's Serena Hotel; wealthy sons of Afghan warlords living in quadruple-decker McMansions surrounded by razor wire and surveillance cameras and sandwiched together on streets of mud, because no one paid taxes. When the Taliban gave up their power, the country they bequeathed the Karzais was bankrupt and broken. Whole industries had to be remade: telecom, banking, mining, petroleum. It helped if you happened to know people in the palace. Since the Americans had invaded, Mahmood had used his family connections to hurl himself into all sorts of business schemes: car dealerships, cement factories, apartment buildings, banks. He was, in a way, the American experiment writ small, the apotheosis of all the big U.S. policy goals: development, wealth creation, jobs, peace. The way Hamid Karzai wanted to be remembered as the man who returned Afghanistan to peaceful governance, Mahmood saw himself as the remaker of its private industry. And Aino Mena would be his greatest legacy.

"I wanted to build a modern city," he said.

As was true for many of the Karzai siblings, most of Mahmood's experience with cities had been in America. In 1976, around the age of twenty, he had said good-bye to his fiancée, Wazhma, and boarded an airplane leaving Kabul. Since then, he had hustled to make a life for himself in the United States. The ouster of King Zahir Shah in 1973 and the rise of the Communists had made things increasingly dangerous for old allies such as the Karzais to live in Afghanistan, and one by one the siblings had fled the country.

The first to arrive in America had been Qayum, a soft-spoken agriculture student, who in 1969 had been sent to Oklahoma by the Afghan Air Force for pilot training; forced to drop out because of recurring motion sickness, he headed east to Washington, D.C. There he met and married an American woman, Patricia Morgan—her family was from Pittsburgh and her mother was the resident manager of an apartment building on

New Hampshire Avenue in northwest D.C., where Qayum was living—and started a career in the restaurant business.

Mahmood arrived in America several years later, accustomed to living among the elite because of their father's position. He had been studying medicine at Kabul University and now had to start with almost nothing. Qayum had scraped together his flight school savings to pay $1,000 for a 1957 Chevy to drive himself to Washington. Mahmood began with even less. "I went to the U.S. with twenty dollars in my pocket," he said.

Mahmood wanted to work, but he wasn't interested in joining Qayum, who was employed at the Devil's Fork, a restaurant inside the Gramercy Inn on Rhode Island Avenue, just off Scott Circle in downtown D.C. It was an upscale but eclectic place; upon its opening, in 1968, it had billed itself as "Washington's newest luxury restaurant." The dining room, with its fieldstone walls, was dimly lit; one review described it as a "dark cave that stretches farther than the eye can see." The Devil's Fork hosted banquets and office parties for up to two hundred people, and it became a regular dining spot for local politicians. It served Polynesian cocktails in the evening and held a Sunday New Orleans jazz brunch buffet for $4.95, where strolling musicians played Dixieland tunes and diners received a complimentary drink. "The culinary emphasis is on variety—roast beef, chicken livers, eggs, fried chicken, creamed seafood, crepes, quiche, macaroni and cheese, Jell-o molds, fresh fruit cup and considerably more," *The Washington Post* wrote in a 1978 review.

Qayum had come to the Devil's Fork after working part-time as a busboy at a golf course restaurant in Olney, Maryland. That job was enough to pay for the studio apartment he rented a block from Dupont Circle for $82 a month, including utilities, which he shared with two other Afghan men. But the manager would only hire him for a couple of days a week, and he wanted something full-time. He found that at the Devil's Fork. Qayum started as a busboy, learned to cook in the kitchen, and later became a waiter.

As a newly arrived Afghan from a conservative Muslim society, he sometimes felt out of place. He was scandalized when one of the owners, a retired colonel, would saunter in with his pals for lunch, flaunting various girlfriends. "They were a bunch of womanizers, my goodness," he said. And when Qayum once stood up for a fellow staff member who was getting berated, he got mocked for it: "Oh, you speak *English*," the owner said, clapping like a child. But Qayum generally didn't mind the work. The tips were good, and they paid for his classes at Montgomery College, a community college in Silver Spring, Maryland, where he studied biology and took classes in American government and economics.

By the time Mahmood arrived in America, on a tourist visa, Qayum and Patricia were living in Wheaton, Maryland, a suburb north of the Beltway, and Mahmood moved in with them. He had a blustery self-confidence and little interest in waiting tables. He felt that handing people their Jell-O molds was beneath him. "It was difficult, for this prestigious family, to be waiting on other people," Patricia Karzai recalled. But Mahmood needed cash. He had enrolled in summer school classes at Montgomery College. He had also promised one of his friends in Afghanistan that he would send money. He was not intimidated by hard work. He decided to become a logger.

Mahmood had seen an advertisement for a timber company in southern Maryland, about an hour south of Washington, on the rural peninsula of rolling tobacco fields and Amish farms between the Potomac River and the Chesapeake Bay. He bought a chain saw and set out to make his fortune. Each day, he left the apartment by sunrise and returned long after dark. "He would come back bruised up, really messed up, tired," Qayum said.

"The first couple days, he came back and said, 'I've only cut down fifteen trees. I'm not making any money at this. I need a bigger saw,'" Patricia Karzai said. "He's always been very ambitious. Always."

The tree-cutting foray turned out to be a short-lived failure, but Mahmood was enjoying America. He and his brother played volleyball and soccer, shot pool, and hung out in a large park near their apartment. He had his favorite pizza joint, where he marveled at how you would take a number and it would show up on a screen when your order was ready.

"I thought the U.S. was absolutely amazing: eating pizza, going to college—everything was beautiful," he said.

Mahmood eventually took a busboy job at the Devil's Fork with Qayum; he also worked at a restaurant in a Sheraton hotel in Silver Spring. He worked two shifts a day, while also taking community college classes. He began by six a.m. and did not get home until after midnight. "He was an extraordinarily hardworking person," Qayum said of his brother.

"I felt like I was made from steel," Mahmood recalled.

He earned enough money to buy a bright red Chevrolet Camaro two years after he arrived, financing the purchase price of $5,900 with payments of $180 a month. He sent money back to Wazhma in Afghanistan; she joined him in the States the following year, when the Soviets invaded.

Mahmood's ambitions were difficult to contain. While Qayum continued to work for years as a waiter, then a restaurant manager at the Bethesda Marriott, Mahmood yearned to become his own boss.

In 1981, the year his first daughter was born, while he was living with Wazhma in a three story brick apartment building on South Buchanan Street in Arlington, Virginia, Mahmood decided to buy his own restaurant. He had saved about $30,000, and he wanted to invest. He settled on Cagney's Restaurant, a D.C. lunch spot that doubled as a trendy New Wave nightclub (David Bowie stopped by one night during his Glass Spider Tour), nestled amid boutiques and bookstores on Dupont Circle. The deal ultimately fell through when the owners backed out. Mahmood tried to recoup his $17,000 deposit in court, but the sellers had filed for bankruptcy, and Mahmood never saw his money.

On January 14, 2002, less than a month after Hamid Karzai was sworn in at the palace, Mahmood registered a new company, AFCO International, LLC, with the state of Virginia. In the two decades since his failed restaurant venture, he had recovered nicely. In partnership with Qayum, he had opened a successful Afghan restaurant, the Helmand, near Wrigley Field in Chicago, then branched out on his own with two more Afghan restaurants, in San Francisco and Cambridge, Massachusetts, whose total gross sales in 2001 exceeded $2.5 million. Mahmood would go on to open two Mexican restaurants, the Viva Burrito, in Boston, and the Tampico Mexican Grill, in Baltimore, while dabbling in real estate in Oakland and owning buildings and parking lots in Baltimore. He had two daughters, and he lived in a spacious house on Shady Lane in Glenwood, Maryland. Mahmood had separated himself from Afghanistan more than almost any of his siblings—Hamid had stayed in politics while in exile in Pakistan, and Qayum was active in diaspora circles in Washington—but for all of the family members, the lure of the country of their youth remained strong. With Hamid installed in the palace, and the U.S. government eager to pay for rebuilding Afghanistan, Mahmood saw an opportunity to expand his business ambitions on an entirely different scale.

For many Afghans living in exile, September 11 presented a fork in the road, a chance to return to the homes they'd fled because of war or oppression or lack of opportunity, to use the skills they had developed in the West to help rebuild their broken country. They saw a way to make money, but just as real was the rekindled patriotism, an eruption of nationalism that had lain dormant through years of foreign invasions and civil war. Mahmood was full of enthusiasm for new ventures. He would talk at length about the virtues of an unfettered free market economy, the theories of Adam Smith, the rebuilding of postwar Japan. Dubai and Singapore and the boomtowns of Asia and the Middle East were his rivals and role models. If Afghanistan could be pulled into the modern world, Mahmood believed, businessmen, not soldiers, would get them there. What his country needed, more than reconciliation with the Taliban or ethnic unity, were jobs, industry, wealth.

Within the first year of the war, Mahmood had helped establish the Afghan-American Chamber of Commerce and become its first chairman. His enthusiasm for private enterprise and rebuilding his native country won him new friends among business-minded Republicans in Washington. At the first large Kabul gathering of the chamber, a fellow Afghan-American businessman, Abdullah Nadi, gave a heartfelt endorsement of his friend, telling the crowd that Mahmood was a man whose heart and mind were devoted to all Afghan people, regardless of ethnic group or social status.

"I believed in him," Nadi told me.

Abdullah Nadi's life had run parallel to the Karzais'. He had immigrated to the United States in 1973, three years before Mahmood, and in early 2001 was living at the end of a cul-de-sac on a wooded lane in Alexandria, Virginia. Nadi was an imposing man, with a bald head and stern bearing. As a young man, he had been a standout volleyball player at Kabul Polytechnic University, where he'd studied civil engineering. In the States, he had worked as an engineer for the Virginia Department of Transportation, reviewing plans for its compliance with zoning ordinances and traffic laws. He had developed a small shopping center in suburban Virginia and owned a string of Jerry's Subs and Pizza franchises in the suburbs. Nadi had talked with Mahmood about the prospect of opening a wedding hall like those popular in Kabul. He helped Mahmood review potential sites for the project, but their plans ended abruptly one sunny Tuesday morning. "September eleventh happened," Nadi said. "And that changed everything."

Almost immediately, Mahmood began outlining his plan for modernizing the city of his birth. Kandahar was a rough crossroads town in the desert of southern Afghanistan. It was all dirty peasants, opium traffickers, danger. It was where the Taliban movement was born, and it had been a place for smugglers and invaders and tribal war since before Alexander the Great. There was suffocating heat, sporadic electricity. Vendors sold marble headstones on the sidewalks next to the fruit stands.

Mahmood's Kandahar would be different. It would have clean water, a sewage system, electricity, paved roads, streetlights, cul-de-sacs—a lifestyle he had discovered in San Francisco, Chicago, Boston, and Washington. Mahmood was by then an American citizen, and he wanted to bring Afghanistan up to American standards. He envisioned a place of solar-powered homes, with air-conditioning and indoor plumbing; trash trucks that ran on schedule twice a week; a neighborhood with zoning and building codes, with homes for the poor and the middle class, as well as the rich, with environmental standards and tasteful architecture, unlike the garish Pakistani-style layer-cake homes in vogue among the Kabul wealthy—a place where Afghans could for once feel civilized. He would tell his relatives that he wanted to build a place like Columbia, the neatly ordered suburban subdivision in Maryland that had been designed in the 1960s as a racial utopia, where his sister, Fawzia, lived.

Through contacts in Washington, Mahmood soon assembled a team of Afghans and Americans undaunted by the prospects of doing construction work in a war zone. Mahmood wanted to include Americans to give the project more credibility and help secure U.S. financing. One of them was Terrance C. Ryan, a West Point graduate with a PhD; a twenty-year veteran of the U.S. Army Corps of Engineers, he had helped build a military academy in the Saudi Arabian desert. Ryan had started the Civil Engineering Institute at George Mason University, then run it for a decade, and had also opened his own firm to help train others, the Engineering and Surveyors Institute, which was based in a low-slung office park in Chantilly, Virginia. Ryan's office was cluttered with rolled-up schematics, stacks of bar charts, enough computer screens and rolling chairs for a small tech start-up, and one plastic mounted bass. He had a white beard and the friendly, direct manner of a former soldier.

"My early impressions were these guys, this bunch of Afghans, were motivated by an altruistic, idealistic notion of jump-starting their country and bringing it back to the cosmopolitan place it used to be decades ago," Ryan told me when I visited his office. "It was intended to be a modern city. Not quite Dubai, but something that would take them into the next century. The plan was large. Huge."

John Howell, one of Ryan's former West Point classmates and a colleague of his from George Mason, also joined Mahmood's team. Lawrence Doll, a former U.S. Marine and Vietnam veteran who owned Doll

Homes, which built subdivisions across the Washington suburbs, signed on as an investor. The other AFCO partners were Afghan-Americans: Hamid Helmandi, who ran a construction firm in Los Angeles, and Hashim Karzai, one of Mahmood's cousins, who owned a small telecom company and had lived in the Washington region for years. Mahmood deemed himself chairman of the board, while Abdullah Nadi was president and chief executive. Each of the five paying partners would own 20 percent of the company.

Mahmood and his partners had plenty of ambition but not very much cash. They estimated they would need $10 million to get it off the ground. They started to shop their idea around Washington, taking meetings at the World Bank and the Asian Development Bank. Their idea received the warmest welcome at the Overseas Private Investment Corporation. OPIC was the U.S. government's development finance corporation; its mission was to fund projects abroad to help spur growth in foreign countries while furthering American foreign policy goals. At the time, OPIC had projects in more than 140 countries and a financing portfolio of about $3.7 billion, funding telecom, oil and gas, mining, and manufacturing projects from Argentina to Madagascar.

Mahmood already had a plot of land in mind for his new city: thousands of acres of desert on the east side of Kandahar. It sat along the ring road and was within a few miles of the airport. Kandahar appealed to Mahmood because it was his hometown, and also because he could conduct this grand experiment with fewer red-tape entanglements than in the capital. "Further away from the central government, the better," Mahmood told me. "Less bureaucracy." Plus, Mahmood's family connections and the strength of his Popalzai tribe in Kandahar would protect him against rivals. The Karzais had just banished the Taliban; there was goodwill in abundance. There was enough land there, he calculated, for thousands of houses and more than a million people. It would be the largest residential development in the country—a gated community he hoped would someday contain more people than the city that surrounded it.

A few months after they registered AFCO as a company, Mahmood and some of the partners flew to Afghanistan to survey the site. Since no commercial airlines traveled to Kandahar in those days, the group flew on a United Nations humanitarian flight to the Kandahar Airfield, then occupied by the U.S. Marines and Special Forces hunting for Taliban and al-Qaeda fighters. The white passenger plane touched down on the base tarmac next to jets and helicopters and the brown tents where the troops slept side by side on cloth cots. Ryan felt like he was back in Vietnam. Driving out to the site was hardly more encouraging.

"It was god-awful," said Michael Ogden, a civil engineer who specialized in wastewater treatment. Ogden had worked in the developing world—Mexico, Costa Rica, China, Panama—but looking at the sand-blown plain, he found it hard to imagine a worse place to build a new city. "There was no development potential at all. It was barren desert. No roads, no water, no power, none of the basics. There was absolutely nothing there."

Over the course of three days, the group crisscrossed the terrain on dirt tracks and open desert, traveling in SUVs with an Afghan security detail Mahmood had assembled and navigating by GPS. During their drives, they stumbled upon old military equipment—tanks, trucks, artillery pieces. Ryan thought the area could have been a military range or camp. This was to be the site of Aino Mena. Mahmood gave them the impression that the land could be theirs with a bit of finesse: "Potentially claimable by the family based on some hereditary rights" was how Ogden remembered it. "Of course, if your brother was the president, you'd have a better chance." To others, it was even murkier: "I never did understand the ownership," Ryan said.

What the Americans didn't realize at the time, and Mahmood and his partners didn't bother to spell out, was that the land was owned by Afghanistan's Ministry of Defense. The area was known as Kishla-e-Jadeed, or New Garrison, a tract of desert that stretched north to the foothills of the Kotal-e Murcha mountains. This fact was well known to the Afghans involved in the project.

"It was a military site," recalled Hamid Helmandi, who oversaw the building in the early years. "This place was just mines and all kinds of things. It was a war zone."

But for Kandahar, this was prime real estate. Despite the arid appearance, there was groundwater below the surface. Wide canals, which ran from the Dahla Dam, built by the American engineering firm Morrison Knudsen in the 1950s, crossed the property. Ogden found the type of native plants that would flourish in the wetland water-treatment system he envisioned. The team began work on a topographic survey. They gathered soil and water samples.

Real estate in Kandahar bore little resemblance to the American system. Afghanistan did not have mortgages. New homes for the wealthy in Kandahar were selling for $50,000 or less. It was customary to pay the total agreed-upon price before construction began. The typical home is known as a *qala*—what American troops called a "compound." There is a house, often made of earth, and an interior yard enclosed by a tall mud wall. Wealthier Afghans have gardens and multiple buildings inside their *qala*, with separate houses in which to entertain guests so that women can be kept out of sight. Mahmood wanted an American design, but some local flavor was included. In Islamic countries, for example, bathrooms should not be oriented to face Mecca, and women's bathrooms would be separate from the men's. They also wanted the neighborhood's main boulevard, a four-lane divided highway with a thirty-foot median in the middle, to face toward the Muslim holy site. The partners assumed people would flock to Aino Mena. They wrote in their business plan that "once on site mobilization occurs, a large demand will appear."

The partners had little trouble convincing the new governor of Kandahar, Gul Agha Sherzai, to back the project. Sherzai was a beast of a man—American soldiers called him Jabba the Hut because of his big blubbery lips and hands like catcher's mitts. During the initial battle against the Taliban, as Hamid Karzai had moved on Kandahar from the north, Sherzai led his militiamen into the city from the south, along with a group of American Marines. Without coordinating with Karzai, Sherzai seized the Kandahar Airfield and would not let go. Sherzai and his Barakzai tribesmen used that early advantage and relationship with American troops to corner the market on American dollars flowing in to expand, supply, and defend Kandahar Airfield—the greatest source of wealth available in southern Afghanistan outside of the opium trade. Sherzai had installed himself in the governor's mansion, where he took in sacks of American cash and disbursed it to his supplicants in envelopes.

The power was out in the governor's mansion the night Mahmood presented his plan to Sherzai, so the meeting was illuminated by flashlights, Nadi recalled. They taped the plans to a wall and described their idea. Sherzai, enthusiastic about the plan, asked them how much land they wanted. Nadi suggested ten thousand *jeribs* (equivalent to five thousand acres). Mahmood, always thinking bigger, said:

"No. We need twenty thousand."

On September 10, 2002, Governor Gul Agha Sherzai ordered the Kandahar municipality to transfer twenty thousand *jeribs* of government land to Mahmood Karzai. The terms of the transfer stipulated a price of $6 million, or $600 per acre, that Mahmood would pay in the future as he sold the houses and shops he planned to build. The governor took the project to Kabul and presented it to the cabinet, which gave its approval, and Hamid Karzai, as chairman of the interim authority, issued a decree authorizing the governor to transfer the land from the Ministry of Defense ownership to the city. The fact that Mahmood had to put nothing down for this sought-after land pleased his business partners, who considered the transfer almost a gift for the president's family. "It was an extremely good price," Nadi said.

In a letter to Kandahar's municipal court three months later, Governor Sherzai explained why he had granted Mahmood the land: "As you are aware that our country was devastated in the past quarter century of occupation and internal strife. Today, however, our countrymen and humanitarian world community have intended to rebuild Afghanistan. They are very eager to see it prosper again. The fact that the number of our countrymen is increasing day by day, and immigrant families return home, it is incumbent on us to expand residential area and housing facilities for them."

The plan Mahmood and his partners submitted to OPIC in early 2003 gleamed with ambition. On the ten thousand acres, their model city had the potential, they claimed, to contain ten thousand to twenty thousand homes, plus public amenities such as parks, hospitals, and mosques and a type of modern infrastructure unknown in Kandahar. They projected that sixty thousand people could live inside, and that the gated community would eventually be worth $150 million. The entire build-out of what they were calling Kandahar Valley would take a decade, by which time, they expected, American troops would be long gone.

Nobody involved had attempted anything of this size. To convince OPIC of their qualifications, they printed glossy brochures touting the business prowess of their team. Mahmood's bio highlighted his ownership of the Helmand restaurant in Cambridge and his role as "chief strategist" of his brother's Baltimore restaurant, which he described as one of the country's top 100 eateries. "Karzai has exceptional talent in budget and project management," the brochure assured readers.

At the time, several partners, both Afghans and Americans, believed that Mahmood's motives were driven more by patriotism than by greed. He did not seem to be trading on his name as the new Afghan leader's brother, or demanding VIP treatment.

"I traveled with him several times to Afghanistan," Nadi recalled. "He always traveled economy, and when we got to the airport, although he could go through diplomatic channels, he never did. At the beginning, he refused to do that and stood in line next to me like any normal passenger. That's what attracted me to him. He never used or abused his position."

Mahmood was always pushing the team to go faster. An e-mail from him arrived in John Howell's in-box at 3:33 a.m. on February 4, 2003. "First," he wrote, "I like to congratulate everyone involved in Afco." The governor's letter selling him the land had been signed by the Ministry of Justice, and the deed would be transferred to AFCO that very day. There would be a scramble for government contracts soon, Mahmood wrote, and they had to hurry: "this I am sure of that time is not on our side."

In the OPIC offices in Washington, Mahmood's project looked appealing. Those assessing the loan application assumed that many of the millions of Afghan refugees would be returning home, and the housing stock was low. The project would put impoverished Afghans to work, bring modern amenities to a backward place, and generate goodwill for the Bush administration.

"Mahmood Karzai was their golden boy at the time," recalled Virginia Sheffield, an American business consultant who helped Mahmood negotiate with OPIC.

His biggest asset was his last name. The Bush administration was willing to do almost anything to help him succeed.

"We knew he was from a very prominent family," recalled an OPIC lawyer on the project. "We undertake a pretty thorough character-risk due diligence. There was no negative information about Mahmood Karzai."

When OPIC gave initial credit approval for a loan to AFCO, the sterling reputation of Mahmood and his partners was an important factor in its decision: "Four of the five sponsors of this project are successful Afghan-American businessmen, and two of the four are brothers of Afghanistan's current President," an internal OPIC memo said of the concept, albeit misstating the last fact, as Hashim Karzai was a first cousin of Hamid Karzai's.

Over the next few months, however, officials at the agency started to realize that the arrangements in Kandahar were not exactly as they had been led to believe. While the land documentation mentioned that some people were living on it illegally, the OPIC officials reviewing the loan application had assumed this meant squatting nomads or temporary refugee camps that could be relocated easily. Within weeks of the initial approval, OPIC learned from Karzai's team that the squatters included a "warlord" living in a compound guarded by his entourage of gunmen. Another problem was that Karzai's team didn't have enough money. By OPIC's standards, loan recipients should contribute a down payment of 25 percent. In this case, that would have been $750,000 on a $3 million loan. But Mahmood and his partners had only cobbled together $100,000. To make up the difference, OPIC had initially wanted to count construction equipment that Hamid Helmandi owned—graders, loaders, tractors, dump trucks—as $615,000 worth of equity for the project, but Helmandi refused to sign over the equipment to AFCO because he wanted it available for other construction projects in Kandahar. Eager to find some way to push the project through, OPIC decided to value the land at $615,000, "in order to maintain the original leverage," as Dan Horrigan, the project lawyer, and Deborah Smith, an investment officer, wrote in an internal memo to one of their superiors.

"We have no data upon which to base this valuation," they admitted. "The right to build on the land could be worth much more than that, or it could be worth nothing." It was simply a way "to get the project off the ground," and it would be a "significant exception" to the agency's normal credit standards.

The invented valuation was made worse by the fact that it was becoming less clear who actually owned the land. Governor Sherzai's order did not amount to a "deed," as Mahmood claimed, because it did not convey ownership immediately but, rather, granted the right to Karzai and his partners to build in the desert. OPIC learned after the initial approval that these rights could be rescinded if the builders did not make enough progress on the project. "The land arrangements, upon which the whole project depends," Smith and Horrigan wrote, "are not as solid as in normal circumstances."

Despite the credit risk, the unmet loan criteria, and the questionable land ownership, the agency decided that the project had "strong developmental and foreign policy benefits," in a country where OPIC was clamoring to do business. President Bush, in a 2002 letter to President Karzai, wrote that he agreed with Karzai's "economic focus to use aid as a magnet to attract trade and private investment," and he touted how OPIC had made $50 million available to finance U.S. private investment in Afghanistan. Now that money had to be spent. And so on September 12, 2003, the Bush administration agreed to give $3 million to Mahmood Karzai to build a gated city in Kandahar.

Just as American officials had intervened to help Hamid Karzai reach the palace, they had ignored their normal procedures to help Mahmood realize his outlandish dream. Eight years later, when I stood with him in the second-story office of Aino Mena's headquarters, behind the barricades and blast walls and police guard booths, I could not deny that there was much he had accomplished. But in front of the room-sized diorama, he seemed gripped by anxiety about all he still needed to do—all the parks and lakes, restaurants and mosques, schools and clinics to be built. He had plans for a new six-megawatt coal-fired power plant. He was going to build the biggest mosque in Kandahar. He wanted thirty-story apartment buildings.

This should have been a moment for him to relish. His city was being made. But he felt harassed and misunderstood. His business practices that had helped realize Aino Mena and his other companies were being called into question. The U.S. government, which had once helped and defended him, was now leafing through his bank records and listening to his telephone calls. Agents had subpoenaed his daughter's Georgetown University tuition records and were reviewing his tax payments. Federal prosecutors in Manhattan were building a case against him. The U.S. military had blacklisted his company. Hamid Karzai was furious with him. His brother Shah Wali wanted to take Aino Mena from him. His business partners didn't trust him. He had become the living symbol of the corruption that was eroding faith in the government and encouraging citizens to join the Taliban. Normally gregarious and funny and outspoken, he had become bitter and conspiratorial.

"There is a vast power in the U.S.," he said. "They can literally destroy a person."

5

BECAUSE WE SEE MORE, WE DO MORE

BEFORE DAWN ON THE MORNING of his daughter's wedding, Mohammed Zia Salehi stared down into the darkened parking lot from the window of his modest third-floor apartment in a boxy, Soviet-built complex
known as Microrayon. Still groggy from sleep, he could make out what
looked like police trucks and gunmen in balaclavas and black body armor.
Voices echoed in the concrete stairwell. Someone was banging on his
door. Salehi knew that the Taliban often masqueraded as police when
they attacked. His mind, he recalled later, was a frazzle of panic, but he
was sure this was a kidnapping. He picked up his cell phone and began
calling everyone he knew.

After three decades in the Afghan government, Salehi knew almost
everyone. He was a consummate insider and political survivor: discreet
and loyal, but canny at reading the winds and helping the powerful. He
had worked in Afghanistan's Soviet-backed intelligence agency and Ministry of Foreign Affairs during the Communist era, and had served as a
low-level diplomat in India. He'd been the personal translator for the
Uzbek warlord Abdul Rashid Dostum. He had gone on hundreds of official government trips and had even met President George H. W. Bush.
In Hamid Karzai's government, he ran the palace Situation Room, where
he worked on sensitive issues, including the transfer of Afghan detainees from the U.S. military prison in Guantánamo Bay to holding cells at
Bagram Airfield; later he was director of the administrative affairs department of the National Security Council. Inside the palace, his benefactor
was a man named Ibrahim Spinzada, a top aide to Karzai whom Salehi
helped handle the dark arts of governing Afghan-style: covert operations,
liaisons with CIA officers, payouts, deal making—all the patronage dis-

pensing that was so central to how power was exercised in Afghanistan and that the American countercorruption officers found so repellant.

In some respects, Salehi was not an important government official, such as a cabinet minister, or someone whose name appeared in the papers. He was a functionary, but one who tiptoed through politically delicate ground. As administrative affairs director, Salehi handled the money. "He's the bag man," one of his colleagues told me. He paid salaries, bought government vehicles, gave out money for cabinet ministers' rent, and dispensed rewards to pro-government allies from the palace slush fund, much of it provided by the CIA. Palace staffers estimated these secret funds totaled roughly $10 million per year. A separate palace slush fund, referred to as Code 91, was filled with a similar amount each year and could be dispensed at Karzai's whim. One of Ibrahim's assistants told me that the palace paid more than seventy people—cabinet ministers, warlords, tribal elders, Islamic clerics—up to $7,000 a month to be "advisers" and to ensure their loyalty. The CIA had been paying him as an informant for years, I had been told by American officials, a common arrangement for palace staff. When I asked Salehi about that, he said, "We have a very good relationship with the CIA. This is part of the job." But he played down the covert nature of his work.

"I just buy the palace toilet paper," he said.

Salehi was not the type of guy who would do well in Taliban captivity. Nothing about him was tough. Chubby and boisterous, with a happy laugh, he enjoyed whatever small pleasures a Kabul lifestyle could afford. He didn't take his work too seriously. He referred to his boss, National Security Advisor Rangin Dadfar Spanta, as "Comrade Spanta" because of his old Marxist sympathies. He liked to make sex jokes with the head of Afghanistan's intelligence agency. He was a proud hedonist who enjoyed the company of women, openly drank whiskey, and struggled to quit smoking. "A little bit of enjoyment never hurt anyone," he told me one night, raising his glass. Life was too short, in his opinion, for the ridiculous dictates of Taliban law.

Pressed up to his apartment window that dark summer morning, Salehi didn't know who was coming for him, but he knew whom to call. In a matter of minutes, he talked to the national security adviser, the attorney general, and the country's spymaster, National Directorate of Security director Rahmatullah Nabil, whom he woke up by saying, "I'm being kidnapped." Within minutes, Nabil dispatched a quick reaction force to Salehi's apartment, a few blocks from the U.S. embassy. The spies drove into the parking lot, and Salehi could hear shouting as they confronted the other group of gunmen.

"They were about to clash," he said.

The masked gunmen were not kidnappers, it turned out, but Afghan police officers with the Major Crimes Task Force, an FBI-mentored police unit under the command of a slight, grandfatherly general named Nazar Mohammad Nikzad. The general hadn't known very much about that morning's target. He had been given the arrest warrant, signed by the attorney general and a judge with the anti-corruption tribunal, and he'd dispatched one of his trusted subordinates, a colonel, along with ten of his men in three police trucks, to execute the arrest. In the parking lot, the colonel showed the arrest warrant, and the intelligence agency response team stepped aside. "I came out," Salehi recalled. "I didn't want to cause problems." The morning ended without gunfire, and Salehi was driven to the American-built counternarcotics detention center behind the Kabul airport.

The man responsible for Salehi's arrest was a singularly determined DEA officer named Kirk Meyer. It was Meyer's investigation, conducted with the blessing of the U.S. embassy, that resulted in a team of Afghan policemen speeding through the empty streets of Kabul that morning, July 25, 2010, to arrest a man as close to the center of President Karzai's palace as it was possible to get without aiming for the president himself.

The resurgence of the Taliban, and the inability of the U.S. or Afghan troops to decisively defeat them, provoked a roiling undercurrent of soul-searching among the leadership of the American war effort. Why were we losing? By the time President Obama's "surge" forces had arrived, and more than 150,000 U.S. and NATO troops were fighting and some-times dying on behalf of the Afghan government, finding an answer to this question became more urgent. When Obama announced his troop buildup, he also established its duration. Within eighteen months, the soldiers would be coming home. The American commanders and diplomats had one last chance to win.

Everyone had a theory about what was going wrong. It was because of the sanctuaries across the border that kept Taliban leaders safe. Or because Afghans didn't respect their puppet president. Or because they were culturally ingrained to drive foreign invaders from their soil, as they had done for millennia. Or because Pakistani intelligence officers were funding and arming the insurgents to fight a proxy war to keep the Afghan government weak while allowing Islamic terrorists to flourish and therefore attract for Pakistan billions more in American foreign aid to confront the very problem they were creating.

During the first half of 2010, another explanation became ascendant. The war was being lost, the argument went, because regular Afghans were angry. They were angry about cabinet ministers who bought their confirmation votes from corrupt parliamentarians; about the fact that Afghan police demanded bribes at highway checkpoints; that judges and lawyers required payoffs at every turn; that just to acquire the right to pay your taxes you had to grease someone's palm. During this phase of the war, a growing number of senior American officials believed that Afghan farm boys were picking up their AK-47s and joining the insurgency because they were angry about corruption. "Afghan government corruption was manufacturing Taliban," Sarah Chayes, a former radio reporter who became a U.S. military adviser and leading advocate for this position, wrote in her book *Thieves of State*. "I was sure that unless they recognized the danger it presented and addressed it head on, they would never win the war."

The U.S. embassy in 2010 had a budget of $4 billion. Ambassador Eikenberry told Karzai's foreign minister—in a plea for Karzai to show some public gratitude—that it would be the largest foreign assistance budget for any one country in American history. Since 2008, the embassy had quadrupled in size to more than one thousand staffers, making it the largest embassy in the world. The diplomats filled up the embassy apartments and spilled over into a trailer city that looked like a shipping container depot. There was more of everybody: State Department political officers, Treasury Department economists, intelligence analysts, forensic accountants, USDA farming and livestock experts, wiretapping specialists, logisticians, cooks, cleaners, mechanics. Once fixing the problem of Afghan corruption became central to the American strategy, this cause generated its own unstoppable momentum. "There were more justice lawyers on the ground than anywhere in the world," Ambassador Eikenberry told me. "More DEA agents. More U.S. marshals. And consistent with my guidance—we've got two years here, and we're going to go as fast as we can. With so many more people, we start to see a lot more, we get better awareness of what's going on. And because we can see much more, and potentially do much more, we do."

When Kirk Meyer first got to Kabul, in 2006, the Drug Enforcement Administration had just twelve people on the ground in Afghanistan, a country that produced 80 to 90 percent of the heroin consumed in the United States. As deputy attaché, Meyer developed a reputation as a dogged agent, albeit one who abraded some colleagues. "I don't think Kirk really had interpersonal skills," one of his bosses told me. Near the end of the Bush administration, Meyer was asked to stand up a new team dedicated to interrupting "terrorist" financing, which meant trying to block the flood of money the Taliban used to run their thirty-thousand-man insurgency. The model for the new unit was another American team, the Iraq Threat Finance Cell, which had been started in Baghdad four years earlier to block funding for the Sunni insurgent groups and Shi-ite militias. In Afghanistan, the Taliban had a multiheaded fund-raising machine: the opium business, Middle Eastern donations, the Pakistani government, taxes and extortion, protection payments, and safe-travel fees that American-funded development contracts would pay to pass through areas the insurgents controlled. "The Taliban was generating enormous amounts of revenue," recalled Mike Braun, who was the DEA's chief of operations in Washington at the time. "We needed to have a more robust presence in Afghanistan or it was going to bite us in the ass."

American soldiers and diplomats didn't know much about how all of this worked or how to deplete the Taliban's income. Stuart Jones, the twenty-eight-year-old Treasury Department attaché in Kabul, recalled spending an excruciating day at ISAF headquarters trying to come to a collective agreement on how much money the Taliban raised each year, and where it came from. The soldiers and civilians made broad assumptions based on scant evidence. The final conclusion was somewhere in the hundreds of millions. "It was a guess in the end," Jones said.

Much of the money moved through the *hawala*, a money-transfer network akin to a low-tech Western Union that was common throughout the Islamic world. In Kabul, the Shahzada *hawala* market was located in the old city, in a crowded bazaar on the banks of the trash-clotted river, where vendors squatted on the ground leafing through fat stacks of currency. A customer would deposit cash at one *hawala*, and the recipient could pick up his money in another country, with the debts, written by hand in ledgers, being settled later between brokers. It was a world poorly understood by foreigners. The *hawaladars* often intermarried and relied on family partners to exclude the untrustworthy. One study estimated there were more than nine hundred *hawalas* in Afghanistan, whereas there were fewer than twenty banks. The State Department estimated that 80 percent of all Afghan financial transactions were executed on the *hawala* market. With no government oversight, smugglers and drug traffickers preferred this system to move their profits. The Afghan government officials who were supposed to regulate this industry were so intimidated by these businessmen that they wrote their reports on blank paper, with their names omitted, in case they were leaked into the wrong hands.

The largest of the 170 registered *hawalas* in Kabul was called New Ansari. Twice a week, the central bank held auctions where they sold off excess U.S. dollars to keep the currency stable. New Ansari would buy 90 percent of the U.S. dollars and set the country's exchange rate. The business had been started two decades earlier by Haji Abdullah Barakzai Ansari, a black-bearded Kandahari man who allegedly made his fortune during the Taliban era by selling opium.

Over the years, key posts in the company were passed on to relatives and other associates, who diversified its operations. The Ansari relatives owned a bank, Afghan United Bank, which had a branch inside Mahmood Karzai's gated community in Kandahar. They also owned a fuel import company, an Internet provider, and construction companies and held exclusive license to sell Thuraya satellite phones in Afghanistan. They had donated to Hamid Karzai's reelection campaign. New Ansari's customers, and their methods of doing business, became a fixation for law enforcement officers at the U.S. embassy. The Americans believed the company was moving Taliban funds and also that its owners were considering relocating to America. The company's president and its day-to-day manager had moved their families to Dubai and were educating their children in English-language schools. They had explored buying businesses in the United States as a way of securing U.S. visas, and they had set up corresponding banking relationships with the New York branch of a Pakistani bank. "They would have gotten into the U.S. financial system," recalled an American official who tracked them. "And that was one of the things we were trying to stop."

The Afghan Threat Finance Cell opened in the fall of 2008. At the beginning, the "cell" was three people. In addition to Kirk Meyer, the director, there were two deputies: a Marine reservist dispatched from Centcom and Frank Calestino, a squat thirty-two-year-old Treasury Department official with swept-over brown hair and the streetwise style of a Boston cop. Several Afghans had told Meyer that Ansari once had a personal relationship with Mullah Omar. As the story went, Omar asked Barakzai to stockpile opium. When the Taliban banned all new production, the opium price skyrocketed, and they split the proceeds. While Meyer didn't have evidence the story was true, it had become part of New

Ansari's origin story. Calestino had served on the Iraq team, amid gun battles and IED blasts, and helped Meyer write the concept paper for the Afghan version. Nobody in Kabul had prepared for their arrival. Neither the embassy nor the military headquarters really knew why they were there or wanted to help them. When Calestino's plane touched down at Bagram Airfield on November 17, 2008, he didn't even know where he would sleep. He hitched a ride to his office, which turned out to be in a dilapidated trailer with a leaky roof and failing plumbing. Its electrical wiring ran out the back of the trailer and hung on a broken tree branch. In one of the rooms, Calestino saw a dusty computer, along with a note of greeting from Meyer. "I found a laptop," he read. "See if it works."

The trailer became both home and office. They had started working before the interagency process in Washington had approved their creation. Without a budget or staff, they fended for themselves. Calestino made a PowerPoint presentation about what he wanted to do and Meyer shopped around to military officers asking for help. They cadged bathroom supplies and bottled water from the soldiers on base. They borrowed a Defense Intelligence Agency conference room at Bagram to go over their classified intelligence. When the Treasury attaché Stuart Jones visited Bagram, he found Meyer and Calestino mostly fighting logistical battles rather than the Taliban: finding secure communication lines to read intel reports, procuring a television. "Stu, we can't even buy toilet paper," Calestino complained.

As the months went on, Meyer's team would grow to more than seventy people—soldiers, civilians, and officers from a broad swath of the government, the FBI, the Department of Homeland Security, and the Pentagon think tank the Institute for Defense Analyses. Eventually, they moved their main office to a fenced-in section of ISAF headquarters in Kabul. Meyer added staff at the Kandahar and Bagram Airfields and at military bases in Jalalabad, Mazar-e-Sharif, and Helmand Province. As a DEA special agent, Meyer could recruit and pay and run informants. He could enter the Bagram prison and talk to detainees because of an exemption that allowed agents to act as interrogators.

During Meyer's earlier tour, he had helped the DEA create an Afghan police team known as the Sensitive Investigative Unit (SIU). This was a "vetted" unit, where the officers got special training and underwent background checks and regular polygraph tests to ensure their loyalty. A tandem team, called the Technical Investigative Unit (TIU), ran a wiretapping program. The DEA could use these police to get search warrants and develop the intelligence needed to capture drug bosses operating in

Afghanistan. Afghan law allowed wiretapping, with certain restrictions. Terrorism cases offered the most flexibility; investigators could listen to phone lines for an unlimited duration. For drug cases, the law allowed authorities to wiretap a single phone line once, for a period of 120 days, after judicial approval. One benefit of these law enforcement wiretaps to Meyer and his team was that they were unclassified and, thus, could be shared widely within the Afghan government and the coalition. There were plenty of other eavesdropping operations in Kabul—run by the NSA, the CIA, and British intelligence, among others—but what they recorded was so highly classified it was difficult to organize large groups of people to act on the tips.

One day in early 2008, Meyer sat down to lunch with an Afghan customs official who had requested a meeting and received one such tip. At the small Kabul restaurant, the customs official pulled out documents recording bulk cash shipments worth millions of dollars in various currencies headed for Dubai. On each one, the courier was employed by New Ansari.

"I don't know what they are doing, but it must be illegal," the customs official told Meyer. "The country doesn't have this kind of money."

When Meyer started the Threat Finance Cell, the Afghan SIU was working out of a house in downtown Kabul and not getting much done. "Nobody was really using them," he said. He started building a relationship with the SIU's commander, Colonel Asadullah Babakarkhel, an Afghan cop since the Soviet days, and started training and mentoring programs. With these police teams, Meyer had access to bilingual Afghan eavesdroppers who listened to calls and typed out thousands of pages of translated transcripts. At its height, as many as 250 Afghan "monitors," working from cubicles inside a large metal building, were producing intelligence for Meyer.

In May 2009, three months before the Afghan presidential election, the Threat Finance Cell began to intercept the first cell phone calls of the New Ansari *hawala*. In retrospect, that was the moment the scales would fall away for the Americans in Kabul. Those conversations in effect unmuted the chattering hive mind of the war's underworld, and began to reveal a scale of crime, theft, and deception that even the most jaded among the investigators had not envisioned. Meyer had worked in Southeast Asia for years but had never seen crime anywhere near as brazen as in Afghanistan. On one level, the Taliban and Karzai's government were at war, but that did not mean they were constantly at odds. Meyer began to believe that agendas of people who appeared to be enemies often overlapped, particularly when it came to making money. "The bad guys are interlocked with corrupt officials, drugs, insurgents and select people in the financial community. We are attacking those networks," Meyer told a Kabul visitor. "Corrupt government officials are talking to the Taliban to ensure that they get their cut of the drug profits. It's a lot more complicated than we ever imagined."

The FBI, along with Britain's Serious Organised Crime Agency, had created a similar organization that worked in tandem with the Threat Finance Cell. Their group was known as the Major Crimes Task Force (MCTF), and it had been established to pursue kidnapping cases (occurring at a rate of about five per day), organized crime, and, increasingly, public corruption cases. It became the largest international task force the FBI had ever operated, including more than one hundred Afghan police and sixty Afghan intelligence officers.

On October 19, 2009, officers from the MCTF arrested Afghan brigadier general Saifullah Hakim, the chief of the border police in Kandahar, and two of his subordinates, for theft, bribery, and money laundering. Using wiretaps and financial records, the investigators had found that Hakim and his men were falsifying police pay records, claiming that 2,800 police were on their rolls, while only 1,200 of them actually existed. The salaries for the "ghost" policemen were being skimmed off for their own use. For those fighting crime in Afghanistan, the arrests were a rare win, but the tactics used proved even more important. As a classified U.S. embassy cable noted, "these arrests show a significant step forward in anti-corruption efforts," as "it is the first use of evidentiary intercepts for non-counternarcotics activity."

Wiretapping was spreading beyond drug cases and showing results. New Ansari was moving $3 to $4 billion a year, and now the Americans could listen to its lenders talk about where it was going. An embassy cable reported that the available intelligence "strongly suggests" that the "New Ansari *hawala* network is facilitating bribes and other wide-scale illicit cash transfers for corrupt Afghan officials and is providing illicit financial services for narco-traffickers, insurgents, and criminals through an array of front companies in Afghanistan and the UAE."

Meyer had been tasked with fighting the Taliban, but his attention was soon drawn toward bankers, ministers, and palace advisers—the elite of the government that America was ostensibly in Afghanistan to defend. "Every case we ever did began with New Ansari," one U.S. official said.

The cargo truck drove slowly down the barricaded lane and pulled to a stop outside the entrance to the U.S. embassy. It was dark and the street was deserted, except for the idling armored vehicle on permanent standby. A few hours earlier, the twenty-three-year-old son of one of Afghanistan's wealthiest financiers had called Stuart Jones, the Treasury Department's attaché. A lanky southerner with an Arkansas drawl, Jones was a charming guy and made friends easily. The man on the phone, Haji Bashir, told Jones he had received a shipment of pomegranates from his family home in Kandahar, and he wanted to present some to the U.S. embassy as a gift. His father, Mohammad Jan, the manager of New Ansari, would be happy if he would accept.

"That's very kind of you," Jones said.

"I'm coming tonight."

Jones laughed. That wouldn't be possible. He was busy with work. Maybe next week.

"No, it has to be tonight."

The sight of a large diesel truck rolling up to the embassy gates after nine p.m. did not please the Nepalese Gurkhas assigned to guard the compound. They muttered into their radios as several muscle-bound Afghans stepped out to unload the cargo. The guards sent out their bomb dogs to sniff the vehicle. Jones strolled outside to meet the banker's son. When he saw the truck, two scenarios flashed into his mind. "This is either a bomb, or this is a lot of pomegranates. If it's a bomb, it'll be quick. If it's a bunch of pomegranates, then surely they're not all for me."

Jones looked into the cargo hold. It was stacked floor to ceiling with crates and crates of pomegranates. Should he just take a couple from one of the crates? he asked. "Oh no," the man said. "These are all for you."

Jones laughed. There must be some mistake, he said. He couldn't accept this many pomegranates.

"It will be a great insult if you don't take all of them."

So for the next hour and a half, until nearly midnight, the Afghan men unloaded dozens of crates and carried them one by one into the U.S. embassy. The Americans feasted on them for weeks—glazes, juices, sauces, parties dedicated solely to martinis made with Stoli vodka and pomegranate—so much, that "if it had been a Trojan horse of poisoned pomegranates," Jones said, "it would have killed the whole embassy."

Jones was a loose, casual guy, not well suited to all the self-serious rules and restrictions that came with a posting in Kabul. He believed that accepting a truckload of fruit from a notorious Afghan money mover was one of those cultural goodwill gestures required in a foreign land. Kirk Meyer didn't like it. He had been investigating Mohammad Jan and the rest of the New Ansari crew and considered them to be a dangerous mafia family helping to corrupt the Afghan government. Meyer would tell Jones that he had him on videotape accepting the late-night pomegranate shipment. He told him that his wiretaps had picked up New Ansari associates gloating about bribing all the key people at the U.S. embassy with pomegranates and that Jones had been duped by this elaborate scheme. Meyer began referring to it as "Pomegranate gate."

"I think he was pulling my leg, but he was enjoying the opportunity to watch me squirm," Jones recalled.

Meyer made some people uncomfortable at the embassy. Because of his recurring insomnia, vampirish intensity, and exhausting work habits, his nickname was "the Count." He had a quiet voice and a dry, far-off way about him, a cynic in a land of sinners. But there was also something idealistic and prone to outrage in his manner, particularly when it came to injustices against the American taxpayer. He could berate his underlings but would also offer gestures of his time and attention that showed people how much he cared. To his adversaries, he had a beat cop's tenacity and would not be intimidated by either Afghan mobsters or his American bosses. The crimes he was investigating genuinely galled him.

"He was a pit bull. Passionate. He refused to back down," one embassy staffer said of Meyer. Another colleague called him a brilliant law enforcement officer, "an amazing talent." A Chicago native, Meyer used to compare himself to lineman William "Refrigerator" Perry of the 1985 Super Bowl champion Bears. "I've got one play," Meyer would say. "Up the middle."

He and Calestino made an odd couple of war-zone gumshoes. Meyer was tall with a grim demeanor and a doomsday view of the war. Calestino, about two decades Meyer's junior, was short (5 feet, 4 inches), scrappy, and easily excited. While other American diplomats stayed behind the blast walls and barricades, Meyer and Calestino constantly ventured into the Kabul throng. They would hop into their up-armored SUV, without guns or bodyguards, and drive themselves around the capital, listening to Tom Jones. They met scores of Afghan bankers and politicians and *hawaladars* at their homes and in Kabul restaurants and hotels. They hopped on DEA airplanes for meetings in cities across the country and flew to Dubai to track down leads among the Afghan business community.

Meyer first met Mahmood Karzai in early 2010, after an interview that

Meyer gave to National Public Radio where he mentioned some illicit land deals in Kandahar involving Ahmed Wali Karzai. Mahmood called the office of the deputy ambassador, Earl Anthony Wayne, who wasn't around, so Wayne's secretary walked the phone over to Meyer.

"You don't understand my family," Mahmood told him, as Meyer recalled.

"Well, let me talk to you."

Meyer seized the opportunity and drove over to one of Mahmood's homes that was located a few minutes from the embassy.

"You don't have a security detail," was the first thing Mahmood told him.

"Why?" Meyer asked. "Do I need one?"

In that first meeting, Mahmood sought to impress on Meyer the probity of his business dealings. He offered documents and tax records, and explained his associations with Aino Mena in Kandahar and the country's most successful financial institution, Kabul Bank. Meyer saw Mahmood as a salesman, a man earnestly trying to hawk the notion that he was clean.

From Mahmood and his other contacts, Meyer began learning more about New Ansari. The picture kept getting uglier. Every day, the company's couriers were toting carry-on luggage stuffed with cash onto commercial flights out of Kabul's airport. Afghanistan did not have currency controls, so anyone could declare unlimited travel cash. Some of New Ansari's employees lived in Dubai. They would take a morning flight to Kabul, collect their cash, and fly back in the afternoon, repeating the commute several times a week. Meyer's team found one Afghan traveler carrying three suitcases stuffed with $3 million in American currency and $2 million more in Saudi Arabian riyals. In April 2010, one New Ansari courier declared $700,000 on a flight to Dubai. Upon inspection, the customs agent found $600,000 more. The man had so much cash, one American official recounted, "he did not realize how much he really had." In the last half of 2009, New Ansari's couriers had declared $948 million at the Kabul airport, almost all of it headed for Dubai. The Afghan government collected less in revenue that entire year.

That summer, Meyer's team made one of its first breakthroughs in the New Ansari case. His Afghan eavesdroppers heard the deputy chairman of Afghan United Bank talking about payments with one of Karzai's cabinet ministers, Mohammad Sediq Chakari. Chakari, a member of the Northern Alliance and a respected Arabic scholar, was in charge of the Ministry of Hajj and Religious Affairs, the government office that organized annual travel for thousands of Afghans to the holy Islamic site Mecca, in Saudi Arabia. A hajj trip was a highlight of any Muslim's religious life. For most who made the journey, it was a once-in-a-lifetime experience. In a place as poor as Afghanistan, families saved up for years for the chance to go. From the New Ansari phone intercepts, Meyer's team came to learn that Chakari was profiting from an elaborate kickback scheme. As they explained the scheme, the Afghan government allotted a fixed number of pilgrims to more than ten travel agencies based in Dubai, Saudi Arabia, and elsewhere. Chakari made it known that to win one of the contracts, the agencies had to pay a fee per pilgrim. Each agency ended up paying an average of $75,000 to him to secure licenses to transport and house Afghans on their journey. Here was an obvious target, a man the embassy described in a cable as "known for being corrupt." Chakari was not close with Karzai, so he would likely have little palace protection, and his crimes were cheating Muslims, in a country that prided itself on its reverence for Islam.

"We were trying to find a high-level government official who could be arrested, to try to start the whole idea that you could deal with these major corruption issues," Meyer said. "It was just assumed that this would be a no-brainer."

Meyer's investigation would ultimately help the Afghan government recover more than $1 million. In addition to the kickbacks, Chakari also sold Saudi visas for $2,000 each; five had gone to former Guantánamo Bay detainees with links to Pakistani extremist groups. The bribery was increasing the cost for average Afghans to travel to Mecca by hundreds of dollars, making it the most expensive country in the region for pilgrims. Meyer had been told that Iran had opened its borders to Afghan Shiite pilgrims who wanted to make the trip from there, as it cost so much less. There were also phone calls that indicated that Chakari was talking with contacts from a range of insurgent groups, including the Taliban, the Haqqani network, and Hezb-i-Islami. In October 2009, an Afghan intelligence officer had arrested two hajj ministry employees acting as couriers for Chakari and seized $362,000 and some Saudi riyals. At the couriers' trial, the judge played recorded conversations between the Afghan United Bank vice chairman, Haji Mohammad Rafi Azimi, and the minister, Chakari, discussing bribes.

On the day the Afghan Sensitive Investigative Unit moved to arrest Chakari, one of President Karzai's aides called the deputy attorney general and told him to drop the case. Meyer was in the deputy attorney general's office when he took the phone call. "I was a little shocked," he said. Despite a travel ban in his name, Chakari, a dual Afghan-British citizen, arrived at the Kabul airport waving a letter from the attorney general's office, saying he had cooperated in the case and was free to leave. After he touched down safely in London, the attorney general's office insisted that since Chakari had not been convicted of anything, they could not stop him from traveling.

These types of events were testing the patience of the Western leaders who were giving their taxpayer money to Karzai's administration, while debating whether to send even more troops. Around the time of Chakari's escape, British prime minister Gordon Brown gave a speech threatening to limit British support for the war. "Sadly, the government of Afghanistan has become a byword for corruption," he said. "And I am not prepared to put the lives of British men and women in harm's way for a government that does not stand up to corruption."

In Kabul, Meyer was appalled. When he brought up the escape, Attorney General Mohammad Ishaq Aloko wasn't interested in discussing it. Aloko wanted to talk about another case: the Afghans had just caught Dutch and American nonprofit workers carrying some gospel music in their backpacks.

"He was all excited about that, but he could care less about the guy who was overcharging people who'd saved their entire lives to go on an Islamic pilgrimage," Meyer said. "One would think that the fact that he was stealing money from the hajj would be something nobody would countenance. Little did we know this would be something that many people would countenance."

Chakari's escape didn't deter Meyer, and he continued to pursue New Ansari. Because of the difficulty of getting firsthand information about the *hawala* business, Meyer regularly met with the New Ansari leadership in Kabul, at a suite they kept at a downtown hotel, over lunches and dinners at the Serena, and at homes of their associates. The money exchangers dismissed Meyer's questions about their customers and the exodus of cash out of the country. They were moving bags of cash to Dubai, Haji Mohammad Jan told him, because the United Arab Emirates was a major trading partner. Afghans sent their money to buy goods that were shipped back home, or they bought houses and apartments because the real estate market was booming. Some people shipped cash on commercial airlines because they wanted to avoid paying bank transfer fees, he explained. If anything untoward happened at New Ansari, he said, he was not aware of it.

His family business was no money-laundering scheme.

The embassy leadership generally encouraged Meyer's investigations and allowed him to keep following leads. But some of Meyer's tactics worried his colleagues. Fellow diplomats worried that his investigations were too politically explosive; others just wanted him to be careful as he drove around Kabul.

Part of Stuart Jones's job as a Treasury official was to teach Afghans working in the financial sector about modern banking practices and to train *hawaladars* to follow the law. Meyer saw this as a way to get to know them but also as an opportunity to gather intelligence. When the Afghan financial intelligence unit invited top bankers and money exchangers to the Serena Hotel for a training session, the session was videotaped in part so that Meyer could review the faces of the bankers for his investigation files. Jones got upset when he found out.

On another occasion, the New Ansari chief executive, Mohammed Khan, asked to meet Meyer at the Serena to discuss bulk currency shipments and show Meyer his records. Over lunch, the executive presented Meyer one of his ledgers as he was making a point. Meyer seized the opportunity. "You don't mind if I photocopy this?" he asked. Khan agreed and Meyer paid the hotel staff to make the copies. The records confirmed his suspicions when Meyer later compared them with New Ansari's cash declarations at the airport. The company was underreporting their shipments by several million dollars per month.

Meyer still felt he needed better information and started planning a raid on New Ansari's offices to seize records and customer logs. Jones was worried about the operation. Before coming to Afghanistan, Jones had worked on strategic issues at the National Counterterrorism Center. In Kabul, he regularly briefed ISAF leadership and senior officials in Washington. He tried to keep the larger goals of the war in mind. What would they accomplish by chasing around every corrupt Afghan official? How much did they actually know about New Ansari's alleged misdeeds?

Jones brought up his concerns with his superiors at the embassy. He didn't want to stop the raid, but he was worried about its aftermath. Other diplomats saw Meyer as smart and dedicated but lacking in diplomatic finesse. They also worried that the Afghan team working with Meyer might get burned because of its association with him. "Kirk was a loose cannon," another Treasury Department official said. "He wanted to be involved in what was sexy. He went looking for action. And he found it."

Meyer's determination to push ahead struck others as arrogant. His attitude, one colleague recalled, was "If you get in my way, fuck you. If you disagree with me, you're uninformed." When questioned about whether New Ansari actually represented a strategic threat to the American mission, or whether the U.S. embassy should be stalking dirty *hawala* dealers, Meyer argued that he had better information. "He would say, 'These guys think we're all complete idiots. They do. They think we're all out to lunch. They think we think they like us. They don't like us. They see us as an opportunity to steal a bunch of money, and that's exactly what they're doing. If you don't think that, then you're deluded.'"

Both Meyer and Calestino took corruption personally. They felt taxpayer money was being squandered by backstabbing Afghan partners. They felt an example must be made. No amount of disapproving démarches or finger-wagging warnings could move Karzai to discipline his thieving ranks. The problem required real consequences: convictions, prison sentences, lost jobs, blocked dollars. Calestino would muse about going into President Karzai's office in the palace, taking him by the back of the head, slamming his face against his desk, and telling him the United States is in charge, and if Karzai wanted his failed country to survive, he would do what was told. "Kirk used to say all the time his goal was to take down the Karzai government," one colleague recalled.

Meyer had his own fantasy scenario he sometimes joked about. On a tour of the Central Bank, he'd once watched, stunned, as *hawaladars* holding battered suitcases swarmed around the tellers' barred windows; each either filling their suitcases with fistfuls of cash or thrusting it at the tellers. As Meyer looked around at the mayhem, he noticed there were hardly any security guards. The main bank vault looked like it had been constructed in the nineteenth century. In his fantasy, after taking down Karzai, Meyer would rob the Central Bank. He would have Frank Calestino, his deputy, strip down to his underwear in the fountain outside the Central Bank. Every Afghan in the building would want to come look at a diplomat in his underwear in a fountain. And while that was happening, Meyer would be inside the Central Bank's ancient vault.

"Have you ever seen the vaults in the Central Bank?" Meyer would tell his colleagues. "They're full of cash. And I'm going to grab all of it. Because it's our money."

On January 14, 2010, the Sensitive Investigative Unit, under Meyer's supervision, had carried out its raid on two of New Ansari's branches in the Shahzada money market in Kabul, as well as one of their satellite phone shops, carting away computers and forty-two thousand documents. Targeting such a politically connected company had been an enormous risk for the Afghan police involved, particularly the SIU commander, Colonel Babakarkhel. To avoid leaks, Babakarkhel had not alerted Central Bank regulators, or the attorney general's office, or even his own boss, Interior Minister Haneef Atmar, about their operation. He had, however, convinced a friend at the Interior Ministry to provide backup police in case things turned violent. The timing of the raid, on a Thursday afternoon, had been chosen specifically to minimize the political blowback, as the Afghan government would be closed on Friday, part of the Muslim weekend. Meyer later came to believe that New Ansari bosses had transferred some of their files to a secret storage facility before the police moved in, but even so, he netted more than he'd hoped. "It was boxes and boxes and boxes," Meyer said. "It was a huge trove."

Because New Ansari was so important to the Afghan economy, and because the vast majority of its clients were law-abiding citizens moving small sums of money, absconding with all of their company records was bound to be disruptive. To avoid panicky customers, and assure people this wasn't simply a robbery, the police posted notices in Dari (the type of Persian spoken in Afghanistan) on the doors of the New Ansari offices, explaining the situation. For two days inside the SIU offices, police working around the clock scanned and copied reams of documents, so the files could be returned by Saturday morning.

"This raid was unprecedented," one of Meyer's subordinates said. "These guys were operating with impunity. And this was the first time there was an attempt to enforce Afghan laws on money laundering."

It also took Karzai's palace by surprise. For the clique of wealthy and politically connected Afghans unaccustomed to being challenged by rules or laws, this was an unusual warning. Haji Naqib, who ran the New Ansari–affiliated business Afghan United Petroleum, called Karzai personally to alert him to the operation. "A lot of important people have money with New Ansari," Naqib told me later. "If these people don't receive their money on time, there could be protests."

Within two days, New Ansari representatives held two meetings in the palace to complain. A large group of elders and businessmen from Kandahar—250 of them, by Naqib's count—came to the palace to see President Karzai. Some of these same men had financed Karzai's first days in Kandahar in 2001. They were men he listened to, fellow tribes-men and leaders from his hometown, and they played on his already heightened suspicions about U.S. motives. The Americans had singled them out, they argued, not because they were guilty but because they were Kandahari Pashtuns.

Not long after the raid, Naqib and Haji Mohammad Jan came to the U.S. embassy to meet with Stuart Jones and Earl Anthony Wayne, one of Eikenberry's deputies who oversaw economic affairs. The Afghans were confident and suave. Haji Mohammad Jan, in particular, exuded wealth and sophistication. He was around forty years old and had started in the *hawala* business as a teenager. He often wore luxurious white robes and expensive watches. "He looked like money that hadn't even been printed yet," Jones said.

The intelligence reports that the Americans had on Mohammad Jan suggested that he was moving away from the drug trade and illicit finance operations and toward his more respectable businesses. Afghan United Bank already had nine branches across the country and had plans to open twenty-one more. He had purchased a 7.5 percent stake in Aino Mena. The homes are so nice there "you would not believe they were in Afghanistan," Mohammad Jan told the diplomats. Just in the past year, he'd invested $85 million in Afghan businesses. He also planned to fund an insurance business, a fruit-harvesting facility, a bottled-water plant, a group of carpet weavers, and a university in Kandahar. "Reputation is the key currency of business in Afghanistan," he boasted. And his was sterling: he was "*the* business leader of the south," he said. When Wayne raised the allegations about laundering money and financing terrorists, Mohammad Jan waved them off.

The New Ansari bankers kept their cool with the American diplomats, but they were furious. They were particularly angry with Haneef Atmar, the interior minister, who oversaw the police and whom they assumed had approved the raid. Atmar had not been in Karzai's favor for a while. Any-one with the stature of a cabinet minister, particularly one as important as the interior minister, would have enemies in Afghan politics. He also car-ried the stain of his affiliation with the Communist government during the Soviet years. But to Karzai and others in the palace, his true badge of dishonor was being beloved by the Americans. Atmar was a young, edu-cated, English-speaking Pashtun, a potential future president—the type of politician American diplomats constantly tried to cultivate, and that Karzai worried about. Two weeks after the raid, Atmar told the Obama administration's drug czar, Gil Kerlikowske, that the operation had hurt him. People were calling him the "American minister."

"These are powerful people," Atmar told him. "And they raise hell."

Within a few months, Karzai fired Atmar from his cabinet post. The proximate cause was a barrage of rockets that fell during a high-profile peace conference in Kabul, an embarrassing security breach. But Atmar believed that this was just an excuse. He privately blamed his taking part in the New Ansari raid for causing his demise. Palace aides confirmed his suspicions. "Atmar was never trusted after that," one of them told me.

Meanwhile, over at Camp Falcon in Kabul, because of the raid on New Ansari "the wires went crazy," as one of Meyer's team members put it.

The ever-attentive eavesdroppers had been recording all the acrimonious fallout: New Ansari and Afghan United Bank officials calling the palace to complain; parliament members and bankers urging the attorney general to shut down the case. A series of phone calls between Haji Naqib, the Afghan United Petroleum chairman, and Mohammed Zia Salehi, the palace aide, were particularly interesting. Naqib asked Salehi to help stop the investigation into New Ansari. In return, according to investigators, he promised to buy Salehi a car for his son. The details played out in further conversations: the men would buy Salehi's son a red 2009 Toyota Corolla, worth about $10,000. Naqib and another associate, Mirwais, would make the purchase and deliver the car. Salehi later informed his boss, Ibrahim Spinzada, who in turn told a man referred to as "the Chief." Investigators assumed that man was President Karzai.

Salehi would later insist that the conversations had been misinterpreted. He said he was the one buying the car for a pro-government mullah, one of the regular palace payoffs he made to fortify the support for Karzai. "And I even bought the cheapest model," Salehi claimed.

The tapes recorded Salehi talking about more than just car prices. In conversations with a prominent Afghan female parliament member, Salehi also made comments that were, according to a person who heard the tapes, "very sexually explicit, even by American standards." In one, Salehi asked the lawmaker, at the time traveling in India, to return for a dalliance, saying he'd pay for the ticket. These recordings were so shocking to the Afghan wiretapping monitors that some didn't want to translate them.

After thousands of man-hours investigating the minister of religious affairs, only to have the Afghan government let him slip out of the country, Meyer did not want to make the same mistake again. From what he had learned about Salehi, Meyer believed he was involved in several layers of shady and possibly criminal dealings. He thought Salehi helped pad the palace slush fund by selling the release of Taliban prisoners, and that he was smuggling gems to India. But Meyer didn't need another labyrinthine investigation; he needed a conviction, an open-and-shut case. The car provided one.

"This was the simplest thing that we could identify with the Afghan police, for them to pursue," Meyer said. "It was a very simple crime. Easily understood by anybody. And that was the reason the focus was on the car."

Ambassador Eikenberry recognized that the case was veering into dangerous terrain. He made sure that Salehi's boss, Rangin Dadfar Spanta, the national security adviser, was aware that an arrest was coming. Spanta wanted to hear the evidence for himself. Eikenberry invited him to his embassy residence, an elegant rooftop apartment with an expansive outdoor patio. Eikenberry and his wife, Ching, regularly held dinners and receptions in their home, and they used it as a more private meeting space for Afghan officials and visiting dignitaries. On occasion, journalists would be invited to the residence for interviews or for gatherings that were supposed to remind people of home but could be somewhat awkward—like the time they hosted an evening of Halloween pumpkin carving, complete with a PowerPoint presentation on how to properly handle a knife. Spanta normally preferred not to visit Eikenberry in his home. He already had enough trouble at the palace with Karzai assuming that he was one of the pro-American ministers. But the case was sensitive enough that he made an exception. Spanta sat with Eikenberry in a small side living room while he listened to the recordings.

When they'd finished, Spanta stood up, agitated, and paced the room.

"Our system is more rotten than I thought, Karl. It's horrible," Spanta said. He hung his head, and tears welled in his eyes. "It's terrible."

"Now do you see the point about Salehi?" Eikenberry asked.

On the scale of Afghan bad behavior, a $10,000 bribe and marital infidelity, even if true, hardly merited a second look. Passing cash in and out of the palace was a tradition as old as the war. Karzai's chief of staff, Umer Daudzai, kept a money-counting machine on top of a safe in his office. (When asked about it by an American diplomat, Daudzai replied calmly that "part of my responsibility is to distribute resources to our friends.") But American officials were convinced that government corruption lay at the heart of their problems in Afghanistan. And Meyer had found a way to do something about it.

"It was about as clear a case of what we would call honest services fraud in the U.S. as you could imagine," an American official involved told me later. "A quid pro quo."

In the palace, President Karzai exploded when he learned of Salehi's arrest. After the election, explosions were becoming his default reaction. Everything the Americans did tended to set him off. But the New Ansari operation took his fury to a new level. The manner of Salehi's capture, with masked gunmen in the early morning darkness, reminded Karzai of the Soviet jackboots of an earlier era. Until that point, Karzai had not followed the work of the American-mentored police units very closely. But he felt the Americans had crossed a dangerous line, opening a new front in their campaign to unseat him and aiming further into his inner circle than ever before. "It was seen as an American attack on the palace. An entry point," recalled Waheed Omar, Karzai's spokesman.

Salehi was being held in an interrogation room at the counternarcotics prison. He was not cooperating. At one point, a group of Afghan police were around Salehi, including Colonel Hamed, who had taken him from his apartment that morning. Salehi asked him who the commander was.

"Hamed pointed at me," General Nikzad recalled. "Then Salehi said, 'I swear if I don't put you in jail for two years, I will change my name.'"

Salehi refused to be questioned. "He said, 'If you guys could keep me one night in this jail, then I will answer all your questions tomorrow morning. If you cannot keep me tonight, I'll be the one interrogating you.'"

General Nikzad was taking calls all day from angry Afghan officials demanding Salehi's release. His FBI mentor told him to ignore them. But by four p.m., Nikzad had received a new letter from the attorney general ordering Salehi freed. President Karzai had personally initiated it. By early evening, Salehi was out of jail.

It took a week before anyone outside of a small group of palace and American insiders heard the name Mohammed Zia Salehi. Then *The Wall Street Journal* published an account of his arrest, and the political crisis broke into the open. Karzai quickly went on the offensive by publicly blasting the operation and its American backers.

"This man was taken out of his house in the middle of the night by thirty Kalashnikov-toting masked men in the name of Afghan law enforcement," Karzai told Christiane Amanpour during an interview with ABC on August 15. "This is exactly reminiscent of the days of the Soviet Union, where people were taken away from their homes by armed people in the name of the state and thrown into obscure prisons and some sort of kangaroo courts. It reminds the Afghan people of those days with immense fear.

"So I have intervened," Karzai went on. "As I am the president of this country, I must uphold the constitution and do things legally from now onwards." He announced that by the next day Kirk Meyer's team and the Major Crimes Task Force would be brought under "Afghan laws and within the sovereignty of the Afghan state."

In subsequent meetings with Eikenberry, Karzai demanded to know who else in the palace the Americans were wiretapping. The president could only assume that his calls were also monitored. Karzai had no secure communications; he made his office calls on a normal cell phone. He had been worried about this for years. When he wanted to share something particularly private with an American commander or ambassador, he would sometimes invite them into a small sitting room behind his main office that he believed was free of bugs. Once, at a palace lunch for NATO secretary-general Anders Fogh Rasmussen, Karzai made droll quips about his office being a den of spies, with the Iranians lurking around every corner, the Brits surveilling the Iranians, and the Americans sucking up every word with their high-tech NSA listening devices. "He was joking about how the Americans listen to every word that's said in the palace, and he's absolutely right," a NATO official at the lunch recalled. It became a dark joke for Karzai: "When he said things on the phone about Americans, he'd say, 'Let the bastards listen,'" an aide related. "Or he'd say, 'You know, I do this intentionally so they know what I think about them.'"

Karzai and his aides, even those critical of him, considered the Salehi case a ridiculous witch hunt. "They came up with some bullshit excuse to get the warrant," one of his aides said. "That he's a front man for Afghan United Bank? He's a front man for narcotics? The courier? Bullshit. They wanted to use this wiretap to figure out the Karzai patronage network. To be frank, it was a white coup d'état against the Afghan government. It's like us trying to take down [David] Axelrod and you wonder what the problem is."

Karzai saw the episode as another blatant attack by an American government bent on destroying him. "Clearly politically motivated. Clearly politically motivated," he told me when I asked him about it. "That's why I intervened and had him released. Clearly." If Salehi hadn't been freed, Karzai said, he would have broken him out of the American prison. "I was ready to send Afghan forces, actually."

Ambassador Eikenberry had rarely seen Karzai so infuriated. He seemed to be in an alternative universe when he talked about the case. The two men exchanged words, but it was not a conversation. In subsequent meetings, embassy officials tried to mollify the Afghans. The investigators wiretapping Salehi were Afghan, they said, while the Americans were simply mentors. Arrests at five in the morning were perfectly normal. They're safer, because there are fewer people on the streets. The masks protect the identities of the police. Arresting the powerful, no one needed to mention now, was dangerous. Besides, Salehi had diplomatic visas for foreign travel, so he could have gone to Germany or the United Kingdom, the American officials explained; Salehi's investigators had wanted to preserve some element of surprise.

American momentum for a Salehi style showdown with Karzai's government had been building for months. At U.S. embassy meetings, Eikenberry often said this was the "decisive year" for fighting corruption and establishing the rule of law. Yet Karzai's ministers had consistently defanged other attempts to graft American-style accountability onto the Afghan government. Attorney General Aloko, hounded by his ever-present Justice Department mentors, had agreed to opening an anti-corruption tribunal, but neither Aloko nor anyone else in authority would presume to bring members of Karzai's coterie before such a court. To the dismay of the U.S. embassy, Aloko and the Supreme Court had also agreed to exempt soldiers and police officers from the tribunal, even though a cursory glance at the security ministries would lay bare elaborate frauds and criminal rackets. The investigative prosecutors with the Attorney General's Anti-Corruption Unit were supposed to take thirty days or less to decide how to handle a case, but these decisions often dragged on for months. Usually, they chose to move on a case depending on if bribe money was paid.

Seemingly simple reforms frittered in limbo. Embassy staffers wanted to raise the paltry salaries of Afghan judges and prosecutors, in the belief that higher pay would lessen their reliance on bribes. Provincial judges and prosecutors at the time earned less than $200 a month. Such remuneration hardly compensated for the risks they faced in adjudicating, as the Taliban saw it, on behalf of the puppet regime. The American embassy kept a prominent female prosecutor in Herat under surveillance because they feared her assassination. The chief judge in the northern city of Mazar-e-Sharif told American diplomats that the Taliban would call him at night threatening to kill his children. The Taliban had their own system of justice that traveled by motorbike between dusty towns and villages, listened to local complaints, with no lawyers or juries needed, and anointed the winner and sentenced the loser, sometimes with lashings or death. No bribes, no interminable meetings or inconclusive results, no wait for punishment.

After the arrest, Karzai's instructions would effectively block the Major Crimes Task Force from ever again taking on politically sensitive cases. The day after Salehi was picked up, Karzai issued a decree creating a commission to investigate the work of these teams and what had happened to Salehi. He would form subsequent commissions on the same matter and the people he appointed demonstrated how seriously he took this issue: two vice presidents, his national security adviser, the attorney general, and a top legal adviser. By the end of September, the group had recommended sweeping changes: all detention facilities should be secured by the Afghan police and not foreigners, and everyone in the Major Crimes Task Force should be replaced with people of their choosing.

Karzai's government demanded an agreement, on paper, to set boundaries on the work of the MCTF. His administration saw such police teams as American tools to pursue unfavored members of the Afghan leadership. The female Afghan prosecutor who had been in charge of the Salehi case, Zargouna Sediqi, was ordered by one of her superiors to drop the investigation, and referred to as the "whore of the Americans" by her bosses. Aloko ordered his prosecutors to steer clear of their American mentors from the Department of Justice.

General Nikzad, the MCTF commander, was ordered to hand over his files and sat through rounds of interrogations by three Karzai-assigned generals—one police, one army, one intelligence—who worked in the palace administrative affairs department. "They were not actually asking me about how I arrested Salehi," Nikzad recalled. "The questions were mainly about how closely I was working with the Americans."

"The atmosphere of the office changed 100 percent," Nikzad said. "One or two weeks later, I wanted to arrest another general on corruption. I went to the Ministry of Interior. The minister said he'd talked to Karzai and Karzai told him, 'Even if I talk on the phone with my wife, I think Nikzad is listening to our conversation.' All of our authority disappeared. We were not allowed to make any arrests on corruption. Our activity dropped to zero."

In the months after Salehi's arrest, the number of Major Crimes Task Force investigators trained and the hours of training both dropped by half. The Afghans on these teams faced more than a crisis of morale.

Their association with the Americans suddenly put their lives in danger; their president saw them as traitors. Nikzad received phone calls from people threatening to kidnap him. "The law in our country is like a spiderweb," Nikzad told me before leaving Kabul. "If mosquitoes or flies land, they will be trapped there. But if a bird or a falcon comes, it will destroy the whole thing. I don't want to face the falcon anymore."

In February 2011, the FBI arranged to fly Nikzad and his family out of Afghanistan and settled them in Fremont, California, a Bay Area city popular with the Afghan diaspora. He had served in the Afghan police for four decades, including twenty-five years as an instructor. The transition to life in America, at sixty-five, was not easy. He enrolled in adult education classes to try to learn English. He survived on money sent to him by his children. When I talked to him two years later, he said nobody from the U.S. government had helped him in any way.

"They just brought me, threw me here like an animal, and disappeared," he said.

Most of the Americans involved in the case came to regret the Salehi arrest. Even though the war on corruption was just starting, in many ways that episode marked America's defeat, and it intensified the feeling that those obscure distant fighters, the Taliban off in their rugged hideouts, were almost irrelevant; the real enemy was the Afghan government, which was supposed to be an ally. But at the same time, the Americans were unwilling to cut off aid, or take any other significant move, to fight that new enemy. The leaders of the Obama administration had spent millions on law enforcement efforts only to be confronted with the fact that they did not have the courage of their convictions.

"The fallout from the Salehi case has had a ripple effect throughout the Afghan programs with which we work," concluded an internal memo circulated within the American rule of law community in Afghanistan nearly a year after the arrest. "We have lost influence and access.

"Those who suffered no consequences because the international community led by the US did nothing meaningful to stand up to the palace in the Salehi matter are less likely now to believe that there will be significant consequences if they interfere in investigations or prosecutions," the memo went on. "One thing for certain, the situation as it exists in Afghanistan when it comes to corruption at the highest levels will not get better if we don't insist that the palace lead and demonstrate the necessary political will to aggressively attack corruption in the political and criminal elite in Afghanistan. We will look weak across the board, not just in rule of law, but in other areas as well, if we continue to back down when presented with situations like Salehi."

It took a while for Salehi to cool off, but eventually he could joke about himself as "the internationally famous Mr. Salehi," as he did the first time we talked on the phone, inviting me, with a guffaw, to his "lavish and luxurious apartment." He had survived, and President Karzai had prevailed. Over drinks at his apartment, Salehi told me that Brigadier General Herbert McMaster, the commander of a U.S. military counter-corruption team, had even given him a certificate of appreciation.

"For me this was a really difficult period," Salehi said, swirling his whiskey. "If they needed me, they could have just called."

6

GOVERNMENT IN A BOX

THE SENSE THAT HAMID KARZAI WAS either unwilling to address the greedy thieving within his government or incapable of doing so effectively was one of the basic strains on the country's relationship with the United States. The other was his position on what to do about the Taliban. The U.S. military, given the troop presence and the size of its financial commitment, wanted an Afghan president who would act like a bold commander in chief, publicly leading his Afghan troops into battle against the evil Islamic terrorists and taking responsibility for American soldiers' actions, even when tragic, as a necessary cost in the struggle for a greater good.

Karzai would do no such thing. He was in no way a military man. He loved poetry and literature and following television news. He could avidly debate geopolitics and grand strategy for hours, but he would get bored when the discussion got into the weeds of military tactics or troop movements. He would often cut short his weekly National Security Council meetings. American military commanders were always encouraging Karzai to give speeches in front of Afghan troops or discuss their bravery and sacrifice, but he rarely took them up on the offer. Diplomats who spent a lot of time with him could watch him begin to fidget as he sat through U.S. military PowerPoint briefings. Sherard Cowper-Coles, a British ambassador to Kabul, wrote that Karzai didn't even have a map available in his office when they were discussing an important battle in Helmand Province, so the ambassador pulled a Royal Air Force map from his briefcase to finish the chat. "He had no idea of distances. He can't read a map. He'd be saying to me, just move your soldiers from there to there. [U.S. General Dan] McNeill would be getting crosser and crosser," one

European diplomat told me. "Karzai had very little authority over his own Army. He wasn't really interested in military dispositions or military campaigns." William Wood, the U.S. ambassador before Eikenberry, found the same thing. "Karzai did not want to hear, or at least did not want to hear from the foreigners, about military developments." General McNeill offered to give Karzai a military briefing every morning and respond to any concerns from the battlefield, but Karzai declined. His interest in his own forces also seemed limited. In a meeting with his defense minister, Abdul Rahim Wardak, Karzai predicted that two weeks after American troops pulled out of Afghanistan, Kabul would fall to the Taliban. "That is what I think of your military," he said.

President Obama's decision to ratchet up the war against the Taliban had been debated endlessly in Washington, as well as within the U.S. military command in Kabul, but it had been presented to President Karzai as basically a fait accompli. One of General Stanley McChrystal's first orders from Defense Secretary Robert Gates had been to write a strategic assessment of the war, and McChrystal's diagnosis was that the "overall situation is deteriorating," with a "crisis of confidence" among Afghans, and a "resilient and growing insurgency." McChrystal knew that the assessment would be the basis for requesting thousands of additional troops. The only question was how many. Karzai had strong misgivings about more troops.

For years he had listened as delegations of elders from all corners of Afghanistan told woeful tales of slain sons and neighbors, bombed-out homes and trampled fields, women disgraced, men zip-tied and hooded, rooms ransacked and roads blocked, home invasions after midnight by bearded Americans and their terrifying attack dogs, the sad accumulation of fatal mistakes and outright atrocities entirely beyond his control. Karzai had explained his basic viewpoint countless times. He felt the war was headquartered and orchestrated in Pakistan by the ISI and its Taliban clients and that American violence in Afghan homes and villages served to swell the rebel ranks and prolong the war. He had said this to anyone who would listen.

In late 2006, during a trip to Kandahar, Karzai told a crowd that the government of Pakistan "wants our children to serve as doormen at their hotels in Karachi instead of becoming doctors and engineers." He went on: "Pakistan wants to rule a land where great empires of Genghis Khan, Alexander the Great, Britain, and the Soviet Union have been brought to their knees. Great empires have not been able to occupy this land; how can Pakistan dream of doing so?" When Obama was a senator visiting Kabul, Karzai insisted to him that if Pakistan stopped "using Islamic radicalism as an instrument of policy," it would find a "true friend and ally" in Afghanistan. In June 2008, Karzai had threatened, at a press conference, to send his troops into Pakistan. "If these people in Pakistan give themselves the right to come and fight in Afghanistan, as was continuing for the last thirty years, so Afghanistan has the right to cross the border and destroy terrorist nests, spying, extremism, and killing, in order to defend itself, its schools, its people, and its life," Karzai said. The American diplomats at the time took their normal stance and warned Karzai against publicly criticizing Pakistan. The next evening, at a dinner reception in the home of an Afghan official, one of Karzai's national security aides, Daud Yaqub, told the deputy U.S. ambassador that Karzai "meant every word.

"This wasn't emotion or an attempt to deflect attention," Yaqub told him. "The president genuinely feels this way and has for a long time."

But Karzai had long since lost any real desire to fight the Taliban inside his own country. He believed the collateral damage to civilian lives would exceed whatever might be won by attacking those foes. The Taliban spokesmen ridiculed Karzai relentlessly as an American stooge, a "captive in his palace." He was far kinder toward them. Karzai tended to see the Taliban as fellow Pashtuns—he often called them "disenchanted" or "upset" brothers—and advocated reaching out to them for negotiations and reconciliation. He proposed hosting a peace conference in Kabul in 2010, at a time when the American position called only for attracting low-level insurgents to switch sides but not reaching out to the Taliban leadership. During one military briefing that spring, Karzai listened as McChrystal gravely informed him that Barg-e-Matal, an embattled town in a remote northern province, had fallen to the Taliban. "So it was liberated," Karzai responded. In a moment of anger during the election crisis, Karzai had told a group of parliamentarians that if the international community kept pressuring him, he would join the Taliban himself.

Americans in Kabul got outraged when they heard such comments. How could this man, installed and propped up and still alive only by the grace of the United States, be so ungrateful? Many people within Karzai's government disagreed with his soft approach to the Taliban and thought he expressed far too much sympathy with the insurgency. Some of them believed that Karzai had not just lost faith in the U.S. military's chances at winning the war but had actively begun to undermine American goals in an attempt to hasten the superpower's withdrawal. "Almost every day the agenda has been: do something to defeat the West in Afghanistan," one of his colleagues told me that spring. "We are trying on a daily basis to get the U.S. out of Afghanistan."

Hamid Karzai's views on the Taliban almost seemed to have come full circle from the spring of 1994, when he'd burst into Richard Smyth's office at the American consulate in Peshawar saying, "Richie! Richie! I've got exciting news! A new group has formed in Afghanistan!"

Back then, a small cabal of mullahs and religious students from Uruz-gan and Kandahar Provinces had taken a stand against the warlords of their day. Most of the leaders of this inchoate rebellion, a one-eyed country cleric named Mullah Mohammed Omar among them, were not of Karzai's social class, educational background, or branch of the Pashtun tribal tree. They tended to be poor men from rural areas and descendants of the Ghilzai side of the Pashtun schism. Within the early Taliban ranks, the Popalzais, Karzai's tribe on the other side of the divide, were not completely shut out. Some of the movement's senior leaders were family friends of the Karzais', such as Mullah Mohammed Ghaus, who went on to be foreign minister in the Taliban regime. Another friend was Mullah Khairullah Khairkhwa, who would be the Taliban governor of Herat and then a Guantánamo prisoner, until he was released in May 2014 in the exchange for American prisoner of war Sergeant Bowe Bergdahl.

At that time, Karzai considered the Taliban a positive development because he hoped they would end the brutal civil war. He also saw them as a hedge against his family's other political rivals in Kandahar. Some have claimed that Karzai went as far as donating $50,000 and weapons to help the Taliban spread, although others in the family dispute this. It is true, however, that Karzai at that stage was urging Pakistan's intelligence service to do more to support them.

By October 1995, the Taliban movement had already spread far beyond Kandahar. That month, they captured the western city of Herat, near the Iranian border. Their arrival set off protests, and they angered city residents with their decree closing girls' schools and firing female teachers and civil servants. A few days after the Taliban took the city—part of their rapid conquest of Afghanistan—Karzai met with political officers in the American consulate in Peshawar. The new Taliban governor of Herat, Mullah Yaar Mohammad, was Karzai's friend, and although Karzai acknowledged that the people of the city were "not entirely happy," he said the Taliban were "trying to be nice." The governor was doing his best, Karzai assured the Americans. When the governor learned some Talibs were running around the city with scissors, threatening to give locals haircuts, Karzai said his friend had the "would-be barbers publicly beaten to belay fears that the Taliban planned to impose drastic change upon the Heratis." The Taliban in Herat was a "Popalzai show," Karzai noted. He had some mixed feelings about this. He was happy his tribesmen were leading the Taliban in the west, but he worried that they were being sent away from the highest ranks of Taliban leadership in Kandahar.

The Taliban thought highly enough of Karzai that he was offered the job of ambassador to the United Nations in New York. Some who knew Karzai well in that period debate whether he accepted, but at least for a time, Karzai presented himself as the Taliban's representative in his meetings with American diplomats. On December 10, 1996, three months after the Taliban had taken Kabul, Robin Raphel, the State Department's assistant secretary responsible for Afghanistan and the region, met with "Taliban-designated UN rep Hamid Karzai" to give him a five-page letter outlining the State Department's views on the new regime. In the letter, Raphel urged the Taliban to reassure Russia and Afghanistan's northern neighbors about their "non-aggressive intentions," because "to many, the Taliban are an unknown entity, perhaps misunderstood and misperceived.

"I note from your letter that you have chosen Mr. Hamid Karzai to be Afghanistan's permanent representative to the United Nations in New York," she wrote. "You should be aware that gaining acceptance of the Taliban's credentials for Afghanistan at the U.N. may be difficult and protracted. Unfortunately, the Taliban's gender policies have cost it the necessary support of the international community."

Karzai was not taking a particularly radical stance by supporting the Taliban at that stage. Many moderate Pashtuns also endorsed their cause. The early rhetoric from these humble clerics seemed to herald a better future: they professed a desire to collect the warlords' weapons, hold a *loya jirga* to choose the next government, and perhaps reinstate the exiled king. That winter, Zalmay Khalilzad, an early Taliban supporter who had been working at the RAND Corporation, spent Christmas in Munich visiting his wife's family. Hamid Karzai sought him out to ask for his advice about the Taliban's job offer: Should he accept the U.N. post? Khalilzad inferred, from how Karzai was discussing the position, that the job hadn't been offered to him in an authoritative way.

Within a month, however, the issue was moot, as Karzai was out of the job. The Taliban had rescinded the offer, once again under mysterious circumstances. Karzai relatives believe that Mullah Omar and others got suspicious of Karzai after he visited with the Uzbek warlord Abdul Rashid Dostum, an anti-Taliban fighter, trying to lobby his support. After that brush-off, Karzai drifted further away from the Taliban. In his diplomatic rounds, Karzai was also reporting growing tensions between the Taliban and his Popalzai tribe. On January 12, 1997, he told John Holzman, the deputy chief of mission at the American embassy in Islamabad, that the Taliban had beaten a senior Popalzai commander a few months earlier, and another one had been shot. They had also moved his friend Mullah Yaar Mohammad from the governorship of Herat to a less important post. Karzai said there was "little clarity" about the Taliban's harboring of Osama bin Laden but that their support for radical Islamists in general "cuts across" the ranks of the movement. Karzai still felt the United States had to work with the Taliban, in order to moderate their views. And his tribe, he insisted, was still relevant in the movement. "The Popalzais are a formidable part of the Taliban, and they know this," Karzai told Holzman.

By the summer of 1998, as Mullah Omar was denouncing the American missile strikes on Osama bin Laden's al-Qaeda training camps as "a brazen manifestation of enmity against the Afghan nation," Karzai had turned completely against his former friends. He later claimed he discovered that the mullahs were being controlled by Pakistani intelligence and were aligned with Islamic radicals, and that the Taliban was not the homegrown nationalistic movement he had believed it to be. Eager to pass tips to the Americans, Karzai told U.S. diplomats in August 1998 that he had heard from several Taliban sources that bin Laden was "on the move," fearing another American strike. Karzai said he and his father were in favor of the U.S. bombings, which he believed sent a strong message against terrorism.

Hamid Karzai got married in 1999 in Quetta. At his wedding, Hamid's father convened the relatives and other Pashtun leaders at a late-night meeting in the family compound. As his elder brother Qayum recalled in *Ghost Wars*, their father told them, "Our country is gone and it's somebody else's country now, and it [will] remain that way unless we [resist]." His father urged them to ally themselves with the Northern Alliance commander Ahmad Shah Massoud. Hamid worked from the family compound that year to organize resistance to the Taliban among prominent Pashtun royalists. He coordinated meetings with tribal chiefs and even wrote to Mullah Omar, inviting him to attend but also warning that the Taliban must reform and "remove the foreigners that [are] with them here killing and destroying our country, ruining our lives."

In the remaining time before September 11, Karzai advocated for regime change. He begged American diplomats to pay more attention to the Taliban atrocities and asked for money and weapons to foment revolt. Bill Milam, a U.S. ambassador to Pakistan during this period, felt Karzai was being reckless. "His third question was always: Can I have some weapons?" Milam recalled. "I would tell him, I can give you a pen and paper."

Karzai's anti-Taliban activism fell on deaf ears. "I would go every week to Islamabad," he said. "I would go to the Americans, I would go to the French, I would go to the English, I would go to the Germans, I would go to the Italians . . . [and] tell them about the readiness of the Afghan people to move against the Taliban. They wouldn't trust me. They wouldn't believe me. . . . They didn't see it."

During the summer of 2000, Karzai testified before Congress about the miseries in his home country. "Our economy is in ruins," he told the legislators. "Our people are pushed into destitution and despair. Our land is turned into a training camp for terrorists, gun-runners, drug dealers, and criminals. Our agriculture is destroyed because of land mines. Worst of all, Afghans are still dying in a foreign imposed war.

"I was among the first to actively support the Taliban movement," Karzai said. "I personally knew and worked with the majority of the leadership during the entire period of Jihad. They were neither radical nor against Afghan values and culture. They entertained no ambition to hold on to political power nor to remain involved in politics. Thus, my knowledge of and experience with the Afghan Taliban makes it very clear to me that the presence and militancy of terrorism in Afghanistan are not the product of Afghans, but rather the product of non-Afghans who have come to our country in disguise to appear as Afghans and as Taliban."

Karzai begged the United States to help. "The time to watch is over and the responsibility to act is long overdue," he said. "Further delay will dramatically increase the political and economic cost of the resolution of the conflict in Afghanistan and the region."

A couple of months before delivering his assessment of the war's failings to his bosses in Washington, General Stanley McChrystal presented it to Karzai and other senior officials in a Cabinet Room briefing with a colorful PowerPoint deck. Karzai understood that this particular briefing was rather momentous. The slide show was supposed to convince him to accept, and endorse, thousands more American soldiers, as well as the attendant collateral damage that would accompany such an escalation. What would ultimately be one of Karzai's most important decisions of his political life would be justified in two dozen slides. Karzai paid close attention. He even took notes.

"Well, General, the first thing is, you called the situation dire," Karzai said when it was over, as a person in the briefing recalled. "Is it really dire? What do you mean by 'dire'?"

Karzai wasn't lacking in vocabulary; he spoke immaculate English with a patrician, vaguely British lilt. He was mulling the implications: How was "dire" different from "awful" or "grim" or "catastrophic." What would that word do to Afghans' confidence in him? The men debated the synonyms for a while before Karzai got stuck on another problematic word: "insurgency."

"We don't have an insurgency in Afghanistan," he insisted.

A historian of Afghanistan, Thomas Barfield, has written that "nothing undermined the legitimacy of any Afghan government faster than the charge that it was beholden to foreign masters." This was something that Karzai knew intuitively, and he returned to this point with anyone who would listen. It was one of his spiels. Afghanistan, in his mind, had a problem with "terrorism." American troops were here to fight that. If there was an insurgency, that meant ordinary Afghans were fighting their own government, and that meant people saw his government as illegitimate. And if the American infidels were here fighting on behalf of this illegitimate government, that meant, he explained to McChrystal, that "I'm a puppet." And if I'm a *puppet*, he went on, and you are *infidels*, then those fighting us can declare this a *jihad*. And in this country, *jihad* is politically and religiously accepted. And if that's the case, we're in trouble.

"So this is not an insurgency," Karzai said.

After that briefing, Ambassador Eikenberry reported back to Washington. His message: *We really do have a problem.* Eikenberry was frustrated by the gulf separating how he and Karzai saw the war; he felt that the interests of Karzai and the United States were not aligned. After his two tours in the military, and then the chaos of the election, Eikenberry had become one of the war's chief skeptics, and many of his misgivings had to do with Hamid Karzai.

He believed that Karzai was misjudging America. Karzai's conspiratorial view of American plans readily assumed there were ulterior motives beyond the Taliban, that the United States wanted to use Afghanistan as a base for operations against Iran, Pakistan, China, and the wider region. Eikenberry also didn't like how Karzai would regularly tell visiting high-level American delegations that the United States had "failed" in Afghanistan. Eikenberry felt this "blame America" tactic was just Karzai's way of deflecting responsibility from his own government.

At President Obama's request, in November 2009 Eikenberry had written a cable expressing his candid views about the prospect of more troops. His reservations centered on Karzai, that he was "not an adequate strategic partner." The troop buildup, Eikenberry wrote, would cement Afghanistan's dependence on American money and protection, and it would delay the day when Afghans fought and governed for themselves. Karzai "continues to shun responsibility for any sovereign burden," Eikenberry said, "whether defense, governance or development. He and much of his circle do not want the U.S. to leave and are only too happy to see us invest further. They assume we covet their territory for a never-ending 'war on terror' and for military bases to use against surrounding powers." Eikenberry believed that a surge in troops would only accomplish prolonging a corrupt administration that has "few indigenous sources of revenue, few means to distribute services to its citizens, and most important, little to no political will or capacity to carry out basic tasks of governance."

The day that cable was leaked to *The New York Times*, Eikenberry's job as ambassador dropped a notch, from difficult to almost futile. I saw him that morning, November 12, 2009, and followed him on his scheduled trip to Bagram Airfield to give a speech at a naturalization ceremony for soldiers receiving U.S. citizenship (joining the military offered a fast track to citizenship) and a routine meeting with military commanders. He was grim the whole day. He would neither confirm nor deny that he had written the cable, a position he would not deviate from in the years that followed. In the cramped military conference room, Eikenberry had to swallow his true feelings. He told the Regional Command East commanders that there was a "consensus" about the need for more troops and that his relationship with McChrystal was "extraordinarily good." His concerns about Karzai represent a "difference of nuance and perspective," he told the room, adding that "it's not a black-and-white divide."

The reality was far different. Eikenberry and McChrystal were fight-

*Hamid Karzai talks with U.S. Defense Secretary Leon Panetta
during a lunch at the Pentagon on January 10, 2013.*

ing over a litany of issues, including the creation of village militias and
the military's plan to buy generators and diesel fuel for Kandahar, and
the two men didn't get along. McChrystal felt blindsided by Eikenberry's
cable. Eikenberry believed he'd made his feelings well known in the
weeks prior. "My analysis was not going to change his mind," Eikenberry
said. "His mind was made up." McChrystal told me he considered Karzai
a "great partner" who has been "absolutely straightforward with me and
been reliable."

Karzai was traveling in Istanbul when the cable was leaked. When
Karzai returned, he met Eikenberry in the palace. Karzai shrugged off
the criticisms in the leaked cable, saying he was used to these things now.
Karzai himself was a political animal; these types of bureaucratic knife
fights were familiar. Eikenberry told me later that Karzai's reaction was
that of a seasoned survivalist. At one point, Karzai looked at him closely.

"Well, Ambassador," Karzai said. "My conclusion is: you have an
enemy."

To inaugurate President Obama's troop surge, the commander of coalition forces in southern Afghanistan, Major General Nick Carter, a gar-
rulous, confident Brit, had orchestrated months of military maneuvers

across the opium tracts of the Helmand River Valley, a crescendo of preparations that reached their climax on the evening of February 12, 2010.
That afternoon, Carter sat surrounded by his top NATO and Afghan
officers inside a command center at Camp Bastion, a military base in Helmand Province, waiting for approval from Kabul. On airstrips and gravel
lots across the province, thousands of U.S. Marines and Afghan soldiers
waited in anticipation to board their CH-53E Super Stallion transport
helicopters for the largest military operation of the war, an assault on the
small farming hamlet of Marja. The first waves of airborne troops would
be followed by more moving overland, laying down mobile bridges to ford
irrigation canals that had become defensive moats of a Taliban fortress.
Predator drones and Apache attack helicopters would prowl the moon-
less night from above. Hulking bomb-sweeping armored vehicles would
blast paths through the minefields. One hundred and fifty-five square
miles of farmland, and the Taliban foot soldiers who lived there, would
witness the full fury of American war power at the apex of its empire. If
Hamid Karzai would say yes, that is.

In reality, Marja was an obscure, no-name, dirt-poor village of only
marginal importance to the Taliban or the overall conflict. The location

Marine commanders take a tour of the town of Marja,
in Helmand Province.

had been chosen mostly because the Marines already happened to be stationed nearby. But the troop "surge," as its name implied, needed a fresh boost, a new publicity campaign for a tired old war. Marja was designed to be the first victory in America's comeback win, a momentum builder and propaganda coup, counterinsurgency theory laid down with overwhelming force. There was a waiting list for reporters to cover it; many journalists had flown in from Washington for the show. After the Taliban were blown away, McChrystal assured the world, a "government in a box" would spring forth. Marja would set the tone, and the whole thing needed to look right. McChrystal wanted Karzai's approval. He was the commander in chief, after all.

Since he'd arrived, McChrystal had been making deference to Karzai central to his political approach. The first time they met, on June 14, 2009, McChrystal ditched his usual fatigues and wore his green army dress uniform, to show respect. He took Karzai's complaints seriously. "No more civilian casualties" became his mantra. When an American F-15 fighter jet bombed two fuel trucks in Kunduz Province, killing more than ninety villagers who were gathered around them siphoning off the gas, McChrystal borrowed his executive officer's cell phone to call Karzai and apologize. "As I promised you when I arrived, I am working to prevent this kind of loss. I'll redouble that effort," he said. After another fatal mistake, McChrystal slammed his hand down on the table and cursed his subordinates. "What is it that we don't understand? We're going to lose this fucking war if we don't stop killing civilians."

Karzai's ego allowed him to appreciate McChrystal's solicitousness, but that wasn't enough to change his opinion about the U.S. military.

"By that time, the president's view on the whole war on terror had shifted," Waheed Omar, Karzai's spokesman, told me. "He was not in favor of more war and fighting. He was very skeptical of the Americans. He was not very keen. One of the reasons the president didn't react too forcefully to it was because of McChrystal's relationship with the president. He liked McChrystal, so he didn't really resist."

By the evening of February 12, some 3,500 Marines, soldiers, and airmen and 1,500 Afghan infantrymen, plus thousands more in support roles, were waiting for the order to attack Marja. But Karzai still had not blessed the operation. After seven p.m., McChrystal drove to the president's home, tucked behind his office across a wall from the Chinese embassy. The two-story residence had a circular driveway with a swimming pool and tennis court in back (Karzai's preferred exercise was forty-five minutes on the elliptical trainer, three times a week). The home was a boxy, gray concrete structure that McChrystal said "had the feel of a prosperous but not wealthy American home, circa 1964." Another writer described it as "graceless." The president's wife lived as a virtual prisoner there, rarely venturing outside. Her days as a practicing gynecologist were long gone. She kept purdah, as Muslims call the practice of female seclusion, and avoided the many male guests, relatives, friends, and advisers who sat with the president until late in the evening.

That night, Hamid Karzai had a cold. This was not uncommon. Karzai was constantly beleaguered by some ailment—coughs, sore throats, fevers. He had a well-scrutinized eye twitch whose intensity seemed to ebb and flow in parallel to the state of relations with America: easing at the calmer moments, then tweaking into furious spasms during crises. He loved effervescent vitamin C tablets. Ambassador Eikenberry's wife had given him Chinese ginseng root powder as an herbal remedy for his illnesses. A palace doctor confided to me that five people were employed to taste the president's food as a test for poison. "He is a hypochondriac," one European ambassador told me. "He's always talking about his health."

McChrystal waited in the downstairs living room, with its floral print furniture and wood-paneled walls, along with Karzai's security ministers. When the president arrived, he listened to McChrystal's spiel. Karzai was "resistant," recalled Amrullah Saleh, the nation's spy chief, who was at the residence that night. "He was against the use of airpower and was puzzled why nearly thirty thousand people had assembled to attack such a little area."

One of Karzai's servants overheard McChrystal's war plan and rushed back to the kitchen in alarm: *The Americans are planning to invade the United Arab Emirates!* He thought McChrystal had said "Sharjah," meaning a city near Dubai. The name Marja meant nothing to him. ("We still call the guy Sharjah," one of Karzai's aides told me years later.)

Down at his Camp Bastion command post, Nick Carter sat in a frustrated heap. Earlier that week, he had told a reporter that "the Afghan government is fully behind this operation." This giant kickoff offensive had been named "Moshtarak," which meant "together." This was bluster. The regional commander of the Afghan police, Mirwais Noorzai, had an idea. Maybe his sister's husband could help? He was referring to Ahmed Wali Karzai. If anyone could change the president's mind, it would be his half brother. This sounded like a good idea to Carter. Noorzai dialed his number and passed the cell phone to Carter, who told Ahmed Wali they had to launch the operation that day or it might get pushed back for a month. Could he help?

Ahmed Wali called the palace and talked it over with the president.

By nine p.m., word had filtered to the southern commanders.

"President Karzai agreed to the operation," Brigadier General Lawrence D. Nicholson, commander of the 2nd Marine Expeditionary Brigade, told his senior staff. "We're a go."

Karzai had agreed to the mission reluctantly. He wasn't happy about the prospect of more fighting, but what were his alternatives? "In his mind they were going to do an operation with or without his permission, and they were just trying to drag him into it," a palace aide said.

"He had no other option," Amrullah Saleh noted. "It was the beginning of the surge."

Yet even in this moment of weakness, Karzai was not completely without options. Always attentive to his political leverage, he took advantage of the momentary rise in bargaining power. The day after McChrystal's visit, Karzai's cabinet voted to "nationalize" the Electoral Complaints Commission, booting the foreigners from the watchdog panel. It was another slap in the face to the partners.

American priorities, at the moment, were elsewhere. The U.S. could withdraw funding for the upcoming parliamentary elections, they speculated in an embassy cable, but the way money was allocated, this would mean cutting support to the United Nations. "Ever the agile tactician, Karzai appears to have timed the decision to nationalize the ECC to coincide" with the Marja offensive, an embassy staffer wrote, "likely calculating that we would not wish to challenge him at this crucial juncture."

McChrystal's aides would later boast of his political savvy for soliciting Karzai's buy-in.

"To this day," Carter said, "I suspect Stan McChrystal doesn't know it was actually Ahmed Wali Karzai who got this done."

7

AN ORDINARY AFGHAN

THERE WERE TIMES, as I landed in Kandahar, when I couldn't distinguish the ground from the sky. Until you felt the jolt, there was nothing to orient you within the monochrome ochre, the layer of haze and hot dust that flared out in all directions, a stratum you dropped into with the feeling of a deep-sea diver leaving the rail. When you stepped out of the plane, the air was scalding and smelled like burned hair. Then you went into the city, in a whine of dirt bikes and clattering cargo trucks, along a thread of desert road under brown crags that looked like rotted teeth. The landscape had been scavenged and exhausted: evaporated riverbeds, baked and desiccated plains, gravel lots commandeered so that car parts and bright plastics could be sold out of the back of sawed-off shipping containers. During the day, the U.S. military's surveillance blimps hung like low planets tethered over bases surrounded by razor wire. At night, you could listen to distant concussions and then watch the slow yellow drift of the illumination flares, leaving tails of white smoke against the dark sky. Everything about the city felt like a higher-proof distillation of the Afghanistan I had come to know in Kabul: more closed off, conservative, inscrutable, violent; more foreign in custom, and more brutal and unforgiving in its daily tournament for survival.

The ruler of that city was Ahmed Wali Karzai. His men addressed him as *Agha Mama*, or "Father Uncle." He lived in downtown Kandahar City in a concrete house on a barricaded street, guarded by Afghan police and his large retinue of bodyguards. Every day in the foyer of his home you could see hundreds of shoes, normally sandals of dirty plastic or dusty leather, discarded by the dozens of supplicants who crossed his threshold to seek his favor or to get one. The old and young men in turbans sat on the floor along the walls and in hallways, waiting for their chance to scale the stairs to the carpeted room on the second floor, ringed with red couches and hung with rose-print drapes, where he would be fingering a string of yellow prayer beads. He often wore a dark vest over a white tunic and usually went barefoot. The group that cycled before him represented a diverse cross section of Kandahar society: elders from tiny villages, gaunt farmers, policemen, parliamentarians. Whenever a new person entered the room, he would kneel before Ahmed Wali or kiss his hand. During the course of these rolling discussions, he would take calls on his multiple cell phones every few minutes, without the slightest regard to interrupting the speaker addressing him, and he conversed in Pashto, Dari, and English with equal ease. I once saw a man hand him a note; he read it quickly, then tore it into shreds.

Ahmed Wali Karzai often gave one the impression of grim and harried impatience, a man who had too much to do, very little of it pleasant. His stubble had gone gray, and his mouth was pinched into a dour scowl. His foot tapped incessantly. He wore a pistol in a shoulder holster.

He had many decisions to make, and he did not belabor them. One morning at his house, I watched him deal with the needs of seventy-three people in two hours. One group of men came to ask for a police checkpoint in their village; they were followed by another group who requested that their checkpoint be removed. Nine tribal elders needed his approval for the guest list of an important assembly. A young truck driver begged for a job recommendation—"if you'll just sign this letter"—while an old man pleaded for his son's release from American custody.

"Is he in the Taliban?" Ahmed Wali asked.

"Yes," the old man said.

"I cannot do anything now. Come on Saturday and we will talk."

His phone calls were brief. "I'm too busy," he told a caller who wanted an invitation to an upcoming peace and reconciliation conference in Kabul. "Call me tomorrow at nine-fifteen and then we can figure out something and we'll meet. What? Again you are removed from the list? Okay, I already talked to Wardak [the defense minister] about that. You will be on the list."

To the two women from Zabul Province who wanted his blessing to run for parliament, he immediately decided yes, but on one condition. "Please do not mention my name," he told them. "There are many people who want my support."

He greeted everyone with the customary Pashtun greeting, *stere meshe.* Its meaning seemed particularly apt coming from him: "never be tired."

King Abdur Rahman, a nineteenth-century ruler of Afghanistan, once said that "the kingdom of Kabul, without Kandahar, was like a head without a nose, or a fort without any gate." The city and the surrounding region of Pashtun tribes were central to the fortunes of anyone attempting to govern the country, which in the past couple of thousand years has tended to be done with a light touch. Afghanistan has rarely had anything resembling a strong central government. The British writer William Dalrymple described Afghanistan as less a state than "a kaleidoscope of competing tribal principalities governed through maliks or vakils, in each of which allegiance was entirely personal, to be negotiated and won over rather than taken for granted. The tribes' traditions were egalitarian and independent, and they had only ever submitted to authority on their own terms." He noted the Afghan proverb *Pusht-e har toppe, yek padishah neshasti* "Behind every hillock, there sits an emperor."

These mini-emperors, who came to be called warlords, tended to expect that whatever government was "in power" in Kabul would respect their authority and pay them for their loyalty and good behavior. Dealing with these men—modern-day examples were Ismail Khan in the western city of Herat or Abdul Rashid Dostum and Atta Muhammad Noor in the north—had been a central challenge for Karzai's government. These people had initially been paid by the CIA to rally their militias to drive out the Taliban, then pushed by the Bush administration to demobilize their troops and turn in their large caches of artillery and other heavy weapons. When asked about Hamid Karzai's greatest failures, critics within his government would often point to his coddling of these types of men.

"That was always a big debate: Should we include them?" recalled Said Tayeb Jawad, one of Karzai's early chiefs of staff. "Karzai insisted that we had to include them and they had to be part of the system. That was a source of some frustration among the more idealistic people who were around him. In his calculation, there was really no force to confront these people."

Jawad remembered that Karzai set this tone at the emergency *loya jirga* in June 2002, the gathering of some fifteen hundred Afghan delegates to choose their transitional government. Jawad had worked on the seating chart for the event and had agreed with the international community that Afghans who had attended the Bonn conference would sit in the front row, facing the stage. At the opening of the event, Karzai noticed that old jihadi commanders like Abdul Rasul Sayyaf and Burhanuddin Rabbani were sitting farther back. From the podium, he called out to them and told them to move up to the front row, forcing newly selected cabinet ministers to move back. "A minister stands up and vacates his seat for someone who has no role in the government?" Jawad recalled years later, still incredulous. "This was a small gesture, but of great symbolic significance."

Instead of sidelining or even arresting the warlords, Karzai brokered deals that gave them governorships and cabinet posts, where they could siphon customs revenue from border crossings or divert funds from ministry budgets for personal use. Karzai saw it as a necessary sacrifice for national unity and to prevent further civil war. He also had few other options at his disposal. Karzai never had much leverage of his own, apart from the implicit military backing of the United States, and that support tended to be unreliable. In the early years of his presidency, the United States had Karzai on what one military commander called a "dual-key system." The United States did not allow Karzai to deploy Afghan forces anywhere without American approval. But his accommodation of the warlords sent the message that nearly any crime was acceptable as long as the criminals were not openly fighting his government.

"A lot of people who are now significant players in Afghan politics and the parliament, we were thinking they'd end up in Guantánamo Bay," Jawad said. "But instead what took place was to allow them to loot half of the national resources, the lands, the government resources. That was the mistake."

By the time the Obama administration came to power, Ahmed Wali Karzai was the preeminent warlord in Kandahar, fully sanctioned by his brother's government. On paper, his job was chairman of the Kandahar Provincial Council, but his duties far surpassed that humble position. On one level, he served as a bridge between the new government—a democratic experiment obviously funded and largely designed by the Western coalition—and the older ways of the Pashtun tribes. It was his duty to extend the feeble writ of that government to Kandahar and the southern region by whatever means required, including coercion or bribery or threat. He faced the task of ensuring that his Popalzai tribe was satisfied with its share of U.S. military contracts, the primary spoils of war available for Afghans. There was also the job of keeping other tribes subservient but not so disenfranchised that they would defect to the Taliban. In addition, he had to supply American soldiers and diplomats with whatever favors they demanded. He was always pragmatic and unsentimental in these duties.

All of this played out in the daily procession to his well-fortified door.

In the meetings I saw, Ahmed Wali often made a perfunctory attempt to refer people to the official channels—the governor, the police chief, the intelligence service—but most of them took such suggestions as little more than a polite gesture. Even the illiterate peasants knew that very little got accomplished at the governor's mansion. Kandahar's governor, Toryalai Wesa, who has dual Canadian-Afghan citizenship, would spend months debating with his coalition advisers all sorts of barely relevant minutiae: whether solar-powered streetlights were a good idea and, if so, what the proper voltage would be; whether Wesa should have his own newspaper, as he wanted, or if print media was passé. Nothing ever seemed to get done. "You're the only real man in the government," one of the villagers told Ahmed Wali one day while I was visiting. "You have the power. I'll always keep coming to you."

Just like his siblings, Ahmed Wali had lived in America and had gotten his start in the restaurant business. In Kandahar, he loved to host lavish feasts for hundreds of people. He would personally make sure that everyone had been served before he sat down and picked up a plate. He embodied the Pashto adage "There is no *khan* without the tablecloth." Even at his most powerful, there was something of the caterer about him.

One hot day in the summer of 2010, I spent the morning at his house, watching as he catered to people with a wide range of problems. After a few hours, he paused and looked at his Rolex. It was noon. He stood up, hurried downstairs, and slipped into the back seat of a white armored Land Cruiser. I sat next to him. One AK-47 was propped between us; another rested on his far side. He had to be careful wherever he went. There had already been several attempts on his life, including attacks on his house and ambushes on his convoy. "The seventh bomb to target me was so big that hundreds of cats fed on human flesh for days afterward," he once said.

Ahmed Wali didn't like to make well-publicized appointments or telegraph his movements. He varied the routes on which he was driven and always had plenty of security. I looked behind and saw that three trucks filled with armed guards were following us. "I'm the most wanted person by the enemy," he said.

As we drove, Ahmed Wali indulged in a moment of self-pity. He was forty-nine years old and felt underappreciated. He saw himself as a selfless public servant, "the Nancy Pelosi of Afghanistan," as he'd once told me. "All I try to do is help people. I gain nothing from this," he said. "I feel responsible for the people, you know. This is our society. Our society is not an educated society. People are still living in a very old traditional way. They think I am the president's brother, I can deliver. They come to me, and it's good. I talk to the police, I talk to the governor, to help."

"I know how to talk to the people," he said. "I know how to deal with these tribes. I know what their needs are. I know how to address their needs. This is the skill I have learned."

He told a story about when he'd lived in Chicago, as a younger man. He had sent in his green card to apply for a U.S. passport, and it disappeared. He tried calling the appropriate agencies and couldn't get a straight answer. "I would be on hold for twenty minutes, and it was a long-distance call," he said. So he looked up the name of his local congressman and called his office. "I called his staff and said, Look, I voted for him, and now this is a problem." He got the name of an immigration official to call and soon had his green card and passport back. The moral of his story was that politics involved a social contract. "They give you something and you have to return it. This is how it is," he said. "You have to return the favor."

A few minutes later, we pulled in to the Mandigak Palace, where the provincial council held its meetings. A week earlier, Ahmed Wali had unilaterally declared that the council was on strike after the Defense Ministry had angered him by accusing him and his brother Mahmood of illegally confiscating government land for Aino Mena. The attorney general had subsequently agreed to lead an investigation into the issue, which satisfied Ahmed Wali, who believed the inquiry would clear his name. So he'd come to announce that the provincial council was now open for business. He adjourned into a back room with the governor and other top officials, then emerged an hour later and stepped up to a bank of microphones. "In front of the media I want to say that if I have ever confiscated one handful of land, I am ready to be brought to justice," he stated. "The authorities should treat me like an ordinary Afghan."

By this time, Ahmed Wali's behavior had made him a painful dilemma for the United States. On one hand, he was consistently helpful to the American, British, and Canadian soldiers who sought his assistance, as well as the CIA and MI6 officers who had been paying him a salary since the early days of the war. And yet years of accumulated stories etched a portrait into the popular culture of a power-mad politician who traded on the family name to dominate the business life of Kandahar: opium, private mercenaries, NATO development contracts, transit trade, cross-border smuggling, used-car sales, real estate, arms trafficking—anything southern Afghanistan had to offer. When you met Afghans in Kandahar in those days, it was common to hear Ahmed Wali blamed for extortion, kidnappings, political assassinations, and drug trafficking, as well as manipulating army, police, and civil service appointments and demanding cuts of foreign military contracts. He was the most dangerous man in the country's most dangerous town. American soldiers referred to him as the "Godfather"; Afghan newspapers, as "Little President."

Kandahar was not just the most valuable prize in the war against the Taliban; it was also to be a model for local government serving the people, which made such arrangements of convenience with questionable allies like Ahmed Wali harder to justify. Even as the fighting in Helmand trudged on, U.S. military planners were looking past it, toward a summertime offensive in Kandahar, where they felt the war would be won or lost. If the Americans were going to beat the insurgents in Kandahar, it would mean coming to terms with Ahmed Wali. The strategy of McChrystal and his aides didn't allow for people like him, though; as they saw it, the Afghan government had become so painful to the common man, so accustomed to bribery and extortion, so ineffectual at solving crime, adjudicating property claims, supplying electricity or clean water, fielding an impartial, or even sober, police force, doing anything that a government might be expected to do, that scores of the young and unemployed were taking to the hills with their Kalashnikovs to join the Taliban. The Kandahar offensive would be more than foot patrols and house searches. The goal looked more like a reinvention of Afghan society.

I had traveled with State Department officers as they counted the men showing up at village councils and calculated how many from each tribe should be attending in order to have a representative sample based on area population estimates. In air-conditioned offices at Kandahar Airfield, U.S. military contracting officers scrolled through their road-building and ditch-digging contract spreadsheets to find out how many dollars were going to each tribe and who was going without. They wanted a new democracy that would be inclusive and responsive and provide services—power, water, health care, justice—to people who had none. Many people trying to defeat the Taliban in Kandahar felt that none of their efforts would be credible if they allowed a mafia boss like Ahmed Wali to run the town.

When Bill Harris arrived in late November 2009 as the senior American diplomat in Kandahar, he was eager to take Ahmed Wali on. Harris was sixty years old, balding, with the amiable gruffness of a man happy to be out of a cubicle and on the front lines. He'd spent most of his career in Latin America but was familiar with Afghanistan; in 2002, he'd spent a few months as political adviser to General Dan McNeill, then the top military commander. Harris's roommates at Bagram Airfield had happened to be the guys running the war nearly a decade later: Stanley McChrystal, Nick Carter, the military intelligence officer Mike Flynn. Harris had since retired and was living in Colorado Springs, but he'd quickly agreed to another tour when the Kandahar job had come open. In his pre-deployment briefings at the State Department and elsewhere in Washington, Harris had sensed a confrontational mood. "There was kind of an appetite for, you know, 'We didn't get Hamid in the election. We missed. It was not the head shot we were looking for. So what we're going to do is teach them a lesson. Teach them to heel. And the way we're going to do that and help ourselves at the same time is to get rid of this pesky brother, so that we can have good governance in the south.'"

"I was ready to do battle with AWK," Harris said.

One of the ways he planned to do that was to freeze out Ahmed Wali and throw American support fully behind Toryalai Wesa, the appointed governor. The operating theory was that insurgents were fighting because there was a weak government, and if Wesa could make it stronger and create a connection between the people and their government, that would dry up the insurgency. The problem with that theory was that many Kandaharis considered Wesa a carpetbagger and a foreign stooge. The son of a newspaper editor, Wesa had founded Kandahar University, then immigrated with his wife to Canada in 1991. In his years abroad, he got his doctorate in agricultural economics and taught at the University of British Columbia. He was squat and placid, tortoise-like in demeanor. He cared about agriculture and education but had little flair for the combat of tribal politics. Unlike Ahmed Wali's home, an incessant hive of commotion, the governor's mansion was a tranquil backwater, an eddy of inactivity.

"Wesa was a wet fish," one of the American generals in Kandahar told me.

Wesa got his job because of his friendship with the Karzai family and served at their pleasure. His "service," however, left both Afghans and Americans unenthralled. He had scant backing from any of the Kandahar tribes. He sat under chandeliers in his wood-paneled office, books about agricultural extension on his desk, treated largely as a token to America's democratic experiment. His weakness meant he rarely challenged Ahmed Wali, who was dismissive of the governor in his discussions with the U.S. military, on different occasions calling him "half Canadian" and saying that "he does not act like a leader in Kandahar should act."

"Whenever Wesa received instructions from the Karzai brothers, he never objected to that, even if it was sacking department heads," said Hameed Wafa, who worked with Wesa in his office for three years as a translator and cultural adviser for the U.S. military. "He was basically an assistant for Ahmed Wali Karzai."

Ahmed Wali would regularly attend the meetings at the governor's palace, and his word, everyone acknowledged, was last and final. Everyone, including Wesa, owed their jobs to him. Across the province, he could choose or fire local officials, police chiefs, prison directors, intelligence operatives. Kandahar had 110 local water representatives, one for each of the canals that thread through the province, and they regularly met to divvy up the supply of water, the region's scarcest and most valuable resource. For most of the war, these meetings took place in Ahmed Wali's house.

"People did defer to him, even people who came down from Kabul, it was quite evident," said Neil Clegg, a Canadian diplomat who served as Wesa's adviser.

Hamid Karzai had removed Gul Agha Sherzai from his governorship in Kandahar in 2003—far later than Ahmed Wali wanted—and summoned him to Kabul. Sherzai's new position, minister of public works, was the equivalent of exile. He was eventually granted another lucrative governorship in Nangarhar Province, which he held for years, but his family's contest for the spoils of Kandahar never ceased. Before Sherzai's departure, "Wali Karzai was not a factor" in national politics, recalled Amrullah Saleh. "He became a factor after President Karzai pushed Gul Agha out."

Subsequent governors who didn't serve at the pleasure of Ahmed Wali weren't in their jobs for long. As a young man, Rahmatullah Raufi had served in the military forces under Uzbek warlord Abdul Rashid Dostum and worked in a Kazakh meat factory cleaning sheep intestines. He rose through the ranks of the Afghan army and became a general in the mid-1980s, and later a corps commander in Kandahar and the deputy head of operations in the Ministry of Defense. He had a regal bearing and a bushy black mustache. He had resigned after disagreements with the minister, and he was taken aback when President Karzai summoned him to the palace to offer him his first civilian post, as governor of Kandahar.

"It was really surprising for me, but I think the reason they decided to send me to Kandahar was that I had experience working there before, and I believe they thought I would say yes to whatever they would tell me, and they expected me to be part of their corruption," he told me in his modest home on a hillside in Kabul. He took office in August 2008, and shortly thereafter "some sticking points started appearing between me and Ahmed Wali Karzai."

They disagreed on personnel decisions within the local government. For example, Raufi did not support Ahmed Wali's representative to lead the education ministry, a man he believed was uneducated and had forged his résumé. Ahmed Wali, as Raufi recalled, had a "long hand" and would appoint district governors and police chiefs—often fellow Popalzais—some of whom Raufi approved; others he tried to fight. Through the Ministry of Information and Culture, Ahmed Wali could censor local newspapers, radio, and television broadcasts, give speeches, and issue decrees. He would send letters to the local judiciary, the police, and customs officials with personal instructions. He would call Raufi on his cell phone and issue orders. "I told him, 'Look, I am the representative of President Karzai and I report to President Karzai himself. You are the head of the provincial council. You have a certain job, I have my own certain job. If you want to cooperate with me, you're welcome, and if you need my help, I'm more than happy to offer it, but I don't want to work under a second authority.' By the time I was appointed governor, Ahmed Wali Karzai was so powerful, and he had been controlling all of my predecessors. And he expected me to obey him and work under him."

Raufi's salary was $700 a month. He believed it was unfair that Kandahar's mayor, Ghulam Haider Hamidi, a lifelong friend of the Karzai family, earned several times more. As governor, he ordered Hamidi's salary frozen for three months, until repeated pressure from Qayum Karzai and others changed his mind. Raufi further provoked the ruling family when he arranged to have a large *shura* gathering of Pashtun tribesmen and refused Ahmed Wali's request to chair the meeting.

During his first months in office, Raufi was told of other, darker activities carried out by top officials in the provincial police and intelligence service, men who he believed had the approval and complicity of Ahmed Wali. "They didn't spare any wrongdoing. They were involved in drug trafficking, they were involved in assassinations; they were involved in raping boys and girls. They did all sorts of horrible things. It was a team," he said. "When I was appointed, they wanted me to be part of their team. That was something I didn't want. And that was how the problems I talked about started emerging between me and Ahmed Wali."

One lucrative sideline for these complicit officials in the customs office, border police, and transportation department was the trade in used and stolen cars. The vehicles would be dismantled in Pakistan and shipped into Kandahar to be reassembled in warehouses and sold along the road. The main area for this trade was Shorandam Hill, in the eastern part of the city, where a couple of dozen dealers had car lots. American military convoys also regularly passed by, so the Taliban planted IEDs in the area and waited for the passing targets. The explosions often killed and injured civilians. After at least three such bombings, Raufi decided that the car dealers should be moved to another part of the city so that the customers would not be blown up.

One day, Ahmed Wali visited the governor's mansion. He asked Raufi if he could make an exception and allow one of his friends, a Popalzai named Mohammed, to keep his car lot in the same place. Raufi assumed that Ahmed Wali stood to gain financially if his friend was the only dealer left in the old location. As Raufi recalled, the conversation rapidly deteriorated:

"I said I cannot do that because people will start talking. The other dealers will come and grab my collar and they'll say, Who is this guy and how much money did you get from him that you allowed him to keep his dealership there? And Ahmed Wali said, 'Mohammed is a very nice guy, and I promised him.' I told him, 'I didn't say he was a bad person. To me he is a car dealer like any other car dealer, and I cannot make an exception.' When he insisted, I told him, 'Look, I'm telling you again, I'm a representative of President Karzai, and I only report to him, and obey his orders. You are his brother, I respect you, but you are not my boss.' Then he got angry and we started shouting at each other. And then I told him that he should leave my office. And when he continued shouting at me, I shoved him."

Ahmed Wali left the office, and Raufi suspected that things would not turn out well. Within the hour, he had received a call from a deputy minister of the Independent Directorate of Local Governance, summoning him to Kabul. When he arrived, he was told that his services as governor would no longer be required. Raufi was out of his job on December 4, 2008, less than four months after being appointed. He never spoke with

President Karzai, nor did he talk to Ahmed Wali afterward, or return to Kandahar.

Like his brothers, Ahmed Wali Karzai had lived a double life. He was the second-to-last sibling in the family, born in Kandahar to Abdul Ahad's second wife. Along with Hamid and his other siblings, he had attended Habibia High School in Kabul, built in 1903 for the education of the children of the elite. His classmates remembered him as a good soccer player and an unassuming student. Sayed Shalala Bakawali, who would go on to become headmaster of the school, was his classmate there for four years. He found Ahmed Wali "quiet, polite, and tidy." Ahmed Wali graduated in 1980. Years later, he donated a few thousand dollars to the school for a rose garden and to fix the electricity—and then fled the Russian invasion and joined his siblings in Maryland.

He followed the path of his older brothers. He worked as a busboy at the Bethesda Marriott Hotel and later joined them when they moved to Chicago to open their first restaurant. By that time Qayum, Mahmood, and Ahmed Wali all had experience in the restaurant business, having worked as waiters and managers around Washington, D.C. Mahmood's failed attempt to buy Cagney's had not dimmed his ambition to be his own boss.

In the family lore, this is a key moment in the brothers' American lives. In Quetta in the early 1980s, their father, Abdul Ahad, had been appointed the head of the Afghan National Liberation Front's local office, overseeing the party's southern efforts for the jihad against the Soviets. Because of his prominence in the Afghan parliament and as a tribal leader, and to honor his time in prison, the party bosses, including Sibghatullah Mojaddedi and his relatives, felt that Abdul Ahad would be an effective leader. After the Peshawar headquarters, the Quetta office was the most important. They directed their rebel efforts across the southwestern Pashtun provinces. His job was to distribute weapons and money—from the CIA and others, funneled through Pakistan's intelligence service—to the anti-Soviet fighters. Abdul Ahad held the job for about a year. "Unfortunately, he was not successful," Zabi Mojaddedi, the party's secretary-general, said. "I think he failed to understand the mechanism of the resistance.

"His approach was more of a tribal approach, while ours was about the war of attrition, the guerrilla war. What he would do when he received weapons to distribute was, he would give them to each tribal leader. While our policy was, we would concentrate on particular groups," Mojaddedi said, meaning those that were effective in battle. Some believed that Abdul Ahad's priorities were to the former king, and not to the party. There were rebel commanders in Kandahar, such as Haji Magash, who were unhappy with the weapons dispersal and felt they had no tools with which to fight. In late 1984, the two men got into an argument. As Mojaddedi recalls, Abdul Ahad scoffed at the commander, in a particular Afghan way. "He told me, 'Who is this Haji Magash? I told Haji Magash I'm going to hang my shoes on the door of the gate of the office. He wouldn't even dare touch my shoe.' I thought this was too much to say to anyone, let alone a commander."

Magash didn't seem to care for it, either. He gathered a number of his rebel fighters and seized the office and threw out Abdul Ahad. Zabi Mojaddedi was dispatched from Peshawar to take over the office.

"I found everything in shambles," he said. "There were no operations coming up. The mujahedeen were all in despair and distress. All the furniture was in the yard, and people were there—these tribal leaders who were receiving weapons were using that as their sleeping quarters. Everything was a mess. I feel bad about this because he was a person of good repute, and I'm sure this hurt him very much."

Before Abdul Ahad left the office, there were allegations of another important development. People who know the family, as well as some relatives, believe that Abdul Ahad sold some of the weapons he was given to distribute, earning a couple of hundred thousand dollars, and that some of that money made it to his sons in the United States, a claim the brothers deny. Before 1985, the Karzai siblings had been restaurant employees: busboys, waiters, managers. The next year, they would become owners.

"This was the seed money," one of the Karzais said.

Ahmed Wali and his siblings Mahmood, Qayum, and Fawzia moved to Chicago in the mid-1980s to start their own restaurant in a city that was a barren culinary landscape for Afghan food. Mahmood, who complained about the overcrowded Afghan restaurant scene in the Washington, D.C., area, arrived first, along with his wife and daughter, and took a job as a waiter at the 95th restaurant, atop the John Hancock building, where he received his education in wine. Qayum set to work finding a location for their new restaurant, securing permits, and buying furniture. Fawzia, who had been working in a grocery store in Washington, also moved to Chicago with her husband, Zaki Royan, to help.

The Karzais found a location they liked on the corner of North Halsted Street and Belmont Avenue, a one-story brick building with bay windows and cheap rent. The neighborhood was bustling and eclectic, its garbage-speckled grittiness being swept up in a gentrifying wave, casual by day and frenzied in the evening, a hodgepodge of antiques shops, vintage toy stores, dive bars, bakeries, boutiques, factories, cafés, and a few of the city's best restaurants. Neighbors had fought to keep fast-food chains away but welcomed exotic ethnic fare. The Karzais' building had once housed a grocery store but was a barren box when they took over. The brothers spent about $40,000 to renovate the space and pitched in on the painting and construction. The expenses exhausted their resources and ran up their credit cards. They were two months behind with the rent on the building before the restaurant opened, but the owner allowed the lapse. "We took such a huge risk in the United States," Qayum said.

Although it was situated next to a hot dog place called Relish the Thought, their restaurant aspired to an air of civility. They draped the tables in white tablecloths and decorated them with fresh flowers. Ahmed Wali and the other waiters wore starched button-down shirts and black bow ties. The family members all shared duties in the kitchen and serving the customers. A review in the *Chicago Tribune* in January 1986, not long after the Helmand opened, described the Karzais as "gentle spokesmen for the food of Afghanistan." More people than they expected arrived the first night, and the restaurant ran out of food.

"People loved it," said Wiroj Worrasangusilpa, an immigrant from Bangkok who owned Relish the Thought and went by "Victor." "Packed every night."

The Helmand was profitable. A business biography Mahmood later wrote said that the restaurant grossed $250,000 per year. In the cities where they opened, the Helmand restaurants tended to flourish. The restaurants were elegant, some with fireplaces, wood-burning ovens, and Afghan rugs. The menu featured warm dishes of eggplant, okra, and lamb, spiced with cardamom and cinnamon. Reviews touted their home-made ice cream with sprinkled pistachio or the baked pumpkin dish, *kaddo bourani*, with its garlic-mint yogurt and coriander meat sauce.

"In capitalism, you invest," Mahmood told one reviewer.

The Karzais all shared an apartment in Westmont, a suburban community west of the city. They seemed to their friends in Chicago to live comfortably; they didn't complain about money.

The Karzais recall both the difficulties and the rewards of those years.

The winters were crushingly cold. As Mahmood remembers it, his car, when he was lucky enough to get it started, was endlessly skidding on the ice and snow. He and his wife worked day and night and took no vacations. At home, exhausted, they would stare at the television before falling asleep.

"I sometimes drove her home at night," Victor said of Fawzia. "She would say, 'I can't do it anymore.' There was too much work."

Ahmed Wali was popular with the neighbors around the Helmand. He liked to play the lottery inside the New Modern Grill, a diner across the street. People found him polite, well mannered, approachable. He dressed well. He was thin and handsome, with a thick black mustache. "I thought he was gay," Victor said. "People would come in and ask about him. He was good-looking."

The Karzais were open about their desire to return to Afghanistan, if the regime changed and their family was not at so much risk. "They said the Taliban wanted to kill them," Victor said. "When they came here it was to survive, it was not to get rich running a restaurant. They wanted to go back home. They were waiting for their time."

"They were political people," he added. "They seemed to know about power."

Two years after the restaurant opened, Mahmood sold his share to Qayum and moved with his family to San Francisco. Qayum returned to Maryland when he and his wife decided to buy the insurance company she worked for. Ahmed Wali stayed on in Chicago for several more years. This period, he would tell the American generals and diplomats he met in later years, was formative for him. "I love America," he told one of them. "It really pains me that people in America think I'm a bad guy. Because I'm not a bad guy."

One day, he stepped into the hot dog shop to say good-bye to Victor. He told Victor that his brother Hamid was the new leader of Afghanistan. "I couldn't believe it," Victor said later. "He was just the guy across the street. I thought he was bullshitting me."

Harry Karountzos, who owned the diner, saw Ahmed Wali the day he was leaving Chicago. He was waiting for the bus on the sidewalk, holding a small suitcase.

"I'm going home," Ahmed Wali told him. "My brother's going to be president."

"Where?"

"Afghanistan."

"Get outta here."

Years later, Karountzos would see Ahmed Wali on TV in exotic Afghan attire. On the sidewalk that last day, Ahmed Wali fished in his pocket. He pulled out a winning lottery ticket.

"Here," he said, handing it to Karountzos. "Cash it for me."

Even if Governor Wesa had been inclined to challenge Ahmed Wali, he had little ability to do so. As the public face of the American occupation, Wesa lived with the perpetual threat of violent death, and his security was guaranteed by Ahmed Wali. Two of the deputy governors had already been killed. At night, Wesa slept in a bunkerlike downstairs room at the mansion as a precaution against rocket and mortar fire. He had about two dozen Afghan security guards, all chosen by Ahmed Wali, who worked with former British military advisers. Even among his own tribe, the Mohammadzai, Wesa had little support.

"People go to see him and they wait for a month. He doesn't have the time to see them. That's not how you run a province," remarked Sardar Mohammad Osman, the deputy head of the tribe. "I don't see a single person in the entire government who has competence and capability. It's like appointing a doorman as head of an administration."

Hameed Wafa, one of the governor's aides, had watched Ahmed Wali order the governor to fire a British guard's translator after the man engaged in an argument with one of his own security guards. "Within five minutes, the interpreter was gone," Wafa said.

Wesa was a Karzai loyalist. He reserved his hatred for other local strongmen, particularly Gul Agha Sherzai, whom he detested, and he referred to Sherzai's tribe, the Barakzais, as "scorpions." And Wesa was no risk taker: the U.S. embassy described him in a cable as "usually supine." But in his private conversations, Wesa let it be known that he would be in favor of the Americans clipping Ahmed Wali's wings. He had to be careful about such statements; even his two personal secretaries had family ties to the Karzais.

"My recollections were that the governor thought it would probably be a good idea to diminish AWK's power," said Neil Clegg, the Canadian adviser. "I did detect there was some resentment."

General Nick Carter asked Wesa whether Kandahar would be better off without Ahmed Wali. He did not equivocate. Ahmed Wali "had to go," Wesa said, according to a person familiar with the exchange.

For the Americans, their research into Ahmed Wali's activities was picking up. The more people learned, the more they worried.

"As the kingpin of Kandahar, the President's younger half-brother Ahmed Wali Karzai (AWK) dominates access to economic resources, patronage, and protection. Much of the real business of running Kandahar takes place out of public sight, where AWK operates, parallel to formal government structures, through a network of political clans that use state institutions to protect and enable licit and illicit enterprises," the embassy wrote in a cable in early December.

> The overriding purpose that unifies his political roles as Chairman of the Kandahar Provincial Council and as the President's personal representative to the South is the enrichment, extension and perpetuation of the Karzai clan, and along with it their branch of the Popalzai tribe. This applies equally to his entrepreneurial and his alleged criminal activities. AWK derives authority and legitimacy from his relationship to President Karzai, from the relative discipline and elite position of the Popalzai tribe and from his access to resources. In Kandahar's political realm, he is the unrivaled strongman.

Accusations against Ahmed Wali had accumulated like sediment over the course of the war. For years, the Canadian military had been the primary foreign presence in Kandahar, and it had its own rich history with Ahmed Wali. When Canada's top diplomat in the south had been killed by an IED explosion, there had been rumors that Ahmed Wali had had a hand in it. Richard Colvin, the slain man's successor, found that Ahmed Wali's dominance was "sucking up the political oxygen in Kandahar."

"He sat at the top of everything," Colvin told me. "Anything that existed, whether it was legitimate or criminal, it had to get his say-so, and he would collect and kind of manage the whole system. He wouldn't get his fingers dirty because he was sitting on top of it, kind of pulling the strings like a puppet master. Not [quite] a puppet master, because these are independent actors. He was the godfather for the whole system. And the whole system was an unhealthy and corrupt system because there was so much money coming from drugs. This was the big problem. He was the top guy in the south. And the south was awash with drug money. He's making decisions based not on what's in the interest of the government or us but what's in the interest of him, his family, and the drug empire. That becomes a problem.

"His interests and our interests did not really coincide. He was seen by local people as that kind of mafia godfather. And therefore to the extent that we were propping him up, our firepower was keeping him in power. We had the airpower and the heavy weaponry. We'd installed these guys and were fighting and dying to keep them in power. And if locals looked at us and just saw us as foreigners coming in to prop up the local drug lords, then we're not going to win a war on that basis. People are going to kick us out. And, frankly, we deserve to be kicked out, if that's all we're doing. Why are we in Kandahar? Are we just there to prop up some local drug baron?"

Frank Ruggiero, a square-jawed American diplomat with graying hair, visited the governor's mansion to see Ahmed Wali for the first time. They met, along with Toryalai Wesa, in the governor's wood-paneled office, under a giant photo of President Karzai. The Ahmed Wali mythology had Ruggiero expecting a glowering crime boss. Instead he found an anxious, diffident man in a crisp white *shalwar kameez* and a pin-striped vest. "He was so shy and quiet and nervous," Ruggiero recalled. "All he wanted to do is offer assistance. That's what he kept saying to me. 'Whatever you need to get done. Whatever you want to get done. Just tell me and I can help you.'

"He was not what I expected," Ruggiero said.

Under the slow ceiling fans, Ahmed Wali lobbied Ruggiero for large-scale development projects—akin to the Kajaki and Dahla Dams USAID had built in the 1950s. He had often offered himself as the organizer for projects that came with large foreign-aid price tags. Earlier that summer, after a devastating truck bomb had killed more than forty people and leveled a city block in Kandahar, he'd proposed to the Canadians that he could oversee the rebuilding—for $2 million. Ahmed Wali also told Ruggiero that the United States needed to empower councils of local elders to resolve disputes between citizens, because so few judges worked in the province. "You can easily bribe the chief of police or a judge, but you can't bribe fifty elders," he said. The governor acknowledged that the local administration had little credibility. They could not provide enough electricity for the residents, he said, and more than 150 factories had closed as a result.

Ruggiero didn't want to push too hard, as it was his first meeting with Ahmed Wali. In his write-up of the encounter, he noted that given Ahmed Wali's reputation for "shady dealings," his recommendation for large, costly infrastructure projects should be viewed with a "healthy dose of skepticism." He added, "The meeting with AWK highlights one of our major challenges in Afghanistan: how to fight corruption and connect the people to their government, when the key government officials are themselves corrupt." Before forwarding the memo to Washington, someone at the embassy in Kabul inserted an additional note in the cable: "While we must deal with AWK as the head of the Provincial Council, he is widely understood to be corrupt and a narcotics trafficker." (When the cable later came out on WikiLeaks, Ahmed Wali complained to Ruggiero about the line: *Why say such a thing? You never asked me about drugs.* "And he was right. I never did. It never came up," Ruggiero said.)

On Christmas Eve, McChrystal dispatched a helicopter to Camp Nathan Smith, where Bill Harris was working on the Kandahar provincial reconstruction team, to ferry the diplomat across town to Kandahar Airfield for dinner with himself and General Carter. It was late in the evening, and the chow halls had closed. They met in Carter's office, snacking on packets of cheese and crackers. McChrystal wanted to hear his colleagues' thoughts on Ahmed Wali. Harris described the situation as a manhood test: removing Ahmed Wali would send a strong message to President Karzai that this was a new era in the war, one where impunity would not stand. Other senior American military officials held similar views. "We were getting to the endgame of this war; we needed President Karzai to fall in line and be a wartime leader and be an ally and shut his fucking mouth. And McChrystal was really buying it," Harris recalled. Harris recognized that ISAF didn't have a smoking gun: no one could point to cell phone intercepts of Ahmed Wali talking about heroin sales or colluding with the Taliban. Everything was circumstantial, a lot of rumor and innuendo. But if you added up all the stories, "It did seem to be rather damning.

"McChrystal was tilting, and Carter and I were both avidly in favor of removing Ahmed Wali," Harris said. They agreed that President Karzai would have to do it, even if it took a call from President Obama. At the end of the evening, Harris thought he'd made his case. "I left believing I had convinced him that AWK had to go. If he didn't, we couldn't really credibly win the war."

And according to several other military officials, Harris, at that moment, was correct. Both McChrystal and his chief of military intelligence, General Michael Flynn, "were convinced that we'd be far better off with Ahmed Wali Karzai going," said a top NATO military official. Kandahar, to them, was the war's center of gravity, and if President Obama's surge was to be effective, they needed to build a local government that didn't respond solely to the whims of the president's brother.

The Regional Command South military intelligence chief, Steve Beckman, had pored over all of the reports, including those concerning heroin and arms dealing. He was determined to find the "smoking gun" piece of evidence that ISAF could take to President Karzai to convince him to remove his brother from power. There were wiretapped phone transcripts about land speculation that suggested financial corruption but nothing solid.

The CIA, which had been working with Ahmed Wali at least since the start of the war, presumably had its own thick files on him, as he had been a partner for so many years, but nothing materialized. CIA officers in Kandahar spoke highly of Ahmed Wali to U.S. soldiers, and for good reason. He had worked with American spies at least since the start of the war. Back then, Ahmed Wali had taken up residence in Mullah Omar's old house, living alongside CIA officers and special operations troops, using his contacts in the city to outfit the residence with a house staff and guards. When the first CIA officers arrived in Kandahar, "they didn't know the city very well, so we got them everything they needed," recalled Fazel Mohammed, one of Ahmed Wali's personal security guards. "The Americans would provide us with money and weapons, and we would give them intelligence and information."

In the spring of 2002, Ahmed Wali helped the CIA create the Kandahar Strike Force, a paramilitary unit of Afghans who were used on kill-and-capture raids against the Taliban. The force would eventually comprise about four thousand people, with bases in Kandahar, Khost, Paktia, Paktika, Kunar, Jalalabad, and Kabul. They were considered highly trained and elite troops. They had regular physical training, including jogging and calisthenics, target practice, and class work such as lectures on choosing targets. While Ahmed Wali did not command the unit, he arranged for many of his loyal Popalzai tribesmen to fill these jobs. Given his connections and influence in Kandahar, he was also one of the CIA's regular paid informants. "He would pass intelligence, a request for a strike, but he was not guiding them," Amrullah Saleh, the country's longtime intelligence director, told me. "Through utilization of his tribal networks, he was providing a lot of tactical intelligence to the Americans about Taliban cells in the southern part of the country. He was also providing political support and creating political space for some of their operations, or justifying these operations."

American soldiers and diplomats knew that the CIA was an active supporter of Ahmed Wali. In the debates about how to deal with him, they always came out on the side of continuing to use him as an informant. Harris had never seen a full dossier on Ahmed Wali, although he imagined it existed. "What went unsaid was that a really in-depth excavation of this guy's life and past would of course unearth his CIA connections, and I think that's what really put the brakes on any serious investigation," he said. "Ahmed Wali enjoyed maybe not an active protection, but a passive or a de facto protection."

Many of President Karzai's senior aides remember asking their American counterparts about the allegations. "They would always say, 'No, we don't have anything,'" one recalled. "Especially people who worked closely with him at the agency, they would always say, 'He's very helpful.'"

From the war's beginning, American officials had taken for granted that Ahmed Wali profited from the opium trade, southern Afghanistan's most lucrative crop. There had been rumors from the first year of his connection to opium-loaded planes touching down at remote airstrips. Embassy diplomats reporting back to Washington repeatedly referred to his drug-world connections. A classified cable from March 2007 argued that President Karzai "should use his authority to remove corrupt officials from office (including his drug-running brother Ahmad Wali Karzai, in Kandahar)." Two years later, discussing Ahmed Wali and his brother-in-law Muhammad Arif Noorzai, the embassy said, "Both have well-known reputations as narco-traffickers willing to engage in anything necessary to advance Hamid Karzai's fortunes."

"Given his suspected ties to narco-trafficking (and possible militant activities)," the embassy said in another October 2009 dispatch, the Canadians were looking for help dealing with Ahmed Wali. "The Canadians believe the ideal situation would be to have him removed from power, but given his status as a strong power player within Kandahar, the Canadian Ambassador is likely to ask for the U.S. to lead on the issue."

And yet each time an effort was made to document these claims, the United States seemed to come up empty. One day in the fall of 2004, U.S. ambassador Zalmay Khalilzad was in a morning meeting of senior embassy staff when his cell phone rang. It was President Karzai, and he sounded distraught. An article had appeared in that morning's *New York Times*. It was a modest eleven-hundred-word story about a United Nations announcement that Afghanistan's poppy crop was now larger than ever before. Almost as an afterthought, the reporter mentioned that the minister of tribal affairs, Muhammad Arif Noorzai, and the governor of Helmand Province, Sher Mohammed Akhundzada, "are widely believed to profit from the drug trade, although both have denied any involvement and voiced support for the government's anti-narcotics stand. Diplomats say there are even reports linking Mr. Karzai's brother, Ahmed Wali Karzai, an influential figure in the southern city of Kandahar, to the trade."

On the phone, Karzai, an avid reader of the foreign press, particularly anything regarding himself or his relatives, had waved such stories in the faces of visiting American officials, angrily insisting that their comments were no way for friends to speak about each other's families. He told Khalilzad that these articles were devastating to his family name. He wanted to know what evidence the U.S. government had on his brother's involvement, and he said that if there was proof, he would deal with Ahmed Wali himself. Karzai also asked Khalilzad to summon Ahmed Wali to Kabul to talk about the allegations directly. Later, when Khalilzad asked the CIA station chief about Ahmed Wali, he was told that Ahmed Wali lived in the Kandahar house of Haji Azizullah Alizai, a known drug trafficker.

When Ahmed Wali came to the embassy to meet Khalilzad, he appeared to be exasperated. "Do you know who my father is? Do you know who my brother is? We have been given an historic role. Do you think I would do anything to jeopardize that?" he said.

"Yes, I know, and you're not supposed to be asking me questions. I'm supposed to be asking you," Khalilzad said. "Why are you living in a drug dealer's house?"

"Mr. Ambassador, can you name one nice house in Kandahar that is not owned by a drug trafficker?" Ahmed Wali replied. "That's what I want from the U.S. embassy. Find me a house in Kandahar that has no links to a drug trafficker, and I will move in there."

Two days after the *Times* article appeared, at the weekly Sunday cabinet meeting at the palace, President Karzai was still upset. Under U.S. pressure, Karzai had made eradicating poppy farming a top priority during his first inaugural speech the month before, even declaring a symbolic "jihad" against opium. But he had always been ambivalent about the issue, and he was particularly opposed to aerial spraying of farmers' fields, which he believed not only threatened livelihoods but posed a public health risk. Khalilzad had watched Karzai get worked up about the issue, shouting, waving his arms, vowing to lead his own jihad against American soldiers if they persisted in spraying herbicides on the Afghans. Before his ministers that Sunday, Karzai mentioned reports of overnight spraying in the eastern city of Jalalabad that had sickened children.

He claimed that he saw a "British hand" behind the *Times* article, according to the meeting notes. The British had been involved from the beginning in the coalition's counternarcotics campaign, including an early, and failed, effort to buy up and burn a large portion of the poppy crop. The Brits, Karzai speculated, had told the *Times* to "start a negative propaganda campaign against me."

"This is a warning for you all. It is a threat. They have even brought your brother into this," one of Karzai's ministers told the cabinet. "These people are our national figures. This is animosity. I suggest that our embassy in Washington should be ordered to start the preliminary work of suing *The New York Times*. I consider this an insult to the people's will, the cabinet, and the people of Afghanistan. They should apologize. And they should compensate us. We should take a diplomatic and a judicial approach."

Near the end of the discussion, Ashraf Ghani, one of the most accomplished technocrats in the Afghan government, who had lived in the United States and Europe for years before the war, called for discipline and unity among the cabinet and tried to put things in perspective. "It would take us ten years to sue America," he said.

News stories with allegations of corruption, drug trafficking, and other criminal behavior against Ahmed Wali occurred with ever-greater frequency as the war progressed and intensified. On January 9, 2006, Karzai met with U.S. ambassador Ronald E. Neumann and British ambassador Rosalind Marsden, as well as the CIA and MI6 station chiefs, and complained about a *Newsweek* story that had raised fresh drug allegations against Ahmed Wali Karzai. That story, by Ron Moreau and Sami Yousafzai, veteran reporters in the region, quoted an unnamed Interior Ministry official saying that Ahmed Wali "leads the whole trafficking structure" in Kandahar. In the palace meeting, according to a U.S. embassy cable, President Karzai was described as "flailing" and asked the intelligence officials "whether they had any evidence to back that up and repeated the question to the ambassadors. We all said that we had numerous rumors and allegations to the effect that his brother is corrupt and a narco-trafficker but that we have never had clear evidence that one could take to court. Karzai fulminated, talked about taking the case to court for libel."

Later that year, before one of President Karzai's visits to Washington, Neumann's embassy recommended Ahmed Wali's banishment from Afghanistan. "One of the most symbolically important things Karzai could do would be to persuade his brother Ahmed Wali Karzai, widely understood to be corrupt and a narcotics trafficker, to leave the country. Karzai must understand that failure to move in this area undermines his leadership at home but also invites questions from Congress and the American People," Neumann reported back.

"We did raise it, I raised it, the British raised it," Neumann told me later of the drug allegations. "Karzai's response was always: 'Show me the evidence.' And there was no evidence. In my time there was no evidence of Ahmed Wali's corruption or drug dealing. There were any number of stories—everybody knows it, that level of thing—but there was not one piece of hard evidence, hard intelligence, classified or unclassified, which I had that I could bring forward to Karzai. None. Zero. And that was true of the British as well." Neumann's successor, Ambassador William Wood, who spent two years in Kabul, told me the same thing: "I asked the question, repeatedly, and the reports that came to me said that none of our sources had a smoking gun. Accusations were rife. Probabilities were high. Smoking gun? Never got a smoking gun."

The cycle of accusation and denial continued. In the year and a half that General Dan McNeill commanded American forces in Afghanistan, European diplomats came to him at least four times asking him to push President Karzai to force Ahmed Wali out of Kandahar. His response was always the same: "I've got nothing on the guy." Many Afghans blamed Ahmed Wali for the July 2008 murder of one of his prominent rivals, Habibullah Jan, an elder of the Alizai tribe, who was shot while returning from a meeting with the Canadian military. The U.S. embassy brushed the claims off as the unreliable assumptions of "conspiracy-minded Afghans." On October 4, 2008, the *Times*'s James Risen published the most detailed account to date of allegations that Ahmed Wali Karzai was involved in the heroin trade, citing unnamed U.S. investigators and a jail-house phone interview with an Afghan informant. The story focused on two drug shipments, from 2004 and 2006, where Ahmed Wali Karzai had allegedly intervened to release trucks that had been stopped by Afghan authorities. Risen would write a series of articles over the years about the Karzai family's business dealings and feuding that often drew strong reactions from the subjects. In response to these stories, President Karzai met again with the American ambassador. And he once again demanded to see the evidence that his brother was involved in the drug trade, while refusing to remove him from his position as provincial council chief in Kandahar. The United States was never able to provide any proof.

It was easy to find Afghans in positions of authority who spoke in detail about Ahmed Wali's connection to the drug trade. I heard the stories from former governors, soldiers, spies—though few who dared to give their names. I sat on the carpet in a Kandahar hotel room and listened late into the night as an Afghan intelligence officer mapped out in detail Kandahar's drug routes and Ahmed Wali's perch at the top of the pyramid. The way most people described it, he didn't dirty his own hands with buying or selling but operated as a fixer, an intervener, his weapon his cell phone, to keep trucks moving, free men from prison. His loyal policemen, the militia commanders who followed him, served, the story went, as escorts just as capable of chaperoning opium loads as accompanying deliveries of fuel or gravel or spare Humvee parts for American military bases.

"Yes, of course he was involved in drug trafficking," said General Noor ul-Haq Olomi, a former Army corps commander in Kandahar. "We live there. We have a good relationship with the people. People over there know very well that he was involved with that. With narcotics trafficking and smuggling. Everybody knows who was working with him."

The accusations drove Ahmed Wali wild. He held press conferences to rail against what he called the "libel" against him. He screamed curses and threatened to beat up a reporter who asked him questions about the allegations. He repeatedly warned that he would sue the newspapers who published the claims. Bill Harris saw him finish reading a newspaper story and stand up in the middle of a large meeting and go berserk. "He went just apoplectic and purple, all twisted up, then he jumps up out of his chair and starts yelling, in English, screaming about 'Why are they doing this to me? I'm going to sue these guys. I'm sick of this. I never did any of this,'" Harris recalled. "If it was a performance, it was an Academy Award."

Ahmed Wali was always categorical: "I was never in the drug business. I never benefited. I never facilitated. I never helped anyone with transportation of any kind," he once told ABC News.

But there were always tantalizing leads. One of the new interagency units that came to Kandahar with the surge was known as Task Force Nexus; its job was to investigate the connection between drugs and the insurgency. The task force's first operation was targeting a district police chief near the border town of Spin Boldak who was believed to be moving marijuana into Pakistan. The American intelligence—the DEA had wiretapped his phones—suggested that the police chief oversaw several large farms and warehouses containing dozens of tons of hashish for shipments and deliveries. His police trucks—donated by the United States— were used to move the drugs. DEA officers eventually lured the police chief to Kandahar Airfield for a meeting and arrested him and five of his bodyguards.

"The reason we picked him was because he's a district-level chief. We didn't know of any connection to anybody. He's a low-level guy. We can go get him and get an early win. We won't hit that point where we've suddenly tripped a political connection that negatively impacts on the [counterinsurgency] campaign," said one person involved. "So we intentionally went after this guy because we thought he was low."

Within a day of the arrest—as they tracked the phone calls—the arrested police chief had called the young border police commander in the area, Abdul Raziq, to complain. He, in turn, had called Ahmed Wali Karzai, who'd called the president. The American officials got berated for making the arrest. The Afghans insisted that the police chief had done nothing wrong and should be released. And they complained that the Americans should not be arresting police chiefs without informing them first.

"It was interesting because okay, that's the first time Ahmed Wali popped up for us," the person involved said. "Ahmed Wali wasn't trafficking, but he was using his influence to say, 'Why was this guy arrested?' This guy's a major trafficker. Why is he interceding on his behalf?

"But in my whole time there, that's the only hard connection I ever saw."

By late January 2010, Steve Beckman was coming to the conclusion that "while AWK was clearly crooked and capable of undermining our efforts" in southern Afghanistan, "we didn't have the goods on him."

Even if the United States planned to demand action on Ahmed Wali, there was no consensus on what that action should be. Some wanted him arrested. Others felt his departure from Kandahar would be sufficient. Ambassador Eikenberry had been trying to persuade McChrystal not to present Karzai with an ultimatum. "Do we really want to go to Karzai and ask him to get rid of his brother? Do we really want to do that?" one of his subordinates recalled Eikenberry asking. People in the palace discussed the possibility that Ahmed Wali could be appointed ambassador to Saudi Arabia or Oman.

In late February, despite growing concern from his subordinates in Kandahar, and hesitance from the U.S. embassy, General McChrystal visited President Karzai in the palace and told him he felt Ahmed Wali had to leave. Given the history of Karzai's responses to this very question, McChrystal should have been able to predict his response. McChrystal was, however, "rather surprised," one of his subordinates said, when Karzai replied, in effect: "No problem. Bring me the evidence."

In the following days, McChrystal ordered his subordinates to collect all the available intelligence on Ahmed Wali Karzai. They would finally settle the question of what Ahmed Wali was really doing. This "deep dive," as they called it, would provide the evidence that President Karzai had demanded. Military and civilian agencies would comb through their records and report back in a classified briefing to McChrystal.

Before the briefing, Ruggiero met with Ahmed Wali again, one-on-one, in late February, to deliver a sterner message. The military focus of the war would be shifting to Kandahar, and the U.S. government would not tolerate people who were working against American aims.

"Nobody is that stupid," Ahmed Wali replied. He insisted to Ruggiero that he was not involved in selling drugs, and he offered to take a polygraph. He said he had hired a lawyer in New York to help clear his name. The allegations were just a campaign to discredit him, he said, and the media ate it up, "like a spice added to a dish to make it more enticing to eat."

The briefing took place on March 8, 2010, at ISAF headquarters in Kabul, the Situational Awareness Room, a high-tech command post with a horseshoe of desks facing a wall of flat screens. The room was packed: Eikenberry, McChrystal, their subordinates. Generals at the Pentagon and Centcom and Kandahar Airfield all videoconferenced in for the performance. One of General Mike Flynn's military intelligence subordinates walked the audience through a series of PowerPoint slides. As he talked about Ahmed Wali's alleged misdeeds, the air seeped from the room.

"It started off with a lot of 'we believe' and 'we guess' and 'we assume,'" one of the participants recalled. "McChrystal's a four-star. 'What do you mean, you assume? Do you know that?' 'No.' 'What do you mean, you don't know that? How do you make that statement?'"

As his subordinate went over the PowerPoint slides, McChrystal grew frustrated.

"So there's nothing?" he said, as another participant recalled. "So I went to the president of this country and I had nothing to go on?"

At the end of the presentation, McChrystal looked toward the flat screens, at the faces of the military officials beamed in by videoconference.

"Nick [Carter], what do you think? You're the tactical commander down there."

Carter and his subordinates had already decided that they could not succeed in southern Afghanistan and also work at cross-purposes to Ahmed Wali. In distant capitals, one could argue with righteous conviction against the wisdom of aligning with Ahmed Wali, and be right, and still not convince the soldiers who had to sit staring at a cross-legged circle of tangled beards and unfathomable Afghan faces, day after day. The soldiers in Kandahar felt the Kabul headquarters' obsession with forcing out Ahmed Wali was reckless.

"Well, sir, you're not going to like this, but I'm afraid he hasn't made the case for me. I can see no reason to remove him based upon what you've told me."

McChrystal went around the room. Others agreed with Carter. They had nothing left but anodyne pronouncements. They would ask Ahmed Wali to "reinforce the central role" of the Afghan government and its institutions. Seek his help finding "political equilibrium" and representative local councils. They would, as Ambassador Sedwill put it, "manage and constrain" him.

McChrystal circled back to Carter at the end of the meeting, more than an hour after they began.

"What do you think we should do?" McChrystal asked.

"We're going to work with him," Carter said. "We don't have any choice."

McChrystal's order was unequivocal: "We're going to stop saying bad stuff about AWK. Okay? Stop."

8

SMASHING THE CHINA SHOP

THE SALEHI DEBACLE FORCED AMERICANS in Washington and Kabul to rethink their whole approach toward Hamid Karzai. The debate came down to this: What will cost more, billions of squandered dollars or a three-sided war? Can we risk losing Karzai as an ally and start fighting both the Taliban and his government, just to save a few bucks and frog-march some perps to the slammer? The counterinsurgency credos had been ball-peened into the collective military skull enough times that everyone knew that nothing could be accomplished without an oblig-ing "partner" government. All the propagandistic slogans dreamed up at ISAF HQ, the soldierly assurances that everything with the Afghans was *shona ba shona* ("shoulder to shoulder" in Dari; or the more cavemanesque version in Pashtu: *ooga pa ooga*) ultimately sought to express this hoped-for result. But the fact remained that the Taliban, drawn predominantly from the president's own ethnic group, had won over growing portions of the country on the argument that Americans were occupiers and Karzai nothing but a foreign stooge presiding over a godless government. Even an emotionless analysis would conclude that Karzai had to demonstrate some of his own authority over, if not outright opposition to, his Ameri-can partners.

But did that explain his outbursts? Was the puppet just posing as anti-American or did he really hate us more than we hated him? And did we need him more than he needed us? These questions could go round and round. Should we confront him about the behavior he seemed so happy to condone in his government: the theft, extortion, drug trafficking, the endless enrichment of his loyalists? Or should we preserve a veneer of civility in the hopes of securing future cooperation when we needed it most? Or had the time when we needed it most already passed?

Inside the embassy, some of the senior diplomats were skeptical about what the United States would gain from rooting around in the sludge of Afghan bad business practices. A country with $1 billion of its own annual revenues was taking in more than $10 billion in American aid. The prospect that such a transaction could be done without kickbacks and quid pro quos seemed naïve. The American project in Afghanistan had never seemed capable of holding in its mind any fixed definition of its enemy. There were always allusions to "al-Qaeda" and "extremists" when it came time for the president to stand at a podium at West Point or Annapolis and justify sending more of those young faces in front of him to Afghanistan, even though the day-to-day combat these men and women would encounter had nothing to do with al-Qaeda. "The Taliban" itself was an elusive term for an unknown quantity of people with unclear motivations and conflicting allegiances. If the upper strata of Afghanistan's business and political elite, a group of people actively encouraged, paid, protected, and enriched by the American government throughout most of the war, were now considered the most dangerous enemies, what would defeating them accomplish?

"The challenge was, the further we got into discovering this, the further we saw how widely corruption had spread," one of Eikenberry's deputies at the embassy told me. "There were more corrupt people than there were noncorrupt people, and even the relatively uncorrupt people would not do everything we would say was the straight and narrow way of doing something. It was a hard situation. And then a number of our people were just sort of like, 'Straight ahead. We're just going to do this. This is a bad target.'"

Brigadier General Herbert R. McMaster, ISAF's point man on corruption, was a straight-ahead type guy. In his ascent through the U.S. Army, McMaster had checked all the boxes of a rising star in the counterinsurgency era. A West Point graduate, he had earned his doctorate and written an influential book criticizing the failures of generalship in the Vietnam War, called *Dereliction of Duty*. After winning a Silver Star in the Gulf War, he'd earned a reputation as a maverick during the Iraq war, commanding an armored cavalry regiment in the northern city of Tal Afar with aggression and creativity. Lieutenant General David Barno, who commanded coalition forces in Afghanistan for a time, said McMaster "might be the 21st century Army's pre-eminent warrior-thinker." McMaster was loud and brash and smart. A former tank commander, he was also physically imposing, a former rugby player with a broad chest, a bald head, and a flashing grin. He resembled an armed Mr. Clean. "He looks like somebody who could strangle a Taliban by himself," one of his subordinates said.

McMaster got to Kabul right around the time of the Salehi arrest. Unlike others who took the political crisis as instruction to back off, he wanted fresh scalps. He came into his job frustrated by the failures of American officials to push harder for prosecutions, and by the sense of resignation and futility starting to seep through the American mission in Kabul. The teeth-gnashing at the embassy over Karzai's tantrums looked to him like sissy weakness and capitulation. McMaster believed that Afghans were no more inherently greedy or deceitful than anyone else, and so any suggestion by his colleagues that this problem was some irredeemable cultural defect offended him. This view was "bigotry masquerading as cultural sensitivity," he would say, his subordinates recalled. Much like Kirk Meyer of the DEA, McMaster felt outrage that criminals had hijacked the Afghan government, and he wanted to stop them because what they were doing was morally and legally wrong and threatened, at a fundamental level, the future of the country. "Our main goal was to keep Afghanistan from becoming a failed state," Pete Orchard, an FBI agent and one of McMaster's deputies, told me. "All the other stuff is gilding the outhouse. If you do nothing, over time it's going to collapse."

When General David Petraeus became the new commander of the Afghan war in July 2010—after President Obama fired McChrystal over inflammatory comments in a *Rolling Stone* article—he decided to make fighting corruption a priority. And as was Petraeus's way, the world's most powerful military—*his* military, not the tentative bureaucrats down the road at the U.S. embassy—would be in charge. Petraeus was also hyper-attuned to the politics in Washington, as well as his reputation and his legacy, and he saw the benefits of appearing proactive on this issue. Setting up an ambitious military-run countercorruption program could help shield him from a Congress increasingly vocal about wasted tax dollars in Afghanistan. Also, some influential Washington insiders had been lobbying Petraeus with the argument that the military risked failure in its mission if it did not do something about the predatory nature of the Afghan government. Within a few weeks of assuming command, Petraeus chose McMaster to lead his anti-corruption effort. The group became known as Task Force Shafafiyat (using the Dari word for "transparency"), and it was supposed to coordinate the work of the disparate teams of soldiers and civilians—such as Meyer's group over at the embassy—trying to deal with this problem.

From the start of his command, Petraeus took a harder line with Karzai than his predecessor had; McChrystal had won Karzai's affection with his deference. When Afghan civilians had been killed by soldiers under his command, McChrystal had apologized publicly and profusely, then passed down orders intended to minimize such casualties, to the point where some soldiers felt hamstrung by the restrictions. He'd regularly invited Karzai to be flown around the country on military aircraft and had treated him as if he were McChrystal's own commander in chief.

Petraeus, when he took over, felt that McChrystal had capitulated too often to Karzai. Petraeus couldn't believe that McChrystal had agreed to Karzai's demand to transfer all American-held prisoners to Afghan control by January 2011. Petraeus canceled that agreement, angering some in his own command who felt he had recklessly broken a promise to Karzai. Petraeus would ratchet up the violence level far beyond what it had been. His soldiers dropped five times as many bombs. Special operations troops launched kill-and-capture raids at far higher rates. Everything that troubled Karzai about the American military posture in Afghanistan—the intrusiveness and collateral damage and his own inability to change anything—intensified under Petraeus. Before Petraeus arrived, Americans were releasing more prisoners than they were taking in, partly as a

U.S. Ambassador Karl Eikenberry, right, walks with General David Petraeus, center, at the Camp Phoenix military base in Kabul, July 24, 2010.

concession to Karzai's demands to let all but the most dangerous insurgents go. Under Petraeus, the release rate dropped toward zero and the detainee population at Bagram Airfield's prison soared.

Petraeus set the tone in one of his first meetings with Karzai in Kabul when he informed the president that he would be expanding the number of American-paid Afghan militiamen across the country, mirroring the Sunni Awakening plan he'd championed in Iraq. Karzai, who was against the prospect of blindly adding to the ranks of armed vigilantes, opposed the project, and his relationship with Petraeus stumbled from the start. "Many people didn't want to play hardball with Karzai," recalled one of McMaster's aides. Under General Petraeus, "ISAF wanted to play hardball with Karzai."

With Eikenberry and McChrystal, the embassy and the military had fought each other on issue after issue—whether to arm militias in Nangarhar Province, whether to buy diesel generators or rebuild the hydroelectric dam in Kandahar, whether more troops were ultimately needed for Afghanistan—and Petraeus's most obvious public relations problem was defining just who the U.S. military was actually there to fight. At a Fourth of July party (held on the third), under the harsh glare in the embassy courtyard, with hot dog and ice cream tents, Petraeus and Eikenberry engaged in some stage-managed reconciliation for the Afghan crowd, which included Abdullah Abdullah, the losing presidential candidate, wearing a polka-dotted pocket square, a female Afghan pop singer, and the chairman and the CEO of Kabul Bank, the country's most booming business, in dark pin-striped suits and heavy cologne (I stood behind them). The army band from the 101st Airborne Division (Air Assault) from Fort Campbell, Kentucky (motto: "Rendezvous with Destiny") struck up an anthem. Eikenberry took the podium first.

"What a great day to be in Afghanistan," he began. "On this occasion, as our attention turns to our founding fathers of the United States of America, the birth of our own nation, and it's fitting at this time to recall Samuel Adams, the American revolutionary leader who said, 'True peace is not merely the absence of tension. True peace is the presence of justice.' We come here to support the Afghan people with this spirit in mind in hopes that they, too, will enjoy true freedom, true peace, and true justice for hundreds of years to come."

That was the tone of these kinds of gatherings. The Americans always hewed to optimism, right till the end. Eikenberry said America was "committed for the long term" to Afghanistan because this country, "free of extremist threats, will contribute directly to America's safety and for our security."

He quoted President Obama: "We keep at it, we will persevere, and together with our partners, we will prevail. I'm absolutely confident of that."

"Now," Eikenberry concluded, "let me introduce a great friend and our military partner here, General Dave Petraeus, just having arrived in Afghanistan yesterday. Dave, before I turn this podium over to you, I'd like to hand you our very own United States embassy access badge," Eikenberry said, to tepid laughter. "It lets you know, on behalf of the over one thousand civilians serving here in Kabul and around this great country, our note to you: Welcome aboard. And you're welcome at this embassy, as we say, twenty-four/seven. We look forward to being your teammates and to our continued combined success. Ladies and gentlemen, General David Petraeus."

Petraeus had achieved celebrity status by then. He was the most famous man in the military, come to preside over his second surge. I had met him several times during his first one, in Iraq, which started as he stood under Saddam Hussein's crystal chandeliers and marble columns, now converted into Camp Victory, and spoke in his earnest way about America's "rucksack of responsibility" in a fight that was "hard but not hopeless." It had been only three years since then, but Petraeus seemed far older. Although it had been somewhat obscured by his missionary haircut and Princeton-man credentials, the *Top Gun*–style cockiness would frequently peek through during his Baghdad years. On tours of bases in Baghdad, I'd seen him drop and challenge nineteen-year-old Marines to push-up contests, ripping off dozens or hundreds (I'd lose count) until the kids would fall out one by one, maybe out of deference to the chain of command, and Petraeus would pop up, beaming. He'd expect other generals to brief him while also trying to keep up with him on some grueling five-mile run in the searing Baghdad heat.

He typified for me an attitude that many top officers seemed to share (McChrystal and his one-meal-a-day regimen, with almost no sleep, was another): that an ascetic lifestyle, a punishing physical routine, and a numbingly long workday would translate somehow into a winning war strategy, as if self-denial were a weapon. Or maybe they just felt guilty that they were so far from the combat and didn't want to appear soft.

The way Petraeus looked—to the audience back home—always seemed so important to him. I'd had colleagues who would do phone interviews with him during which he would speak his punctuation—for example: "The war is hard comma the hardest of my life comma but it is not hopeless period." He was a good general for the media age: expert at appearances. He'd gotten angry during an interview with me one day when the photographer took a shot of him in his reading glasses as he scrutinized a document to reference some statistic. He said he didn't want a glasses photo to undercut his image as a tough fighting man, and we all laughed at the joke. But he hadn't been joking, and his spokesman called later, demanding that the photo be removed immediately from *The Washington Post*'s website.

In Kabul, he seemed different. Not just older, but slower, less engaged. People always quipped that he was recycling ideas from Iraq—the Afghan Local Police initiative an early and obvious example, hoping to re-create the Sunni Awakening project that helped take Anbar Province back from al-Qaeda (before ISIS then took it)—and how he would confuse place-names from the two countries. Some just assumed that he could tell that the Afghan war wasn't a winner and he'd rather not have it stick to him too closely.

"Well, good morning to you all, *salaam alaikum*," Petraeus said stiffly when he got to the podium. "And thanks, Ambassador. Thanks, Karl. For this wonderful badge. I feel like one of the team now. *Persona grata*."

In this same flavor—attentive to appearances, but awkward and forced—the month after his arrival, Petraeus asked Sarah Peck, an elegant auburn-haired diplomat in the rule-of-law office at the American embassy, to join McMaster's anti-corruption task force as its civilian co-director, on paper the general's equal. At the time, Peck had a month left on her year-long tour at the embassy. The job offer no doubt surprised her. She had no prior relationship with either Petraeus or McMaster. But she was committed to the cause, both trying to avoid the waste of American tax dollars and improving the Afghan judicial system. The corruption issue had heretofore existed largely out of the military realm. Her job could bridge the civilian and military worlds. Eikenberry gave his grudging approval, although he made it clear that McMaster's task force was not anywhere among his priorities.

As it turned out, Peck would not be entering the collaborative environment that Eikenberry and Petraeus sought to portray. In his first weeks, McMaster had already managed to infuriate many civilians at the embassy. He had no background in money laundering, organized crime, or state-sponsored corruption. He began recruiting experts he came across in his background reading and other soldiers and civilians he had known from earlier tours. The group was a hodgepodge of specialties: former fighter pilots, Rhodes scholars, counterintelligence officers, and Scotland Yard investigators. There were FBI officers and Treasury Department financial guys, military officers from the prestigious social science program at West Point, itinerant professors and brainy kids fresh out of grad school. The task force worked out of a small windowless double-decker metal shipping container. Peck's desk was in an area known as "the pit." Their offices sat close to the ISAF headquarters building, a white-shuttered, yellow concrete lodge at the center of the coalition's walled-off mini-city in Kabul.

The ISAF HQ had housed an Afghan military officers' club before the Soviet war; even earlier, the grounds had served a British cantonment from the First Anglo-Afghan War, in 1842. This was the campaign often invoked darkly by coalition soldiers on the base. The British general at the time, William Elphinstone, led an ignominious retreat from the base, a wintertime death march by thousands of troops and families, survived by a lone British army surgeon. When McChrystal took command in Kabul, he placed a replica map of Elphinstone's route under his dining room table's Plexiglas top—"to warn against hubris," he said.

Military brass from forty-two nations traversed the grounds, a clashing coalition in their various epaulets and berets. HQ life was far removed from the rigors of the combat bases out in the field, where soldiers slept on cots, ate MREs encased in plastic, and burned their own feces. At headquarters, soldiers smoked cigars over poker games and wheeled away hours at spinning class. They could pray at morning mass and dance salsa at dusk. The U.S. military couldn't drink, but the other soldiers could—by one count, fourteen bars could be found on the campus (until McChrystal decided to ban booze on campus, dampening the festivities). But ISAF still had an easy-living feel, with gardens and basketball courts and pine-tree-dappled shade on the gazebos. When you bought your cappuccino at the main base café, they gave you change in euros.

Inside the task force's trailers, the atmosphere McMaster cultivated was one of desperate urgency. Soldiers usually receive lengthy orientations when they come into a country, a slow-motion weeks-long baton pass from their predecessors known as a "right seat ride." His team had no such guide. They just had a vague goal: change the behavior of a country that Transparency International was ranking, at the time, as the second most corrupt country on the planet, behind Somalia. (Afghanistan would later fall into a tie for first.) McMaster wanted to understand the extent of the rot within the Afghan government, so his team began a months-long, round-the-clock research binge to write ISAF's countercorruption strategy. This document would ultimately become codified as a classified annex to the war's overall campaign plan. Such an intellectual pursuit, in the middle of days packed with appointments, briefings, and meetings, felt, as one participant put it, like "finals on steroids."

McMaster's bravado and intensity instilled in the mission a frenetic energy. He maintained the type of punishing pace that was demanded of ambitious generals. He worked seven days a week, often past midnight, racing by helicopter and Humvee from palace briefings to Afghan dinner parties to country team meetings at the U.S. embassy, swapping between fatigues and business suits. His staff bragged that he slept four hours a night. Even those who hated and feared him regarded him as brilliant. He was gregarious, profane, funny, impatient, and demanding. "He's not a bull in a china shop," said Paul Rexton Kan, a professor at the Army War College, whose book on Mexican drug cartels caught McMaster's attention, and who spent a month in Kabul at his invitation helping to write the anti-corruption strategy. "He's a bull who picks up the china shop and just smashes it."

McMaster had a strong appetite for study and set aside time each day for reading. While working out on the elliptical trainer, he would jot notes and highlight magazine or journal articles. He'd then charge back to his office, the pockets of his cargo pants bulging with folded articles, which he'd drop off on his subordinates' desks, pointing out new thoughts or observations. He loved ten-point lists. He would stay up all night rewriting papers. He would describe a problem and say, "We're going to crush this."

"What McMaster articulated was a charge to eradicate corruption in Afghanistan," one of his team members recalled.

But how to define "corruption"? Which of its many varieties mattered to them, militarily? The way graft seemed to be interwoven in the politics and economy of the country defied easy categorization. Soldiers need an enemy. In this messy new economy overwhelmed with American cash, who was the enemy? Would they go after the people ripping off crates of hand sanitizer and paper plates from NATO cargo containers shipped in from Pakistan? Or Afghan civil servants charging bribes for driver's licenses? Or couriers shuttling gold bars and bags of cash out of the country on airplane flights? Or policemen demanding roadside "donations"?

Or Air Force generals running drugs? Or ministers getting kickbacks? Or Beltway bandits inflating contract costs? Or mercenaries paying off the Taliban? Or palace relatives and cronies? Or President Hamid Karzai himself?

It was the most important question that no one ever quite answered. McMaster had articulated a goal, but what exactly was the mission, and how would they complete it? As the team members sat at their laptops writing and rewriting campaign plan drafts, the scope only widened. Their "lines of effort" branched far afield of traditional soldiering, into economics and development, counternarcotics, civil society, rule of law, in addition to mapping out networks of criminals and reforming the Afghan national security forces. Days dragged into weeks, then months, and the task force still had not finished writing its plan. A Pentagon official flew to Kabul to tell McMaster that he was taking on too much. That the work was straying too far into high-level Afghan politics. That he didn't have the staff to do a quarter of what he was proposing. His team began to worry about their mission. "The plan was a pig. It had no focus. It was across the entire spectrum," one team member said. "Is he going after all corruption in Afghanistan? Because, wow."

When the task force started looking, the stories of graft, greed, and insider deals poured into their offices faster than they could handle them. They selected cases from intelligence reports, detainee interrogation transcripts, newspaper articles, and from tips McMaster was picking up in conversations at the palace and parliament and government ministries around town. The scope of theft, bribery, and graft left them dazzled. An example of their startling conclusions: the rate of money being stolen, siphoned off, or pilfered from U.S. government contracts—what they called "shrinkage"—was as high as 50 percent. They believed that three-quarters of the money, weapons, and other supplies given to the Taliban were moving through official Afghan police checkpoints, rather than the mountain passes, goat trails, or dirt tracks that might be employed to try to avoid the authorities. Even those on the task force who had studied organized crime as academics or practitioners in other third-world countries felt like astronauts bounding on a new planet. "This was so much bigger than we realized," one of them recalled.

"This was the first live kleptocracy I'd ever actually seen," another said. "It was amazing what they were doing. Hundreds and hundreds of millions of our dollars just disappearing. It was mind-boggling."

"I think corruption, broadly defined, was really at the core of why we were failing," said Timothy Sullivan, a civilian who spent a year working under McMaster in Kabul.

In their early briefings around Kabul, members of Task Force Shafafiyat articulated a vision that declared that not even the petty corruption common in the region, or around the world, could be ignored. Low-level bribery had been "systematized into pyramid networks to prey on Afghans," they explained at a conference in Kabul in late September 2010, according to the notes of one participant. So the idea of just treating this as petty corruption "would be to misunderstand the problem." The task force would also attack the "criminal patronage networks" they saw as attempting to monopolize entire sectors of the economy: construction, mining, petroleum, trucking. Their recommendations—stop American aid that worsened corruption; cut off diplomatic support to the criminal networks—seemed to ignore the fact that thousands of new American troops and billions of additional dollars had just come to Afghanistan to fight on behalf of the Karzai government. But the disclaimer at the end of the briefing said a lot: "Beware that there is no example of an outside power ever solving the corruption problem of another country."

When Peck started working in the pit, she was given no staff to help her. McMaster rarely had time to speak with her. His military staff would not inform her about his meetings or tell her which Afghan officials he was speaking with, or what they had talked about. Peck prepared a list of priorities she believed would narrow the scope of their work: McMaster should focus his reformist zeal on finding the fraud and waste in the money that the U.S. military was spending in Afghanistan. The Afghan military and police force was costing taxpayers more than $10 billion per year, and following that money would be difficult enough.

McMaster and his military aides dismissed her ideas and mocked her behind her back. One of them referred to Peck, a slender woman with reddish hair, as having a "head like a sun-fucked orange," another task force member wrote in his diary.

("If you had to go to the men's room to take a dump, you'd say, 'I have to go to the embassy to drop off a cable,'" Paul Rexton Kan recalled. "That's how rancorous it was.")

"HR just ignored her," one of his team said. "The staff treated her like shit."

Embassy diplomats started referring to the general as "McMaster-Disaster" and ignored his requests for information. What angered them was not just his rude behavior but also the grandiosity of his vision. He was proposing direct attacks on the government they were supposed to support. He made it clear that locking up corrupt members of President Karzai's inner circle should be their goal. McMaster told them they were failing. Such bluntness, coming from a general with no experience in the subject, was galling, "a slap in the face," as one embassy staff member put it.

"McMaster came in guns blazing: 'We need to take down Karzai's networks; we need to indict Karzai's brother,'" the staffer recalled. "He had a preconceived notion of how to fight corruption, which was to hit Karzai over the head with a giant hammer."

One State Department official in town from Washington asked McMaster how he planned to do all of this.

"First we're going to go after the chumps, then we're going to go after the pussies," McMaster shot back. "Any questions?"

The idea for Kabul Bank began in the months following the American invasion, when business opportunities, for those undaunted by risk and violence, seemed boundless. Whole industries—telecom, private media, oil and gas, automobiles, construction—that were either undeveloped or nonexistent under the Taliban had to be built anew. Logistics and security firms funded by the American taxpayer were springing up to cater to the arriving foreign troops and their expanding network of bases. Aid money from America and Europe was inventing a new wartime economy. Before businesses could take off, they needed financing. In banking, Afghans with free-market plans, a bit of English, and some friends in the right places were discovering that they could become fantastically rich.

"Kabul Bank was my dream business," Mahmood Karzai told me.

With his gated city under way in Kandahar, Mahmood began looking to extend his empire. Early in the war, he had been named chairman of the newly established Afghan-American Chamber of Commerce, an organization USAID had given $6 million to so that it could expand along with affiliated business groups. Mahmood was a relentless networker and constantly hatching plans for new business deals in Washington and Kabul. He had teamed up with several other Afghan entrepreneurs to start the Afghan Investment Company (AIC), with the intention of buying a cement plant in northern Afghanistan to supply the construction boom he imagined. After his friend Jack Kemp, the former NFL quarterback and U.S. senator, helped arrange some introductions, Mahmood flew to Tokyo to meet with Toyota officials and won the concession to sell

Brigadier General Herbert R. McMaster, the head of ISAF's anti-corruption task force, gives a speech at the National Military Academy of Afghanistan on December 8, 2011.

Toyotas in Kabul when there were still few cars on the roads. A decade later, the streets would be in perpetual gridlock with Corollas. During one visit to Kabul by U.S. Commerce Secretary Carlos Gutierrez, Mahmood gave him a presentation on the obstacles to developing the Afghan private sector. There was a shortage of electricity; the few paved roads were potholed and in disrepair. Access to land and capital was difficult, and there was no clear economic vision, Mahmood never failed to mention, from his brother's government.

The relationship to wealth, as well as a larger interest in or knowledge of the economy, separated President Karzai from his siblings. While Mahmood was the clearest example, the other brothers, including Ahmed Wali in Kandahar, and Qayum in Baltimore, had a great hunger for wealth and ambitions for business dominance. Part of this seemed to come from their experiences in America, where these men from a distinguished Afghan family had had to gut out years as waiters and busboys in suburban chain-hotel restaurants. Hamid Karzai had had an easier path when it came to money. After college, he'd been welcomed into the fold of one of the political parties in exile in Pakistan, thanks to his father's connections, and eased into his career as a politician and diplomat. But he had never been particularly interested in wealth or material objects. Many of his childhood friends and acquaintances have remarked on his penchant for giving things away. An old man who'd been a servant for the family in their village of Karz once told me a story about Hamid and his pet horse, Almond Blossom. The servant used to spend hours walking alongside Hamid as he rode down the dirt lanes that wove through the grape orchards. Hamid wanted to repay him for all his time, but he didn't have any money. Instead, Hamid offered his bicycle. "He told me, 'Look, I don't have cash, but I'll give you this bicycle and you can sell it.'" The servant remembered him as unusually generous for a child.

"He always had an enormously soft heart," Qayum said. "Beggars used to come to our house and ask for Hamid."

In the palace, Hamid Karzai lived an almost ascetic life, rejecting many of the perks of his position. Early on, he ordered the palace chefs to scrap the lavish menu that had been favored by earlier regimes. He replaced multicourse meals with basic Afghan fare—rice, salad, bread—and limited meat to three days a week. He once issued a presidential decree that he did not want to inherit any of his father's land in Kandahar. These views on wealth and privilege informed his politics in unexpected ways. At times he argued against his own defense minister who wanted the United States to pay for a larger, more powerful military; Karzai worried that it would create an entitled military class, like in Pakistan, and dominate Afghanistan's domestic politics. He complained that his military officers drove expensive cars and believed they should live more Spartan lives. Karzai preferred reinstating a military draft to encourage nationalism and a more egalitarian force (although that didn't come to pass). "He is probably the cleanest, most uncorruptible Afghan I've ever met," recalled Javed Ludin, who served as Karzai's chief of staff. "He has no economic interest in anything. He's a poor man."

Karzai's relatives often mocked his seeming disinterest in money. A Persian Gulf dignitary had once given Karzai and his wife diamond-encrusted watches, but Karzai took them away and had them cataloged and held by the government, to Zeenat's frustration. "I don't think he's ever lived an extravagant life anywhere," Patricia Karzai, his sister-in-law, said. "He likes nice things. He's not necessarily going to shop at a Walmart for his clothing, but he's never led an extravagant life."

"Afghan families tend to try to live beyond their means," Karzai had once written. "They overconsume. Everything is taken to excess. They put too much food on the table, they spend money they don't have on clothes, and there is no notion of saving. It's a strange characteristic of Afghans that is quite puzzling to me."

The president's attitude toward money, and his lack of interest in helping others get rich, infuriated many of his relatives, who thought he acted too superior. This was something that the U.S. anti-corruption investigators were missing as they sketched their criminal patronage network maps inside ISAF headquarters: the president wasn't the godfather pulling the strings on a family mafia.

"He doesn't want any of his relatives to get rich," his cousin Hashim, who was one of the partners in the Aino Mena development, complained to me one afternoon over fried chicken at a Popeyes fast-food joint in Dubai. "You know what the president wants? He wants us to live in, what do you call it, a soup kitchen? Or live in a shrine. Or an orphanage. Something like this. You tell him, 'Oh, I saw your cousin, he's a big businessman in Dubai. He owns a hotel.' He'll be very upset. If you tell him, 'I met your cousin, he's living in a shrine, he's smoking tobacco and he doesn't have any money for his food,' he'll say, 'Oh, what a great guy.'"

When the war started, Afghanistan was basically bankrupt. By 2001, there were six state-owned banks, confined largely to Kabul and virtually defunct. Management was inexperienced. Audits had not been conducted in years. The IMF first visited in late January 2002, and as a consultant wrote in a subsequent report, "It soon became clear that in reality, none of these financial institutions had been operating in a normal fashion for years." Most of the staff did not know how to use a computer. All the money in circulation in the country totaled about $270 million. Government employees had gone months without salaries. The Central Bank vault was nearly empty, the few stacks of remaining bills wrapped in rubber bands. The Taliban had run off with gold bars and cash in U.S. dollars and Pakistani rupees. A diminutive central banker with a nasal voice, Abdul Qadir Fitrat, went on the BBC the same month as the IMF visit and informed the world that "if the international community as a whole fails to provide us with immediate short-term and long-term assistance, we have no choice but to resort to printing new bank notes, which is a disaster for the economy and would put much pressure on the already existing inflationary pressure." He said "we need at least $25 to $30 million per month to meet both military and civilian employees of the government alone. Let alone other government expenses, furniture and other day-to-day expenses.

"At least provide us with some security," Fitrat pleaded to the world. "That promise alone would mean a lot."

To handle the incoming foreign aid and make the country more amenable to American companies, Bush administration officials believed Afghanistan needed to move away from the *hawala* money-transfer network and toward a modern banking system that could interact with Western banks. Besides New Ansari, the *hawala* that Kirk Meyer would later investigate, the biggest player in the Afghan market was Shaheen Exchange. It was run by a short, pale, balding, overweight Afghan businessman named Sherkhan Farnood. When the Soviets invaded Afghanistan, Farnood, an ethnic Tajik from the northern province of Kunduz, relocated to Moscow, where he could avoid conscription into the Afghan army. He learned the language, studied at the Moscow Textile Institute, and started a *hawala* out of his dorm room to move money between Russia and Kabul. After the collapse of the Soviet Union, his *hawala* took off. By the late 1990s, Farnood's business in Moscow had run afoul of the law. Ten of his employees were arrested and convicted of illegal banking activity. Meyer learned that Russian authorities had seized one million dollars when they executed their search warrant. Fearing arrest in Russia, Farnood headed for Dubai, the burgeoning hub of Islamic finance. The Persian Gulf emirate, flooded in oil wealth and racing to build new skyscrapers and malls, was paradise for freewheeling businessmen. In 1996, Farnood, who was a fugitive on charges of illegal banking, money laundering, and organizing a crime syndicate, opened the Shaheen Exchange, a *hawala* named after his son, out of an office near the Gold Souk, a market for platinum, diamonds, and gold. His business flourished. One former Shaheen employee estimated that the company made $100,000 a week in profits. His colleagues were impressed by his acuity in mathematics and his calculating ruthlessness, his competitiveness and cunning. In 2003, Afghanistan had passed a banking law, written with the help of advisers at the USAID contractor BearingPoint. That year, Farnood moved to transform himself from fugitive *hawaladar* to respected international banker.

How to begin?

"It started with a bribe," Naseem Akbar said.

Akbar was deputy director of the Afghanistan Investment Support Agency, or AISA, a small government agency across the street from the Foreign Ministry that licensed companies to work in Afghanistan. On December 28, 2003, not long after the country drafted a banking law,

Farnood submitted a preliminary application for a license for Kabul Bank. Akbar was in his office one day not long after when a colleague came to him with an envelope holding $5,000 in cash given to him by one of Farnood's employees, in order to speed along the bank's first license.

"At the time, that was quite unusual," Akbar recalled. "They wanted a simple license—you didn't even need to pay a five-thousand-dollar bribe."

Kabul Bank started when the country had little experience in enforcing banking rules or regulating this new industry. The law required background checks on the shareholders and management. The names of Farnood's first partners in the bank—including his brother, body guard, and driver—were submitted to the Interior Ministry for review and cleared in September 2004, three months after the bank had already opened. The check, if it happened at all, raised no alarms; nor did it note that Farnood was a fugitive or that his brother's curriculum vitae was, almost word for word, identical to his own.

"Sherkhan was never doing business according to the law. He was thinking, I am the law," Kamal Nasar Kroor, whom Farnood had recruited from his job with the United Nations refugee agency to join Shaheen Exchange and, later, Kabul Bank, told me. "He did not consider the government as real. He thought, I'm Sherkhan. I'm the one."

Kabul Bank's first office was a storefront on Flower Street, a pleasant Kabul shopping lane populated with florists. When it opened, in June 2004, Farnood also brought over employees from Shaheen Exchange; they would continue their money transfer services from inside Kabul Bank. The two companies merged seamlessly, their staffs in regular contact from Kabul to Dubai. Farnood's casual approach toward following rules wouldn't be much of an obstacle; it was nearly three years before any Central Bank regulators visited Kabul Bank. As late as February 2010, an audit by A. F. Ferguson & Co., a member firm of PricewaterhouseCoopers, noted that the bank had no compensation committee to look at management salaries and no code of ethics or conflict-of-interest policy; furthermore, it was missing a slew of loan documents such as borrowers' financial statements, tax clearance forms, trade licenses, passports, and credit reports.

Farnood's vision for Kabul Bank was simple: he wanted a pool of money from which to finance other investments for himself and a small group of allies. Within five years of Kabul Bank's founding, he would come to own or have major stakes in an airline, a television station, a fuel import company, an oil storage complex, a cement plant, more than a dozen Dubai properties, more than two hundred cars and motorcycles, and a Mi-8T helicopter. Because Farnood's banking license came through early, he lent to other entrepreneurial Afghans who needed financing. The rates varied widely: competitors would sometimes pay 35 percent interest; allies paid none. Farnood's willingness to lend massive sums to bank insiders and his cronies helped popularize Kabul Bank among the political elite, including Mahmood Karzai and Haseen Fahim, the brother of the vice president, both of whom became major shareholders, paying for their stocks with loans issued by Kabul Bank itself. Kabul Bank was a major donor to President Karzai's 2009 election campaign, contributing tens of millions of dollars. The bank also purchased dozens of vehicles for Karzai, including bulletproof SUVs, for the campaign to distribute as gifts, and paid for his media advertising campaign, billboards, and television ads. All this despite an order from the Central Bank's governor, Abdul Qadir Fitrat, that said banks were "required to remain politically neutral and strictly refrain from campaigning for any of the presidential candidates," as such contributions from depositors' funds were "immoral and inappropriate."

Among the average Afghan, who lived on a few dollars a day, the big attraction to Kabul Bank was the lottery. Big prize giveaways had become popular among banks in Dubai and in other Islamic countries, where offering interest is a religious taboo. On the second anniversary of the bank's opening, Farnood began holding drawings for his depositors, offering cash prizes, first on a monthly basis, then weekly. The first lottery winner took home one million afghanis, or $20,000. As one early employee put it: "The bank was a runaway success."

"Kabul Bank's relentless journey in pursuit of excellence is on course," Farnood wrote in the bank's second annual report, illustrated with cover photos of a pile of bills in multiple currencies and a line of sprinters leaving the blocks. At that time, Kabul Bank had issued about $100 million in loans. The headquarters had moved into a building in the Shar-e-Naw neighborhood with a blue glass façade. It had twenty-one branches in eleven provinces—numbers that would triple in a few years—and planned to open a network of ATMs. The bank's customer base by that time had reached a "whooping 165,000," Farnood wrote, and the "financial highlights of the Bank depict a glorious picture.

"Let us make Kabul Bank the nation's pride."

Within a few years, what the bank had made was Farnood and his friends fabulously rich. Mahmood Karzai soon owned about 8 percent of the bank and was living in one of Farnood's villas on Palm Jumeirah in

Dubai, a home worth several million dollars. That was just one example of their taste for luxury. In the span of six weeks during the summer of 2009, Farnood's former bodyguard turned bank chief executive, Khalil Ferozi, racked up $121,000 in bank expenses on shopping trips. In Dubai and India, he charged thousands at Tom Ford, Taherian Jewellery, Versace, Dolce & Gabbana, Yves Saint Laurent, and the Taj Palace Hotel. In Paris, he swung through Christian Dior, Chanel, Louis Vuitton. Ferozi had once sold emeralds to raise money for Ahmad Shah Massoud, the anti-Taliban guerrilla commander. During Ferozi's rise to Kabul Bank's chief executive, he was gifted a large portion of the bank's shares. Farnood loved to gamble with his money and considered himself Afghanistan's best poker player. He played for high or low stakes, against anyone who wanted a game. In 2008, he had won an event in London at the World Series of Poker Europe.

Farnood had also been pouring his depositors' money into Dubai real estate, as the emirate was booming, snapping up properties in his name and that of his wife, Farida. He owned at least sixteen properties, including several villas on Palm Jumeirah, the man-made island shaped like a palm tree, which cost more than $4 million each, and two office towers under construction, the Wave and the Dolphin, in an area of Dubai known as Business Bay. These seemed like sound investments until the shock waves of the 2008 world financial crisis reached the Persian Gulf and the value of Dubai properties started to fall. A city that had once been renowned for its bountiful supply of construction cranes began to be known for its high-rises standing empty in the blistering desert.

The losses began to create friction between Farnood and his business partners, and it didn't take long before rumors of his spending began to circulate in Kabul. In October 2009, Afghanistan's intelligence agency notified the Central Bank that two Afghan institutions—Kabul Bank and a rival, Azizi Bank—were buying hundreds of millions of dollars in Dubai property. The intelligence report stated that the financial crisis had eliminated at least 40 percent of the value of their holdings. It warned of the banks' growing instability. And it noted that millions of dollars were flowing into the accounts of Kabul Bank's leadership, including Mahmood Karzai. The bankers, the report added, "are in collusion with drug smugglers and people turning black money into white."

Newspaper articles published in the following months laid out many of the problems and conflicts of interest at Kabul Bank, information that terrified the governor of Afghanistan's Central Bank, Abdul Qadir Fitrat.

Unlike others in the Afghan diaspora who'd returned from exile to join Karzai's government, Fitrat was unusually well qualified. His career in Washington, with the International Monetary Fund and the World Bank, had given him a solid understanding of first-world macroeconomics. He had helped write Afghanistan's post-Taliban banking law. As the leader of the Central Bank, he was proud of the chance to help guide the country's fragile financial system in this new democratic era. A fastidious man, Fitrat wore conservative suits and wire-rimmed glasses. He tried to keep a low profile and focus on his work. Among the Afghan cabinet, he was well liked by the U.S. embassy. Eikenberry viewed him as an ally and a strong advocate for reform. The DEA's Kirk Meyer, who worked with Fitrat on his financial investigations, called him "the real deal." For an Afghan official, this was doubled-edged praise.

Any increase in esteem for Fitrat from the U.S. embassy was matched by rising suspicion from President Karzai. Karzai viewed Fitrat's letter to the banks about campaign contributions as a political attack, and he subsequently ignored repeated requests for meetings. Fitrat once complained to Earl Anthony Wayne, a deputy U.S. ambassador overseeing economic affairs, that his attempts to regulate the banks were putting him in political danger, which in Afghanistan meant real danger. "Good people are under attack in Afghanistan because they are the minority," Fitrat told him.

"While rumors continue to swirl about Governor Fitrat's future, we remain convinced that his leadership has improved the financial sector," the embassy wrote in a cable at the time. "Unfortunately, his work to uphold the law and enforce regulations may have made him a target of power banks like Kabul Bank."

Fitrat worried that the revelations about Kabul Bank's outlaw style could spark panic. A run on the bank, he felt, could devastate the nation's fragile economy. He considered resigning. The U.S. embassy had similar worries, and believed Kabul Bank's failure would "severely" undermine American goals in the country. Two days after a lengthy *Washington Post* article about Kabul Bank, Fitrat sat down at his desk and wrote President Karzai a letter.

"I, with all due respect, want to remind you that it's been several months that I've tried to consult with you about highly important and sensitive issues that the life of the banking system depends on," he wrote. In the preceding months, "tens of my requests to meet with you" were rebuffed by the palace protocol department. Now that the presidential elections were over, Fitrat noted, "it's time to make serious decisions and bring key corrections to the leadership structure of these banks. From my point of view, further delay will result in the decrease and destruction of Afghanistan's banking system."

The USAID contractors tasked with helping the Central Bank oversee the banking sector had failed to raise any warnings about Kabul Bank. Since 2003, USAID had been paying to build capacity at the Central Bank. It had awarded a four-year, $79 million contract to BearingPoint for the work in 2005, followed by a five-year deal for $92 million with Deloitte in August 2009, after Deloitte purchased BearingPoint's public services business. Many of the same advisers stayed on. In that period, there were "several opportunities to learn about fraudulent activities at Kabul Bank," a USAID inspector general's report would later conclude. But despite the exorbitant contracts, nobody looked very closely. Some BearingPoint advisers had received death threats, and the company banned its staff from visiting the banks they were hired to inspect. The USAID banking staff fell into turf war squabbles with the Treasury attaché's office—the same type of backstabbing so common whenever different slices of the American government attempted to work together in Afghanistan. The Deloitte advisers and the Treasury team rarely cooperated, or even spoke. The woman who ran USAID's Economic Growth and Governance initiative in Kabul wouldn't let Stuart Jones, the Treasury attaché, talk to her staff at the Central Bank. When he finally arranged a meeting, she made sure it took place on the USAID side of the embassy compound, marking her territory.

One Treasury Department official who looked at Kabul Bank's balance sheet in the spring of 2010 immediately noticed fewer than 1 percent nonperforming loans among the more than $1 billion issued, whereas it was common for banks in the developing world to have problems with as much as 10 or 15 percent of their loans. The official had worked in bank compliance for decades. Even the best banks made loans that did not get paid back on time. The official recalled thinking, "This can't be true." But when he raised his concerns, the adviser responded, "We don't work for the U.S. We work for Deloitte."

"I knew right then there was a major problem in the loan portfolio, and those guys never spoke to me again about that kind of issue," the official said. "That was a bellwether right there."

Even some of Mahmood Karzai's business partners were starting to get worried about the Kabul Bank's health. That's where the proceeds from their gated city in Kandahar were being held. Abdullah Nadi, the developer living in Virginia who'd been one of the original Aino Mena partners, wrote an e-mail to Mahmood urging him to move their money elsewhere.

"Kabul Bank as the largest bank in Afghanistan with over 4000 employees and branches in 34 provinces has many enemies," Mahmood wrote back. "IMF and the [Central Bank] are watching and monitoring Kabul Bank closely because it hold over 600M USD in deposits from Afghans, all report indicates that the Kabul Bank is doing good."

Mahmood told Nadi he could trust such respected international institutions.

"We shall not," he concluded, "believe unofficial sources and rummers [*sic*]."

On August 5, 2010, Abdul Qadir Fitrat was attending a U.S. Department of Defense–sponsored conference at Grosvenor House, a complex of two glistening forty-five-story towers that rose seven hundred feet above the Dubai Marina and were striped with colored lights that shimmered at night on the slack water. The purpose of the conference was to discuss establishing a consortium of Afghan banks that would cooperate on mobile banking and whose ATMs would be linked. After lunch on the second day, Fitrat departed to the Dubai Mall to show his young son its indoor aquarium.

They were on a shuttle bus back to his hotel when his cell phone rang. It was Mike Pisa, the U.S. embassy's new acting Treasury attaché, and he sounded worried.

"Mr. Fitrat, we have received news that Kabul Bank's shareholders have split into two groups," Fitrat recalled Pisa saying.

Pisa explained what the embassy knew about the crisis at Kabul Bank. Money was leaving the country. The shareholders were at one another's throats. The bank's assets were dissolving. Its collapse appeared imminent.

The embassy had learned this information largely from the work of Kirk Meyer and his team at the Afghan Threat Finance Cell. During his investigations into the New Ansari *hawala* business, his attempts to understand why millions of dollars in cash were leaving on daily airline flights to Dubai, and the work to arrest the palace aide Mohammed Zia Salehi, Meyer had become well known among Afghanistan's business elite. He would meet businessmen for dinners in their gaudy

Kabul homes, with their cedar-paneled living rooms and basement liquor cabinets, or in Dubai high-rises, and he picked up much of the gossip about new deals and shattered alliances. In his conversations, he'd heard increasingly troubling things about the *hawala* called Shaheen Exchange and its partner business, Kabul Bank. Part of what he learned came from a parallel interest of Meyer's: President Karzai's brother, Mahmood.

Since Mahmood held U.S. citizenship, he was subject to American financial laws and was thus an easier target for arrest and prosecution than the average corrupt Afghan businessman. Mahmood had come to the attention of Meyer's team in part because Haji Mohammad Jan, one of their targets at New Ansari, was a part owner of Aino Mena. But going after Mahmood was particularly dangerous, given the political sensitivities. If President Karzai had threatened sending in Afghan troops to free one of his mid-level aides, the prospect of how he would respond to the arrest of his brother was daunting.

As part of the investigation, Meyer and his team wanted to conduct a covert operation against Mahmood and catch him in the act of committing a financial crime. For such a prominent and politically connected figure, it was necessary to run the decision through a high-level interagency review. The group in charge was known as a Special Activities Review Committee, or SARC, and consisted of representatives from the Department of Justice, the State Department, Treasury, and others. The rough plan was to send an undercover agent posing as a businessman looking to start a venture in Afghanistan. The man's invented company would have a website documenting its fake credentials. Mahmood would eventually, the investigators hoped, ask for a bribe from that person as they worked out the deal. And then he would be caught. One day in July 2010, Calestino was in Charlottesville, Virginia, attending a threat finance conference, when his cell phone rang. Kirk Meyer was calling from Kabul.

"Eikenberry just signed the SARC," Meyer told him.

After the Obama administration authorized the investigation into Mahmood, Meyer's team gathered information that was shared with federal prosecutors in the U.S. Attorney's Office for the Southern District of New York, who were also on the case. They began looking into a range of allegations against Mahmood, including tax evasion, racketeering, and extortion, as part of a possible indictment.

Close to midnight one evening, after it began appearing in the newspapers that Mahmood could face a grand jury indictment, Kirk Meyer's cell phone rang. He was in his embassy apartment, standing next to his bed, as he held the phone to his ear.

"This is Mahmood," the caller said.

"Okay," Meyer replied warily.

"Kirk, is there anything you really want?" Mahmood asked.

"No," Meyer replied.

"Okay," Mahmood said, and hung up.

What Kirk Meyer really wanted was information about Mahmood's business life, a record that was long and somewhat checkered. As an entrepreneur, both in the United States and in Afghanistan, Mahmood had some successes, such as the Kandahar gated community, but other projects had failed or become embroiled in scandal. Often the reality wouldn't live up to his outsized visions. Some of his restaurants in the States flourished but others encountered various legal problems over the years from customers, suppliers, and employees. He had been sued for unpaid invoices by a company that washed the linens at one of his restaurants and for a few thousands dollars' worth of unpaid soda bills at another. A real estate company had sued him for breach of contract over an agreement to sell two of his Baltimore properties that went sour. At least two women who'd fallen in his parking lots and injured themselves had sued him. His restaurant in San Francisco, on a street with a view down to the Golden Gate Bridge, had to close in 2007 after a boulder crashed through the kitchen during a landslide on Telegraph Hill.

In 2000, Mahmood got into a legal dispute with one of his dishwashers, Juan Carlos Yeh Gutierrez, who worked at Helmand Restaurant in San Francisco, which Mahmood had opened in 1989. Gutierrez and other employees regularly worked seven days a week without receiving overtime pay. Mahmood contended that there was an understanding that Gutierrez's salary of $350 per week included overtime, but the California labor commissioner's office disagreed. Mahmood did not record the hours worked by Gutierrez or other employees, paid them in cash, and required them to put in seven-day weeks regularly for more than a year, in violation of state law. Mahmood, who was ordered to pay Gutierrez $25,000, argued that Gutierrez had threatened potential witnesses in the case, but the labor commissioner's office found that this claim was "a mere smoke screen to divert attention" from his "failure to pay the plaintiff and other employees full wages earned."

One of his more serious run-ins with the American legal system came three years later, after Mahmood had opened the Tampico Mexican Grill on North Charles Street in Baltimore, just four blocks north of Qayum's restaurant the Helmand. The $450,000 needed to open the grill came from Mahmood himself as well as his brother-in-law, Zaki Royan, and Ali A. Tokhi, who had worked with Mahmood in the San Francisco restaurant and would become a manager at Tampico.

One of the bartenders, Robie Allen Thomas, soon began complaining about sexual harassment from Tokhi. She accused him of regularly rubbing up against her, looking down her shirt, calling her stupid, speculating that she must be from "Africa or Haiti" because of her skin color (although she was Native American), and laughing at her, "especially," she said, "when he sees me about to cry.

"I've asked him constantly to not talk to me like dirt or humiliate me," she wrote.

One night in August 2003, Tokhi followed Thomas out to the parking lot after her shift. In her handwritten account, she said that Tokhi had kept asking to walk her to her car, "pushing me to comply.

"He grabbed me by my right arm and leading me towards some building stair steps," she wrote. "He pulled me towards him . . . took his other hand and felt me up. He felt my breast and then ran his hand . . . down to my crotch area touching me down there."

Thomas said she was able to extricate herself from Tokhi, rush to her car, and speed off "while he was staring at me through my car window."

Thomas told the Baltimore City Circuit Court that she had already mentioned Tokhi's harassment to Mahmood even before the incident in the parking lot, something he would deny. She said Mahmood had never disciplined Tokhi but had, instead, reduced her bartending hours. When Thomas found a lawyer and complained in writing to Mahmood about Tokhi's attack, Mahmood fired her.

Thomas responded by filing criminal charges against Tokhi, who was convicted of assault. She also sued Mahmood for sex discrimination, retaliation, and civil rights violations.

Mahmood denied to the court that Thomas had complained to him about sexual harassment and said she had been fired for a different reason. Mahmood stated that he and Thomas had worked together on developing the restaurant's menu and other tasks. "At the beginning I was impressed, but she became quite problematic," he said. "She was not getting along with people. She was bossing everybody around, and she would not cooperate and she was very demanding and making noise and just the behavior was very bad for our restaurant." He said he had reduced her hours, and when the harassment issue surfaced, "I just fired her."

While these allegations were playing out in court—one of the chefs had also sued Mahmood and Tokhi for harassment—Mahmood decided to sell the Tampico Mexican Grill, which was losing money from the start. He created a new limited liability company and used the remaining assets of the Mexican restaurant to open a French restaurant called Limoges Gourmet Bistro in the spring of 2005. That restaurant didn't fare much better, and less than a year later Mahmood sold it to Sam's Italian Restaurant for $300,000.

Thomas and her lawyer accused Mahmood of "fraudulent conveyance," arguing that he had sold the Mexican restaurant to place its assets out of her reach. The court ruled in favor of Mahmood. Thomas also lost the battery and discrimination arguments, but she prevailed on her civil rights claim, and in December 2007 a judge ordered Mahmood to pay $14,500.

The Tampico Mexican Grill was open for just eighteen months and was, in Mahmood's words, "a complete disaster."

The American restaurants became a sideline to Mahmood's primary focus on building his businesses in Afghanistan. After Aino Mena, he swung his attention to an aging state-run cement factory in the hills of northern Baghlan Province. Mahmood believed the Soviet-era relic, known as the Ghori Cement Factory, could be overhauled to serve Afghanistan's wartime economy. With the United States pumping more money each year into building roads, schools, clinics, and military bases, Mahmood expected that demand for construction materials would soar. Ghori was the country's only functional cement plant, and as shabby as it was, it was set amid rich deposits of limestone and clay—ingredients needed to make concrete—and near four coal mines that kept the kilns burning. A paved highway led to Mazar-e-Sharif, the largest city in the north. Mahmood felt the payoff could be huge. "The cement plant was government-run on the Soviet model. It wasn't producing any cement. It was a robbery, just like other government-owned projects. It was a filthy dump, with no sewage," Mahmood recalled. "I really had an idea of how to bring the country forward."

Mahmood's plans were characteristically outsized. He envisioned spending hundreds of millions of dollars to renovate the existing plant, finish a second portion started and abandoned by the Soviets, and build a third plant from scratch that alone would be capable of producing four thousand tons per day, or twenty-five times the current output. The company would also renovate the four neighboring coal mines and build two new power plants to run everything. On the campus for the employees there would be clinics and kindergartens and parks. Mahmood recruited many of the country's most prominent and politically connected business-men, including several with U.S. citizenship, to partner on the Afghan Investment Company venture. The initial arrangement was to have fifty businessmen invest $500,000 to reach the $25 million Mahmood felt was needed to begin. Sherkhan Farnood and Khalil Ferozi, who ran Kabul Bank, were involved, as was Haseen Fahim, the vice president's brother. Mahmood, along with several others, took loans from Kabul Bank to finance their shares, rather than putting up their own money.

Mahmood pestered the Ministry of Mines and Petroleum and the U.S. embassy to help push through his project. He "clearly has great expecta-tions for the AIC," the embassy wrote back to Washington in early 2006. He had even talked about "possible plans for the company to go public in the future."

But he was having trouble executing the sale. These types of insider deals—a state-run plant being sold to the president's brother—didn't look particularly ethical, and the minister of mines, Mir Mohammed Sediq, was against it. The U.S. embassy also found the negotiations "worrisome," writing that "other investors without his family connec-tions would likely not be as successful. This bodes poorly for the future."

Not long after this, however, the situation was resolved in Mahmood's favor. In March 2006, President Karzai fired the minister of mines, and the deputy, Mohammad Ibrahim Adel, was appointed to take his place. Adel moved forward on the sale of the Ghori Cement Plant. While there was a bidding process, the other companies believed that the minister put up unrealistic obstacles. In the final days of bidding, Adel informed them that they needed to present $25 million in cash as a guaranty. One of the bidders, Nasir Khisrow Parsi, told me he complained to the minister about the last-minute requirement. "In a country like Afghanistan, a per-son cannot carry even $100,000 from one place to another," he said. But Mahmood's business partners didn't have a problem cobbling together $25 million: they had Kabul Bank. Ministry staff members watched as gunmen entered the ministry carrying a cardboard box filled with cash and placed it on the minister's desk. One deputy minister worried that the gunmen were Taliban coming to kill the minister.

Mahmood's company won the right to rehabilitate and expand the fac-tory. But in the end, it wouldn't turn out as he'd hoped. The costs were too high for many of the renovations. Demand was filled by cheaper cement from Pakistan. The output at the Ghori Cement Factory remained

*Workers stack bags of cement at Mahmood Karzai's Ghori Cement Factory,
in northern Afghanistan.*

as anemic as ever. The AIC partners started moving their money out of
the cement plant and into Dubai real estate. "They didn't even pay the
salaries," Abdul Ghafar Dawi, one of the AIC investors, told me. "When
I saw that everybody was moving his money to Dubai, I resigned."

When I asked Adel, the minister, about the bidding, he mildly defended
the process but acknowledged that he had since changed his procedures.
"It was unusual," he said. "It was our first bidding."

If it succeeded at anything, Mahood's cement factory showed the value of
Kabul Bank. For a small group of Afghan entrepreneurs, it was like having a pool of free money to start the businesses of their choosing. Such a
business, in a country with so much to rebuild, was enticing. Mahmood
owned a small share of the bank. But he wanted more. The fact that his
relationship with the bank's chairman, Sherkhan Farnood, continued to
deteriorate only increased his appetite. Mahmood disagreed with many
of Farnood's investment choices as well as his authoritarian style. Every
few weeks, Mahmood would call Fitrat, the Central Bank governor, to
complain about Farnood's behavior, especially how he made unilateral
decisions and never took input from other shareholders. Mahmood didn't
like it that Farnood had opened a luxurious office in Dubai for Pamir

Airways, his commercial airline, when Mahmood felt the office should be in Kabul. He felt that a Kabul Bank call center should also be relocated. Farnood ignored some of Mahmood's proposals, such as starting an insurance company and establishing a pension fund for employees. "Most of the time Mahmood said, 'Farnood is very stupid. He doesn't know how to do business,'" Fitrat recalled. Farnood had also been spending more time outside of Kabul, leaving his chief executive, Khalil Ferozi, in charge. The real issues ran deeper: the shareholders wanted control of a vastly lucrative bank to finance any number of business ventures. Ferozi and Mahmood, along with the vice president's brother, had discussed taking over the bank.

Through their various contacts in the Afghan businessworld, Meyer's investigators had learned about the growing rift within the top ranks of Kabul Bank, including fights that got so heated that Farnood had hurled a teacup at another shareholder's head. Calestino suggested to Meyer that they send a DEA agent to Dubai to meet with Farnood, to see if he was disgruntled enough about the situation to share information with the Americans. "It was sort of like the priest showing up at your house for confession; you didn't even need to go to the church," one team member put it.

Farnood, it turned out, was so angry about the brewing coup d'etat at Kabul Bank that he was ready to list, in graphic detail, all his sins. After the initial meeting in Dubai, Meyer and Calestino realized that the Kabul Bank problem was going to dwarf the scandal they had uncovered at New Ansari. They summoned Farnood to Kabul and over the course of dozens meetings, Farnood described the inner workings of what amounted to a bank heist. At first, those meetings took place in the polished calm of the Serena Hotel. Soon, however, the Afghan monitors who worked with Meyer and wiretapped calls throughout the Afghan business and political elite tipped him off to the fact that Farnood's rivals within the bank were following his movements, and had the license plate number of the SUV that Meyer and Calestino drove to the hotel. Until then, the armored car was mostly frustrating because the wiring was shoddy and the battery would often die, forcing the two men to whip out jumper cables in the Kabul gridlock. After they learned they were under surveillance themselves, they brought Farnood to Meyer's apartment in the embassy, which they knew was not bugged.

In those meetings, Farnood provided reams of documents and bank records, spilling out details that incriminated himself and his partners, explaining what a forensic auditor later concluded: "From its very beginning, the bank was a well-concealed Ponzi scheme." Farnood was surprisingly candid about many aspects of his business, including his notorious connections. He told Meyer that before September 11, he moved money for both the Taliban and al-Qaeda. He described how he had brought on Mahmood Karzai and Haseen Fahim to give him political cover with both Pashtun and Tajik leaders in Afghanistan and how that decision eventually backfired as they formed an alliance against him. If there was an appropriate war-zone metaphor for this soul-bearing, it might be that of the suicide bomber. In order to prevent his business partners from stealing his bank, Farnood was willing to destroy it. But why? "Every time I talked to Sherkhan and asked that question," a member of Meyer's team recalled, "he said if he's going down, he's taking everybody with him."

In a way, Farnood, with his scam, had achieved what many other reformers in Afghanistan had failed to do: seamlessly meld the old customs of Afghan culture with modern Western technology. The key to the deception was how he'd combined his *hawala* money-transfer business, Shaheen Exchange, with Kabul Bank. Farnood would move money between these two institutions, which allowed him to keep two sets of books. Money would often be sent—by wire transfer or in stacks of cash on a Pamir Airways flight—to Dubai, where the *hawala* would provide it to the ultimate recipient. In the records of the bank, a loan would be attributed to one name, while the Shaheen records would indicate the true recipient. "Shaheen Exchange was the front for the insider loans," one former senior official who worked at the bank for several years told me. "All the insider loans were given in different names, and the loan proceeds were credited to Shaheen Exchange. From that account the funds were either transferred or withdrawn."

Farnood and Ferozi would give millions of dollars to people of their choosing: business partners, shareholders, politicians, friends. This was illegal for several reasons. There were rules for "related party" lending, giving money to owners or employees of the bank, which were disregarded. The size of the loans also exceeded the legal limits. Another problem was that Kabul Bank had no expectation that these loans would be paid back. In essence, they were gifts.

To mask their loans, the bankers would break them up into smaller pieces so that they wouldn't attract attention or violate the legal lending limit. A large loan intended for one person would be issued in several parts in the name of various fictitious companies, often named after the recipient's relatives, employees, servants, or bank bodyguards. The bank's loan portfolio had grown from about $100 million in 2006 to more than $900 million by the time Farnood sat down with Meyer. In its official filings, Kabul Bank claimed that 80 percent of its income came from interest payments on these loans. In fact, the bank had collected hardly any interest and had become insolvent within a year of its inception. The challenge, as this illicit lending increased, was to find ways to mask the recipients of the money and give the impression the loans were being paid back. This required some invention. When the business licenses of these front companies would expire, after a year, the credit department would dip into the bank's deposits to issue a new, larger loan, to create the appearance of repayment. For example, a $1 million loan that went unpaid would be followed by a $1.5 million loan—to a new fake company— to give the appearance that the initial loan had been paid off with interest. This operation could work only with a growing pool of deposits to draw from, which Farnood had, thanks to his popular lottery drawings, as well as the support for Kabul Bank from the U.S. government and foreign donors.

To help facilitate the scam, the bank's credit department operated like an arts-and-crafts class. After the money had been given out, the staff would create a loan file for the fictitious firms, with business licenses, articles of association, tax returns, and business plans. Several auditing firms—such as Best Solutions Accounting, Naweed Sahar Accounting, and Oriental Consultants, some of which were run by people with family relationships to the Kabul Bank leadership—provided audited financial statements for the front companies. Sometimes their work would get sloppy. Investigators looking back on the bank's operations found that financial statements for different companies were often almost identical; in other cases, the paperwork didn't match the company. On one loan file, the credit appraisal claimed that the company's industry was "furniture and carpets," while the supporting invoices showed purchases of cement, steel, and wood. The same photographs of construction materials, intended to portray a functioning company that was actually making a product, were used in several loan files. When investigators inspected the bank's premises, they found 114 rubber stamps in the names of fake companies—Jamal Naser Trading, Abdul Mahmood Trading—used to make loan applications look official. The bank records would show that Mahmood Karzai had taken out $22.2 million. This had been recorded as ten separate loans under names such as Abdul Rahim, Dawood, and Sultan Mohammad Hafizullah LTC.

"I've seen some really, really bad banks, but I'd never seen one with so much fraud," Kat Woolford, an International Monetary Fund official who worked in Kabul, told me. "These guys were crooks, real honest to God crooks. I've never seen anything like it."

Meyer and Calestino laid out their findings to Ambassador Eikenberry. Once they understood how the bank operated, and how severely it had been looted, they became convinced that it could not survive. The embassy notified Fitrat and explained the gravity of the situation. Fitrat went to President Karzai and told him that he needed to demand the resignations of the Kabul Bank leadership and have the government seize control of its operations. Karzai's government would then have to try to get the shareholders, including his brother, to pay back nearly $1 billion in loans. Otherwise, the country's financial system would be on the brink of collapse.

9

CLOSE COUSINS

FARID KARZAI WAS TALL AND HANDSOME, a young man with thick, dark hair and an open, intelligent face that showed a clear resemblance to President Karzai and his brothers. But those were the "Big Karzais," Farid told me the first time I met him, and he was not one of them. "In Afghanistan, someone could be your cousin, but that doesn't mean they'll stand by you," he said. "He might do whatever it takes to destroy you."

This wasn't hyperbole. The history of Afghanistan reads as one convoluted backstabbing family treachery after another. For generations, rulers have reached the throne by vanquishing their relatives, and when they fell it was often at the hands of their own kin. The empire that began in the late eighteenth century with Ahmad Shah Durrani and marked the founding of modern Afghanistan spawned a multigenerational dynastic competition among a small circle of relatives and descendants, all grasping for control. Durrani's son Timur Shah succeeded him on the throne only after putting down a revolt that supported his brother and executing its leaders. When Timur Shah died, his many sons carried on the fight among themselves. As Afghan historian Thomas Barfield wrote, "Each contender waited for an opportunity to betray his rivals, and at least a half dozen proclaimed themselves king at one time or another. They fought and replaced each other at such a dizzying pace that it was hard to keep track of even the successful plots, coups, and murders that brought three rulers to power, let alone the more numerous ones that failed and left their perpetrators blinded, exiled, or dead." In Pashto, "cousin" and "enemy" are the same word.

One of the first things foreigners tend to learn about Afghanistan is the concept of Pashtunwali, the tribal code of conduct that makes the

Pashtun such an exotic specimen to outsiders. It includes concepts like extreme hospitality: the insistence on offering food and shelter to anyone who arrives at your door, even a hated rival. It calls for loyalty, faith, courage, and the "protection" of women. Yet I found that the closer one looked, the harder it was to see these customs in daily life. They seemed to be characteristics that Pashtuns liked to remark about themselves collectively but did not bother practicing individually. One of the more intriguing, and visible, of the Pashtun principles, however, was the celebration of revenge. It was known as *badal*, and it was necessary whenever one's honor and reputation were called into question. "If René Descartes had been a Pashtun," one of President Karzai's former advisers told me, "he would have said, 'I have enemies, therefore I am.'"

This tradition had surprisingly tangible consequences throughout the war. The U.S. military was constantly forced to sort through whether some act of violence had been motivated by the insurgency or the result of blood feuds within families and tribes. Afghans realized the limits of American understanding about their culture and could exploit this ignorance. It wasn't uncommon to hear stories of how Afghans fed faulty intelligence to the U.S. military so they would take out "Taliban" targets that later turned out to be family rivals. American soldiers also had to navigate delicate negotiations over family honor. When they killed civilians or damaged property, soldiers would decide on condolence payments in money or livestock so that order was restored and wider tribal revenge averted. Some of the customs could make Americans feel very far from home. After one particularly heinous crime, when a U.S. soldier massacred several Afghan civilians, the commanding general called Qayum Karzai, the president's elder brother, and asked what Afghans would do to settle such an enormous debt. "Well, you can't do what the Afghans would do," Qayum told the general. "Because we would give them a daughter."

I met Farid Karzai when he was on the run, a frightened twenty-year-old caught in one of these family feuds. There were lots of pressures on the Karzais from the outside: the president's fights with the Obama administration, the investigations into Ahmed Wali and Mahmood, the threats from the Taliban. But there were also internal stresses that were harder to unravel. One thread that kept emerging was a dispute that reached back decades yet still appeared to influence the politics of Kandahar and the wider war. I hoped Farid, a minor character in the vast drama of Karzai relatives, could help me understand this backstory and explain the rivalries that were pulling the family apart. He agreed to meet me at the Continental Guest House, one of the few places in Kandahar, outside of military bases, where foreigners could stay.

The hotel was pretty grim. If you spent enough time there, you could hear all sorts of violence outside: car bombs, mortar blasts, gunfire. Breakfasts were particularly depressing, with muttering clusters of Indian engineers or Pakistani agronomists eating stale bread and swirling their Nescafé, seemingly wondering if their NATO seed-distribution contracts or road-building projects could possibly be worth the risk of living here. Half the time the power would be out. The sign on the gate showed a picture of a pistol, but it had been misspelled in Pashto so that instead of "No Weapons" it read, "No Grace."

We sat at a white plastic table in the back garden under a hot morning sun. Farid was wearing a brown *shalwar kameez* and held a string of black prayer beads. He spoke in a high-pitched, nervous way. As we talked, I tallied fourteen gunshots in the background before I lost count.

"I believe there is a great threat to my life," Farid said. He was not sure if he should have come to meet me, but his desire to explain his predicament won out. "I am taking some security precautions. I cannot distinguish between the Taliban and the government. After what happened to my family, I'm scared of them both."

Farid told me a bit about himself. He had moved out of his home village of Karz and was living in hiding with his mother, Farida, and his youngest sister, Sonia, in a shabby apartment in Kandahar City. He was broke. While the other Karzais traveled in armored Land Cruisers and lived in fortified mansions, he got around Kandahar hitching rides in rickshaw taxis. And with his sixth-grade education, finding work was difficult. In an attempt to raise money for his wedding, he bought a tiny tarp-covered plywood stall in the outdoor market known as Charsu, or "Four Directions," to sell brightly colored children's clothes imported from India. The market was a claustrophobic warren that smelled of boiling vats of oil and platters of herring-sized fish left out in the sun. You could buy cheap plastic necklaces or bags of okra or a small green parrot from a rickety wooden cage. Farid disliked the work. The environment was oppressive, and he wasn't making much money. In an average day, he would earn four dollars.

But his more pressing concern was his safety. Both his father and his brother had recently been murdered, leaving him the family's lone surviving male. Explaining their deaths required a story that started quite a ways back. But it was a story Farid was desperate to tell.

*Farid Karzai in the alley leading to his house
in the village of Karz*

"Everyone knows what happened to my family," he said. "And everyone knows it is just a matter of time before somebody comes for me."

The origins of Farid's story go back to the late 1970s, before he was born. After Hamid Karzai graduated from high school in Kabul, his family sent him to study in India. The decision was a bit spontaneous, his relatives recalled. Hamid had a cousin, Masoom Kandahari, in medical school in New Delhi. Masoom remembers visiting Hamid's house and Hamid's mother, Durkho, asking how he liked his studies abroad. Masoom, who would go on to be a hematologist in Arlington, Virginia, told his aunt he enjoyed medicine but the weather was unbearably hot and the food too spicy.

"Then my aunt said, casually, 'Hamid's not doing anything. Why don't you take him with you?'" Masoom remembered.

Hamid traveled with his cousin to Delhi, with the intention of studying medicine as well, but after a few months he moved to the northern town of Shimla, an old British garrison post in the mountains, where he preferred the cooler weather. His interest in medicine soon flagged—he'd always had trouble in science courses while in high school in Kabul—and when he enrolled at Himachal Pradesh University, he took classes in English and political science.

As a teenager in the 1970s, Hamid had adopted a bit of the hippie style popular even in Afghanistan. His sister recalled how she would sew flowers onto his bell-bottom jeans. At university, he liked to affect the style of what the British writer William Dalrymple described as a "bookish fop," wearing a suit and carrying a sun umbrella as he walked to the mall. Hamid lived in a large Georgian cottage in Summer Hill, just west of the town, an area that appealed to Hamid because it was near where Mahatma Gandhi stayed on his visits to Shimla.

The language was difficult for him in the beginning, and he failed his first-term English course. He studied diligently and worked with an Anglo-Indian tutor, who helped him develop his British-accented English. He soon adopted "the old-fashioned English of newspapers in the subcontinent, addressing women as 'ma'am' and using expressions such as 'turning turtle' and 'miscreants,'" the journalist Christina Lamb has written. Hamid also developed a fascination with British colonial history and literature. In Shimla, he recalled, "there was a lovely cinema called the Regal by the ice-skating rink. Fridays I would go and see Peter O'Toole movies . . . *Goodbye, Mr. Chips* and *Man of La Mancha*." He read Thomas Hardy and Alfred, Lord Tennyson, Percy Bysshe Shelley and George Eliot's *The Mill on the Floss*. He seemed uninterested in the usual youthful rebellions.

Another cousin, Hashim Karzai, who was studying at Punjab University at the time, often came to visit. "The guy did not have any habit of anything," Hashim recalled. "No smoking, no drinking. Nothing. That really bothered me. I was smoking back then. He would sit in the window. It was very cold in the summer. He would say, 'Hashim, is that your last cigarette? You swear you're not going to smoke anymore?' And I'd say, 'Yes.' And he'd close the window."

Hamid lived simply. When his elder brother, Mahmood, would send money from the United States, Hamid would spend it the first few days by giving it away and helping to feed others.

"Then he would eat salad or boiled eggs," Mahmood said.

A friend, Ezzat Wasifi, recalled how boys from Kandahar who visited Shimla would rib Hamid about his formal, cautious nature. He recalled one episode where they kept pushing Hamid to show them a Shimla brothel until he shouted back at them in embarrassment and demanded that they walk on the other side of the street. "Hamid said, 'You guys are rascals, I'm not going to walk with you,'" Wasifi remembered.

While his Afghan friends in India don't remember him as particularly active in protests or gatherings, Hamid began to develop his political consciousness while at university. He started paying closer attention to the changes in Afghanistan as communism, and the opposition to it, began to take hold. Hamid had grown up in Kandahar and Kabul during the last peaceful years of the reign of King Zahir Shah, before the Soviet invasion and subsequent civil wars scattered his family into exile. The family business had always been politics, but initially Hamid wasn't sure if that was the path for him. His grandfather Khair Mohammad Khan had been a military man; he had served as a brigadier in the Afghan army. He lost a hand and earned a medal for bravery fighting the British in the Third Anglo-Afghan War, in 1919. He was also a Popalzai tribal leader and became an adviser to Sardar Mohammad Hashim Khan, who served as prime minister from 1929 to 1946. Khair Mohammad was a devout Muslim known for his recitations of the Koran. A family friend of the Karzais' recalled that for a period, one of Khair Mohammad's roles in the palace was to entertain the king, telling jokes or stories or offering religious interpretations. His title in the king's court translated as "jubilant companion." At other times, he also served as the number two official in the Interior Ministry and as a deputy to the prime minister. He was known to friends and family as Moin Khairo Jan, *moin* being the word for "deputy."

Hamid's father, Abdul Ahad Karzai, was Khairo Jan's second oldest son, born in 1925 in the village of Karz. As a younger man, he held a series of local government posts around Kandahar. One of the first was in the municipal office that regulated commodities such as sugar, oil, and gasoline, products imported to Afghanistan whose prices could be manipulated by unfair market practices. He was later appointed *hakim*, or chief, of a small village in Kandahar. Slender and balding, with a trim mustache and no beard, Abdul Ahad was described by his friends as quiet, thoughtful, discreet, wise, and cautious in his political strategies. As his influence grew, he was chosen as district governor in two parts of Kandahar that would become notorious for their Taliban violence during the American war: Arghandab, the fertile river valley of lush pomegranate orchards to the north of the city, and Panjwayi, the farmlands to the southwest.

Abdul Ahad and his other male siblings had inherited land from their father in Kandahar, as much as thousands of acres of farmland in Karz and elsewhere in Kandahar. But the Karzais were not the wealthiest landowners or the most powerful merchants. They had a reputation as educated government bureaucrats whose power derived from their political, rather than economic, influence. Abdul Ahad had inherited the leadership of the Popalzai tribe, and he was also an ally of the king, who ruled for four decades until he was overthrown by his cousin in 1973.

"In those days, even a low-level government position afforded more prestige than having thousands of acres of land," said Sardar Roshan, who was close with the family and went on to serve as Afghanistan's ambassador to Pakistan. "People wouldn't trade a government position for land. No matter how poor or rich, if you were in government, you'd be respected, you'd be special, you would feel important. Abdul Ahad's political weight was due to his close relation to the royal family."

The government positions and affiliation with the king added credibility and influence within their tribe. But the king's authority didn't impinge very heavily on his rural subjects, so local leaders such as Abdul Ahad had great autonomy to solve the issues of their tribesmen.

He was a conduit for patronage passed down from the royal palace and also saddled with the responsibility of helping the impoverished farmers of his tribe. The job of tribal leader had many duties: judge, counselor, headhunter, benefactor. Villagers from all over southern Afghanistan would come to his house with their problems. These could be a plea for a new canal or irrigation system; a verdict on which family owned a plot of land or which son had the rights to a daughter's hand in marriage; a request to free a relative from jail or to find a job. It was a leadership style followed a generation later by his sons Ahmed Wali in Kandahar and Hamid in the palace. Abdul Ahad's children remembered that sometimes there would be so many people waiting to see their father that they would spill out of the guesthouse and line up along the walls in the spacious courtyard. If they had come from far-off villages, they would often sleep there, too. "He couldn't always afford to give them all food, because settling disputes with them would take weeks and months," his son Qayum said.

This job required endless patience for listening to complaints and an orientation toward consensus and compromise. Poverty was a fact of life in Kandahar. Most people were peasant farmers whose lives depended on the vicissitudes of drought and harvest. Abdul Ahad, in his tribal rulings, made distinctions, as the rest of the villagers did, between crimes of necessity and those of predation. He allowed flexibility according to the level of need of his tribesmen. "I remember as children, we used to define the difference between good thieves and bad thieves," Qayum recalled. "There were stories of a good thief who went to rob a bus, and when he saw that the bus would be filled with children, women, older men, he would apologize for trying to steal, and leave. A bad thief, on the other hand, would have stolen from the children and the older men and women. That is a man who has no limits. We used to dance when the bad guy was caught. But we would be sad if the good thief was caught."

Karz was a small village—fewer than one thousand people—and the Karzais lived in a home clustered closely with those of several other relatives. The children all remember their youth as idyllic, spending their days outside playing all manner of games: baseball with a ball fashioned from rolled-up cloth, marbles, cards, chess. They played a game called "carrom," popular in India, that uses a square board and is similar to billiards, and a version of bocce but with stones. They put up a makeshift net on the dining room table to play Ping-Pong. For their barefoot soccer games, they used a tennis ball. In the sweltering Kandahar summers, they would swim in the silty water of the creek that ran through the grape fields near their house. They would often bicycle miles from home for picnics. Each night, between the early evening prayers when the sun was still up, and the late evening prayers when the sun had set, there was an hour of downtime, when the villagers congregated outside to talk about the day's happenings. The kids were free to run around in the evenings without fear for their safety. The only dangers came at night, when they'd fall asleep to their mother's warnings to watch out for scorpions.

"The whole town was like your own house," Qayum's sister, Fawzia, recalled. "It was so safe and secure."

In those first years, their lifestyle was not lavish. When I asked Qayum what he remembered about his childhood village, the first thing he said was: "I remember a scarcity of food." He recalled how his father would give him one pair of shoes per year. On his walks to elementary school, he didn't want to get them dirty, so he would put them in a cloth sack and walk barefoot, then put them back on for class.

"It was a very humble life," Qayum said. "But it was peaceful."

Abdul Ahad's first wife, Durkho, was also from a wealthy family in the Popalzai tribe but grew up in Kabul. She was known as a devoutly religious woman, and one with a penetrating intelligence. Hamid has written that his mother fasted often and that he learned from her "a great deal about high moral standards." Neighbors spoke of her generosity: she donated food and cooking oil to other families in Karz. She gave birth to the first five of the Karzai siblings—Abdul Ahmed, Qayum, Mahmood, Fawzia, and Hamid. Several people close to the family remarked on the special bond she had with her youngest.

"She was with Hamid all the time," her daughter, Fawzia, recalled. "She really loved Hamid."

She would not live to see Hamid move into the presidential palace—she died in 1999 from cancer—but she had predicted that the palace was where he would end up. "Everybody in the family heard her say that he will be the president of Afghanistan," Fawzia said. "She would tell that to everybody."

Shortly after Hamid was born, Abdul Ahad took a second wife, Nazo, the daughter of a farmer from the Babur tribe who lived in the Arghandab Valley, where he served as district chief. Multiple wives were common in Afghanistan then, as they still are. But according to some accounts, Hamid's mother was against Abdul Ahad marrying Nazo, and it left lasting strains on their relationship even though they never divorced. Hamid was the last child of the first marriage, before his half brothers Ahmed Wali, Shah Wali, and Abdul Wali were born. As author Bette Dam has written, "Abdul Ahad Karzai never really bonded with his son Hamid."

Hamid was a bit of an unusual child. He would play games and sports with his siblings, but he was also more bookish and introverted. Where his elder brother Mahmood would be the ringleader of many little adventures and schemes with the neighborhood kids, Hamid had other solitary pursuits. He described himself as "quiet," usually spending time with a "small circle of friends." As an older boy, he liked to ride his horse and play guitar. He listened to the radio for news of the world. As Khalid Pashtun, a Kandahari who knew the Karzais in their youth and later became a parliamentarian, described it: "He was not normal, from the very beginning."

Ezzat Wasifi, another Kandahari from a rival tribe, believed that Hamid's aloofness stemmed from a strained relationship with Abdul Ahad, particularly after he married his second wife. Hamid "was kind of downgraded," Wasifi recalled. "To be ignored, to be not loved and cherished, and to see other kids getting all the love of the father: he was totally discarded."

Some believed that Hamid kept himself apart because he was a shy, intelligent child, mature beyond his years. "He never fought with anybody," Fawzia said. "I think for some reason God gave maturity to young people like that. To prepare them for the future."

Political changes in the monarchy sometimes trickled down to the villages. Halfway through King Zahir Shah's reign, he appointed his cousin Mohammed Daoud as prime minister. Daoud developed a reputation as an economic and social reformer. He cultivated ties with the Soviet Union to attract foreign aid to build factories, airports, and roads, and to modernize the Afghan army with Soviet weapons. He tried to pit the Soviets against the United States to encourage investment from both sides. "I feel the happiest," he once said, "when I can light my American cigarettes with Soviet matches."

While Daoud was not a Communist, the economic ties with the Soviet Union increased to the point that they could even be seen in places such as Karz. One evening, a short man carrying a stick knocked on the Karzais' door. It was unusual for an outsider to show up, and the man didn't speak Pashto. He informed Abdul Ahad that the district chief now wanted the village to grow cotton, which would be purchased by the government and exported to the Soviet Union. The family hosted the stranger for dinner, and he left the house before the morning prayer the next day without saying good-bye.

The villagers were left to work out the details of the plan. The normal family arrangement would be to devote a third of one's land for grape vineyards, a third to grow wheat for bread, and a third for cash crops, such as tomatoes or eggplants or cucumbers. The Karz villagers debated the mandate for hours in a public gathering. In such settings, the traditional customs prevailed. If one person objected to a decision, the elders would consider the meeting disrupted and continue until there was unanimity. Silence was taken to mean consent. The Karz villagers agreed to devote just one-third of their fields, the cash-crop portion, to cotton. The village *malik* informed the district chief of the decision, and it was respected. Soviet airplanes soon began touching down at the Kandahar airstrip and loading up bags of cotton.

The villagers of Karz hewed to more conservative religious customs than did people in the major cities. In the late 1950s, after Prime Minister Daoud moved to relieve women from wearing head scarves, Saleh Mohammed Khan, a cousin of Abdul Ahad Karzai's, rebelled against the measure. He led a mob from the village into Kandahar City and torched the cinema, which he saw as a symbol of dangerous, un-Islamic ways. Afghan soldiers entered Karz and hauled Khan off to prison for seven years. Four decades earlier, Karz villagers had revolted over a decree from the king ordering women from every province to come sing at the prince's wedding. The angry villagers went searching for the governor of the district but found an unlucky judge instead. As the story went, they bludgeoned him to death with pumpkins. "People from Karz didn't want a woman to sing," one of the elder Karzais told me. "Karz is famous for rebellions."

The Karzai family was far less conservative. At home, Abdul Ahad stressed education and achievement with his children. He wanted them to aspire to top jobs in medicine, business, engineering, and politics. He had a tutor come to the house and teach them English from a young age—a man who later got a job in President Karzai's palace. The boys started school at about age five, but there was no school for girls in Karz, so Abdul Ahad sent Fawzia, his only daughter, to live with one of his brothers in Kabul when she was a little girl. When she was in the third grade, she returned to Kandahar and attended the Zarghuna school for girls.

Abdul Ahad's children had greater access to the outside world than most kids in Kandahar. Afghanistan was a popular destination in the 1960s and 1970s, a famous route on the hash-smoking "hippie trail." American and European travelers would hitchhike through Kandahar, and Abdul Ahad would rent them rooms. American Peace Corps volunteers taught at their boys' middle school and showed them how to play basketball. Sometimes there would be copies of American magazines, and they remember listening to the radio in stunned silence when the news of John F. Kennedy's assassination was broadcast. Abdul Ahad was also more cosmopolitan than other Afghan leaders. He wore dark suits and bow ties and drove his Land Rover or green Mercedes around Kandahar. "He was a modern leader," his nephew Hashim said. "He was not a guy with a big turban."

King Zahir Shah ended his cousin Daoud's tenure as prime minister in 1963, after a decade, and began experimenting with democracy. He had a committee draft a new constitution, and he established a new parliament. Abdul Ahad was chosen as a member of that first congress to represent Kandahar, a position that was still somewhat ceremonial. Even though it generated spirited debates, the legislature did not allow political parties, and the royal family still held all meaningful control. The next term,

Abdul Ahad was chosen as deputy speaker. To fulfill his parliamentary duties, he moved his family back to Kabul. The Karzais lived in a spacious house downtown, with a modern kitchen and a stone fireplace. There were fishponds and gardens with enough room that Hamid could ride his horse inside the walls.

In 1973, while the king was traveling in Italy, Daoud staged a coup d'état against his cousin and captured the palace. To avoid civil unrest, the king stepped down from the throne. Daoud abolished the monarchy and created the Republic of Afghanistan. His five-year rule was marked by increased repression, rising Communist sympathies, and deteriorating relations with the Soviet Union.

On the morning of April 27, 1978, while Hamid Karzai was back in Kabul on a break from school, the 4th Tank Brigade of the Afghan army rumbled up to the Arg palace. The shooting started at noon while President Daoud was hosting a cabinet meeting to discuss the arrests he'd ordered against leading Communist agitators. Hamid was visiting a friend in a house near the palace when the tanks laid siege, and he could hear the blasts of artillery shells rattling the windows. At 7:05 p.m., the music on Radio Afghanistan stopped, and air force colonel Abdul Qadir Dagarwal, speaking on behalf of the military revolutionary command of the Afghan military forces, announced that "for the first time in the history of Afghanistan an end has been put to the sultanate of the Mohammadzais." The Mohammadzai were a Pashtun tribe who had been a part of the dynastic rule of Afghanistan for the previous 230 years. The nation's new Communist leader and the chairman of its revolutionary council was Nur Mohammad Taraki, a sixty-one-year-old son of a shepherd.

As the battle intensified throughout the night, pilots loyal to the rebels flew bombing runs out of Bagram Airfield that strafed the palace. Tank rounds crashed into the French embassy nearby and destroyed the consular building. Before dawn, the last of the presidential guard had surrendered to the Marxists. Two dozen members of Daoud's family gathered unarmed in the ground-floor living room. Daoud, holding a pistol, confronted his overthrowers in a marble hallway of the building where Hamid Karzai would take office twenty-three years later. "It is said that he was holding the Afghan flag as he faced them," Hamid Karzai would recount later. Daoud was gunned down, along with most of his family, and dumped in a ditch.

The Communist takeover—known as the Saur Revolution, for the month of the Afghan calendar when the coup took place—"laid the foundation for the devastation of Afghanistan," as Hamid Karzai later put it, and also marked the moment of great fracture for the Karzai family. The Soviet invasion would come the following year and suck the United States into one of the defining Cold War battlegrounds, leading to the deaths and forced displacement of millions of Afghans. Prominent political allies of the former king, such as the Karzais, were now seen as enemies of the state. The new government also saw Abdul Ahad as a threat because it did not want him to rally opposition through his Popalzai tribal network in Kandahar.

The day after the coup, Abdul Ahad's eldest son, Abdul Ahmed, an engineer who was working at the Ministry of Mines, was told he should go home and not come back. A few months later, while driving through town, Hafizullah Amin, then the Communist leader of the country, saw Abdul Ahad walking along the sidewalk in Kabul. Amin's car stopped. He got out, grasped Abdul Ahad's hand, and greeted him warmly. But two days later, intelligence agents pulled up in a military jeep at the family's home. Abdul Ahad's daughter, Fawzia, was home, with her baby daughter, Minna. "We were scared," she recalled. "We were under so much pressure." Fawzia remembers that the spies were respectful as they escorted her father away. *We just want to ask you some questions. You should come with us. We will bring you home soon.*

Abdul Ahad Karzai was taken to Pul-e-Charkhi prison, on the eastern outskirts of Kabul. From the air, Pul-e-Charkhi is shaped like a wagon wheel. Built by the Germans from a Czech design, the prison has a circular perimeter with eight rows of cell blocks arrayed like spokes. The roofs, covered with copper sheeting, "glowed in the evening," according to one British writer, "with a bloody colour." The guards put Abdul Ahad on the second floor of Block 3, along with many other political prisoners from a cross section of the opposition. There were former senior officials of the monarchy who still supported the king; Muslim clerics and scholars who felt that left-wing propaganda undercut Islamic values; Communist opponents from rival factions; and parliament members, cabinet ministers, governors, and military officers of the former regime. All were thrust into captivity together.

Abdul Ahad's younger brother Khalil, who had been arrested in Karz, ended up in the same part of Pul-e-Charkhi. The prison, which was still under construction, had been designed to hold five thousand people. But during the time of the Karzais' imprisonment, the American embassy estimated that it held between twelve and fifteen thousand. The prisoners were crammed into cells by the dozens or hundreds; many were forced to sleep in the corridors or take turns lying down. The place stank from the shortage of toilets. Fleas and lice and other vermin ran wild. Some of the higher-level inmates lived in solitary confinement or with small groups. Abdul Ahad had two cellmates; Khalil lived with others down the hall.

Pul-e-Charkhi's commander, Sayed Abdullah, was known for brutality and sadism. He enjoyed flaunting his lists of prisoners to be tortured and killed. From their cells, the Karzais could listen to the firing squads dispatching new victims each night. Khalil would later tell his children about the nightly roundups, how the guards would choose prisoners, bind their hands, and lead them away to be shot inside the prison, then bulldozed into a pit grave. The American embassy, under chargé d'affaires J. Bruce Amstutz, complained to Taraki's government about the deplorable conditions at Pul-e-Charkhi. "At a minimum, 3,000 political prisoners had been killed since last September," Amstutz wrote in a June 25, 1979, cable. "Not a week passed but we did not learn of further political arrests. And I surmised that few households existed in Kabul that did not have a relative or friend who had been purged from his job, imprisoned or executed."

When Taraki's short reign ended, less than three months after the cable was written, the subsequent government began publishing lists of some twelve thousand names of prisoners purportedly killed in Kabul jails. An Amnesty International delegation found that in addition to the murders and disappearances, torture had been systematically practiced in the prisons, and its interviews confirmed "frequent use of electric shocks, prolonged beatings, pulling out of fingernails, burning of the skin, threatened executions and sleep deprivation." The most common torture device of the period was known as the "telephone." It was a small square machine about the size of a phone, with wires that attached to a prisoner's armpits or ears or toes or penis or tongue. The torturers doused their victims in water and pulled or cranked a handle to inflict the electric shock.

The prisoners endured smaller daily deprivations. The guards ordered them not to discuss politics. Inmates could not listen to radios, read newspapers, or write letters. One poet locked up in the prison convinced a guard to dismantle a pen and slip the inner ink tube to him inside a chunk of black bread. He wrote his poems under a blanket on scraps of cement bags.

The two Karzai brothers approached these restrictions in different ways. Abdul Ahad tried not to anger his captors and wanted to serve his time quietly. "He was trying to keep himself safe," one of his fellow inmates recalled. But Khalil was brash and bold and seemed to enjoy provoking the guards. The two had become Popalzai tribal leaders and had grown up together in Kandahar, but they struck their friends and relatives as a study in contrasts (they were half brothers, born to different mothers). Khalil was as bombastic and impulsive as Abdul Ahad was quiet and shrewd. Abdul Ahad was the distinguished politician who favored tailored suits, while Khalil wore a flamboyant Taj Mahal–brand black turban and Italian loafers. When Abdul Ahad moved to Kabul to join the parliament, Khalil stayed in Kandahar and took over some of his problem-solving duties for the tribe. Khalil had been the fifth of seven children of Khair Mohammad's fourth wife. He had left school as a teen and joined the military. In his tribal role, he had a macho swagger and a reputation as a ruthless enforcer, armed with his ever-present Kalashnikov. Noor ul-Haq Olomi, an Army general and corps commander in Kandahar during the 1980s and 1990s, described Khalil as a "bully" and an "outlaw" who jumped at any chance to fight. A fellow inmate of Khalil's in Pul-e-Charkhi, Sulaiman Laiq, said that Khalil reminded him of "an American cowboy."

Staying alive in Pul-e-Charkhi took some luck and connections. Before Abdul Ahad's imprisonment, he had befriended a security guard who worked on his street. Each day as he was driven home for lunch from the parliament, he would pass the small security guard shack, and he got in the habit of instructing his driver to drop off food for the guard. When he found himself in Pul-e-Charkhi, he discovered that the same guard had moved on to prison duty and was stationed in his block. "It was unbelievable," Fawzia recalled. "The guard told him, 'Anything you want, I can bring it to you.'" Twice a week, the guard visited their home, and Fawzia would prepare his favorite dishes: *khajoor*, a deep-fried, sugary oval-shaped pastry, and *rote*, a circular, slightly sweet bread. She stuffed packages with grapes, pineapples, and cheeses. Through the friendly guard, Abdul Ahad asked for mementos from his family. One day he requested photos of his youngest son, Abdul Wali, and of his two-year-old granddaughter, Minna, to keep in his cell. When the photos were discovered, Fawzia remembered, he was beaten.

Khalil flouted the rules with more gusto. The other inmates marveled that he always seemed to have money and new clothes. He smuggled a radio into his cell and even carried around a large knife. The guards routinely beat and tortured Khalil for his transgressions. On one occasion, a prison guard hammered a nail into his foot. On another, a guard used the butt of his AK-47 to smash out four of Khalil's bottom front teeth. "He never gave in," one of his brothers recalled.

The punishments emboldened Khalil, and with each new provocation he mounted, his legend for bravery and generosity grew. Abdul Ahad was a fastidious man, and the prison's filthy conditions made him miserable. Khalil earned another beating by arranging to find water so his brother could bathe. Sibghatullah Mojaddedi, a prominent politician who was imprisoned at the same time, befriended Khalil after he stood up for Mojaddedi's female relatives in the jail. One day in the prison yard, an inmate taunted Sulaiman Laiq about his position in the former regime. Laiq had been a minister overseeing radio, television, and film, and a member of the revolutionary council. The argument intensified and was heading toward a fight until Khalil showed up and whipped his knife from his belt. "He showed it to the man bothering me and warned him that if he touched me again he would kill him," Laiq recalled.

One of Khalil's brothers recounted an exchange he'd heard about between Khalil and the prison commander, Sayed Abdullah. The commander said hello to Khalil as he passed him in the prison one day. Khalil ignored the greeting.

"Why didn't you greet me?" Abdullah wanted to know.

"I'm an ordinary prisoner. Why do you need my greeting?"

"You know what this is?" Abdullah asked, pointing at his holster. "You're a man of the gun. How many people do I kill each night?"

"I don't know. But I hear the sounds."

"Your death to me is like the death of a bird," Abdullah said.

"If Allah has not made his decision," Khalil said, "then you cannot kill me."

Outside the prison walls, the tumult of Afghan politics was churning through leaders. After less than a year in office, Taraki was arrested and killed, suffocated by pillows. His successor, Hafizullah Amin, was himself killed when the Soviets laid siege to his palace. The Soviet-installed leader Babrak Karmal issued a decree freeing most of the political prisoners. Sulaiman Laiq got released before Khalil. On the day he left, Khalil called out to him from a prison window. "You are leaving us here alone," Khalil shouted with a grin. Laiq told him he would be out soon, too. After eighteen months in one of the world's most notorious prisons, the Karzais were set free.

For Hamid Karzai, his father's imprisonment, and the subsequent

Soviet invasion, changed his own life plans. Throughout his childhood, Hamid had chafed at some of the restrictions of being the son of such a prominent figure, and the stultifying tribal obligations of life in Kandahar. He had wanted to travel the world as a diplomat. But he began to feel his life's work needed to be closer to home. "I suddenly realized how spoiled I was," Hamid once told an American journalist about this period. "I realized that I had been consciously rejecting all the things that were really important and now were lost."

Over the next decade, the Soviet war shaped the destinies of many of the Karzais. Hamid and his father lived in exile in Pakistan and worked for a moderate mujahedeen faction fighting the Communists and became prominent on the exile diplomatic circuit, as we've seen. Several of his siblings, of course, established their lives and businesses in America. After prison, Khalil Karzai also joined the anti-Soviet resistance, and he used his position as a Popalzai elder to funnel weapons and supplies to rebels in Afghanistan. He lived surrounded by bodyguards and servants in Pishin, Pakistan, a small town not far from the Afghan border city of Spin Boldak. Pishin was close to a sprawling refugee camp called Surkhab, for Afghans who were fleeing the fighting. The treacherous politics of the capital had translated into devastation and violence in rural Afghanistan. Whole villages had been bombarded to rubble.

Karz was not spared. Within the family, the details of this period blur with the retelling, and little was written down about the events that took place among the mud huts of the small grape-growing village outside of Kandahar. But it's clear that the Karzai family and extended clan endured their share of tragedy.

One night rumors raced among the villagers that the Afghan government wanted to conduct a census of Karz. The governor of Kandahar at the time was a man known as Engineer Zareef, a staunch Communist from eastern Afghanistan. The census was part of an attempt to redistribute land to peasant farmers. As the villagers remembered, the landowners would lose 20 percent of their property under the government's plan. The Karz residents were opposed. They saw the Communists as godless bureaucrats who would only bring them harm. They were also angry about the prospect of the government counting their women. "This was something a lot of people could not accept," Haji Mohammed Karzai, one of the villagers present at the time, told me.

"Zareef was talking about which land should be divided and also that the girls should go to school," another villager remembered. "But the people did not agree. They said no. You are Communists and slaves of Communists. We will not support you and will not agree to your programs."

The villagers refused to allow the census takers into their homes. To solve the matter, the local government told men to gather in front of the village school. The governor himself would be coming to speak with them. Engineer Zareef arrived with a convoy of armored vehicles and large German-made buses. More than one thousand people crowded into the school yard. As villagers remember it, Zareef told the crowd that the government didn't want anything from the women of Karz, that they were also good Muslims. He pointed to one of the old men in the crowd, whose son was a high-ranking Communist. "Look at this person," Zareef told the villagers. "Does he look like an infidel to you?"

"Yes, he is an infidel," one of the village elders shouted. "He is a Communist like you!"

Zareef ended his attempts at persuasion. He told the Karz villagers that they were enemies of the revolution. He had come to the school with a list of names. The people there remember different numbers— thirty-two, thirty-eight, forty, forty-four—but the outcome was the same. The men, most of them members of the Karzais' extended family, were rounded up and loaded onto the buses. None of them returned. As the story goes, the men were taken to the governor's mansion, where the soldiers slaughtered them. "It was brutality," one relative said. "People were hit by stones, stabbed with bayonets."

"The soldiers used shovels and sickles and whatever tools they could find," recalled another Karzai relative.

It was said that some of the men were dropped from helicopters into a lake outside the city, and that others were rolled in blankets and then battered with stones. At the end of the killing, the story went, the blood-stained carpets were washed in the rivers of Kandahar until the water ran red. After such massacres, and the Soviet bombardments of the village, Karz emptied out. Those who lived through that period told me that some five hundred people from the village were killed: "elders, women, children, bombardment, rockets." Ahmadullah, an old grape farmer from the village, said one day as we sipped tea on the floor of his hut, "In that time, they were killing everyone. If they found us sitting here like this, they would just kill all of us. It didn't matter if you were involved in a crime or an incident."

"One day, when the Russians were here, the mujahedeen attacked, and we destroyed two of their tanks," another villager, Noor ul Haq, remembered. "They started killing everything, even the animals that were in their way. There were many people around that day, and the only people who survived were the ones who hid themselves in their gardens."

One day I took a tour of Karz with an old man who had been a servant of the president's as a child and had witnessed the destruction of his hometown. "The entire village left," he told me. He pointed at some decrepit mud structures. "These were the only two houses which are still standing from the old days; the rest of the neighborhood was destroyed. What you see has been rebuilt."

According to lore, on the day of Engineer Zareef's visit, one young man watched the others being loaded onto the buses. He called out to the soldiers. "He said, 'You are taking all these people. How will I go to my wife and what will I tell her? That all my fathers and brothers and family are gone?'" one Karzai recounted. "He said, 'I could never show my face to my wife or family when all these elders have been taken, and I'm still here.' So even though he wasn't on the list, he went along with them. And he never came back. That's the kind of village we lived in."

Among those who fled from Karz was a man named Yar Mohammed Karzai. Yar Mohammed was a cousin of Abdul Ahad and Khalil's, but he'd achieved none of their prominence. He'd attended school for only a few years before quitting to work in the fields. He was a wiry man with close-set eyes, a sunken chest, and a thick mustache. In old photos, he can be seen wearing a worn blazer and a boxy calfskin hat as he stands in knee-high grass or hikes across scrubland carrying a goat. As a twenty-two-year-old, Yar Mohammed was arrested for robbing a bus, and he spent a decade in a Kandahari jail. After he got out, he left Afghanistan with everyone else and ended up in the Surkhab refugee camp. While living there, Yar Mohammed would often see his cousin Khalil, who helped him out with money and food. Khalil had picked up his tribal duties again while living in Pakistan. He thrived on these interactions with his followers. "Among all the brothers, Khalil was the most sociable," one of the Popalzai elders said. "He liked tribal politics and tribal relations." When Yar Mohammed had another run-in with the law in Pakistan, Khalil found him a lawyer and helped spring him from jail. "They were close cousins," one of Khalil's sons recalled. "They were sitting every day together."

Yar Mohammed's status as a single man in his early thirties caused him considerable shame. Afghans marry early—sometimes as children—and often the marriages are arranged within their families or tribes. The weddings themselves are lavish and expensive. At night, the city of Kabul is lit with the neon glow of wedding halls. The groom or his family often have to save for months or years to pay for the wedding, an event that can attract more than a thousand guests.

Yar Mohammed had been promised the hand of one of his young cousins. His father and Hamid Karzai's grandfather had arranged for their daughters to marry each other's sons, a common occurrence among Pashtun families. Some of those marriages came to pass, but his prison term and the outbreak of the Soviet war had disrupted his own. His bride-to-be, Rahima Karzai, had left Kandahar for Kabul, attended school, become a teacher, and married a fellow teacher, Mohammed Naeem. They'd moved to the United States and settled down in the Maryland suburbs. For Rahima, Yar Mohammed was a path not taken. "She was an educated woman. Yar Mohammed was in jail for killing someone else," one of her nephews told me. "She said, 'I can't wait for him for the rest of my life.'"

For Yar Mohammed, a poorly educated farmer, a convicted criminal, and a proud Pashtun man, the loss of his promised wife was a grudge against Abdul Ahad's branch of the Karzai family that he refused to let go. It was an affront to his honor and reputation, a reason for *badal*, revenge.

"So the problem started there," Mohammad Jan Karzai, his brother, told me.

One day in late May 1984, Khalil visited Yar Mohammed where he was living in Surkhab. Khalil carried two guns at the time, a Russian-made Kalashnikov and a Smith & Wesson pistol, purchased in America, a gift from one of his brothers. They talked for a bit while Khalil's bodyguards waited outside. The exact circumstances of what happened next have been in dispute ever since. According to Khalil's son Hashmat Karzai, who would search for answers for years, Yar Mohammed acted intrigued by the Kalashnikov. Russian-made weapons were rare. "Yar Mohammed asked, 'Can I see the weapon? This is a beautiful weapon you've got.' He took the weapon. He turned around and he just stood up and pointed the weapon toward my father. He said, 'I want my woman back.'

"My father said, 'Hey, these things are past. She's married. She has two children. She's in the States.' 'No, people are teasing me. I can't take it anymore.'" The gun fired from point-blank range, and Khalil Karzai fell to the ground.

With Khalil's death, the family lost a charismatic leader: brash, funny, violent, brave, a rough Pashtun tribesman in Italian loafers, a man who'd taunted his jailers and cared for his followers. The grief traveled as far as the Karzai relatives had been scattered around the world. In a three-bedroom apartment in Silver Spring, Aziza Karzai, one of his sisters, sobbed at the news. "When I came home from work she was doing something crazy," her son remembered. "She was hitting her leg. I saw her leg was bruised. She was hitting too much. Before that day, my mother used to be young, strong, working. I've never seen her strong after that day."

"If he were alive," one of Khalil's brothers told me, "the story would be different."

Eighteen years later, once his nephew became president of Afghanistan, Khalil's remains would be exhumed from his Pakistani grave and returned to the family plot in Karz. His headstone reads:

Martyr Khalil Karzai, whose body was temporarily buried in the refugee cemetery in Pishin, was moved to Afghanistan as the new sun rose by his son, Hashmat Khalil, and his dear friends, on January 2nd 2002, and he was buried in his ancestral cemetery may God bless his soul.

The eyes of flowers are brimming with tears.
There is no laughter but only crying in this garden.
The one I was visiting with used to smile;
now I am carrying him to his grave in tears.

"Watch your head," Farid Karzai told me. We ducked off a crowded Kandahar sidewalk, passed through a low metal door, and walked down a dark concrete corridor that opened up into a narrow courtyard. The apartment felt like a safehouse. He didn't know who might be looking for him, and he didn't want the "Big Karzais" to know where he lived. Farid, the son of Yar Mohammed Karzai, was engaged to marry, but his mother, Farida, was so worried for his safety that she'd asked him to postpone the wedding. Sonia, his fourteen-year-old sister, now rarely slept through the night. We sat down in the concrete courtyard on a yellow patchwork carpet festooned with roses.

"Thank you for coming," Farida told me. "Thank God there are still people who come and listen to people and take their messages and their voices." Then she started to cry.

Farida had met Yar Mohammed in the Iranian border town of Zahedan, after he had fled Pakistan following Khalil Karzai's killing. They met through relatives, married, and lived in refugee camp squalor, surviving for a time by selling flour and cooking oil out of their home. For a long time they wandered in exile, welcome neither in Taliban-controlled Afghanistan nor outside it. Then one day American fighter jets appeared overhead, their contrails tracing a white script altogether different.

"My cousin is the president of Afghanistan," Yar Mohammed told his wife. "How long are we going to live in a foreign country?"

By then, Farida had borne Yar Mohammed two sons, Farid and Waheed, and a daughter, Sunita; their youngest daughter was still to come. The family rented a truck and filled the bed with their meager belongings and drove back to Karz. The village was almost unrecognizable. The only thing that remained from the buildings where Yar Mohammed and other Karzai relatives had grown up were the weathered ruins of a few mud walls. The area around was sunbaked dirt and a trash-filled swamp that smelled of sewage.

Yar Mohammed and his sons set about building a new home, living in a tent on their plot of land while the work progressed. Yar Mohammed was

Farid Karzai with his mother, Farida, and sister Sonia in the
courtyard of an apartment they were renting in
Kandahar City after fleeing Karz

too old and gaunt for much physical labor, so Farid and Waheed worked on the house after school. They supervised the work of local masons and builders as they fashioned a small, one-story, L-shaped concrete house with a flat roof. It had four small bedrooms, each with its own door facing the main gate leading into the yard, and a concrete staircase near the kitchen that rose to the roof. The house was simple and crude, but in a village of decrepit earthen homes, a sturdy white concrete house amounted to a status symbol.

Yar Mohammed sometimes sold sundries such as wheat and sugar but often spent his days sitting around the house, his rifle propped next to him. On rare occasions, when his boys were at school, Yar Mohammed would walk out through his yard of dirt and pebbled rock, past the hand-pump well and beyond the gray metal gate. He might pass black-and-white goats, so dirty both colors converged toward gray, or shirtless kids splashing in a fetid canal. In the fields, farmers bent to their grapes. He sometimes saw men riding dirt bikes, their turbans enveloping all but a slit for their eyes, to keep out the dust. Generally the path was empty, the only sound his footfalls. The trail ended where it abutted the main road through Karz, the one paved road in the village. At that intersection there was one house unlike all the others. From the outside, nothing was visible but its perimeter wall, a twenty-three-foot-high unbroken façade that ran for nearly a quarter mile along the main road. At the corners of the wall stood forty-foot turrets, manned by gunmen. The front door looked fit for a castle, a huge wooden slab embedded in a brick archway, protected by a metal bar. It was less house than fortress, visible from anywhere in the village, and it literally loomed over Yar Mohammed's tiny home. It belonged to Hashmat Karzai, the son of the man he shot.

Hashmat was a quintessential Afghan striver, an unabashed war profiteer. He'd been an immigrant selling car loans in suburban Virginia who had returned to his homeland and traded on his family name to amass a fortune of American taxpayer cash and command his own mercenary army. By 2007, he'd founded the Asia Security Group with former U.S. military officers and old friends of President Karzai's, and he was soon earning tens of millions of dollars from government contracts to provide private security to U.S. military bases across the country. With his new riches, Hashmat wanted to establish himself as the political heir to his slain father, to challenge Ahmed Wali Karzai as the preeminent power in Kandahar. Karz had become Hashmat's domain, the castle his headquarters. He had hired many of the villagers into the private army—he claimed to employ two thousand men—paying monthly salaries of a few thousand dollars a man, far more than could be earned in the grape fields. Once Hashmat came back to town, you couldn't go anywhere in Karz without seeing the image of his slain father; he'd erected a giant billboard on the main road with a black-and-white photograph of Khalil, who looks down on passersby with his turban and bushy mustache and an expression almost bemused.

On the few occasions when Yar Mohammed passed Hashmat's castle, he would bear right, onto the main road. He would pass the three-story village school where his sons studied, then the Karzai family cemetery, continuing on until he reached the cluster of roadside shops. He made few trips beyond the market, sometimes to the village mosque, the butcher shop, or the family vineyards. He once dressed in his two-toned blue turban and flew to Saudi Arabia for his pilgrimage to Mecca. But for the most part, Yar Mohammed didn't venture far. "He would hardly ever leave the house," his wife recalled.

October 16, 2009, was a Friday, the Muslim day of rest. Three weeks shy of his eighteenth birthday, Waheed Karzai put on a shimmery denim jacket over a white button-down shirt and left for a picnic. Waheed was thin and handsome, with high cheekbones and delicate features, a fine graze of stubble on his cheeks. Some of Waheed's cousins had made money on American contracts, providing construction materials for U.S.

Photograph of Khalil Karzai that was converted
into a billboard and erected in Karz

A photo of Waheed Karzai

soldiers at Kandahar Airfield, and they'd bought new cars they liked to race along the sandy banks of rivers outside the city. That day, as Waheed watched them tear across the sand, he posed for a photograph with a couple of his cousins. He sat cross legged and held his hands together in his lap. His lips curled into a slight smile.

His cousins with him that day were among his best friends. Waheed spent hours with Bilal and Zalal Karzai, the sons of one of Yar Mohammed's brothers. They lived next door in Karz, their houses separated by an eight-foot mud wall. Bilal and Zalal worked for an American company that provided generators at Kandahar Airfield. They would see each other in the evenings after work. Sometimes they would talk until the morning hours in Bilal's room; other nights they explored the city. "We would come home very late, like three or four or five a.m.," Bilal recalled. "Since the doors would be locked, we would come over the wall. Many times Yar Mohammed almost mistook us for thieves or his enemies. He would always curse us." The boys laughed off his worries. "We would go wherever our friends wanted to go. We liked to sleep during the day and chat at night," Bilal said. That Friday, Waheed felt tired and Bilal a little sick. That night, while Farid went out to a friend's wedding in the city, the other two headed home early.

As the sun set, Waheed knelt for evening prayers, touching his forehead to his prayer rug in his bedroom. The space was cramped, an austere and unadorned concrete nook, carpeted in brown. A window near the door looked out onto the dirt-and-gravel yard, empty but for the odd pile of sticks, discarded tires, and a yellow plastic bucket. In the back of Waheed's room, away from the door, a thin mattress lay on top of a rope bed, known as a *charpayee*. His Koran rested on the bedside table. At night, the sky provided the only illumination, by moon or stars. Electricity in Karz was still an unfulfilled wish. Evenings were quiet and only rarely interrupted by the lonely patter of a distant motorbike or a barking stray.

Yar Mohammed had taken his nightly sleeping pill and gone to bed on a floor mat under the window in the next room. Waheed decided to read verses from his Koran before going to sleep. He was the more studious of the brothers. "He loved education, reading and writing," Farid recalled. "He would always tell me that the only way to change our lives was to go to school and go to university and become either a doctor or an engineer."

Waheed took off his shirt. He shook out his blanket and placed it on the mattress. It was at that moment, just before nine p.m., when the visitors arrived. In the story Waheed would later tell several relatives from his hospital bed, the ensuing moments unfolded in confusion and fear. Men broke the lock on the gate and came in fast: at least two Toyota Surf SUVs and about seven men with black military-grade assault rifles. Most of them wore gray uniforms, common among police and security guards, but two were dressed in civilian clothes. One of them, a stocky, balding man, wore a crisp white *shalwar kameez* with a black vest and combat boots. The other also wore a *shalwar kameez*, in greenish-gray. These two men carried pistols with silencers and laser sights. They approached Farid's room, the one closest to the front gate, but it was empty, because he was still at the wedding. They found Waheed in the next room. When they entered, he froze, ducking into a crouch next to his bed, his body turned toward the wall.

"It's not him," one of the men said.

"Shoot him anyway," the other replied. "Don't let him go."

The man in white opened fire. One bullet missed Waheed and lodged in the wall about a foot off the floor. Another pierced his left calf, and he started to scream. The next shot struck him in the gut and he fell over, writhing and bleeding onto the carpet.

The commotion woke Waheed's mother and Sonia, who were sleeping nearby. The two shooters entered their bedroom. The green dot of the laser danced across their faces. Sonia screamed, "It's the Taliban!" and they ordered her to shut up.

"As we started screaming and shouting, one of them raised their gun again and pointed it at us," Farida recalled. "And that's when my daughter held up a Koran and begged them not to shoot. When they saw there were only two women, they left the room."

Yar Mohammed had by that point grabbed his Kalashnikov and staggered into the yard. Bleary from the sleeping pill, he couldn't see well as he sprayed gunfire at the intruders. "Window glass was shattered. Bullets were flying everywhere, as he was exchanging fire with these two men," Farida said. "After a few minutes, they escaped, the car engines roaring."

The gun battle woke Bilal Karzai next door. His first thought was that the shooting had come from the direction of the grape fields behind his house. When he went outside to look, he saw nothing. As he was coming back, he heard more shots from the direction of Waheed's house. He knew that one family in the neighborhood bought and sold weapons, and Bilal thought that the American soldiers might be doing some type of raid on that house. He hoisted himself up the dirt wall that separated his house from his cousin's and peered down into their yard. He saw a welter of commotion: Yar Mohammed firing his Kalashnikov as uniformed men ran through the yard, jumped into their vehicles, and drove off.

When they left, Yar Mohammed helped his injured son into the yard and examined his body. Waheed had taken off his shirt before bed, and now blood streamed from his stomach wound. The cell phones were out—the Taliban would not allow cell phone companies to provide service at night—so a neighbor ran to the nearest police checkpoint to summon help. The police loaded Waheed into the back of a truck. As it pulled away, Farida ran after it, shouting and crying for them to take her along. But as a woman, she was not allowed, and she wouldn't see her son again. They drove Waheed to Mirwais Hospital, the lime-green clinic in Kandahar City that had become the main collection point for the war wounded in southern Afghanistan.

As word spread of the shooting, Farid left the wedding and drove to the hospital. He found his brother lying on polka-dotted sheets in the second-floor emergency room. The sight of his brother's wounds caused him to wretch. He got woozy and fainted, and someone splashed water on his face to revive him.

The doctors removed bullets from Waheed's leg and abdomen. He was able to speak to his relatives, and he described the shooters to them and the sequence of events in his bedroom. But over the next day, his condition deteriorated, and by Sunday morning, Farid knew that Waheed needed more help. He called Fazel Mohammed, the chief of security for Ahmed Wali Karzai, and told him his brother was dying. Ahmed Wali sent another aide to the hospital, and he arranged for Waheed to be taken by ambulance to the U.S. military hospital at Kandahar Airfield. He arrived on a Sunday afternoon.

According to his medical records, by the time Waheed was transferred to the American doctors' care, his heart rate was racing at 145 beats per minute. His blood pressure was 45 over 21, and vacillating wildly. He had massive blood loss from the abdominal trauma. Despite the intravenous fluids, he was unable to urinate. "Overall condition is not good," a doctor wrote. They performed a laparotomy, opening up his abdomen, and inserted a chest tube to help him breathe. He received a dopamine injection for his failing blood pressure and hydrocortisone to stave off renal failure. By then, Waheed had drifted into a coma. His heart stopped beating, and he was revived by defibrillator paddles and an adrenaline shot. Antibiotics—Metrogyl, ciprofloxacin, imipenem—coursed through him. By one a.m. on Monday morning, his blood pressure was "indeterminable," and the doctors were called to his bedside. Yellow pus seeped from his chest tube. Purple bruises had appeared on his skin, signs of internal bleeding. His medical records would later list the cause of his demise as acute tubular necrosis, or kidney failure, the result of septic shock from severe blood infection. By four-thirty that morning, Waheed Karzai was pronounced dead.

Within the family, the question of who shot Waheed Karzai was not much in dispute. On his gravestone in the Karzai cemetery, it says that Waheed was killed "by the enemies of Islam" when he was in his house, sleeping. But most people believed Hashmat Karzai was the killer. The theory went that Hashmat was enacting revenge on Yar Mohammed's family for the killing of his father a quarter century earlier. Perhaps he meant to kill Yar Mohammed himself but took advantage of the first target he found, then fled in the ensuing gun battle. Waheed's relatives believed that the other gunmen in their house that night were Hashmat's guards from the Asia Security Group, the American contractor. Given the risks of accusing the village's most powerful man of premeditated murder, the subject became one that most of the relatives wanted to avoid. "They were not among the people we knew" was all Waheed's mother would tell me. Farid offered a bit more: "Everyone in my family, including my dad, saw those men wearing the same uniforms that Hashmat Karzai's security guards were wearing."

Over the months I spoke with the Karzais, I would always ask about people's thoughts on this incident. Some gave credence to the rumor that the killing was a conspiracy by supporters of Ahmed Wali Karzai to frame Hashmat and drive him from Karz. But most of the relatives I spoke with believed Hashmat was ultimately responsible. Yar Mohammed's brother Mohammed Jan put it this way: "According to Waheed himself, it was Hashmat who went to the house and shot him. He told us that he was wearing white clothes, a white *shalwar kameez*, with a black vest, and he had recognized him. Everybody that night was saying Hashmat had attacked Yar Mohammed's house and shot at Waheed. The next morning, people stopped saying that, because they were scared."

Even one of Hashmat's allies told me that Hashmat had confessed to the killing, and that it was not a mistake or a failed attempt to kill Yar Mohammed. "He told me, 'I want to show Yar Mohammed the way my grandmother felt.' He wanted to break him physically and spiritually and mentally."

I eventually found Yar Mohammed's own written statement about the attack. It confirmed this account. In his letter to Hamdullah Nazziq, the district governor of Dand—the area surrounding Karz—Yar Mohammed wrote that he had been sleeping in the next room that night when he heard screaming and shouting. "And I immediately grabbed my weapon to kill the armed men inside my house. When I fired at them, the murderers escaped."

"Eyewitnesses," he wrote, "had seen two Surf SUVs—one brown and one blue—in the village many times before the incident, and which belonged to Hashmat Karzai, son of Khalil Khan Karzai. According to Waheed himself, who told his relatives at the hospital that one of the killers who had entered his room was a well-built, tall man in white clothes, whose name is Hashmat Karzai, who is the eldest son of late Khalil Khan Karzai. I am submitting this complaint letter and I am hopeful that you arrest the killer Hashmat Karzai, son of Khalil Khan Karzai, who killed my son and who fired at my son that night. His accomplices should be arrested too and should be tried in accordance with the Islamic sharia and should be punished for the crime and sin that they have committed."

10

WHO'S RUNNING THIS PLACE?

MAJOR JEREMY KOTKIN and Lieutenant Colonel Jim Bruha, two mid-level Army officers, were known as "Afghan hands." The program they were a part of had been hatched at the Pentagon as a plug for the leak of institutional memory that was an annual rite of the Afghan war. It had become one of the more tired bromides of the war: American soldiers had not been fighting the Taliban for ten years, as calendars would attest, but instead had waged ten one-year wars, this seasonal wheel reinvention due to troop rotations, embassy summertime turnover, swapped-out ambassadors and commanders. Each year it seemed like the whole American enterprise would revert to learning the names of the provinces or that "afghani" meant the currency, not the people. The idea of the Afghan Hands program was to develop experts that stayed around. Modeled on the U.S. military's China Hands project of the 1930s, the program committed several hundred soldiers to five-year terms. They studied Dari or Pashtu, as well as Afghan history and culture, and they alternated stints in-country with jobs back home that dealt with Afghanistan. The program was also intended to build the sense of commitment to Afghanistan among the officer corps, to underline the idea that this was a long-term problem and fixing it would require patience.

Bruha and Kotkin were in the first class to sign up. Both were career Army planners. Bruha, forty-seven years old, had spent the last few years at Centcom in Tampa. Kotkin, younger and one rank below, felt it was his duty as an American to offer himself for such a long-term commitment. They touched down in Kabul on April 24, 2010, and found their bunks in a trailer on Camp Eggers, a downtown base used by ISAF soldiers who trained the Afghan army. Kotkin arrived believing he would be an adviser for the training command. Bruha expected to sit across town in the head-quarters of U.S. Forces Afghanistan. Someone above them in the chain of command had different plans. A colonel informed them that their bil-lets had changed, and they would be working at ISAF headquarters for the deputy chief of staff for stability, who, in customary NATO fashion, had no idea they were coming and passed them off to the deputy chief of staff for strategic partnership, an Australian two-star general named Ash Power. Three weeks passed before Bruha and Kotkin had their first meeting with the general, who correctly pointed out that they had been "thrown to the wind."

ISAF needed help in the palace. Less than a mile separated Karzai's swivel chair from the flat-screen panels inside ISAF's Situational Aware-ness Room, but as far as perspective went, the two places had almost nothing in common. What was to the military a successful kinetic opera-tion to eliminate a high-value target was to Karzai the murder of an inno-cent Afghan farmer. Close-air support on an enemy compound meant firebombing someone's home. The anti-corruption task forces and finan-cial investigations looked to Afghan politicians like nonviolent weapons for sabotaging the president.

The ISAF generals were frustrated with the public relations disso-nance between their headquarters and the palace—two supposed allies in a state of divorce court disagreement—but their concerns went beyond that. The United States saw its mission as remaking Afghan institutions into something recognizable to the Western world. The way President Karzai did business—long phone calls about tiny matters, endless ram-bling chats with whatever bumpkin wandered into the palace, meetings unshackled by agendas or decisions—did not seem to them very efficient or presidential. Karzai's political style was adopted from Afghan customs and the tribal conventions learned at the foot of his father, but it looked to the United States a lot like dysfunction. Karzai's National Security Council, an institution created with coalition funding to mimic its White House counterpart as a coordinating body for wartime decision making, never seemed to coordinate anything. Karzai made his decisions with-out PowerPoint briefings or position papers, and when they were made, often nobody followed up. Each afternoon, his NSC staff would provide him with a document outlining the number of insurgent, Afghan, and coalition casualties that day, but he hated receiving it and often chose to ignore the report.

As Karzai grew more embattled in his job, the flow of information and advice reaching him began constricting. Even staffers at the palace complained that it was getting harder to see him, as his inner circle shielded him from other views. Karzai was a "lonely and alone man," one of the palace staffers informed the U.S. embassy. He was becoming convinced that everyone was "out to get him." Karzai's deputy chief of staff, Homayra Etemadi, had warned the embassy to be careful about what information they shared with her boss, because he might pass it along to Iran.

The palace had become a web of hidden allegiances and concealed treacheries. "His methodology was consensus," Robert Finn, the first post-Taliban U.S. ambassador to Kabul, told me. "So everything took forever to do, and decisions were often not made. He spent a zillion hours talking about something, he'd get it all decided, and then the next day he'd start it off as if he never had talked about it before. That's not the best management style. It could be any issue—that was just the way things were, the way he ran his government. It was like a late-night TV show. You come in and sit in the chair next to him. You get your fifteen minutes. Then you move over to the couch and someone else comes in. Then you move down one and someone else comes in. By the end of the day, half the government is sitting in the president's office. You know, who's running this place if we're all in here having tea?"

ISAF decided that Kotkin and Bruha would be the ones to help. So the two Army planners ditched their fatigues, bought ill-fitting Afghan business suits, and, on a sunny Saturday in early June, walked under the watchtower and through the ancient fortress walls to go help President Karzai fight the Taliban. "As good Army field grade officers, we attacked our new billets with energy and passion," Bruha would later write to his boss.

"It was a great job," Kotkin said. "On paper."

The National Security Council operated out of a two-story yellow concrete building adjacent to Karzai's office in the Flower House. The Afghan NSC was intended to be Karzai's inner circle, the body that would formulate foreign policy—the issues most important to Karzai—and buffer him against the powerful departments of defense, interior, and intelligence, which were controlled by his ethnic rivals. The Americans and Brits paid for the office and the refurbishment of its decrepit building. At the beginning, what the Afghans lost in sovereignty, they made up in protection. "We were looking for a framework. But we wanted things in return," Daud Yaqub, one of the first members of the National

Security Council, said of that early period. "We accepted the American presence. We knew there were liabilities. But our goal was to get American leverage against our archnemesis, which was Pakistan. We didn't realize from the beginning that the United States didn't see it that way. I hate to use [former CIA director George] Tenet's words, but we thought the NSC in Kabul was a slam dunk. Given our stance against extremists, and Pakistan's double-dealing with the United States, we thought we could replace Pakistan in the region, and America would be happy for us to do that."

In early bilateral arrangements, Karzai's government agreed to pretty much all American demands. There was a notorious 2003 agreement between the two countries that gave free rein to American soldiers and civilians operating in Afghanistan, including immunity from prosecution and tax exemption for private contractors, that Afghans spent many years regretting. The American abandonment after the Soviet withdrawal coursed through the Afghan political fabric. Nobody in the palace, least of all Karzai, suspected that the United States would stay one day longer than its own self-interest deemed necessary. "Not in a million years I would have advised Karzai to sign the [agreement] if I had seen it; it was way too imbalanced," one of the National Security Council staff members recalled.

Before an early visit to Kabul by Defense Secretary Rumsfeld, Enayat Qasimi, a legal adviser in the palace, talked with Karzai about the prospects of formalizing a strategic partnership with the United States, to try to ensure that if they were going to have America as the benefactor and protector, it would be for many years to come. Qasimi researched the diplomatic arrangements America kept with its allies, such as Israel and NATO, and wrote up his concept in a brief memo in English. The policy in the early years of the Bush administration was minimalist: few troops, no nation building, ignore the nefarious characters; there wasn't appetite yet for spending billions of dollars in Afghanistan. After Karzai read it, he told Qasimi he should rip up the memo and delete it from his computer. "It was too sensitive at the time," Qasimi said. "He was not an elected president, he was still in the transition. But he was one hundred percent in favor of it. He would tell me all the time, 'The survival of this country depends on what kind of relationship we can forge with the United States.'"

By the time Kotkin and Bruha arrived, the mood in the palace toward Americans had changed dramatically. The two soldiers had been assigned to work with Mohammad Daud Yaar, who ran the policy and oversight department, one of seven departments in the National Security Council. Yaar was a former Kabul University professor and a Pashtun of royalist tribal lineage. He had escaped Kabul at a time when the Soviets had imprisoned several of his colleagues—a grudge some held against him—and he had been close with Ahmed Wali and other Karzai siblings during their restaurant years in Chicago. Yaar spoke English, and unlike many Afghans in Karzai's entourage, he didn't mind having two American soldiers roaming around inside the palace gates. "He's as American as you or I. His wife was in California," Bruha told me. Yaar had told their superiors, "If you send a couple of Americans over here, as long as they're not in uniform, I can put them to work."

The office in the palace, along a polished marble hallway, had the veneer of officialdom, but it didn't take them long to realize that very little was happening. The formal roster of the NSC listed more than one hundred employees—their salaries paid by the Americans and Brits—but only a third to half that number seemed to be showing up. Those who came to work didn't appear to be approaching it with as much urgency as Kotkin and Bruha had expected. The layers of protocols and security and compartmentalized information that one could find in the White House hadn't reached Kabul. The most sensitive Afghan government secrets were discussed over Nokia cell phones and between Yahoo e-mail addresses. Palace televisions were tuned to Bollywood soap operas. The power would go out for hours at a time.

The Americans tried to be helpful. Bruha scavenged five computers from Camp Eggers to add to the NSC's meager supply. He and Kotkin helped write the policy on transition to Afghan security control that got presented at a major conference in London that summer. They attended working groups on countering roadside bombs, fighting corruption, and controlling narcotics, and they helped write Afghanistan's national security policy, a fifty-five-page document that detailed several sobering data points, including that the number of "terrorist incidents" for the year, 7,865, was nearly double that of two years prior, and that despite full-bore military operations, the ranks of the Taliban had reached 38,680 men (subdivided into 2,246 insurgent cells), up 32 percent over the previous year.

Communications didn't move through the bureaucracy as they had hoped. For instance, Yaar had approved Kotkin and Bruha to work in the palace, but his boss, the national security adviser, Rangin Dadfar Spanta, had not. That made things uncomfortable from the start. Each morning, palace guards would block the Americans' entry, submitting them to endless pat-downs and body scans, despite their official badges. Carrying their weapons inside was prohibited, but so was carrying food, pens, aspirin, or lip balm (Bruha resorted to smearing a dollop behind his ear each morning, so that he had a supply throughout the day). One palace aide felt sorry for how they had to wait so long each morning just to get to their office. The aide told the guards to hurry them along, that the two Americans shouldn't be forced to wait outside the gates. Only later did Kotkin learn that he was Mohammed Zia Salehi, the man arrested on corruption charges, then freed by President Karzai. "He was the nicest guy we knew in the NSC," Kotkin said.

"By the time Jeremy and I showed up, there was a real palpable sense of wanting us away from the palace," Bruha said. "It was like, Who are these palefaces?"

To help the skeptical Afghans, ISAF had designed elaborate charts brimming with acronyms that mapped out how Karzai's palace ought to arrive at its decisions. The Office of the National Security Council (ONSC) was supposed to function as a "hierarchy of committees," according to an ISAF terms of reference (TOR) paper describing the envisioned work flow. This included the Principals Committee (PC), the Deputies Committee (DC), and its subordinate the Security Operations Group (SOG), all meshing to "ensure that national security policy issues are properly analyzed and prepared for presentation to the NSC for consideration." The DC, with a meeting every second Saturday, was supposed to study all Afghan policies related to national security and review the work of all interagency policy working groups (IPWGs), with the final agenda item of any DC meeting reserved for a backbrief by the SOG chair. The SOG, meeting on the fourth floor of the Ministry of Defense every Wednesday, would monitor the IPWGs and recommend "courses of action" to the DC. Then there was the DC/SOG Secretariat, the "organizing forum" for the above committees, whose duties included proposing agendas for DC and SOG meetings, drafting preparatory paperwork—"PowerPoint briefings, information papers, and reports"—at least two days prior to said meetings, arranging for simultaneous translation (Dari to English), and deciding if any new IPWGs should be created, all while ensuring "appropriate linkages, both higher to lower and vice versa" within the overall ONSC. After their meetings, occurring each Monday morning at ten-thirty a.m. in the small conference room, the chair of the DC/SOG

Secretariat must then "back-brief the SOG and DC Chairs to ensure they concur with the agreed upon agenda and work plan." And then each year these Terms of Reference would be reviewed and reinvented, "or at any time that DC/SOG Secretariat members deem appropriate."

As one might expect, almost none of this happened. NSC staffers regularly skipped meetings or disregarded the agendas ISAF helped them write. The SOG meetings would routinely go so poorly and be so mind-bendingly dull that Kotkin and Bruha would draw straws to see who got to skip them. The deputy national security adviser, Shaida Mohammad Abdali, would occasionally conduct the deputies' committee meeting by telling the group members to talk among themselves.

Rangin Dadfar Spanta, the national security adviser and top boss, was rarely seen by the Americans. He had a complicated reputation among the foreign diplomatic core. He was friendly and avuncular, with his unruly Einstein hair and bushy mustache. In a game where American diplomats chose animals to describe prominent Afghan officials, he got pegged as a koala. Spanta had been a professor in Germany during his exile years. He sympathized with many of the American goals in Afghanistan, particularly taking on government corruption. And privately he could be one of the most cutting critics of Karzai's administration. One evening we sat on the porch of his Kabul home, as we drank whiskey and he smoked a cigar, and he lamented that fate had placed him in Hamid Karzai's government. He told me he was desperate to resign and would do so any day.

Spanta never left the palace. His colleagues there would say that his image as a thoughtful, pro-Western academic belied a much harsher view of America's project in Afghanistan. Kotkin and Bruha, who were supposed to be working for him, hardly ever saw him. Spanta spent far more time sitting by Karzai's side than managing his national security staff. "As far as being hands-off, he was the *chief* of hands-off," Kotkin said.

That lack of involvement struck Kotkin and Bruha as the norm. Many staffers didn't seem to be spending much time on their official duties. Kotkin and Bruha had a running joke about one NSC employee who seemed to have no assignment at all. "He just sat in his office. Never attended a meeting," Kotkin said. "He was a nice little guy. He just wanted to learn English."

The government ministries, controlled by different ethnic and political factions, tended to ignore orders from the palace and rarely coordinated with them. The real decision making happened when President Karzai gathered privately with his aides and ministers, with no foreigners present, and hashed out issues, in the fashion in which Afghan politics had played out for generations. There were administrators: several hundred other palace employees worked in a separate department known as the cabinet secretariat, including many who had served in previous regimes, writing up presidential decrees by hand and carrying out palace business as it had been done since the king's time. One American military adviser called the cabinet secretariat the "beating heart" of the Afghan government, but the United States tended to disregard it.

The way Karzai made decisions was often reactive and ill-supported by study or data or preparation, but it was the way to which he and his Afghan colleagues were accustomed. Trying to shoehorn decisions through a new multilayered NSC meeting process was not. Ambassador Ronald Neumann could recall long arguments with Karzai about how the palace should adopt a system of data-driven briefings to help inform his thinking. "But Karzai's view is: I don't trust staff, I don't trust paper, I don't trust reports. I trust what a good man tells me," Neumann said. "I argued with him, that a good man can produce a bad report because he misperceives, because of partial information. He doesn't have to be doing it deliberately, but a good man can give you a false impression. I absolutely lost. I couldn't rock this view."

Other diplomats observed the same disorganization in Karzai's palace. "He never writes anything down," one British ambassador to Kabul said. "He never has records. There's no follow-up. Sometimes someone takes notes but nothing is ever promulgated."

"They would come up with an agenda every week and they would just completely blow it off," Kotkin said. "They don't want to have meetings like we would have meetings. They just wanted to have a *shura*. We would just go crazy because they're not following the agenda."

Karzai's management style also left his own aides frustrated and off balance. Cabinet meetings would meander through hours of tedium. At one point while Karzai was still interim president, one of his ministers demanded a ten-minute break for every hour of discussion. In these cabinet sessions, Karzai dove into matters that other leaders might have left to subordinates. They chose an eight-hour Afghan government workday, from eight a.m. to four p.m., then, seven months later, shortened it by an hour. They worried over how many cars coming from Pakistan had steering wheels on the right-hand side, as opposed to the customary left, as in Afghanistan. Karzai felt the minimum age limit for mayors was too low. That the available university training on animal husbandry was insufficient. He thought there were too few trees in Kabul and too many potholes. In his war-weary capital, he wanted more five-star hotels. One of Khalil Roman's duties, as deputy chief of staff, was to take notes on all these issues at cabinet meetings. During particularly tense exchanges among the ministers, Karzai would look over and order him to write faster, to capture every word. "He was displaying behavior which was unique to a tribal leader, to a *khan* or a *malik*, rather than a democrat or a modern leader," Roman recalled. "He would be so happy when someone would compliment him. Then he would abuse people. He would use swearwords. He was dictating whatever he wanted, his will."

As the weeks went on, Bruha and Kotkin watched with growing alarm as the NSC autopiloted through a succession of failures. The work on banning the fertilizer used in roadside bombs got snatched away by the Interior Ministry. The National Security Council office flubbed the process of choosing which former Taliban fighters should come off the United Nations sanctions list, with shoddy research and no coordination with other branches of government. The NSC's most important task, to guide the transition to Afghan security control as the American troops withdrew, was taken over by a new office under Ashraf Ghani, who had lost to Karzai in the election. In a memo Kotkin wrote for his boss titled "Observations of ONSC Failures," he noted that the Office of the National Security Council was "completely detached and out of the loop," and that within the Afghan government "it is generally understood that the ONSC does not have the authority to task Ministries to generate reports, answer requests for information, or provide assessments to satisfy Presidential requirements."

The ISAF brass knew that the NSC bureaucracy, despite the millions of dollars poured into it, was not the way to influence Karzai's government. The top generals had created another weekly forum, what they called the Senior Security Shura, as a way for Petraeus to meet directly with the Afghan ministers of defense and interior and the intelligence chief to carry out the war plan. No one bothered to let the National Security Council know what took place at those meetings.

At Karzai's palace, plenty of wheels were spinning, but the advisers knew they were going nowhere. "There was no leadership," Kotkin said. "They were just not doing anything."

Three months into the army officers' job, their Afghan colleague Yaar walked into the office, looking upset.

"You guys have to leave," he told them. "Today."

That morning, an Afghan newspaper had published an article about how two foreign spies were working inside the palace. It claimed these were British spies working for the CIA to steal Afghan secrets. This type of press smear was a common tactic in neighboring Pakistan, where any foreigner who fell out of favor with the government would appear in print as an agent of Blackwater, Mossad, the CIA, or all three. Yaar thought that his boss Spanta, who wrote a column in the Afghan press under a pseudonym, had leaked the story. But many people in the palace resented the presence of these two "Lawrences of Afghanistan," as Daud Yaqub, a senior national security staffer, described them. "Everybody saw them as doing nothing but gathering information for their boss," Yaqub said. Whoever had done it, the message was plain enough. Kotkin and Bruha retreated for a week or so to wait for tempers to cool, whiling away the hours reading books in the ISAF garden under the dappled shade.

Karzai was increasingly sensitive to appearing to be an American lapdog. As he grew into the role of president, he tried to exercise the sovereignty he felt befitted his role as head of state. The problem was that the United States, in one way or another, paid for almost all of the operations of his government and the security forces fighting on his behalf. Despite that, at every turn Karzai sought to distance himself from the United States. Civilian casualties prompted him to demand an end to American air strikes or night raids, to keep U.S. soldiers out of Afghan homes. He wanted Afghans to take control of Bagram prison so that Americans wouldn't be holding his citizens—and predominantly his fellow Pashtuns prisoner. He increasingly left Americans out of the loop when making decisions.

In the late summer of 2010, at the height of military operations in southern Afghanistan, he made the surprise announcement that he would be banning all private security companies within four months, despite the fact that nearly all American military and civilian staff relied heavily on these companies to do their work. When Karzai made that unilateral decision, the United States was employing nineteen thousand private security guards in Afghanistan, from companies such as Triple Canopy and Xe Services, better known as Blackwater. American officials considered these demands at the very least unrealistic and more often saw them as a dangerous threat to the partnership and the mission.

These types of decisions earned Karzai his reputation as an erratic leader. But taken together, they began to appear strategic: by making unrealistic demands for autonomy, Karzai could win small concessions that inched him toward greater authority. These public onslaughts against the United States also earned him some measure of credibility among a population that had turned deeply against the war. The American posture of doubling down on a losing battle gave Karzai that many more chances to attack his allies.

In the fall of 2010, Ambassador Eikenberry went to warn Karzai that WikiLeaks would be publishing a cache of thousands of diplomatic cables with potentially embarrassing revelations about the State Department's view of the Afghan government. At first, Karzai brushed the issue aside. They had already talked about WikiLeaks, he reminded Eikenberry, when Julian Assange's website had published the "war logs" of thousands of military field reports from Iraq and Afghanistan. Eikenberry told Karzai that this was WikiLeaks 2, and it was going to be much worse.

"What's it going to say about Afghanistan?" Karzai wanted to know.

"We don't know what cables might be leaked," Eikenberry told him. He was under strict instructions not to talk about their contents.

Karzai considered this. "Now, is there going to be anything from you about medications?" he asked.

His aides laughed nervously. Karzai was referencing Bob Woodward's book *Obama's Wars*, which had been published two months earlier. Woodward, citing "sensitive intelligence reports," wrote that Karzai was erratic, with delusions and severe mood swings, and that he "had been diagnosed as a manic-depressive" and took medication for the condition. He also suggested that Karzai might sometimes be "high on weed" in the palace.

No one disputed that Karzai wore his emotions on his sleeve and could flip from giddy laughter to rage in a moment. On several occasions, he wept publicly while giving speeches about the suffering of the country or while visiting the war wounded in hospitals. Many people around him did consider it possible that he took medication of an antidepressant or mood-stabilizing variety. But only the most vicious of the president's enemies actually claimed that he took recreational drugs. Karzai was a devout Muslim who did not smoke or drink. Woodward quoted Eikenberry as saying, "He's on his meds, he's off his meds" to describe the president's mercurial behavior—something Eikenberry denied having said. Karzai had seized on the passages as further evidence of America's disrespect for him.

"No, Mr. President," Eikenberry responded. "It will, though, be conversations between your ministers and embassy officials, and they'll be saying things that are going to be controversial in Afghanistan."

Karzai swiveled toward Spanta, his national security adviser.

"Now I will finally know if you are an American spy," Karzai told him.

There was nervous laughter among the other palace aides.

"I'm not an American spy, Mr. President. I speak my piece. I'm a good Afghan patriot."

"We'll see," Karzai said.

During Petraeus's tenure as ISAF commander, American military aggression exploded. Special operations kill-or-capture raids rose to about six hundred per month, or twenty per night. The number of air strikes spiked dramatically, in a reversal of McChrystal's decision to limit bombings that might kill civilians or erode the Afghan public's support for the war. Four months into Petraeus's command, the U.S. military reached its high-water mark for bombings, launching 1,043 air strikes in one month. Civilian deaths rose in tandem. The problems that Karzai cared about were all getting worse. And as America's celebrity general, coming off his tour in Baghdad, Petraeus was a tough man to dissuade. "Karzai was, frankly, scared of Dave Petraeus," an American ambassador told me.

Petraeus was concerned that ISAF and the palace couldn't get on the same page. He and Karzai often disagreed about the facts on the ground, the daily drumbeat of arrests, shootings, bombings. And they found little common ground on the broader strategy. Their problems came to a head in November, six days before an important NATO conference in Lisbon to discuss the war plan. That Saturday evening, Karzai had met me and two of my editors from *The Washington Post* who were visiting Kabul. In the discussion that night, Karzai vented his frustrations with the American war in Afghanistan. He seemed to have concluded that U.S. military operations had reached the point where they were counterproductive, that their actions were making more people join the Taliban than leave them. He wanted American soldiers out of Afghan homes and off their roads. "The time has come to reduce military operations," Karzai told us.

"The manner in which this war was conducted by our allies," Karzai said, "increasingly began to cost the Afghan people in terms that they could not understand. The bombardment of our villages, where we knew there wasn't an al-Qaeda or a terrorist, the pursuit of a Mr. B. Taliban, of whom there are thousands in this country, and in pursuit of bombarding an Afghan home or an Afghan village and causing death and injury to innocent people, women and children, this is what the Afghan people fail to understand. You are really speaking to a skeptic mind-set here in Afghanistan, that doesn't know whether the international community is here to fight terrorism. And if it is fighting terrorism, do they know that they're making mistakes? Whether the international community is here to free Afghanistan from the troubles that it had and strengthen it, or if it's added to those problems?

"The message that I have for the American people is, one, that we know in Afghanistan that America earns money the hard way. That you work hard. I've seen people working in America, that all that you spend there [is] hard-earned, from your younger people to the older people; they wake up early in the morning, they wake up much earlier than us, and go to work, and toil the whole day, shed a lot of sweat before they can earn a dollar. But that dollar spent in Afghanistan doesn't reach the Afghan people the way it should. Second, the intentions that you have in America toward Afghanistan as a people, as a country, is not reflected here in Afghanistan the way it should. It sometimes is reflected in con-tradiction to what you are thinking as an American people. The security firms, for example: How can you have a country grow a police force if you have created a parallel structure of at least forty thousand men with more money, with more salaries, with less accountability to them? And yet expect us to have a strong and effective police force and one that can provide you and the Afghan people with security.

"We have our faults," Karzai said. "We have too many faults. We are a poor country. We are a highly undereducated country. We have cen-turies of backwardness to cope with. We have lots of other difficulties of our own. But we are genuinely trying to emerge out of that misery. We are genuinely trying to fight terrorism. We are genuinely trying to be a country that likes to live well with its neighbors and with the rest of the world. We genuinely want to be partners with America for good and for good causes. The way things are moving, we don't seek clarity on these accounts, whether we are treated as equal—let's not talk of equal—whether we're treated respectfully or whether we're seen as 'Hell, these third-world guys, let's use them and abuse them and confuse them.'

"The Taliban is not a man manufactured in a factory and then brought to—the suicide bombers may be, but not the Taliban; they are people, they have families, they have wives, they have children, they have moth-ers, they have fathers, they have cousins," he said. "And they suffer, too.

They suffer exactly from the hands of the same elements. When there is a bomb blown up by a suicide bomber, maybe a Taliban family member is standing by and gets hurt."

The kill-or-capture raids that American soldiers were launching at record rates were "terrible, terrible," he said. "The raids are a problem always. They were a problem then; they are a problem now. They have to go away. The Afghan people don't like these raids. If there is any raid, it has to be done by the Afghan government within the Afghan laws."

He wanted all of it to stop. From the start of his tenure as president, when he declared, "I would not kill an ant to remain in this position," Karzai had been opposed to violence in any form. His disdain for macho military posturing, and for using the powers of his office to inflict physical harm, only deepened over time. During the Soviet war, he had occasionally carried a gun when visiting rebels on the battlefield but claimed that he never fired it. As president, his office had a backlog of three hundred death-penalty cases that he refused to sign because he could not bear the thought of executing a potentially innocent man. I asked him about the CIA drone strikes in Pakistan. I thought he might be in favor of those, because he'd always talked about how Islamic terrorists were headquartered in Pakistan and should be attacked there. But he didn't seem to want that, either. "My nature is not one that appreciates military. I'm not a pro-gun person, I don't like guns or airplanes, so I can never talk in favorable terms about planes that are shooting people or bombing people, so you'll have to ask a more hard-core fellow. I'm a soft-core fellow."

Karzai seemed to have decided that he wouldn't stand by idly as the Americans sank deeper into their quagmire. He referenced the phrase from Eikenberry's cable, by then famous, about him not being an adequate strategic partner. "If a partner means a silent spectator of events conducted by Washington, if that's the kind of partner you seek, well, I'm not that partner," Karzai said. "Nor will be the Afghan people."

When Petraeus read these comments the next morning, he became enraged. He called up Ashraf Ghani, the former World Bank official who often helped mediate between Karzai and the Americans. Petraeus told him he felt betrayed, that Karzai had abandoned the surge strategy they had agreed on together. Petraeus told Ghani to listen very carefully. "Your president has put me in an untenable position," he said. "Untenable" meant that unless Karzai clarified his position, Petraeus could not go to the conference in Lisbon. He could not work with Karzai. He could not remain as ISAF commander.

Petraeus had issued a similar ultimatum to the Iraqi prime minister early in his tour as military commander in Baghdad, when the Iraqi national security adviser had presented Nouri Kamal al-Maliki's demands: accelerating transition to Iraqi control and pulling American soldiers back onto big bases, essentially reversing Petraeus's elaborate counterinsurgency plan. Petraeus let it be known that if this was truly Maliki's desire, he should let President Bush know as soon as possible, but it would also mean that Petraeus would be on the next flight to Washington. Maliki backed down.

Karzai never publicly retracted his statements, but he stepped back from the brink, and he let his spokesmen announce vague assurances that things were still okay with the Americans. By that time, relations with the palace, one senior American official told me, "were already in a death spiral." I could tell how bleak things had gotten when Karzai's chief of staff e-mailed me the day Karzai's interview was published. "Dear joshuan [*sic*]," he wrote. "Read the story. You have done very well. ISAF is not happy."

Petraeus was frustrated with Karzai's behavior. But he also felt that the palace made many of its decisions based on bad information about what was happening on the battlefield. Karzai carried his own unencrypted cell phone, and he would take calls from around the country. ISAF generals believed that Karzai's ears were poisoned with incessant rumor and unverified gossip, often at their expense. To improve communications, ISAF tried one thing after another. After reports of civilian casualties, ISAF officers would type up their version of events into PowerPoint presentations they called "storyboards" and rush copies over to the palace for Karzai's perusal. They devised a crisis hotline, so that they could reach Karzai at any moment and try to get the facts to him before he heard rumors from elsewhere. They gave one of the deputy national security advisers, Shaida Mohammad Abdali, a special "red phone" that ISAF could call in an emergency. But the few times they dialed the number, Abdali never picked up.

Petraeus wanted more ISAF eyes and ears in the palace, besides Kotkin and Bruha. So he decided to create a new office, akin to the White House Situation Room, modeled on an organization he had established in Iraq. It would operate inside the palace, staffed with American military officers and Afghan liaisons from the Army, police force, and intelligence service. The Presidential Information Coordination Center (PICC) would be staffed around the clock, taking reports of breaking news from across the country, meshing them with ISAF's version of events, and presenting the information to Karzai every morning in a daily briefing. The model was tested during the parliamentary elections that September, and Karzai liked the real-time information flowing into the palace. Petraeus told Captain Ed Zellem, a fluent Dari speaker who had been serving as the senior intelligence officer at the Afghan National Police Coordination Center in Kabul, that he would be in charge of the new operation. Petraeus gave him one piece of advice before he started: "Don't get kicked out."

Zellem embraced the work. He had an unusual fondness for Afghan culture. He discovered Afghan proverbs and began to collect them (he would later publish a book of 151 of them with a grant from the U.S. embassy). He saw his responsibilities as a link between two foreign cultures that rarely understood each other and often suspected the worst. When ISAF security officials suggested that the PICC should have barriers separating the Afghans from the Americans, Zellem flatly refused, to avoid insulting his hosts. When a group of visiting tribesmen spotted Zellem's deputy walking across a courtyard and informed Karzai of their displeasure about foreign spies inside the palace, Zellem and his American colleagues decided to lower their profile as much as possible. They traded in their camouflaged fatigues for suits. They drove to work in an unarmored Land Cruiser. They carried no weapons and wore no body armor, even though the frequency of Afghans killing their American counterparts was picking up. Under the guise of computer technicians, Zellem brought in a Special Forces team to do a security assessment of the office. If his staff needed to be rescued, Zellem was told, the Americans would have to kill so many Afghans that it would probably not be worth trying. In case of trouble, he should just lock the door. Zellem tried not to dwell on those risks. *Da qismat leek na noregey*, the proverb says. "What is written in fate cannot be changed."

The PICC was located in an office under a stone watchtower near a palace soccer field. The staff grew to seven Americans and twenty-six Afghans. The Americans installed flat-screen televisions and computers that operated on the classified NATO network. Since the power would regularly go out in the palace, Zellem had a giant backup battery installed to keep the office lights on twenty-four/seven. Every day at seven-thirty a.m., during Petraeus's morning "stand-up" briefing, Zellem would be beamed in by videoconference from the palace to give his daily update. Since Afghanistan doesn't have a navy, or navy captains, the Afghans in the situation room addressed Zellem by his equivalent Army rank. In

Dari, *zaalem* means "merciless." So to them, Captain Zellem was Colonel Merciless.

One of his basic goals was to teach the Afghans how to verify the reports they were getting from the field. If a low-level police officer in a far-off province called to say that fifty civilians had been killed in a bombing, that should not go directly into a report for President Karzai. They should get names, ages, hometowns. He wanted his Afghan officers to learn Microsoft Word and PowerPoint, and he brought in a tutor for English classes. He felt that if Karzai's palace had access to the best information possible about American military conduct, the relationship would improve.

Even so, he was regularly reminded about how difficult it would be to dispel Afghan notions about American soldiers. One weekend, an Afghan army colonel who worked at the PICC went home to visit family near Bagram Airfield. He told them about his job with the Americans in the palace. The colonel's relatives had seen Americans leave Bagram: suited in armor, draped in weapons, scowling. It must be terrible to work with them every day, they said to the colonel. How often do the Americans beat you? they wanted to know.

Zellem chose an Afghan proverb for the PICC's motto: *"Aaftab ba doo angusht pen han na mey shawad"*: "The sun cannot be hidden behind two fingers." The truth will out.

On the night of February 17, 2011, American Apache attack helicopters and F-15 fighter jets made bombing runs over the forested mountain valleys of the Ghaziabad district in Kunar Province, the remote eastern borderlands where fact and fiction were always in fluid interplay. The provincial governor announced that the Americans had caused "tremendous civilian casualties," slaughtering sixty-five innocent villagers, men, women, and children. That number, if true, would have made it one of the deadliest civilian tolls from one attack in the war. President Karzai immediately condemned the attack and dispatched an Afghan fact-finding team to the site of the violence. ISAF could count on him to provoke further confrontation. The situation became known as "the Kunar 65."

Civilian casualties were fraying the last shreds of mutual respect between the two sides. But these had been Karzai's longest-running complaints, even when he was an eager participant in all of America's new plans and programs. Karzai's comments caused intense discomfort at ISAF headquarters, but his position was remarkably consistent and, in many ways, a legitimate reflection of the common sentiment in Afghanistan, one that the American leadership often minimized or ignored. In May 2006, Karzai had written an eight-page letter to President Bush warning about the growing strength of the Taliban and the harmful mistakes of American troops. "We may have won the war, but we might risk losing the peace unless we review our strategy at this juncture, and take corrective measures where necessary," Karzai noted, asking that "avoidable mistakes should not be repeated.

"Heavy aerial bombings and other practices that are perceived heavy-handed by the population have contributed to the misperception that US forces are distrustful of the Afghans, and worse still that the US do not value the lives of common Afghan people," Karzai wrote to Bush. "Mr. President, I fear we have not only failed to harness the goodwill of the Afghan people, we are facing a certain possibility of losing it altogether."

Zellem and his team at the PICC worked overnight to collect as much information as they could about the bombings in Kunar to share with the palace. His initial assumption was that the Afghan account must be exaggerated. ISAF learned from the soldiers in Kunar that no civilians were killed; nor were their homes attacked. Petraeus's chief spokesman, Rear Admiral Gregory J. Smith, said that Apache helicopters, using rockets, Hellfire missiles, and 30mm Gatling-type guns, had targeted Taliban insurgents. Surveillance drones hovering overhead had videotaped the air strikes, he noted. "I have reviewed the footage and found no evidence women and children were among the fighters," he said. ISAF had intercepted phone calls, he added, between insurgents discussing how they might pressure the Americans to stop bombing by reporting fictitious harm to civilians. But an Afghan investigator who went to the scene documented a far different, and more visceral, story. He reported seeing twenty-seven graves, women's and children's garments, quilts and blankets, dried blood. He described how terrified villagers ran from the sound of helicopters to hide in an old Soviet-era trench, which collapsed under the bombing, burying those below.

Zellem was sure that the Afghan reports were a fiction. He had seen the aircraft gun-camera footage. The video showed what appeared to be armed Afghans moving in small teams down the mountainside. He and the rest of Petraeus's team were convinced that the men killed in this operation were legitimate military targets. But the reports of dozens of dead women and kids? "No way," a member of the PICC said. "This never happened. We knew it wasn't true."

Three days after the violence, Petraeus went to the palace for a meeting of the National Security Council, as was his Sunday routine. The next morning, I received an unusual e-mail from a senior aide to President Karzai, a man who was not normally proactive about contacting reporters. "This is anonymous," it began. "In the National Security Council of yesterday, PK asked Gen. P. about alleged civilian casualties in Kunar. The honorable General furnished the meeting with a very interesting explanation. He claimed that in the midst of the ops some pro-Taleban parents in contact with a government official decided to create a civilian casualty claim to pressure international forces to cease the op. They burned hands and legs of some of their children and sent them to hospital. Ha ha ha. Most interesting explanation i have ever heard."

The story I cobbled together, after talking to other Afghan officials who attended the meeting, was that Petraeus had suggested that it was a customary Afghan form of punishment in this part of the country for parents to discipline their children by dipping their feet in boiling water, and that these wounds might explain what the Afghan investigators had been reporting when they'd talked about casualties among children. I'd come to know many of the Afghan officials in the palace pretty well. As they discussed Petraeus's comments in this meeting, I'd never heard them so angry. "I was dizzy. My head was spinning," one of them told me. "This was shocking. Would any father do this to his children? This is really absurd."

"Killing sixty people, and then blaming the killing on those same people, rather than apologizing for any deaths? This is inhuman," said a third Afghan who was there. "This is a really terrible situation."

I was told later that President Karzai didn't react immediately to Petraeus's comments. At the end of the meeting, however, he walked back into his office and turned to his spokesman, Waheed Omar.

"Did you hear what Petraeus said?" Karzai asked.

"Yes. Which part, sir?"

"He said that children are burned in boiling water as discipline in Afghanistan," Karzai said.

"Yes sir. I heard that."

When I later asked President Karzai about this meeting, he told me he remembered Petraeus's comments "very vividly."

"Very unfortunate for America to have officials like that," he said.

In Karzai's account, the Afghans confronted Petraeus with evidence that American forces had killed innocent civilians. "He said, 'Well, it's not us. It's those parents, mothers and fathers themselves, who burned their children in order to blame us, the Americans,'" Karzai said.

"You know what this means?" Karzai told me, getting worked up. "That the Afghan people hate America so much, that in order to blame America, they burn their own children. So if it is true, it's even worse than the U.S. having bombed. Because it shows the immense anger in the Afghan people. To get rid of the United States, they burn their own children. But perhaps he didn't think of this."

The U.S. military's public relations machine dug in its heels. Admiral Greg Smith said the U.S. military "did have initial reports that the feet and hands of the children appeared to have been burned. We have observed increased reporting of children being disciplined by having their hands and feet dipped into boiling water. No one is claiming this is the case in this instance, but it may well be." Waheed Omar responded by calling Smith's comments "outrageous, insulting, and racist."

Because of mistranslation, cultural misinformation, or just clumsy delivery, the story had now become not about whether sixty-five civilians had died in Kunar, but about whether Afghans like to boil their own children. The offense taken by the palace seemed to overwhelm any desire to come to a mutual agreement on the facts in Kunar.

Even if the Americans could prove they'd acted correctly, they could not dwell on these victories, because sooner or later another tragedy would occur. Just two weeks after the Kunar 65 incident, American helicopters killed nine young Afghan boys, between the ages of nine and fifteen, who were gathering firewood near a military base in the same province. There was no denying this one, and Petraeus issued a contrite apology. President Karzai, on a subsequent trip to Kunar, made an impassioned speech calling for an end to the combat. "With great honor and with great respect, and humbly rather than with arrogance," Karzai told the crowd, "I request that NATO and America should stop these operations on our soil."

Kotkin and Bruha were feeling ever less useful in their jobs. Their purported bosses in the National Security Council clearly didn't want them around. They took on menial tasks to fill the time. Bruha taught rudimentary English to some of the palace staff. He helped set up the NSC library from books donated by the U.S. Air Force. The officers did not feel gainfully employed. The palace staff used their American mentors for personal favors or as messengers to pass on complaints. One time when Vice President Biden was in the country and moving about, the sound of his hovering helicopter bothered President Karzai. The president's aides demanded that Captain Zellem quiet the clatter. If a palace staffer wanted a scholarship to study abroad or help getting a relative a job at ISAF or a visa to the United States, they would pester Bruha or Kotkin.

Once, Zellem received an emergency call about trouble with "the treasure." President Karzai's son, Mirwais, had appendicitis, the caller said, and needed to see a Western doctor. "The treasure has to get to the ISAF hospital," one of Karzai's aides told Zellem. The hastily arranged convoy of palace staffers, bodyguards, and Karzai's wife and mewling son raced across town to the French-run military hospital near the Kabul airport. Zellem and the others waited outside the operating room in a tense cluster to hear the diagnosis. "Well, sounds like Mirwais probably ate too many cookies," the doctor said when he'd finished the checkup. "He had a stomachache. He's fine." The Afghans had a boiled-down proverb for such occasions: *Tu ba ma. Ma ba tu.* "You do for me. I will do for you." These little quid pro quos were about all the allies had left.

Kotkin and Bruha started writing up their complaints about the NSC, and their role within it. They recommended that the American and British governments stop all salary top-ups to NSC staffers, who were earning a few hundred to several thousand dollars a month on top of their government salaries from NATO, depending on their rank. Those salary payments, not to mention the ranks of palace staffers on intelligence agency payrolls, added to President Karzai's conviction that his staff members didn't work for him but were beholden to other agendas. Plus, the money didn't seem to be helping. "None of the work we have ever been associated with in the ONSC has ever been followed through to completion (or even accepted as a viable and actionable effort)," Kotkin noted.

"We have no definable job, we serve no purpose in support of the campaign plan, we have no actionable guidance from which to proceed," he added. "There is simply nothing to occupy 95% of any day at the Palace."

By the first week of February, their NSC colleague Daud Yaar had decamped for a new job at the Foreign Ministry. That month Bruha wrote up a letter for a Navy captain who ran the Afghan Hands program in Kabul, outlining his frustrations in the palace. He described the work helping to write the transition plan and serving as a conduit for information between ISAF and the palace, especially on civilian casualty cases, which laid the foundation for establishing the PICC, and he explained how their responsibilities had steadily diminished. Bruha concluded that "we have to accept that we cannot force the Afghans to conduct business the way we think they should—it is their country and their government, and we have to work within their system and what they are content with."

Bruha had decided that he could stand no more and confronted his Australian boss, Ash Power, with an ultimatum. Take him out of the palace and reassign him, Bruha told his superior, or send him home. "He wasn't particularly happy," Bruha said. "But the bottom line was, I was very frustrated. If the Afghans don't want us there, there's nothing more that I can do. I want to feel like I'm making a difference in Afghanistan, and right now I'm not."

The attempt to mimic the White House in the palace of the Afghan ruler never worked. The graft wouldn't take.

11

WHERE EVERYONE GETS ACCUSED

THE NEW CHIEF EXECUTIVE of Afghanistan's largest and most important bank arrived for his first day at three p.m. on August 31, 2010, the day after the Central Bank forced out its chairman and chief executive. He arrived alone. He walked through the main lobby, past the row of glassed-in booths with young Afghan tellers—dark suits for boys; head scarves for women—past the Western Union window, and up the stairs to the plush executive suites. He was introduced in a conference room, then shown to an office—not the chief executive's, as he'd expected, with its dark wood-paneled walls, leather chairs, and soft blue recessed ceiling lights, but the deputy's desk. Still, he felt surprisingly little hostility. He received the customary warm Afghan greeting for a new boss. The staff surrounded his chair, clapped, and presented him with flowers. A thought crossed his mind: This might not be so bad.

Massoud Ghazi was under orders from Central Bank governor Abdul Qadir Fitrat to freeze all operations at Kabul Bank. Ghazi was a shy, bespectacled accountant who had been working as the Central Bank's chief financial officer. He'd been wary of stepping into the viper's nest that was Kabul Bank, but Fitrat, who considered him the most careful, trustworthy member of his staff, had urged him to accept. Until that afternoon, Fitrat's decision to oust the bank's leadership and have the government take control had been kept a secret.

Ghazi wanted to keep a low profile himself. He was now dealing with the money of Afghanistan's most powerful men, and he didn't want to make mistakes. His first decision was to ask the documents department to issue a bankwide letter to cease all loans immediately. He wrote a second order stating that no shareholders could withdraw any money from their accounts. These were not the types of decisions that could be kept secret, among the country's gossipy business elite. Before Ghazi left the office that day, word had leaked out about the government takeover. And as soon as it did, the panic began. By the morning of September 1, the world knew that Kabul Bank was in crisis. A crowd of angry customers swarmed the sidewalk outside the bank's headquarters in the Shar-e-Naw neighborhood of Kabul, desperate to take out their savings before the bank collapsed.

The day the bank run started, the U.S. Treasury Department dispatched a three-person emergency response team from the Office of Technical Assistance in Washington. If Kabul Bank stopped functioning, the salaries of teachers, soldiers, police officers, and much of Karzai's government would not be paid. Treasury officials were now hearing rumors about Azizi Bank, started by Farnood's rival, and its reckless lending and real estate speculation in Dubai. Financial panic could take down other banks and cause economic catastrophe. Unwilling to risk sending American diplomats into a potential riot, the U.S. embassy dispatched its local Afghan staff to Kabul Bank branches to quietly watch the bank run and report back. American diplomats in the United Arab Emirates also began trying to ascertain the value of Farnood's real estate holdings. The Americans watched with growing alarm as the bank's reserves evaporated. On paper, Kabul Bank had $458 million in cash when the crisis started. Within three days, this would be gone.

Fitrat was frantically searching for money to bail out Kabul Bank. The Central Bank sold its reserves on the *hawala* market in Kabul to buy dollars to ship over to Kabul Bank, but there wasn't that much in the country. Afghanistan had around $700 million in international banks, and Fitrat needed an emergency transfer as quickly as possible. Fitrat begged the *hawala* association to leave large sums of cash in the banks to help keep them solvent. Until money could arrive from overseas, the Central Bank needed access to afghanis. The *hawaladars* agreed, but exacted an exorbitant price.

On the third night of the bank run, he called his colleagues around the world. Fitrat recalled that the United Arab Emirates' Central Bank governor was traveling, his cell phone off. The Bank of Tokyo was closed for the night. He asked the U.S. embassy if the Federal Reserve could send $300 million in two days, but an official told him no. He tried Citibank, Standard Chartered, Commerzbank. Nobody could promise a bulk delivery in one or two days; such transfers usually took at least two weeks. Finally, Fitrat found that Deutsche Bank in Germany could fly $180 million of Afghanistan's reserves to Kabul in two days, plus another $120 million the following day. The fee would be high, nearly $1 million. Fitrat needed President Karzai's approval for such a costly move. He called Karzai that night and told him Afghanistan was out of money. "Take care of it," Karzai said, and don't worry about the fee. "Afghanistan is a country where one gets accused of everything."

The money the Central Bank was spending to bail out Kabul Bank— $825 million when it was all over—was largely American money. The U.S. military and civilian agencies paid the Afghan government in dollars, which they converted into afghanis and paid to the contractors for the reconstruction and development projects. The Obama administration did not want to be seen condoning such a blatant scandal and did not allocate new funds for the bailout. But the reality of Afghanistan's finances meant that whatever pot they pulled from invariably included American tax dollars. "We didn't have any money before donors came to Afghanistan," Fitrat told me. "This was donors' money, U.S. Army money. We didn't bring this money from Venus or Mars; this was U.S. taxpayers' money and other international donors' money. We paid it from the Central Bank's reserves."

This was one of the reasons that the bank episode became, in both Kabul and Washington, the defining scandal of the Karzai government. It was a glaring example of how the greed of a small cabal of relatives and political and business cronies had stolen from both poor Afghans and the U.S. government. The scope of the fraud was enormous: the bailout represented 5 to 6 percent of the country's GDP. But the real problem was even larger, because a lot of people involved in Afghanistan lost hope. Much of the daily war news was bad: another far-off firefight and a helicopter crash, the dead marked as numbers, not names. But the venality of this situation further stripped away the veneer of valor from what was already a very weathered enterprise. After the Kabul Bank fiasco, it was harder to make the case that we were fighting for something worthwhile or paying to build something that would last.

For President Obama and his administration, it represented a turning point. It was well documented that Obama had been wary about sending new troops to Afghanistan. He knew those soldiers could win any direct physical battles they might have to fight, but what would be their larger goal: engineering an honorable and functional democratic government in this war-torn debtor state? And according to U.S. officials who discussed these issues with Obama, the bank scandal reinforced his skepticism about the American mission. Obama seemed interested in the Kabul Bank crisis. He read about it. He asked a lot of questions. "I believe that on Kabul Bank, the president used that as an intellectual litmus test on whether or not this could work," Karl Eikenberry said.

One of the things Obama wanted to know from Eikenberry was whether President Karzai was going to deal with this issue and put the people in jail who needed to be there. Eikenberry believed Karzai didn't have any incentive to confront the crisis. If he attempted to prosecute those responsible, he would be attacking his own political base, as well as his family. If he did nothing, and risked economic collapse, the Americans would pay to prevent that. The best solution would be to blame some marginal figures, accuse the United States of interference, and continue on.

"Mr. President, no. I don't think he will," Eikenberry told Obama.

In the first moments of the bank run, President Karzai ordered Fitrat to hold a press conference and insist that the situation was under control. Karzai told him to announce that the government had not fired Farnood and Ferozi but that they had resigned voluntarily, that the Central Bank had not taken over Kabul Bank, that the bank was healthy and had no problems—in other words, Fitrat said, "all the lies we told in those days." President Karzai also offered Fitrat another piece of advice: "Blame the Western media."

Fitrat complied. He stood at the microphones that afternoon, with Farnood and Ferozi looking haggard and disheveled before him, and told the gathered reporters that the Central Bank's board had decided that bank owners could not serve as managers, so Farnood and Ferozi had voluntarily stepped down. "Reports by certain media about Kabul Bank are baseless. Kabul Bank is safe and sound," Fitrat told the crowd. "Kabul Bank itself has appointed a new CEO."

"The bank is solvent, the bank is solvent," he insisted. "Kabul Bank has no cash problem."

Throughout the Kabul Bank crisis, Karzai dragged his feet. He'd refused to meet Fitrat for months. He'd resisted hiring outside experts to do a forensic audit because he didn't want the United States government to see the results. He reluctantly agreed with Fitrat's decision to oust the bank's leadership. It wasn't that the crisis didn't worry or anger him—he was furious with his brother Mahmood for getting involved with the bank and sullying the family name—but he wasn't willing to concede to American demands for reform or risk alienating his supporters. He believed that the Kabul Bank fiasco, like all the other crises, was an American conspiracy to destabilize his government and oust him from the palace.

Once Massoud Ghazi and his Central Bank team took over the bank, the industrial-scale theft stopped and the bigger test for Karzai—the prosecution of those responsible and the recovery of the lost money— began. Within days, several Kabul Bank employees, including many of the Indians and Pakistanis who had been hired for technical jobs and in the credit department, fled the country. Sherkhan Farnood, who had flown to Dubai after he'd resigned as chairman, said he would return to Kabul only if he could be kept safe. Fitrat worried that the chances of recovering the bank's money were slipping away. In palace meetings, he stressed that the guilty would flee, and it would be shameful for the government.

Ghazi soon realized that he had other problems besides the angry depositors on the sidewalk. The staff kept hiding things and wouldn't answer his questions about how the bank worked. Nobody was heeding his orders, and shareholders were using their connections in the bank to withdraw money. Farnood had wired $5.87 million to Dubai in four installments, starting the night Fitrat forced him to resign. The ousted chief executive, Khalil Ferozi, had still not left his office, and Ferozi's relatives were also withdrawing vast sums. "I realized on the first or second day: How can I trust these people?" Ghazi told me. "Everyone here was involved."

Even more worrisome to Ghazi, the bank's security guards, some fourteen hundred of them, were employed by Ferozi and were still loyal to him. The chief of security at the Central Bank had heard rumors that the guards were planning to attack Kabul Bank, to blow it up or set fire to the building. The government wanted to replace the guard force, but there weren't enough trustworthy police officers to take over. Ghazi worried that the guards were planning to destroy computers and documents and break into the vault. Fitrat believed the warnings were credible enough that he asked Ghazi to sleep at the bank, so that he could raise an alarm if the guards made a move. During the day, the crowds of angry customers kept the guards busy; at night, Ghazi was alone. "The fear," he said, "it was there."

The physical safety of the bank and its remaining staff was eventually ensured when the Afghan intelligence agency agreed to seize control from the guards. Its agents from Department 10, the section responsible for the protection of public officials, performed what amounted to a raid on the bank. The agents ordered all the guards to lay their weapons on the ground and leave the premises. The officers picked up the discarded weapons and took up positions throughout the bank. After that show of physical force, Ghazi was able to work. "If we hadn't removed the guards, I don't think we could have stopped the bank run," he said. "They were here to destroy the archives. They didn't get a chance."

Three weeks after the takeover, Fitrat drafted a letter to President Karzai. He considered it highly sensitive and did not want to deliver it through the normal channels to the palace's department of administrative affairs. Fitrat's personal secretary typed it up, and he decided to carry it by hand. An official lunch with top officials, including the finance minister, national security adviser, and Karzai's chief of staff, was scheduled for two days later; Fitrat would deliver it then. Given that the shareholders could not be trusted to voluntarily stay in Kabul or cooperate with any investigation, Fitrat wanted permission to have them placed under house arrest.

After the meal concluded, Fitrat handed the president his letter. Karzai read over the five-paragraph request in silence.

> To his excellency the President of the Islamic Republic of Afghanistan:
> Respectfully would like to apprise you that since 29 August 2010 until 20 September of the ongoing year, Sherkhan, Ferozi, and Haseen Fahim, by making excuses and arguing with each other, haven't effectively cooperated with the Central Bank and new custodian due to which the progress has been very slow.

The stilted translation of the letter that I obtained said that through loans and embezzlement, these men were responsible for taking more than $500 million from the bank. Fitrat had still been too afraid to include Mahmood Karzai's name among the others.

> Additionally, each of these men hold passports of several countries [and] risk of their escape is expected any minute. If these individuals . . . run off, recovery of the embezzled assets will not only be difficult or even impossible [but] would cause a huge reproof toward the government of [Afghanistan].

Also, it should not be forgotten to mention as every day passes by and the investigation expands, many . . . of these men's felonies, forgeries, counterfeits, ironies, and embezzlements are being exposed. As currently enough evidence exists to put them on trial.

I hope your Excellency will at least issue the order of bringing these men under custody in an appropriate location in order to avoid these criminals' flee [*sic*, translation] and public assets being squandered . . . Whatever be your direction will be implemented.

Karzai turned the paper upside down. Then back the right way. He peered at it. Fitrat noticed that the president's face was flushed as he handed the letter back.

"I'm not a dictator!" Karzai shouted. "What do you expect me to do? Do you think President Barack Obama would do this with Madoff?"

This defensive, obfuscating Karzai was very different from the idealistic man who'd started in the palace a decade ago. In the early days, he would at least muster the energy to rage to his cabinet against the evils of corruption, if not try to stop them. One of the best examples of this was the scandal over the Kabul neighborhood known as Sherpur. In the nineteenth century, the area had been the site of a British cantonment, then later an Afghan army camp. When Karzai took power, the neighborhood was mostly a squatter settlement at the base of a muddy hill. Thousands of refugees were streaming back to Kabul, and the capital's population had soared since the Taliban regime had left. Land was in demand, and this was coveted real estate: close to the palace and the diplomatic compounds. The idea of divvying up Sherpur to the new government elite was presented to Hamid Karzai over breakfast; his vice president, Mohammad Qasim Fahim, told Karzai that there was prime land surrounding the Sherpur garrison that used to be inhabited by the nobles of Kabul. Palace chief of staff Said Tayeb Jawad recalled Fahim's use of that word in particular: "nobles"—in Dari, *ashraf*.

"Now we are the new nobles of Afghanistan," Fahim told Karzai. "And I suggest that we distribute this land to the new nobles because many government officials do not have a place to stay."

The breakfast ended without a decision from Karzai. But Fahim pushed ahead. He ordered a decree drafted by the palace's administrative affairs office to distribute Sherpur among a small coterie of officialdom. The Afghan government in 2003 did not yet have a parliament, nor an elected president. When Karzai was traveling abroad, Fahim, as first vice president, became the acting interim leader, with authority to sign presidential decrees in his name. Karzai's aides worried about such trips for this reason. In their absence, Fahim would sign orders carrying out his whims—"in two days, you'd have a hundred decrees signed," one of the palace aides recalled. Even if Karzai disagreed, he could do little to stop Fahim.

In September 2003, government bulldozers demolished several dwellings in Sherpur and police chased away its residents to clear ground for the new homes. A report by the United Nations' special rapporteur that month warned the Karzai government that it must "come to grips with the prevailing culture of impunity." The U.N. investigator, Miloon Kothari, referred to the Sherpur seizures as a "microcosm of what has been happening all over the city and the country," and he called publicly for the sacking of Fahim. The Afghanistan Independent Human Rights Commission weighed in, fanning the scandal by listing twenty-nine senior officials, including six cabinet ministers, the mayor of Kabul, and the Central Bank governor, as having illegally received land in the neighborhood. The day after the human rights report was released, September 15, 2003, Karzai met with his cabinet in the palace. According to handwritten notes of the gathering and to witnesses' recollections, Karzai opened the Monday meeting by telling his ministers that there had been a lot of talk about them in the media over the past few days. "The world has never paid as much attention to an Afghan as it is paying to us right now," he noted. Their behavior had to change.

"This cabinet has lost its credibility," Karzai said.

From now on, he ordered, they would have to publicly declare their wealth and property. If they didn't want to be misjudged at the end of their term, they needed to follow some rules.

"In the eyes of people, cabinet members are land grabbers, not land givers," he said. "We should not give the impression to people that Karzai and his cabinet have come to get rich and fill their pockets."

As he lectured them, Karzai grew more animated and forceful.

"I have always tried to be nice with you in the past, but you can't expect me to be nice and soft on this issue, too. I don't want to be the president of an infamous cabinet. From ministers to the lowest-ranking government official, all of you have grabbed people's land. Today, I want to know what you are going to do about it."

The cabinet dithered. One man suggested that the government could stop giving land to people who already owned multiple homes. Another said he'd heard that only thirteen families had been evicted, so what was the problem? Mohammad Mohaqiq, a cold-eyed jihadi commander and the leader of the Hazara ethnic group, said he'd been given twelve hundred square meters (less than a third of an acre) but it would be a public "disgrace" if he was forced to return it. "If we give the land back, it would mean we've committed a crime," another added. The education minister, Yunus Qanooni, considered the whole issue a "political conspiracy" hatched by the human rights commission to defame the government. "They have given me a plot of land in Sherpur, too. We all got it," he told Karzai. "Your cabinet is not a toy that the human rights commission can play with. I think the accusers should be punished."

When it was Fahim's turn to talk, he calmly addressed Karzai. He acknowledged that Sherpur had been Defense Ministry land but added that according to the city's master plan, it was zoned for residential housing. "I admit that I gave all the orders but it is also true that nobody got more than one piece of land. If the distribution of this land raises any questions, in my defense I can say that many of the houses around the presidential palace are also owned by a few limited families.

"If we give the land back," Fahim went on, "after we have already demolished people's homes, I don't think this would have good consequences for us. It would be an insult to ask a commander or a cabinet minister to give the land back. We should take people's dignity into consideration."

Karzai was fuming. He looked around the room. "When Fahim Khan came to my office six months ago and brought me this proposal, I warned him not to do it, and today we have to deal with the consequences."

The mayor of Kabul started to say something, but Karzai cut him off.

"Be quiet!" Karzai exploded. "This is a government of thieves! You are giving Afghanistan to a few warlords, and then you try to justify it. I am the one who should be blamed because I am always easy on you. You have come to Kabul only to loot. People's lands have been stolen. You have demolished their homes. . . . Everybody is using force against poor people. We are talking as if we are an honest and just government, but we are not an honest and just government. . . . Either you are deceiving yourselves or you are trying to deceive the world.

"I will issue a decree today and ban the distribution of land," he continued. "No minister and no deputy has the right to get a single plot of land. No police chief, no commander, can demolish people's homes. People are sick of our two-faced government's treason and deception. We are a disgrace to the national interests. We are traitors to our people. We never tried to help them. We never freed them from oppression. Nobody listens to the cry of the poor, the helpless, the have-nots, no matter how loud they cry. This is the government of a few warlords, of the rich and powerful. One cannot see justice and bravery in this government. It is treason, treason, treason!

"We only think about ourselves; we don't think about the people. This government needs to change. If it is a coalition government, it should be broken up. All you do is try to cover up every wrongdoing and crime. The people's cry has reached the sky. The behavior that caused the emergence of the Taliban has come back into our lives."

During his tirade, Karzai slammed his hand down on the wooden table so hard that he injured his wrist.

Was he sincere? Those who knew him best believed he was. Karzai took it as a personal betrayal when he discovered that close aides or associates had taken land in Sherpur. But very little came of his anguish. The Kabul police commander in charge of the evictions, Abdul Basir Salangi, was removed from his post, although he would later get promoted to governor. No one lost his land. And no one touched Fahim. Even Karzai would eventually make jokes to his aides about who got houses. "Sherpur was the first big symbol of corruption," Jawad said. "People would be bitter at me: 'Why are you pushing on this, the president doesn't care.' I said, 'The president does care, this is stealing.' But the president ultimately looked the other way, or he'd joke with them: 'Oh, did you get one plot? Or two plots?' I was so disappointed to see that."

In later years, Sherpur would become the glittering symbol of wartime greed and nouveau riche bad taste. The mansions built there one-upped each other in gaudy splendor. There were colonnaded layer cakes of shimmering mirrored glass and marble, zigzagged funhouses with cruise-ship prows and wavy balustrades, rooftops crowned with eagles and fountains. Everyone just assumed the money was ill-gotten; the design of these "poppy palaces" was termed "narcotecture." One had forty-seven bedrooms and rented for $47,000 a month. Another had a poolside crow-shaped machine that enveloped swimmers in its metallic wings and blew them dry with hot air. It was a neighborhood for warlords and private security companies and American television networks. Inside, the rooms felt drafty and cold, all thin walls and marble. Nomads slung up tents in the vacant lots between them. All of it smelled of sewage.

The lesson seemed to be that even if President Karzai worried about the moral, or religious, or reputational damage that a corrupt government could cause him, those concerns were always subservient to other priorities. Karzai's ultimate goal was to hold in balance his government's fragile ethnic coalition. The militia commanders and regional warlords—and his vice president—had artillery and tanks. He would rather have these men enrich themselves on government—or, more specifically, American government—funds than launch rockets at one another. Another dynamic was that Karzai tended to see the problem as imported. He felt the worst corruption came from American defense contractors or private security companies or expat Afghans, like his brothers, who had a taste for U.S.-style consumerism and had returned to Afghanistan not to help people but to get rich. Karzai would tell Eikenberry that corruption was caused not by "real" Afghans but by the Americanized ones. "The problem is with foreign relatives," he said.

The Americans considered Karzai the master of looking the other way. But he saw himself as less naïve about the type of government this impoverished, violent, undereducated, opium-producing nation could, in the short-term, create. "In public administration, the first principle is that an administration is as good as the people in it," Karzai told me in one of our conversations. "Our administration is as good as we are. That means, our level of education, our level of institutional depth, our level of practice, our level of laws, the workability of laws, and the whole environment that we live in. So you can't detach an administration from the personnel of it. So our ability is commensurate with our education, and our experience. And that's very low."

What American officials tended to forget was that Karzai had sat through waves of emissaries who would come at him arguing with certainty the indisputable, fact-based, essential rightness of whatever policy they had come to present, only to have its opposite argued before him with equal fervor years later. When, in the beginning of the war, he asked for major new highways, he was told that the United States had come to kill the Taliban and did not do nation building—before American officials decided that inundating the country in nation-building money was the only way to defeat those same Taliban. They asked him to sideline dangerous drug-dealing "warlords" while delivering suitcases of cash to the ones of their choosing. They pushed him to drop his vice president, Mohammad Qasim Fahim, from the ticket before the 2004 election, and prodded him to remove appointed governors they disliked. Counterterrorism changed into counterinsurgency only to change back to counterterrorism. "So many messengers," Karzai once told an American military commander. "What's the message?"

"Our whole line on corruption was never really very credible," Ronald Neumann, the former U.S. ambassador, told me. "To Afghan ears, it was 'I won't fire my crooks, but I want you to fire your crooks.' By the time we really got wound up on corruption, we were also becoming very unclear about where we were going, how long we would stay, what we would do. If you're Karzai, what you're hearing is 'I want you to fire people without whom you cannot politically survive, and I know you can't do that unless I stay around and support you, and I can't tell you if I'm going to stay around.' That dialogue is wholly unpersuasive.

"Karzai has very few tools," Neumann went on. "His only tool politically is patronage and positions, and if you don't want him to use that, what is it you want him to do? How do you want him to handle the turmoil of Afghan politics and factional balancing with purity and cleanliness?

"But then we had the added problem of everything you take to him about corruption . . . being processed through a filter of 'What do they really want? Why do they want to weaken me? What is this about?' Nothing you do on corruption is accepted at face value."

Successive American ambassadors and military commanders parried with Karzai over the same questions. Why could he not clean up his government? "It was always a topic," said General Dan McNeill, the former military commander in Afghanistan. McNeill recalled a conversation with Karzai on the subject. In the fall of 2007, a congressional delegation had visited Kabul, railed against Karzai's corrupt government, then returned to complain to President Bush. Bush told McNeill to tell Karzai that if he didn't act on corruption, the money from Congress would dry up.

"My president has asked me to bring a message," McNeill remembered telling Karzai when he got to the palace. "Mr. Bush says that you've got to show more effort on getting corruption under control. If you can't, he's going to have a difficult time keeping these funds coming."

Karzai leaned back and considered the question. "General. What's that thing you have in America? You call it the big something?"

McNeill didn't understand.

"It's in the northeastern part of your country," Karzai prompted.

Boston was almost finished with the most expensive highway project in history, rerouting the main interstate through a tunnel under the city. There had been decades of delays, leaks, cost overruns, and fraud charges, and a woman had been crushed by a falling concrete ceiling panel. Karzai, an avid consumer of news, had read about the project.

"Oh, you call it the Big Dig," Karzai said.

"Mr. Karzai, I understand your message. I'll take this back to Mr. Bush."

"No, no, no, I'm not trying to be obstinate. But I want to make a bet with you. Let's bet that if we can get all fifty of the major newspapers in each of your fifty capitals in each of your fifty great states, in how many, in the first four pages, we will not find an article on corruption in government."

"I will not take that bet, Mr. Karzai."

"Okay, then. Well, how about all of your European allies? Let's go to the major newspapers in each of these European capitals. Let's look in the first six pages."

"Mr. Karzai, I've got your message. I will take it."

"No, no. Here's what I want you to tell Mr. Bush. This is not a failed state. This is a destroyed state. And I'm doing the best I can, but this is really hard stuff."

McNeill realized that when it came to Karzai, negotiating would take more than sanctimony: "He's not a witless guy."

As the Kabul Bank scandal played out, the relationship between Karzai and Fitrat deteriorated. It was humiliating enough to be denounced in front of the government's most senior officials. But as Fitrat kept pressing for action, the obstacles got bigger. It was clear that Karzai had little interest in punishing the perpetrators, so Fitrat decided to make his concerns public. In a speech to parliament, Fitrat named names. He talked about Mahmood Karzai and the other shareholders and how they were responsible for the crisis at Kabul Bank. He said they made their decisions together and that they were aware of the criminal activity and had not reported it to the regulators at the Central Bank. Whatever problems the bank faced, Fitrat said, these men should be blamed.

Whenever Fitrat went to the palace, Karzai's treatment of him was chilly, almost threatening. At one meeting, Karzai announced to the room that "those who want to make themselves heroes at the behest of foreign embassies are going to have a stick shoved up their ass," and Fitrat knew that was meant for him. After May 2011, when he wrote to central banks around the world asking them to freeze the accounts of

Kabul Bank's shareholders—because, as he noted, "all of the shareholders are suspected of embezzlement of funds"—he then had to sit in the palace and face the president and all these men and explain his actions.

He could tell that he'd crossed a line, and he began to worry about his safety. He started preparing for his departure. The governors of South Asian central banks were meeting in Kochi, an Arabian Sea port city in western India, on June 10. Two days before the conference, he booked his travel. Careful not to raise suspicions, he purchased a round-trip ticket. He packed just one suitcase, to suggest a quick visit. The rest of his belongings—books, clothes, furniture—would have to stay in Kabul. He told no one in his office about his plans. Karzai had already warned Fitrat and Finance Minister Omar Zakhilwal that they should not leave the country during this period, as the government needed their services.

On the morning Fitrat booked his tickets, he met Karzai at the palace.

"Mr. Fitrat, you're not traveling anywhere, are you?" Karzai asked.

Fitrat considered whether to lie. Then he reflected that Karzai might have already received intelligence about the trip or could have instructed the airport to report his travel.

"Mr. President, I will be traveling for a three-day trip to Asia."

"No, no," Karzai responded. "You don't need to go there."

Fitrat smiled. He insisted that the trip was necessary. He had made a commitment. On the third day, he would return to Kabul. His office was already swamped with hundreds of thousands of documents about Kabul Bank that his staff was sorting through. He would not be missed. Karzai agreed. They set a date to meet again: June 22, after Karzai returned from a trip to Kazakhstan.

"Wonderful," Fitrat said.

"Make sure you return very quickly," Karzai said.

Fitrat flew to Dubai and on to India for the conference. On the third day, he called the travel agency in Kabul and asked to cancel his return to Kabul. He needed a new ticket: Dubai to Washington. His plane touched down at Dulles International Airport on the morning of June 14. As long as the Karzai government was in power, he would not return.

With little to show for months of work, morale inside General McMaster's anti-corruption task force was foundering. His soldiers were referring to themselves as the "Fix the Impossible Task Force" and the

"Anti-Gravity Task Force." They were putting in exhausting hours to please McMaster, trying to match his four hours of sleep, wandering bleary-eyed to their bunks at one in the morning and shuffling back to their desks by five a.m. But the Kabul Bank scandal had made it clear that Karzai's government didn't want to crack down on corruption, even when it was blatant and threatened the nation's economy. "The whole thing's kind of a fool's errand," one of McMaster's aides said.

McMaster refused to slow down or change his convictions. He seemed to see corruption in moral terms and believed that through force of will he could impress that on Karzai and his government and convince them to change. The Afghans in his administration, though, had lived through three decades of violent regime change. No one had any illusions about their job security or personal safety. Loyalty was something you needed to pay for. They formed alliances for their own protection. The future was too uncertain for them to act otherwise. "They had a way of thinking that the next upheaval is around the corner, and if it comes, I need a group I can trust," recalled Annie Pforzheimer, the U.S. embassy's top political officer in Kabul. "If one of us is in power, they better be helping the rest of us."

Many of the Americans working on this issue agreed that they could not change the Karzai government's behavior unless there were real consequences—that is, if they could turn off the spigot of foreign aid coming from Washington. They called it "conditionality," making donations of U.S. taxpayer money contingent on it being spent properly. Sarah Peck, the civilian co-director of McMaster's team, had written a proposal tying U.S. nonmilitary aid to certain reforms in the Afghan government. But in the post-Salehi environment, where all of the Americans were afraid of antagonizing Karzai, it went nowhere. "It just died," one embassy staffer said. "There was no political will on the U.S. side to do it."

McMaster, for his part, was desperate for arrests. He wanted the Afghan government to put somebody, anybody, behind bars. The pursuit wore on his nerves. One of his staff members assembled a briefing packet for a routine visit to the deputy minister of rural development. Leafing through the folder in the parking lot before leaving, McMaster decided it wasn't complete. "He just unloaded on me," the staffer said. "'What the fuck? What the fuck? What the fuck? Fuck! Fuck!' For like thirty seconds." The staffer was shocked but tried to recover: "And then I was like, Okay, I'm just going to relax, this is absurd. This is a dinky little packet.

"The culture was toxic. I've never seen anything like it."

Members of McMaster's team would pull all-nighters to finish papers. They urged him to stick to more normal civilian hours, to lower his expectations. "I'm like, Look man, this place isn't going to be Sweden with bad roads," Paul Rexton Kan, a professor who came over for a short stint, remembered telling McMaster. "I don't know what you're expecting."

Embassy diplomats were avoiding McMaster's requests for information. They stopped attending the "prioritization board" meetings to pick corruption targets. One day, Earl Anthony Wayne, a deputy ambassador, chaired a meeting in an embassy conference room. He had convened Kirk Meyer, the DEA officer who ran the threat finance cell, McMaster, and several other American officials who worked on corruption issues, to try to reach some agreement on how to move forward. The American mission was deeply divided about whether corruption was even something worth fighting. The CIA station chief had told Meyer directly his work had no bearing on America's ability to win the war. Others remained convinced that government rot fueled the insurgency.

When it came time for McMaster to speak, he reiterated the same talking points he'd been making for weeks. How the Americans and Afghans needed to establish a "common understanding of the problem." How they needed to diplomatically isolate "bad actors" and create "islands of integrity" within the Afghan government. When he told them that the embassy needed to cooperate more with his task force, Meyer rolled his eyes. McMaster snapped.

"Oh, I'm sorry, Kirk, am I fucking boring you?" he said loudly. "Are you tired of hearing about corruption, Kirk? Because you should be *very* interested. You should be leaning forward."

Meyer had already been frustrated with how McMaster was trampling on his investigations. Meyer was a trained law enforcement officer with authority to conduct criminal investigations, and he didn't need this rampaging dilettante getting in his way. McMaster was meeting with Afghans all over town, gathering his own intelligence, talking about sensitive details of Meyer's investigations. Meyer felt McMaster should work on trying to clean up the Afghan army and the police, not duplicate his own work. Meanwhile, he'd been forced to listen to these "Corruption 101" briefings for weeks while nothing changed. Meyer had already told McMaster that he was tired of rehashing the same ground.

"We need to have a common understanding of the problem. I got it.

Corruption's bad. Okay. What are we going to do? What are you *doing*?" Meyer had told him before, one of their colleagues recounted.

When McMaster called him out at the meeting, Meyer started to apologize. He wasn't rolling his eyes, he said; he just wasn't feeling well. Meyer had been sick for the past four days and only attended the meeting because two generals and two ambassadors were present. Then he reconsidered.

"Wait a minute—fuck you," Meyer shot back, as one member of the meeting recalled. "You don't get to raise your voice at me.

"I'm not the State Department," Meyer told him. "I'm law enforcement and you are not going to talk to me the way you have them. Or we can take it outside."

A U.S. embassy conference room was not normally a place where fistfights were proposed. Although McMaster actually hugged Meyer after the meeting, and they would eventually even become friends, the blowup had left the room, as one person put it, "completely stunned."

McMaster "went into Patton mode," another official remembered, "and none of our great leaders said, 'Okay boys, knock it off.'"

The American anti-corruption effort was failing in two ways. The American teams were fighting among themselves, undercutting their own efforts. But that squabbling also arose from a pervasive sense of frustration about not being able to do much to solve the problem they'd been handed. With the U.S. government unwilling to take the political leap of cutting off money to an embattled ally government, they had no effective leverage to encourage change, and no way to force Afghan prosecutions that might make a difference.

In early November, Sarah Peck had flown from Kabul to Bangkok for the Fourteenth International Anti-Corruption Conference, a four-day event that convened experts from around the world. On opening day, a video message was piped in from Secretary of State Hillary Clinton. While Peck was away, McMaster invited Robert Lunnen, the lead justice department lawyer in Kabul, and other members of Lunnen's embassy team to come to his office. McMaster was frustrated that the Afghan attorney general, Mohammad Ishaq Aloko, was not sharing the files his office kept on corruption cases. Lunnen agreed with McMaster that Aloko served as a puppet for Karzai and had no interest in prosecuting the powerful. But he felt reform needed to come from Karzai's palace, or nothing would change, according to his colleagues. McMaster wanted Lunnen's team to push the attorney general harder to make prosecutions.

Since the DOJ lawyers mentored the attorney general's prosecutors and worked in their offices every day, McMaster wanted them to get the corruption case files for him. Lunnen refused. Raiding their file cabinets would be both illegal and a breach of trust with the Afghan lawyers. McMaster's military task force, in any event, had no business with the criminal files.

McMaster erupted and started shouting at the lawyers. He said he had "never been treated so poorly by a dickhead I agree with." McMaster snapped his notebook shut. He stood up, kicked a chair, stormed out of the meeting, and slammed the door.

Sometimes these fights stayed within Kabul, battle scars of the secret war within. This one didn't. The lawyers reported McMaster's outburst to their bosses, all the way to Attorney General Eric Holder. He wrote a letter to Petraeus complaining about McMaster's conduct and demanding an apology. The people in the meeting were asked to give affidavits describing what happened. From then on, the lawyers in Kabul referred to themselves as the "Dickheads of Justice."

"That's the way he handled every meeting," one member of the task force said. "If you didn't agree with him, he threw a temper tantrum."

Peck learned about the meeting only after she returned to Kabul from the conference in Thailand. McMaster didn't mention it to her; she had to learn about the fight from another colleague. For her, this was the final insult. Two days after she learned of the lawyers' meeting, she quit her job and flew home.

The longer McMaster stayed in Kabul, the more blatant the corruption cases that faced his task force seemed to become. An Afghan governor was accused of taking bribes in exchange for government contracts, using donor aid money to build a slew of homes, and colluding with the Taliban. Afghan prosecutors eventually dropped the case. Members of the Afghan air force were suspected of using their aircraft to ferry drugs and illegal guns around the country. One of the Afghan officers thought to be shipping illicit cargo burst into a U.S. military meeting room at the Kabul airport in April 2011 and murdered eight of his U.S. Air Force mentors. The investigation fizzled.

The Dawood National Military Hospital, where Afghan soldiers wounded in battle were sent for treatment, was looted by its administrators to the point that patients were allowed to die of starvation. The American-funded hospital allowed Afghan veterans to languish in soiled sheets with maggot-infested wounds. McMaster's task force helped discover that the surgeon general, an ally of President Karzai, had stolen tens of millions of dollars from the defense ministry and in medicine intended for the wounded troops.

These revelations were almost never followed by punishment. Of the roughly 2,000 corruption cases investigated, only a couple of dozen people suffered consequences and almost all of them were minor figures. With the military hospital, Karzai initially suspended several officials, including the attorney general, but later demanded evidence that McMaster's team had already shown him. McMaster's task force managed to convince an American general to threaten the Afghan minister of defense with a loss of U.S. aid if the hospital investigation didn't proceed, but the inquiry never amounted to much and the scandal eventually faded away.

McMaster's team periodically asked the coalition command that mentored the Afghan security forces to cut funding that benefited certain units, such as an Afghan border police team in western Afghanistan believed to be running drugs into Iran. They debated freezing budgets and halting the delivery of helicopters to Afghan forces. But the American mentors would always decline, saying "it would demoralize the units," one of McMaster's aides recalled. When the task force tried to develop a political strategy to lobby Afghan politicians, NATO's civilian representatives in Kabul shot it down. "They saw any suggestion that Mad Dog McMaster would be meeting with anyone in parliament as dangerous," another team member said.

Some of McMaster's colleagues admired him. They considered him intense, but not cruel, a man with a relentless drive to bend the bureaucracy to his will, to "reverse the slide toward the acceptance of defeat—in the realm of corruption and in our mission more broadly," as one subordinate put it. But by then the battle against Afghan corruption had been lost. The Obama administration ultimately did not have the political will to confront Karzai's palace. In the spring of 2011, the State Department issued guidance to the Kabul embassy that the priority should be on "predatory" corruption, the local cop demanding a bribe on the street, the kind of corruption that supposedly made normal Afghans look to the

Taliban for help. The veterans of the corruption wars saw the guidance for what it was: a warning to stay away from high-level politicians, or anything else that might rile up President Karzai, as the focus turned to withdrawing troops from Afghanistan.

As a postmortem, embassy staffers and members of McMaster's team drafted a long cable deconstructing their failures. The document was both memorial to a dead effort and a lesson intended for future diplomats who might tread this path. The draft cable, dated June 8, 2011, was called "Impunity Incorporated: The Demise of the Afghan Counter-Corruption Program." After input from various agencies within the embassy, it needed to get top-level approval before being shipped back to Washington. But somewhere in the upper reaches of Eikenberry's embassy, the cable got killed, and it never reached home.

There were no brass bands or fanfare when Eikenberry finally took his seat next to his wife on a Safi Airways commercial flight out of Kabul. When he left, in July 2011, he didn't regret his opposition to the troop surge or his diagnosis of the problems with Karzai's government. "When it comes to your reporting and your analysis, you've got to call it like you see it," he told me. "Don't feel under pressure to always say the glass is half full when it might be near empty."

During Eikenberry's tenure, the Americans saw all the problems, but that didn't mean they could solve them. Just exposing corruption, they'd learned, didn't mean anyone would care. That was one regret that would linger with Eikenberry after he got home: that the Americans had become activists. They'd tried to change too much. "I think we just let it get out of control," he said. "Just like we did in Vietnam."

The most frustrating thing for Eikenberry was the view in Washington that he had failed in his most important task, keeping Hamid Karzai quiet. He'd tried to be rational and civil with Karzai, but the fights had become too personal. Even a diplomat could swallow only so much. Not long before Eikenberry left, Karzai gave a speech likening U.S. troops to an occupying army and made another order that all bombings of Afghan homes should stop. Eikenberry stood at a podium in Herat and let his frustration loose.

"When Americans, who are serving in your country at great cost—in terms of lives and treasure—hear themselves compared with occupiers, told that they are only here to advance their own interest, and likened to the brutal enemies of the Afghan people, they are filled with confusion and grow weary of our effort here.

"At the point your leaders believe that we are doing more harm than good, when we reach a point that we feel our soldiers and civilians are being asked to sacrifice without a just cause, and our generous aid programs dismissed as totally ineffective and the source of all corruption, the American people will ask for our forces to come home."

For Eikenberry, a career military man who'd been in Afghanistan for half the war, that time had come.

Two days before he left the city, he visited the Kabul Zoo. He'd always liked that quiet enclosure, despite its rather sad collection. I went along with him for the tour. He brightened up immediately when he saw the animals.

"You've got camels now?" he asked the zookeeper in surprise.

Eikenberry noted with pleasure the four-horned ram from Badakhshan.

"Boy. There's none like them in the world."

But it was the lone pig—people used to call it Afghanistan's only pig— that was his favorite. When he returned home, Eikenberry would get a job teaching at Stanford, including a class about the war and all that had gone wrong. He would drive among the campus's sandstone buildings with their red-tiled roofs in his yellow Mini Cooper. On the dash he kept a pig in a hula skirt.

"There he is," Eikenberry said when he saw the Afghan pig standing in a mud puddle. "Does he have a name?"

"Khuk," the zookeeper said.

"How old is he?"

"Twelve year."

The pig's thatchy white hair was filthy. He was one of two pigs given to the zoo by the Chinese government at the start of the war; the other had died. The pig was an oddity in this Muslim country, and had even been quarantined by the superstitious staff during the swine flu pandemic in Mexico.

"Is he in good health?" Eikenberry asked.

"Yes. He is happy in the water and mud."

Eikenberry squatted in the mud in his khakis and blue blazer and fed the pig a sugar cube.

"Boy. He is happy there. His name is Khuk?"

Eikenberry patted the pig on the back. A small entourage of aides and security guards were watching. Eikenberry had several pictures of himself taken with the pig. He would ask about his well-being long after leaving Afghanistan.

"If he could talk right now, he would be saying, 'I, for one, like the United States of America.'"

The entourage moved on. A young aide turned to a colleague.

"*Khuk*, I think, just means 'pig' in Dari," she said.

U.S. ambassador Karl Eikenberry next to Khuk the pig at the Kabul Zoo

12

COULDN'T BE MORE HELPFUL

THE INTERNATIONAL PRESSURE that was mounting on Mahmood Karzai and the president over the financial scandals and anti-American criticism had all but disappeared from Ahmed Wali Karzai. After the investigation of his possible drug-dealing ties turned up nothing, he became the official ISAF-approved power broker of Kandahar. President Karzai took satisfaction in declaring Ahmed Wali innocent of years of charges against him. He stood at his podium and cast the whole issue as another tired example of foreign attacks on his government. "There have been many things mentioned about my brother Ahmed Wali Karzai, who is the chief of the provincial council in Kandahar, particularly in foreign media and by foreigners. We have been in touch with the foreigners regularly, continuously, and consecutively asking them to put forward their evidence or documents if they have any. . . . No matter how hard we tried, nobody brought us any evidence," he said. "I have called them and talked about it twenty or twenty-five times in the past five weeks."

ISAF officials had decided that they would not harass or investigate or attempt to force Ahmed Wali from his perch in Kandahar. Instead, they wanted to harness his power. This turnaround in relations proved extreme. Instead of being the reason the United States was losing the war in Kandahar, he became central to the military strategy for its next phase.

Nick Carter crafted his political strategy for the upcoming Kandahar offensive with Ahmed Wali at its heart. Carter felt he had to be pragmatic. The line outside the Kandahar governor's office would never match Ahmed Wali's. Afghans knew who could solve their problems. As much as he might want the power balance to match the bureaucratic flow chart, in Kandahar it didn't. Every eighteen hours, one of Carter's soldiers was dying. He couldn't waste time on appearances. Wesa could attend ceremonies and ribbon cuttings and posture all day long, but Carter intended to leverage Ahmed Wali's influence to make appointments throughout local government deemed sympathetic to ISAF's cause. He would rely on Ahmed Wali to pave the way with tribal chiefs for military clearing operations, to gather intelligence on enemy movements, to bend President Karzai's ear when Karzai hesitated about supporting ISAF's plans.

"It really boiled down to a case of realizing that to succeed, we'd have to try and deal with the devil we knew," Steve Beckman, the military intelligence chief in Kandahar, told me. The American strategy was now to build Kandahar through Ahmed Wali, and everyone would abide it. But the generals and diplomats in charge still wanted to keep their meetings with him out of the public eye. On one occasion, when Ahmed Wali came to Kandahar Airfield to meet Carter, he was whisked out a back door, so that House Speaker Nancy Pelosi wouldn't see him as she arrived.

The actual combat was a relatively small part of the military offensive in Kandahar. The American soldiers would make foot patrols through villages or drive their armored trucks to meet local tribesmen. They would hire construction firms to dig new wells or build bridges and roads. If Afghan police needed a solar-powered highway checkpoint so they could more effectively search passing cars for explosives, the American soldiers would comply. If the Taliban were ambushing convoys with homemade bombs placed in drainage culverts, the Army would spend the day installing mesh screens over the mouths of the culverts. The broader goal was to be seen making life better and safer for more people, and to share that credit with the Afghan government. If the government could win the respect of the people and entice the Taliban to rejoin society, that would amount to victory.

But for all sorts of reasons, General Carter's team was not happy with most of the local government officials. In the neighborhoods in and around Kandahar, some district chiefs colluded with the Taliban. Some stole foreign aid earmarked for schools or hospitals or peasant farmers. Those based in the more dangerous outskirts, places like Panjwayi or Zhari, often lived in the city and rarely even made an appearance for these people they purportedly represented. Finding an honest, educated person to take a local government job in Kandahar was not easy.

For years, the Taliban had been systematically picking off bureaucrats associated with the Karzai government, from the presidential palace staff to the lowest district official. In Kandahar in 2010, government officials were dying at the rate of more than six per month. The office manager of the city's Sarposa prison was shot by a bicyclist who pedaled up to his car window during his morning commute. The city's deputy mayor was executed as he bent to pray in a mosque. Six months later, his successor was shot by young men on motorcycles as he drove home from work. And nine months after that, their boss, Kandahar mayor Ghulam Haider Hamidi, a close friend of the Karzais', died when a suicide bomber blew up inside his office.

Threats were often as effective as actual violence. The chancellor of Kandahar University, Hazrat Mir Totakhail, once held his Nokia cell phone out to me with a nervous hand. "We've warned you many times to stop working with the government," the text message read. "Just keep counting the days of your life. Your death has been approved." Of the 120 job slots budgeted for Kandahar's municipal government, about forty people were willing to show up to work. The governor's office had a similar shortfall. Even those numbers tended to overstate the staffing, as many of those employees served in menial jobs such as cooks, gardeners, or tea boys. In the four key rural districts around the city—Zhari, Panjwayi, Arghandab, and Dand—the U.S. military had identified forty-four jobs that were necessary to maintain a minimally functional government. Twelve of those positions were filled. Kandahar City had about half a million residents and hundreds of millions of dollars of U.S. military construction projects, but for months the municipality had a single engineer. The incentives sufficient to entice people to risk working in Kandahar were in other fields. An Afghan in Kandahar working for the U.S. military or an American contracting firm could easily bring home $1,000 a month. At city hall, he would earn $70.

Some of these problems were insurmountable, but Carter wanted at least to staff the local positions with people who wouldn't fight against the NATO coalition. He also wanted to spread the wealth among tribes, to ease some of the rivalries. Tribes that got excluded from political power or the bounty of ISAF largesse had a greater incentive to fight. (Carter's intelligence officers estimated that NATO contracting from Kandahar Airfield—the whole avalanche of goods needed for an installation with thirty thousand people—generated about $1 billion a year, 95 percent of which went to two extended families: the Karzais and the Sherzais.) Therefore, the distribution of government appointments—the first step to dipping one's straw into the aid gusher—should reflect the proportionate tribal makeup in any given area. This made sense as an abstract exercise in fairness (ignoring the fact that it was exactly the kind of gift-giving patronage ISAF was battling with the Karzai administration about).

You could sketch out a rough guide to Kandahar along tribal lines. Achekzais controlled the border out at Spin Boldak. Alokozais ran the Arghandab Valley. Noorzais smuggled whatever they wanted. Barakzais manned the Kandahar airport. Popalzais dominated government. Mohammadzais, the tribe of the governor, boasted royal lineage, education, and bureaucratic standing. Yet dissident factions and cross-tribal allegiances muddied the waters so much that it was dangerous to guide such decisions by tribal maps. And no American on a one-year military tour in Kandahar could know enough about the players and their web of personal histories and back-channel communications to safely assess whether some deputy provincial customs officer Ahmed Wali was nominating would be a service to redistribution and fairness or a lackey to further his empire and enrage his enemies.

The real arrangements existed beyond the knowledge of the American military, in what one Canadian adviser to the Kandahar governor referred to as the "Afghanosphere." But Americans couldn't function in that world. So they needed people like Ahmed Wali Karzai. "We unashamedly used him to manipulate the politics of Kandahar to get the right governors in the right places," one of the people involved said. "Ahmed Wali, throughout that process, could not have been more helpful."

The commanders liked Ahmed Wali because he could decipher the bewildering array of tribal grudges and allegiances of the most obscure village. The Afghans who worked with the Americans were often embarrassed by how little the Americans actually knew about Afghanistan. The basic intelligence presented as fact was often inaccurate, recalled Abdullah Sharif, an Afghan-American adviser to the State Department in Kandahar. "Just the basic stuff was wrong: tribal affiliations, political alignments."

Having lived in the United States, Ahmed Wali could see the war with both foreign and domestic eyes. Soldiers found him astute at anticipating their concerns. Stephen Bowes, a Canadian colonel (later a general) who served in Kandahar in 2005, recalled a provincial council meeting where a human rights group presented complaints about the Pashtun custom of arranging marriages for child brides. As another council member started mocking the presenter, Ahmed Wali interjected, trying to assure Bowes about the societal context and his concern over the issue.

"He was exposed to the Western mentality but was also trying to convey to me: We're living in an area that is very poor and uneducated," said Bowes. "He was trying to sensitize me to the fact that it would take years to change."

Ahmed Wali was valuable. The month after the "deep dive" into his dealings, American diplomats presented him with what they called their "red line" plan. There were five main points. He was not to interfere in government appointments (except when asked by ISAF). He was not to block people from attending tribal gatherings. He was not to disrupt "the rule of law." They wanted him to refrain from taking advantage of Afghan or NATO contracting. And he had to transfer his private militia forces over to the Afghan government. If he violated these rules, ISAF would consider itself justified to act against him. In practice, these rules were vague enough that Ahmed Wali won a free pass to act any way he chose.

Ahmed Wali dispensed advice of all kinds, including where the U.S. military should spend its money. He told a Special Forces commander that townspeople in one village would leave the Taliban once they had jobs. He suggested buying the village five thousand hammers so the men could break rocks into gravel. "I know you need a lot of gravel," Ahmed Wali told the commander. He failed to mention his family was in the gravel business.

During meetings with U.S. military officers, Ahmed Wali lobbied for what he called the Helmand River Project. He wanted the soldiers to build a massive canal running from the Helmand River through the deserts of Zhari and Maiwand, an infrastructure project that would turn swaths of desert into fertile farmland and ignite the local economy. General Terry's military intelligence officers later learned that Ahmed Wali had been buying up land along the proposed canal route. If the Americans built the canal that land would instantly become far more valuable. The soldiers declined.

Ahmed Wali found ISAF new district governors in Khakrez, Panjwayi, and Zhari (although two of the three men would get assassinated). He persuaded Governor Wesa to appoint a new police chief for Kandahar City (who would also be killed). He lobbied President Karzai to support American military operations as they prepared to ramp up for an offensive in Kandahar. Karzai felt U.S. military operations were causing too much damage in Pashtun parts of the country, which happened to be where the insurgency was based. Ahmed Wali, at the behest of the U.S. military, pushed to win Kandahar's tribal support for these operations, and he convinced the president to come to Kandahar and speak to the people directly.

*Hamid Karzai visits Nawa, in Helmand Province,
on January 2, 2010.*

Frank Ruggiero, one of the American diplomats who attended this *shura* gathering, remembered how Ahmed Wali was at his most solicitous during it. Ruggiero had told Ahmed Wali that the gathering was an important gauge of public opinion, and he didn't want it stage-managed in any way. Ruggiero knew that Ahmed Wali would ultimately decide who attended. But he felt it was important for President Karzai to hear a realistic sample of public opinion, not just canned support. Some fifteen hundred tribal elders from across southern Afghanistan showed up to meet with President Karzai in a sweltering room in the governor's compound. One after another, the elders spoke about their fears of a U.S. military offensive. They worried about the harm that would come to innocent civilians and the damage to their homes and crops. They didn't believe the Taliban could be defeated. President Karzai told the crowd that he sympathized with their concerns.

"Afghanistan will be fixed when its people trust that their president is independent and not a puppet," he said. "We have to demonstrate our sovereignty. We have to demonstrate that we are standing up for our values."

Karzai asked the crowd whether they were happy about the upcoming military operation. A loud murmur echoed across the vast meeting room.

"We are worried!" one man shouted at the president.

"Listen to me carefully: until you're happy and satisfied, we will not conduct this operation," Karzai said, to loud applause.

For the Americans, the *shura* was a disaster. The president had distanced himself from their operation. The residents had expressed their anger and bitterness. Once again, the Afghan allies didn't look much like allies. After the meeting, Ahmed Wali rushed over to Frank Ruggiero, beaming with delight.

"So, did I deliver?" Ahmed Wali asked.

"Did you deliver what?"

"All those messages were really negative, right?"

Ruggiero sighed. "Uh, yeah. It was a great *shura*."

A few months after Ahmed Wali's official ISAF exoneration, a distraught Afghan man walked up to the guards at the gates of Camp Nathan Smith, on the east side of Kandahar City. The man said he needed to speak to the foreigners in private. He was ushered past the dirt-filled barriers and down corridors of chain-link fencing, into a compound that had once been a fruit-canning factory. Inside was an oasis, smaller and more pleasant than Kandahar Airfield, larger and more comfortable than the numerous gravel-and-moon-dust combat outposts farther afield. There were fountains and palm trees in a central courtyard, unlimited mini-cartons of Häagen-Dazs in the cafeteria, evening outdoor movie screenings, and a walled-in swimming pool. The visitor claimed that a relative of his was being held in a secret prison run by Ahmed Wali.

The relative owed Ahmed Wali a debt. He had been captured and was being held in a building east of the city, along the road to the Pakistani border. There were other prisoners, he said. The man was beside himself and needed help. He had nowhere else to turn. The news was not necessarily out of context for the local milieu ("The Sopranos come to Deadwood," one soldier called Kandahar). A few years earlier, a former provincial governor, Asadullah Khalid, had been accused of running a secret basement torture chamber inside the governor's mansion. The Afghan mercenaries who guarded Camp Nathan Smith were once led by a man whose nickname was "The Skinner."

Still, diplomats on the base found the torture allegation startling; the Canadian intelligence analyst who took the man's statement was "extremely upset," one of his superiors told me. "He thought we could be accomplices to war crimes." Word trickled up to Bill Harris, the senior American on base. U.S. soldiers from a military police unit followed up and drove to the location. The MPs found a private house with jail-like fortifications: bars on the windows and heavy metal doors, all locked. The soldiers discovered the man's relative languishing inside, along with other prisoners. He told them he owed Ahmed Wali money and that he'd been in jail for six weeks. "They were ransoming him against the debt," Harris said.

The soldiers made another trip to the jail, but that was the extent of it. "The MPs didn't want any part of it after that," Harris said. "That would have been something we turn over to the police. We had a report. It's credible. We're turning it over to you."

A Canadian official on the base would remember that episode for a long time. A CIA officer came to interview the Canadian analyst about the man's visit, but the American spy was inscrutable. The Canadian knew that Ahmed Wali got paid by the CIA. "It was like, 'Okay, you caught us, you know about it,' without making any admissions."

Stories in Afghanistan often didn't have endings any more satisfying than that. This one was no exception. The secret prison would be another ghostly suggestion of the darker side of the American partnership with Ahmed Wali.

"We found that one," the Canadian said. "That doesn't mean there weren't others."

Four of the U.S. Army's eight-wheeled eighteen-ton mine-resistant Stryker armored vehicles had just been bombed into submission. They stood immobilized off Highway 1, at the point where an earlier bomb had blown a hole in the asphalt, forcing traffic to detour through the dirt along the shoulder. The U.S. trucks required to haul away the wreckage had arrived. At the same time, Taliban fighters were reeling a wire used to detonate bombs into a mud-walled compound, the sort of trap the American soldiers fighting there had seen before, while U.S. commanders discussed the potential consequences of firing their own explosives to level the Taliban compound. Right at the top of Lieutenant Colonel Jeffrey French's list of concerns that dangerous day, when fourteen bombs either exploded or were found in the same patch of dirt, was the row of Afghan cargo trucks waiting to get past this complicated mess, a line that stretched far into the desert. "I don't want to be piling up massive amounts of coalition force vehicles," French radioed to his soldiers before leading his convoy out of the congestion and clearing a path for traffic. "It doesn't really send a good message."

For the 5th Stryker Brigade Combat Team, 2nd Infantry Division, deployed around Kandahar, the mission was not killing insurgents but facilitating what they called "freedom of movement." By allowing the safe flow of commerce and travelers on the highways—particularly the ring road the U.S. government had helped pay to rebuild earlier in the war— they hoped to fan to life the region's economic embers. Their mission was central to the overall military strategy for Kandahar. By establishing a cordon of coalition forces around the city, military commanders hoped to encourage people to get on the roads, restoring a semblance of normalcy. One of the biggest obstacles to this mission, French and his subordinates in the thirteen-hundred-man battalion soon realized, were the men hired to protect their supplies. Security guards who traveled with the coalition supply convoys up and down the highways would often fire their guns indiscriminately as they drove through villages. This would provoke the Taliban or the villagers to fire back, frightening people off the roads and adding to the atmosphere of danger and lawlessness.

One of the worst offenders was known to be Watan Risk Management. The company, owned by two Karzai family cousins, Rashed and Rateb Popal, had become one of the most powerful in the world of military contracting. The brothers, who had lived in the States, both had checkered pasts. Rateb Popal had spent nearly a decade in prison in the

American and Afghan soldiers patrol a portion of Highway 1 outside Kandahar.

United States for smuggling heroin. Rashed had also pled guilty to conspiracy to import heroin and received probation. But these blemishes did not dissuade the coalition from rewarding them handsomely. The Canadian government hired the company to provide security on its signature foreign-aid project: the renovations of the Dahla Dam reservoir, outside Kandahar. But the most lucrative contract was known as Host Nation Trucking. Watan was one of eight firms to win a $2.2 billion contract (which amounted to more than 10 percent of Afghanistan's GDP) to deliver U.S. military supplies to bases across the country. Watan's role was to provide protection, in the form of heavily armed guards, for the six to eight thousand NATO supply convoys that each month delivered Pop-Tarts, toilet paper, Humvee fuel, Entenmann's muffins, lobster, sleeping cots, flat-screen televisions, or anything else the two hundred military bases might require.

One of the company's leading mercenaries was a man named Ruhullah, a Popalzai who'd grown up in a village next to Karz. He'd been recruited by Ahmed Wali to work with the U.S. Special Forces early in the war and went on to command a private security guard force of some six hundred men. His nickname was "The Butcher." American soldiers had arrested him for drug trafficking in 2009, after allegedly finding heroin in his house. Both U.S. and Afghan officials told me that Ahmed Wali had persuaded American commanders to free him after less than two weeks in detention. "The Karzais got him out of prison, and the issue was silenced," a senior Afghan official in Kandahar said. "It was covered up." Ruhullah admitted, as part of a later lawsuit, that he was released thanks to his relationship with the Karzais (although he claimed he was arrested because of tension between Watan and ISAF, rather than drugs).

Ruhullah claimed to be responsible for guarding thirty-five hundred U.S. supply trucks each month, and he charged as much as $1,500 per truck for his services. His income, in 2009, was $12 million. From his fees, Ruhullah, and mercenary commanders like him, would then pay to ensure safe passage for their convoys. These were not small operations. The average convoy consisted of three hundred trucks, and they would be accompanied by four hundred to five hundred guards in gun-mounted Toyota pickups. These payments went to Afghan police and army officers, intelligence agents, district and provincial governors, and Taliban commanders—anyone who could claim control over any stretch of road. The price tag per policeman was $1,000 to $5,000 per month, Ruhullah said, but he "must pay them. There is no other way."

In December 2010, after Ruhullah's statements to congressional investigators about these bribes, the U.S. Army attempted to prohibit Watan from receiving future contracts. In a memo justifying that decision, a lawyer with the procurement fraud branch of the Army's contract and fiscal law division wrote that on May 14, 2010, the Afghan government had suspended Watan after two incidents when its guards had fired on civilians. "In the immediate aftermath of this suspension, multiple attacks were made on ISAF supply convoys, resulting in the closure of Highway 1 to further resupply convoys. Two weeks later, after approximately 1,000 trucks were stranded on the highway, this suspension was lifted. No further attacks were made on ISAF convoys following the termination of the suspension."

Watan hired a prominent American law firm, Venable LLP, sued the Army over the proposed debarment, and had it reversed. But the suspicions remained about Watan's behavior on the Kandahar highways. People thought its guards could turn the violence up or down when they chose. Many American soldiers believed that these types of business interests lurked behind many attacks that might otherwise appear to be insurgent violence.

"Why would they go and pick a gunfight like that?" asked Lieutenant Colonel Joseph Cooper, the battalion's officer in charge of governance and development projects. "Well, if you go and you pick that gunfight, it illustrates the need for security. In reality, there wasn't a lot of need for security on a lot of those convoys."

The security guard violence became such an acute problem that French's battalion would lie in wait for its own supply convoys, to catch the guards in the act of shooting into villages so soldiers could document the crimes. The guards were killing innocent civilians while working for the U.S. government, which was making the battalion's job that much harder. "Think about it," Cooper told me. "If every time you've got a convoy rolling through town, and it's got U.S. military shit all over it and some Afghan shooting at you, what do you think if you're the locals? The U.S. military is trying to kill me."

Ahmed Wali always denied that he owned any particular company and never admitted to a salary of any kind, even as American officials at Kandahar Airfield were estimating his annual income at around $250 million. The way he made money, many of his colleagues and relatives insisted, was by making the other military contractors in southern Afghanistan pay him a percentage of their contracts. Rival private security owners all knew that this was how the system functioned. If it was a man as strong and politically connected as Ahmed Wali, you respected his territory. One company owner told me that he wouldn't consider working in four southern provinces—Helmand, Kandahar, Uruzgan, Zabul—without Ahmed Wali's permission. Once, Ahmed Wali offered him part of an Interior Ministry contract to do convoy security between Kandahar and Helmand. The owner would get to keep the contract in his name, but out of the $1,500 per guard it paid—there were two thousand guards—he would receive only $350. The rest would go to Ahmed Wali.

"That's the way it used to work," he said, estimating that Ahmed Wali had that arrangement with at least fifteen companies. "He was a well-orchestrated person. He knew what to do."

On one occasion, a convoy of guards opened fire as it passed through the Hutal village in an area of Kandahar called Maiwand and killed a young Afghan girl of about five years old. An elder from the area, Mohammad Yusuf, led a delegation to Kandahar City for a gathering where Ahmed Wali and other city fathers were meeting. As Yusuf started to complain about the girl's killing, Ahmed Wali "came over and grabbed him and told him to be quiet, very forcefully," said Captain Casey Thoreen, a company commander in Maiwand at the time. "And he wouldn't do it. [Ahmed Wali] grabbed his arm and told him to shut up and sit down and wouldn't let him speak. [Yusuf] was highly, highly insulted and wanted justice, and wanted revenge."

The view on Ahmed Wali looked different depending on where you stood in the chain of command. The generals saw him as a man with the political clout to execute their plans. To the lower-ranking soldiers out trying to make Kandahar's highways safer, he was the enemy. The goals were always out of balance. Local government officials who were staunch opponents of the Taliban might also be stealing aid money; or they could be so accommodating to the Americans that people saw them as foreign lapdogs.

"Does anyone else see this as a problem?" a lieutenant colonel with the Army Corps of Engineers asked some forty soldiers gathered in a muggy tent in Kandahar Airfield one afternoon during a meeting I attended. He was discussing how the Afghan border police commander, General Abdul Raziq, had just offered to give the U.S. military prime land at a border crossing to build a waiting area for NATO cargo trucks. And yet this same Raziq, everyone knew, was believed to earn millions of dollars a year trafficking opium and extorting drivers of those same cargo

General Stanley McChrystal, right, and General Abdul Raziq tour the Afghan-Pakistani border crossing in the town of Spin Boldak.

trucks. Silence followed the lieutenant colonel's question. Raziq was a key ally because he had the ruthlessness to keep his patch of Afghanistan quiet. Corruption was a tricky enemy when it had to compete with security, intelligence, or killing the Taliban. "What is the focus?" Lieutenant William Clark, an American squadron commander at the border crossing, asked me. "Is it security and stability? Or is it governance and anti-corruption? That's a discussion well above me."

It was weird how the Afghan war did actually work in one-year cycles. The embassy emptied out in the summer, and dozens of new diplomats arrived. New military units rotated in, and the old lessons disappeared with the departing soldiers. The same debates got recycled and the same problems rehashed. Carter's successor in Kandahar was a silver-haired American general from Georgia named James Terry, commander of the 10th Mountain Division, the final unit of the surge. At his division's pre-deployment briefings at Fort Drum, Terry would ask his subordinates how, in the ninth year of their stalemated campaign, was the senior American general for the entire Pashtun south supposed to behave. "What role do I play? Am I a soft-touch guy? Am I a powerbroker? Am I a heavy hand?

What face do I wear when I get down there?" One of his subordinates, Brigadier General Kenneth Dahl, recalled telling Terry: "Sir, you're a powerbroker, whether you like it or not. You own all the money. You own all the combat power. Nothing's going to happen without you enabling it. Whether you want it or not, you're a powerbroker."

During their pre-deployment preparation, ISAF advisers and D.C. think-tank types briefed the division's officers on how the Karzais ran the country for their own enrichment and got them well acquainted with Ahmed Wali's reputation. The new American military forces came into Kandahar seemingly oblivious of Carter's change of heart about Ahmed Wali. It was as if the whole fraught soul-searching and deep-diving of the past year had never even happened.

"We were absolutely convinced that AWK was the source of all evil," Lieutenant Colonel Ketti Davison, the military intelligence chief for the division, told me.

Davison and other division leaders designed their strategy to isolate and marginalize Ahmed Wali. They would frustrate him and work around him, bring new people under the tent. They would establish Terry's dominance and the authority of the provincial governor. They would shower their attentions on Afghans whom Ahmed Wali considered rivals or subordinates or peripheral players in the politics of Kandahar.

They made a list of everyone Terry would meet, and "Ahmed Wali was dead last," Davison said. "Well, maybe Mullah Omar was after him." This strategy held for about six weeks. During that time, Ahmed Wali's emissaries made several inquires to Regional Command South headquarters, asking when Terry would be meeting the most important man in Kandahar. Terry eventually accepted an invitation to see Ahmed Wali at Camp Gecko, the CIA base in Kandahar. The setting was familiar to Ahmed Wali: his aides said he visited the base three to four times per week. And just like generals before him, Terry came away impressed with Ahmed Wali's knowledge of Kandahar and eagerness to help. Ahmed Wali promised his support for all the anti-Taliban district governors and police chiefs that the Americans liked. He was ready to cater to all their needs. "That first meeting set the tone," Davison recalled. "It was surprising to us that he wasn't the obstacle we imagined."

The notes of months of meetings between Ahmed Wali and Terry show that above all, he was their guide to a foreign land. Ahmed Wali told them whom to trust and fear. He informed Terry that the reason the town of Ghorak was important stemmed from its relationship with

Sangin and Khakrez, two other violent towns where U.S. soldiers were dying. He described how the Taliban would stage in Ghorak for their attacks elsewhere; they could do this because the appointed police chief was not from the area and not respected by his townspeople. Ahmed Wali explained that the U.S. military needed to worry about a land dispute within the Kakar tribe in Pashmul because the tribesmen were leaning toward the Taliban and this might be enough to push them to the insurgency. He told Terry that the district governor in Maiwand was worthless and should be dismissed.

He lectured the Americans on their propaganda strategies, informing them that by describing car bombs or suicide explosions as "spectacular attacks" they were appearing weak to the Afghan audience. Another time, Ahmed Wali warned Terry that his soldiers patrolling in the city's Loy Wallah neighborhood, who were showing residents photographs of Mullah Neda Mohammad, asking for information, were in danger. Mohammad was a prominent cleric, and even if he sided with the Taliban, his arrest by American soldiers could prove explosive and would only enhance his reputation. Ahmed Wali told Terry that if they planned to capture the cleric, it needed to be with Afghan soldiers, preferably flown in from outside Kandahar.

It is evident from the notes of these meetings how Terry tested his decisions against Ahmed Wali's local knowledge. Terry told Ahmed Wali he believed the villages of Nalgham and Shah Joy were ready for local anti-Taliban militias. Wrong, Ahmed Wali said; Kolk and Sanjeray were better options.

"By far the best intel we would get would be from Ahmed Wali Karzai," Colonel Chris Riga, commander of the 1st Battalion, 3rd Special Forces Group in Kandahar, told me. "They know who people are. We don't. I could go to him for anything and everything. And I constantly would."

The Kandahar where Riga fought was moved by forces difficult to understand and impossible to control. Everything was lies and rumor. He had a mission to defeat the Taliban. He could forgive almost anything for a trusted guide who furthered that mission. He didn't care about Ahmed Wali's bank account, even though his gut told him the drug allegations were probably true. He'd come to the realization, as soldiers and spies had before him, that Ahmed Wali couldn't be marginalized. "I have zero negativity toward him," Riga told me. "We had a common goal. If you're going to assist me, I'm going to assist you."

They met or spoke several times a week. One of his battalion's missions was to set up pro-government militias across Kandahar. The program, known as the Afghan Local Police, had been one of Petraeus's top priorities when he took over as ISAF commander. The theory went that hiring local tribesmen to fend off the Taliban would bolster the unseasoned Afghan army and the incompetent police; it would fill in the holes in security forces spread too thin. President Karzai had opposed the program when Petraeus first proposed it.

Ahmed Wali had none of his brother's qualms. He spoke publicly in favor of the ALP program. If villagers balked at working with the Special Forces, Ahmed Wali intervened. One of the places Riga had trouble was in the Arghistan district, in northeastern Kandahar. He wanted to talk to the elders from the area to pitch his militia idea, but they didn't want to meet him. Riga asked Ahmed Wali if he could convene the Arghistan tribesmen, maybe sometime in the next week? By nine o'clock the next morning, they were all at Ahmed Wali's house. "That kind of thing just doesn't happen," said Andy Feitt, one of Riga's intelligence officers. "This guy can accomplish what you ask of him—it's not just bluster. The military is a results-oriented organization; if you promise something and you deliver, we tend to like you."

Khakrez, a district north of Kandahar, was another problem for Riga. His Special Forces team was fighting every day with young Talibs racing down dirt trails on motorbikes. A provincial councilman from the area, Haji Sayed Jan Khakrezwal, wanted no part in any American militia program. At Riga's request, Ahmed Wali summoned Khakrezwal and the village leaders to his home to meet Riga's men and discuss the problem. Faced with Ahmed Wali, Khakrezwal caved. "The things said about me, and how I do not support the local police, are all lies," Khakrezwal told the gathering.

Ahmed Wali looked around the room. "So now we all understand?"

Ahmed Wali turned out to be insistently and passionately pro-American, beyond what anyone could have hoped. As his brother was railing against the U.S. presence in Afghanistan, Ahmed Wali was begging the American commanders to stay. In the palace, President Karzai angrily condemned American troops for any harm they inflicted on civilians, but Ahmed Wali brushed off such mistakes. One August evening in 2005, American soldiers on patrol in the Zhari district of Kandahar spotted three men at a gas station carrying AK-47s, standing next to their red Toyota Hi-Lux pickup truck. The soldiers called out to the men, who ran for their vehicle. The soldiers fired warning shots, then pumped thirty rounds into the truck, striking the tires, gas tank, truck bed, and all three men. One of them would die from his wounds and another was gravely wounded, shot in the arm, back, and leg, with eight pieces of fragmentation lodged inside him, a military report on the incident noted. The men turned out to be guards for Ahmed Wali Karzai.

"Colonel, this is not good," Kandahar's governor at the time, Asadullah Khalid, told Lieutenant Colonel Bert Ges, the battalion commander responsible.

"I apologize," Ges later told Ahmed Wali Karzai. "I'm so sorry."

"He looks at me and he goes, 'Colonel Ges, things like this happen amongst warriors. We are both fighting the same enemy. Mistakes will happen. We will overcome this.'"

"I was so shocked," Ges said. "I'll never forget it."

When President Karzai's aides claimed that U.S. air strikes had caused $100 million worth of damage in the Arghandab Valley, Ahmed Wali called on behalf of his American friends to tell his brother the information was wrong. Ahmed Wali often insisted that the president, in his heart, also wanted the troops. The cabinet ministers in Kabul fed the president bad information to suit their own personal motives, he said, and Terry should consider sending delegations to Kabul to convey all the good news. He promised that if America agreed to a permanent presence—say, two thousand soldiers based at Kandahar Airfield—the whole southern region would have a solid backbone. But if the United States left, Pakistan would arm more fighters and send them flooding back into Afghanistan. "Leaving" was a very dangerous word, Ahmed Wali told Terry, and should not be uttered by the Americans.

General Kenneth Dahl, one of Terry's subordinates, began to meet with Ahmed Wali more often, usually at the offices of the provincial council or at Camp Nathan Smith. Dahl enjoyed his company. He saw Ahmed Wali as a leader, a man of conviction and action. Their friendship developed to where Ahmed Wali would call Dahl before he traveled to Dubai, telling the general when he'd be away and how he could be reached if anything came up. "This guy is very, very capable. He clearly is the guy who's making shit happen," Dahl said. "We both wanted stability. We both wanted progress. He hated the Taliban as much as we did. Hated the insurgents. I wanted electricity. He wanted electricity. I wanted roads. He wanted roads. He's a very practical guy."

Dahl trusted Ahmed Wali so much that he led him on a tour of the

Joint Operations Center inside the Kandahar Airfield headquarters. On the tour, Dahl showed Ahmed Wali the Predator drone footage broadcast on large flat-screen monitors. He gave him statistics on ISAF medevac missions. This expression of friendship toward a man who was likely manufacturing violence to profit off the U.S. military was something that worried others. Terry even warned Dahl not to get too close.

A year after the first deep dive, the division decided to update the file on Ahmed Wali. Its personnel would do a new assessment of the available intelligence and see whether he had violated the boundaries set for him. Ketti Davison put one of her intelligence analysts, Todd Rump, in charge of the project. He spent two weeks researching Ahmed Wali's actions in the previous year and wrote a paper of about forty pages. That spring, both Ahmed Wali and Qayum had worked with American military planners on a strategy to unite the tribes across a swath of southern Afghanistan, resurrecting the old term for the area: Loy Kandahar, or "Greater Kandahar." The idea was to rally competing Pashtun tribes around a common identity. They wanted the concept to drive efforts to demobilize Taliban fighters. This was, at its heart, the embrace of old tribal ways rather than the grassroots democratic machinery engineered by foreign diplomats on one-year tours.

This type of political cooperation helped convince Rump that Ahmed Wali was a changed man, one whose worst abuses had occurred in earlier years, when the Taliban was stronger and his survival was at greater risk. Now that U.S. military operations seemed to be taking back territory from the Taliban, Ahmed Wali could start governing rather than fearing for his life. As with all his predecessors, Rump found that there wasn't evidence for the drug-trafficking allegations. Rump concluded that Ahmed Wali had not crossed the "red lines." He was proving useful, and he seemed to be walking a more virtuous path. He believed that Ahmed Wali was making Kandahar safer.

"My recommendation was we needed to engage him," Rump said.

On the evening of July 11, 2011, Ahmed Wali came to Camp Nathan Smith to meet Ken Dahl in his office. It would be the last time the two men spoke. Dahl had a couple of months left on his tour before rotating out. The 10th Mountain Division, like the soldiers before them, had won some battles, cleared some villages. But they had not defeated the insurgency. There would be another summer fighting season after they were gone, and another after that, and then another. Dahl was looking ahead. Since the two men were alone, he hoped they could have a candid talk. He wanted to know where Ahmed Wali stood with all of this. He felt they trusted each other enough by now to speak honestly. Dahl told Ahmed Wali that staying in Kandahar, prevailing against the insurgency, would only benefit him. "If you're interested in more money, more influence, more power, then stability in Afghanistan and stability in the south will contribute to that. And contribute in a legitimate way. There is a lot of money to be made here. And your power and your influence will only grow if things go well," Dahl told him.

Did Ahmed Wali plan to take his money and move to Dubai when the American troops left, or was he committed to Kandahar for the long haul? Was he worried about Afghanistan, its future and its people, or just about himself?

Ahmed Wali seemed uneasy that night. He was quiet for a long time.

"Look, General, I've always been the one," he said.

Ahmed Wali felt he had inherited this set of responsibilities from his father, to lead his tribe. He had already survived so much. He believed that the war in Kandahar was 90 percent won. Things might change in the future—he worried about Pakistan, Iran, al-Qaeda—but he was hopeful. The Karzais were ahead of the Taliban. If the United States would just agree to keep military bases in Afghanistan, as a show of force, Ahmed Wali felt, the Afghan government would survive.

Sometimes he was jealous of his brothers, Ahmed Wali told Dahl. They were safe in Kabul or Dubai or America. They could spend their time multiplying their fortunes, meeting with statesmen, enjoying their position in Afghan society. Ahmed Wali knew that he would be staying in Kandahar. There wasn't any other place for him. Dahl recalled, "He was essentially saying, 'This is my burden to bear. I'm responsible for this.'"

Dahl felt relieved. "He had just articulated, very clearly, 'I'm in. It's my responsibility. It's time for us to do this.'"

The last time I asked Ahmed Wali about his relationship with the United States, he insisted all the trouble was in the past.

"I'm telling you honestly, there is no pressure on me from a single American. They treat me with respect," he said. "I'm trying to make things better for Afghanistan and for the Afghan government. And also they are trying to make things better for Afghanistan. Their success is my success. Their failure is my failure."

13

A MOVIE STORY

"HEY MAN, HOW YOU DOING?" asked the guard in a blue striped polo shirt, carrying a black M4 assault rifle, standing in the guest room doorway. "You need anything? Afghan food?"

I asked him when I could see Hashmat Karzai. I had come to visit him at his fortress-mansion in Karz to ask about the killing of Waheed Karzai. Over the phone, Hashmat had invited me to spend the night. I had arrived at the house in midafternoon and been ushered upstairs to wait until Hashmat was ready for me. I'd been sitting alone on the floor for several hours in this carpeted second-story room, and the sun had now set. I was getting nervous, given that this American-funded millionaire had, according to both verbal and written accounts, murdered his own kin. I looked through the window, past the veranda and part of the grounds below, at a walled enclosure of footpaths and rose gardens stretching far into the distance.

"I not seen him," he said. "It is big place."

Command Sergeant Major Abdul Sami was the head of Hashmat's seventy-five-man personal security detail, a trusted cadre within the Asia Security Group. He was a northerner, a Tajik from the Panjshir Valley, the son of a colonel in the Afghan army during Soviet times. Standing in the doorway, walkie-talkie in his hand, Sami told me about how he had joined one of the first Afghan army battalions of Karzai's government and had gotten three months of training by the French. He'd then moved to the Afghan special forces (3rd Battalion, 205th Corps), been retrained by U.S. special operators, and worked at Camp Gecko, the CIA base in Kandahar, in Mullah Omar's old house. On hundreds of occasions he had choppered in on night raids with America's most talented killers, he said.

"Every night. Every day. Every night. Every day. We were a good unit. A *very* good unit. 'Hero, not zero.' That was our motto." He'd earned a spot training with the U.S. Army in Fort Bragg, North Carolina, and had broken his leg while rappelling down a rope from a helicopter. His salary risking his life each day for the Afghan army was $400 a month.

Sami told me that the ethnic rivalries within the organization made cooperation impossible: "Pashtuns hate Tajiks, Tajiks hate Pashtuns, you cannot believe it." That hatred denied him promotion and prompted him to abandon active duty in 2008, moving to the reserves. Hashmat hired him at his private security company, Asia Security Group, badge number 4470, for $3,000 a month for safer work guarding employees at the defense contracting company DynCorp, which was providing services in Afghanistan. Out of the Asia Security Group's thousands of mercenaries, Sami caught Hashmat's attention and was brought into his inner circle, into his very own home, a Tajik in the Pashtun heartland, to worry each day about Hashmat's life and how to protect it. "My hand is on my pistol, and there's a round in the chamber twenty-four/seven."

He hadn't moved from the doorway. He looked sad.

"I'm so tired of this shit," he said. "I could tell you stories. I know many things I cannot tell you. I know many things." He waited a moment. Then he said, "I have a story."

In 2002, he was working on a base in Uruzgan Province. One of the janitors on the base wanted to marry his son to a local woman. The woman's father gave her hand to another man's son. The janitor got angry. He told the U.S. Special Forces that the Taliban were gathering one night at a home in the Deh Rawud district, known insurgent terrain. Sami said he went on the mission with American special ops to raid the house. There was a skirmish, and an air strike was called in on the gathering. Sami and the other soldiers went back the next day to check on the damage. The insurgent gathering turned out to have been a wedding. "We only saw dead women and children," he said. "We called our cleaner: 'Hey, where are you? Come in.' He told us, 'Oh, I've left. I've finished my work.'"

I thought about what he was telling me. A reporter needs only a few hours in Afghanistan before he stumbles into this type of epistemological thicket. Some horrifying story of brutality, incompetence, corruption, treachery, something that hints at the throbbing, venal heart of the whole brutal struggle, but also a story almost impossible to verify and that seems on its face too tragic and absurd to be true. Something must have snagged in the language barrier. Would American soldiers bomb a wedding party on intelligence provided by their janitor? And yet the record of this war would show that the manipulation of American firepower in the service of personal feuds was a recurring motif. "The longer I stayed there, the more I realized I didn't understand," one of the top American commanders in Kandahar told me. "We think we're clever because we're playing three-dimensional chess. They're playing ten-dimensional chess. We don't even know what the other boards are."

It was true that a wedding party had been bombed in Deh Rawud district on the morning of July 1, 2002. In the BBC footage just after the incident Lieutenant General Dan McNeill, three stars across his cap, stands outside, in the wind. "We're not unmindful of the comments made by the Afghans that there were fires celebratory in nature. Supposedly a wedding. It seems to be a very difficult scenario. But I'm confident that we will work our way through it and do our absolute best to determine that if indeed something went wrong, what it was, and we will do our best to make it right."

Six days later, sitting in the palace under a crystal chandelier, to the left of Foreign Minister Abdullah Abdullah, General McNeill was at a press conference he would call "a seminal moment in my life." That day, he told the media, "On the basis of some intelligence that we have amassed over a number of months and subsequent to this operation, we have determined that there were civilian casualties.

"I believe it is forty-eight dead and one hundred and seventeen wounded," McNeill said. "I believe that the more formal investigation will expose a lot more facts."

The U.S. embassy sent a fact-finding mission to the site of the bombing and the team eventually reported their findings to President Karzai. In the palace meeting, Karzai informed them that some of the people who died had cared for him during his initial journey into Afghanistan to overthrow the Taliban. "You killed the women who cooked my meals for me. You killed the women I would talk to at night when I was up there," Karzai said, as one of the Americans present remembered.

"I went to visit the family in Deh Rawud," Karzai told me. "I considered this [bombing] a mistake. And the people understood it as such, as well. And later, when this was repeated, I began to tell the U.S. representatives, the generals and the civilian representatives, that they should stop being reckless. . . . The people began to visit to tell me they were troubled by the way the Americans behaved. Barging into people's homes. Intimidating people. Unleashing dogs against people and their children. And these voices began to increase by 2005. By 2005, I began to speak publicly about it. But in a calculated and careful manner. In 2006, then I began to speak publicly, loudly. In 2007, I began to raise it ferociously. Angrily. To put public pressure on the United States in a manner of confrontation. The real confrontation began in 2007 between us, public and privately."

The American reaction, Karzai said, was often contrite. "Just 'Sorry, we won't do it again.' But they would continue to behave that way. So it was this, telling me, 'All right,' then not doing anything about it, that caused me to believe that the Americans would not change their behavior for as long as we were nice to them. And that talking to them and reasoning with them is not going to change them. That we need to force them to change things. That's when I began to force them to change things," he said. "They would always try to hide the truth. They would deny that they had done it or had that many people killed. Once they were forced to admit to the number of killed, then they would say because the Taliban came we were not at fault. They didn't behave honestly with us. They tried to suppress the truth. It was the intimidation that they did that caused us to suspect their intentions. So that made me speak."

According to an investigation of the incident, declassified in heavily redacted fashion, United States Central Command found that "active AAA [anti-aircraft artillery] weapons [had been] fired into the air and in close proximity to helicopter landing zones and objective area and while U.S. aircraft were overhead" and that "women and children were in close proximity to the AAA fires." Such fires prompted the American AC-130 gunship to respond with "proportionate and necessary force" and "ultimate responsibility for these deaths and injuries was placed on those who deployed weapons to residential areas and willfully placed at risk innocent lives."

The fact-finding team had difficulty collecting evidence because of "the failure of the villagers to preserve the scene; difficult terrain and the lack of helpful guides; and the local Islamic tradition of burying the dead within 24 hours." The team's search of grave sites was inconclusive. The fact finders speculated that areas "may have been 'sterilized' after the air strikes to remove evidence of AAA fire." They also found this: "At the Kakraka Clinic, the team found a six by thirty-foot mural in reddish-purple ink that depicted ground personnel using AAA to shoot down helicopters and aircraft. Initially, the locals claimed that the mural was from the Soviet occupation. After further investigation revealed that

Hashmat Karzai speaks with guests at his mansion in Karz.

the mural was freshly painted with berries, remnants of which were found beneath the painting, the locals stated that children had drawn the mural. However, the height of the mural exceeded six feet."

"The U.S. made many mistakes like that," Sami told me from the doorway. "That was the first one I saw. But there were many. People brought a lot of their family problems to the U.S., and they used the U.S. to solve them."

Sami's radio crackled, and he straightened up. He spoke into it for a few seconds, then told me to stand.

"The boss is coming."

Hashmat Karzai is an imposing man. Thick as a stump, he has dark, hooded eyes, which he covers in the daylight with aviator shades. His balding head, thick black mustache, and rough stubble give him the appearance of an aging member of the Hells Angels. He wears a flashy watch and lights his cigars with a butane torch. Hashmat met me on his second-story veranda, a colonnaded expanse of marble appointed with carpets and cushions. Two of his guards lingered to one side, while an old man stared into a large flat-screen television set up on one side of the porch. The summer evening was warm.

Floodlights in the yard illuminated the domain Hashmat had built for himself. There were several buildings within the castle walls. Next to the white-and-blue, candy-striped guesthouse stood his personal home, a large beige concrete building with a tiled roof; under the portico sat the fleet of four-wheelers used by the staff to traverse the grounds. Across the garden, a stone waterfall had been embedded into one of the perimeter walls, decorated with tropical plants and flowers, the water springing from ceramic gourds at the top and trickling down the terraced steps to the pool below. Gravel footpaths, lined with multicolored roses, cut across the vast lawn, encompassing more than two acres. At the far end was Hashmat's personal zoo. In more than a dozen large metal enclosures he kept peacocks and pit bulls, a pelican, a hyena, and three ostriches from Pakistan. Hashmat called the zoo a work in progress. The chainlink cages were still rudimentary, with dirt floors and little foliage. He told me he had recently purchased a tiger—he left the logistics of the transaction vague—but it had died in Kabul before he could transport it to Kandahar. He was making arrangements to find a replacement. Maybe this time a lion.

Behind the zoo opened another stretch of property, out of view of visiting guests. The grass here was somewhat overgrown, and the footpaths made of dirt. Next to pink-and-white roses, several chest-high marijuana

A guard patrols the grounds of Hashmat Karzai's mansion in Karz.

plants grew with bushy impunity. In a barn there were speckled cows for milking and a shimmery chestnut-colored horse with white fetlocks that Hashmat used for his afternoon rides inside his castle walls. In a series of cages he kept dozens of carrier pigeons of a rare type that his guards claimed cost $2,000 apiece, and there was an elevated circular concrete platform for dogfighting.

Hashmat had just broken the Ramadan fast and sat cross-legged on a carpet, a plate of watermelon at his feet. He lit a cigar and told me about his childhood and memories of his father and other relatives, about what he thought of young Hamid Karzai (that he used to wear a cowboy hat and loved American Westerns and Clint Eastwood, and how he always seemed "mentally sick"). And then we started talking about his father's murder, and about Yar Mohammed, and how he'd decided as a young man that someday he would avenge his father's death. It was dark by then, and his shadowed face glowed as he drew on his cigar. "I'll tell you a story," he said.

"To be honest with you, I had a pistol with me," he said. "I was young, boiling, angry."

It was the winter of 1997, the second year of the Taliban's government in Afghanistan. Thirteen years had passed since Yar Mohammed had hoisted Hashmat's father's AK 47 and shot him with it. After his father's death, Hashmat had immigrated to suburban Maryland with his mother, grandmother, and younger brother, Hekmat. They lived in a two-bedroom apartment on Glenallan Avenue in Silver Spring. Several other Karzais lived in the D.C. area at the time, and they tended to help each other. For newly arriving relatives, the others would donate microwaves or televisions or other appliances. A relative gave Hashmat an old police car purchased at auction. Hashmat drove the Chevy Celebrity, which still had holes for the siren mount, for more than a year, until Hekmat crashed it. "We were broke," Hashmat recalled. "I had to get a job. I didn't have nothing to eat."

The Karzais stuck together in those days. America in the 1980s was not a bad place to be an Afghan immigrant. The nightly news broadcasts portrayed these bearded mountain rebels as freedom fighters relying on faith and grit and Stinger missiles to combat the Soviet occupiers. The war spawned a massive exodus, and thousands of Afghans found refuge in America, with the largest enclaves sprouting up around the Bay Area cities of Fremont and Concord, as well as near D.C. Hashmat and his brother enrolled at Gaithersburg High School, then took classes at

Montgomery College and the University of Maryland, working at night and on weekends throughout. At the time, Qayum Karzai was working as a manager at Bello Mondo in the Bethesda Marriott, the restaurant that employed, as waiters or busboys, nearly all of the Karzai siblings of Hamid's generation—Qayum, Mahmood, Shah Wali, Ahmed Wali, Abdul Wali—as well as some of their cousins. Just as Qayum and his wife, Pat, helped sponsor his relatives for visas and immigration papers, he introduced them at the hotel.

Hashmat joined his relatives at Bello Mondo, taking a job as a busboy. He was young and strong—six foot one and 180 pounds—and when he got into weight lifting, he could bench-press more than three hundred pounds. But working for a living was a shock. The night he came home from his first shift, well after midnight, he sat down, exhausted, and peeled off his sweaty socks as Hekmat watched. "It was ironic, because he'd never worked in his life, as the son of a *khan*," Hekmat said. "He brought this money, it was sixty dollars, and gave it to my mom. He said, 'This is my first honest day's job.'" Growing up, the brothers had always had servants; they didn't even know how to cook the rice they'd eaten every day of their lives. "Imagine," Hashmat said, "you had everything in your mouth, a silver spoon, and you go to the States, and you become a waiter."

For money of his own, Hekmat began working with a cousin who ran a hot dog stand outside the main Silver Spring Metro station. He would wake up each day at five to get to his position before the morning commuter rush. His first task was to brew a giant vat of black coffee for the commuters. He worked six days a week and on a good day earned twenty dollars. "I still hate coffee," he said. When he was older, and studying criminology at the University of Maryland, Hekmat worked nights at Persepolis, an Iranian restaurant in Bethesda. For a time he also took a job as a bouncer at Viva, a nightclub in the District. His nickname at the time was "Sonny."

"I think my brother and I realized we had to start working fast—otherwise we'd be on the streets," Hekmat said.

Money was always tight. In the summer of 1994, when Hashmat was twenty-four years old and living in Gaithersburg, his daughter, Henna Karzai, was born. He had been dating the girl's mother, Awista Salimi, for two years, since the fall of 1992. She was having trouble making ends meet. In the court filings in a subsequent paternity case, she claimed that she earned about $500 a month, but her rent was $400, and with the other costs, she was falling further behind each month. Weeks after her daughter was born, she filed a petition in Montgomery County Circuit Court, seeking child support from Hashmat. A year later, the case was thrown out because the couple decided to get married.

Hashmat eventually found better-paying work at a Toyota dealership along the toll road out to Dulles Airport in Vienna, Virginia. He worked in the finance department, arranging car loans. Even as it stretched into years the brothers felt their time in America was temporary, a holding pattern until they could resume their rightful lives in Afghanistan. The death of their father was one debt that Hashmat still burned to settle.

When Hashmat learned that Yar Mohammed was living in Kandahar, hanging around a jewelry shop, he decided to find him and take his revenge. He bought a ticket to Karachi, Pakistan, then drove to Quetta and over the border into Kandahar. Standing outside the store, Hashmat realized that he'd never actually seen Yar Mohammed before; he'd just been told that the man had blue eyes and wore a turban.

"So I looked inside and there were like five or six people sitting in there. I was wearing a turban and I had . . . maybe a three-week-old beard. This is the Taliban time, nobody could carry a small knife. So I had a pistol in my hand. The Makarov. The big one, with twenty rounds in it. Shit. I was fucking boiling. I stood in front of [one guy]. I said, 'You and I have to talk.' I was holding my pistol. This other guy stood up. I'm looking around. I couldn't see him at first. I see this guy sitting in the corner, almost like a blanket over him. I looked at him. He said, 'Who are you looking for?' I said, 'Not you. Sit down.' He looked at my pistol. I looked at the other guy. Maybe him. 'You. Get up.' So he got up, other guy stood up, too. I said, 'No. You sit down.' I took my pistol. Big Makarov. The big one . . . I said, 'What's your name?' He said, 'My name is Yar Mohammed.'

"At that time I was bench-pressing. I was fucking huge. I was playing football. This guy is standing in front of me. Shit. I could just eat him. Seriously. I said, 'You're Yar Mohammed?' He said, 'Yes.' I said, 'Do you recognize me?' He looks at me. I said, 'Take a guess.' He said, 'Are you Hashmat?' I said, 'Yes.' I said, 'You owe me something.' He starts shaking. I swear. I said, 'Let's go outside.' I didn't even care that he has anything in his pocket or not. I held him by his neck. Like this. Like a ten-year-old boy. I hold him by his neck. The other guy got up. I said, 'I told you once. Next time you get up, all the twenty rounds are going to be in your stomach. Your shit is going to be all over the wall.' I was watching movies and all that."

Hashmat dragged Yar Mohammed out the door, flagged down a rickshaw, and told the driver to take them to police headquarters. The Taliban had been hosting public executions in the stadium in Kandahar, and Hashmat wanted a Taliban judge to order Yar Mohammed to be killed in public. The judge, however, told Hashmat that ordering such a killing required two witnesses to the crime. Since his father's murder had taken place in Pakistan more than a decade earlier, the witnesses had dispersed. Hashmat bargained the judge down to one witness, but he didn't know where he would even find that. He left Yar Mohammed at the police station while he thought about what to do. He couldn't stay with relatives in the city, because of the family trouble he was stirring up. After spending a few days meeting with Taliban representatives, Hashmat returned to the police station. He asked to have Yar Mohammed brought outside. He was torn between demanding a confession from Yar Mohammed and just shooting him and getting it over with. "I was as frustrated as I possibly could be," Hashmat recalled.

"So I'm sitting there, face-to-face. I said, 'Tell me, face-to-face, what's going on? Why did you kill my father?' I recorded this conversation. He was telling me a story, he said, 'I swear, I didn't kill him.' He was crying. 'I didn't kill him. I took a weapon and suddenly the weapon discharged and shot him.' 'Why did you take his weapon? His pistol? His money? His watch? Why did you run away?' He said, 'I was afraid.' I said, 'At least you could have come back to the family. You didn't do that.' He's crying. Sort of. Nose is running." Hashmat asked the police guard to go get some tea. When he stepped away, Hashmat told Yar Mohammed, "Follow me."

"I sat him in the car. Go straight toward Spin Boldak. You could say I was foolish or young. I had two things in mind. I had these things in my mind. On the road he was crying like a baby. I have this on tape. He's crying, 'I haven't eaten. My babies this and this.' I'm sorry."

They drive toward the Pakistani border.

"I'm thinking about this. He's crying. . . . Shit. What am I going to do now? I reach to the Arghasan bridge. Under the bridge. I said, 'Shit. This is getting too much.' Frustrated. Tired. Why don't I just shoot him and get it over with? Get it over with. I didn't care. I get him outside. Park the car under the bridge. About eleven-thirty a.m. 'Let's pray right here. Then we'll go to Pakistan. We pray. We have a long way to drive.' I'm trying to convince him, but he's crying. I get out. I took my pistol out. I come outside. Come on his side. I open his door. He sees the pistol. He knows for a fact that I'm shooting him now. Shit. There's no time to pray. Nothing is going on. I said, 'Get out.'

"As soon as he puts his first step, second step, he falls down. I say, 'Get up.' He said, 'I can't. My feet are not working.' I said, 'What do you mean your feet are not working?' I said, 'It's okay. You need to make your last prayer.' We're talking eighteen years ago. He's crying. Falls down on my shoes. I still have those shoes. I see everything coming out of his nose on my shoes. Begging me. I mean. The *begging*. Unbelievable. 'My kids. I haven't eaten for a month.' This and that. Blah blah blah. Shit. I said, 'We are praying. What's wrong with you? Get up. Just look at me.' He won't look at me. I have this pistol on fully auto. Twenty rounds. Boom. Everything comes out. Or you can do semiauto. I have it on fully auto. I'm not worrying about these freaking Talibs. Worrying about kidnapping. Shit. I have a thing on him. It's my thing. That's not what the other people think about. He's crying. Shit. I put him back in the car. Turn around.

"I couldn't do it.

"I swear.

"I couldn't do it."

Hashmat stopped talking. In the darkness, there was the click and blue hiss of his butane lighter, the brief illumination of his face.

"He was crying. He was crying sitting in the car. I have this thing: if you start crying, I can't do anything. Regardless how pissed I am. The minute you start crying, I can't do it. I said, 'Okay.' So I grabbed some oranges. I said, 'Why don't you peel this?' He was crying. He was shaking. He couldn't do it. I said, 'What tape would you like to listen to?' I had two cassette tapes. This is fucking Taliban times, you couldn't hear tapes. Are you kidding me? I said, 'Would you like to hear Nashnas or Obaidullah?' He said, 'Whatever you want.' One is Kandahar musician. One is Kabul, Pashto singer. Famous. Both of them. He said, 'You play whatever.' 'Okay, I'll play cassette. You peel orange.' He couldn't peel it. I said, 'Okay. I'll play cassette.'"

They drove on, approaching the border.

"I turn the car back off road. We are off the road. Soon as I go this way, he starts crying again. I stopped the car. 'Let's go.' By that time, about one or one-fifteen p.m. I said, 'Get out. Let's go. It's time to pray.' He knew, that son of a bitch. He said, 'Something is going to happen.' This time he wouldn't get out of the car. He put the lock on. He wouldn't get out. I can't shoot him in the car, because the blood is going to fuck up my car. Oh man. I said, 'Okay. Let's do this.' Let's take him back to Pakistan."

Hashmat gave up on his plan to murder Yar Mohammed. But he still wanted the Taliban to convict Yar Mohammed of his father's killing and have the man publicly executed. He traveled to Quetta to meet with his family and convince someone who was there from the time of his father's death to testify as a witness to the crime. In the family meetings that followed, various Karzai relatives, including Abdul Ahad (Hamid Karzai's father) and his brother Habibullah, a veteran diplomat who had been an aide to the king, impressed on Hashmat that he should forgive Yar Mohammed. "This is not a good time," Hafiz, another of Abdul Ahad's brothers, told Hashmat. "Even if you kill half of Kandahar, it will not compensate for the death of your father. Don't do it."

"If you kill him," Habibullah said, "then war starts."

Hamid also weighed in on the family dispute. He wanted to convene an official tribal reconciliation. They would assemble the elders and use an old Pashtun custom for forgiveness: tying shoes together by their laces and draping the shoes around the person's neck like a garland. One of his aunts pleaded with Hashmat to give up his desire for revenge. Hashmat remembered her standing there, so many years ago, wrapped in a white shawl, her eyes red from crying; her eyes reminded him of his father's eyes.

"Look at me," she said. She handed him a Koran for him to kiss its cover.

"Let him go," she said.

Hashmat bought a plane ticket the next day and returned to the United States. He did not go back to Afghanistan until the American invasion. And until he did, he understood, he wouldn't be satisfied. "Where's the justice? You're telling me to forgive him and let it go and that's it? Nothing happens? That's it? That's not good enough."

That was the story he told. It was Hashmat's way of arguing that he hadn't been the one twelve years later standing in Yar Mohammed's house that night, shooting his son in the stomach and the leg. Hashmat called the story of Waheed Karzai's death a "movie story." "Guy goes in. Brothers and sisters doing homework. First of all, what homework? Which school you going to? Fine. Guy comes into the room and shoots him. When he shoots him? What happens next day? Why wouldn't he tell the police I came in and shot him?" Hashmat's alibi was that from five to ten o'clock that evening he was at a funeral. "How could I be there the same time? How come son not saying, 'I was shot by Hashmat'? Why he waited and waited and waited. Written on grave son was killed by enemy of Islam. Why wait all this time? Why would he go to police eighteen days later and do the report? Eighteen days later he does the report. Yar Mohammed goes eighteen days later and did a report."

I asked him who killed Waheed Karzai.

"I don't know, Josh." He laughed. "I don't know. Whatever it was, I don't know. Okay?"

A popular conception of the Karzai family was that of a united cabal of colluding interests. The reality was far more complicated. President Karzai was keenly aware of their reputation and often intervened—or gave the appearance of intervening—to block his relatives from profiting off his name. The Karzais have all sorts of stories of Hamid thwarting their plans. Early in the war, after a relative demanded that a Kabul high school make him its principal, Karzai sent a letter to all government ministries ordering them to report to him any time one of his family members attempted to win preferential treatment. Jamil Karzai, a cousin, told me that his brother had been considered for a commerce ministry job in Kazakhstan until President Karzai personally intervened to block his selection. "He ignores his family," Jamil said. Another cousin, Hashim, complained that the president stepped in to keep him from obtaining a license to open one of the first cell phone companies in Afghanistan. "If it wasn't for Hamid Karzai, I would have two or three hundred million dollars today," he said. When Ahmed Wali wanted money from the palace safe for his political activities in Kandahar, the president demanded that his aides give him an exact accounting of the funds. When Qayum visited U.S. ambassador Zalmay Khalilzad and asked for his help being named speaker of parliament, Khalilzad shot him down; President Karzai then applauded the decision, saying, "God be with you. I agree with you."

Why couldn't he give his relatives government sinecures? they wanted to know. Or pay for one hundred Karzai kids to study in India? Or let them start a few contracting companies?

"The president is responsible to the Karzai family, and he has benefitted nobody," Hashim said. "The Americans will not give you a job because you are a Karzai. The president will not hire you because it's nepotism. In the history of Afghanistan, he will be remembered as a president who has done nothing for his family."

When Mahmood Karzai got the license to sell Toyotas in Kabul, President Karzai complained to Ambassador Zalmay Khalilzad that the deal would ruin his reputation and solicited Khalilzad's help to cancel the arrangement. President Karzai later told me that he had written to the Japanese embassy in Kabul to oppose the contract and asked Mahmood to back out. "I told him, clearly. That's not the right thing. That doesn't suit our name and our way of life. I explained it to him: When I wasn't the president, when you were not here, did Toyota ever come to you to offer you a deal? So naturally, they're coming to you because you're my brother. The brother of the president. So it's my position that has attracted them to you. They wouldn't have come to you if I were not the president, if I were a district administrator in Kandahar. They would not have given a damn."

Karzai's critics would insist that this outrage was just for public consumption and that he was privately pleased to profit from his family's exploits. That never felt true to me. Karzai's political legacy and his place in the history of Afghanistan seemed to mean far more to him than material wealth ever would. President Karzai believed that by lodging these complaints against his family's attempts at government jobs or contracts, he had fulfilled his moral and political obligations. Whatever his siblings did after that was up to them. "The U.S. media accuses me of cronyism and nepotism, which I have completely and at great cost avoided and not done," he said.

Hashmat was one of the president's most determined enemies. He was steadily trying to chip away at Ahmed Wali's control over Kandahar to become the most powerful Karzai in the south, to thereby restore some of what had been lost when his father died. He'd been staking this claim for years. When Abdul Ahad was killed, in 1999, Hashmat insisted that he should be the new leader of the Popalzai tribe, rather than Hamid. At the tribal gathering in Quetta where Hashmat made this appeal, Ahmed Wali turned to his assistant and whispered, "What a motherfucker."

But to be recognized as a leader, Hashmat needed to deliver for his tribesmen. The Karz villagers, much like many rural Afghans, felt frustrated by the government's failures over the previous decade. The grape farmers here had won no particular benefit from residing in the ruling family's home village. They could list the accomplishments of President Karzai's father the parliamentarian, including bringing new roads and canals to the village. But the only recent aid they'd received had come from foreigners. They had grown to depend on organizations such as IRD, a USAID contractor, which gave six-dollar cash handouts for day-labor work planting seeds or dredging canals. It was the United Nations that had paid to put up a rock retaining wall along the riverbed to keep the one paved road from washing out in floods, and the U.S. government that had paid to fertilize the fields. "The government itself has not done anything," Abdul Ali, a village elder, told me. "I can tell you that the president has not served the tribe. He has not done good things for the people."

"Many of our young people are jobless now," said another old farmer, Ahmadullah. "And the main reason for insecurity is when people don't have jobs."

Hashmat had plans to build a hospital and a new mosque in Karz. He wanted to start a new *shura*, a council of his own loyal followers, which he hoped would become more influential than the official provincial council, run by Ahmed Wali Karzai. Using profits from his security company and from a hotel he ran for foreign contractors outside Kandahar Airfield, Hashmat paid more than $2,000 to repair all the broken windows in the Karz school after a bomb went off nearby. He claimed to have spent $70,000 of his own money to bring power lines to Karz, which had no steady source of electricity.

Hashmat had loyal followers, but he was still not widely recognized as a leader of his tribe by the other Karzais. The president and his siblings had opposed Hashmat's power grab each step along the way. In 2010, when Hashmat campaigned to represent Kandahar in parliament, he came in first place in the preliminary results. But during the review process, election officials threw out thousands of his votes, citing fraud, and disqualified him. Hashmat attributed the result solely to the dirty work of Ahmed Wali and the president. He later told me that Ahmed Wali had offered him the parliament seat but only in exchange for $1 million. "Originally, I got thirty-seven thousand votes. At the end, I was left with fifty-eight hundred," he said. "Why was I kicked out of parliament? The president doesn't want anybody who's not kissing his hand."

The same year, when President Karzai decided to shut down certain private security companies, the Asia Security Group was one of the first to close. Hashmat and his partners felt this decision had been motivated by the family rivalry. The company regularly clashed with the government. On another occasion, Hashmat had tried to get some imported pickup trucks out of customs, but President Karzai had ordered the Afghan spy agency to seize them until all taxes were paid, a former senior British official who had entered the private security world told me. Company insiders saw the presidential decision to close Asia Security Group as an extension of this family feud. "It is my understanding that this was politically/personally motivated due to the friction between the President and Hashmat," Hashmat's business partner Asad Khan, a former U.S. Marine, wrote to me. "In reality the two did not get along.

"My sense is that the President and AWK were threatened by the following Hashmat has in the south," he said. "Hence they tried several times to undermine him politically."

The decision infuriated Hashmat. He appealed to the president, the interior minister, and other high-ranking officials to reverse the decision. Some private security companies remained in operation, including those linked to relatives of senior Afghan officials, but Hashmat's failed. "Why mine?" he asked me. "Because I'm a Karzai? Because I created two thousand jobs for Pashtuns? We were told, 'We're shutting you down because you are relatives. You are high-ranking people.' What? So if I know somebody in my family or somebody, I can't have a job? That doesn't make sense. That is basically a crap."

Hashmat's exclusion from the inner circles of Karzai power ate at him. He had risen in a few short years from the loan department at a suburban Virginia car dealership to become a wealthy Afghan baron living in a castle and running a private army. But he hadn't won respect. "I don't know what it is," he said. "Why they think of me as an outsider? My grandfather started this, what do you call it, dynasty. And it has been passed down over generations. So why suddenly I'm an outsider?"

After his brother died, Farid Karzai dreaded living in Karz. He assumed that his father had been the intended target. Since he had survived, what would stop them from coming back? Staying in Karz, you could not miss the billboard of Khalil Karzai or the ominous walls of Hashmat's castle. To protect them, Ahmed Wali, who was Hashmat's rival in Kandahar, gave Yar Mohammed four Kalashnikovs and two policemen as bodyguards. The policemen, Khairullah and Atta Jan, were known to the family and lived in the village. They would come to the house each night, sleep on the roof, and depart in the morning. Yar Mohammed remained wary. He never went anywhere without a gun, and he started sleeping with a Kalashnikov under his mattress and a pistol under his pillow. He would sometimes wake during the night and shine his flashlight through the window at the gray metal gate to make sure it remained closed and locked.

On the evening of March 9, 2011, a year and a half after Waheed's death, Yar Mohammed was asleep in one room while Farid, his mother, and Sonia slept in another. Neighbors would later report hearing helicopters flying low over the village. But this wasn't unusual anywhere in

Kandahar, and the rotor blades didn't wake the family. Only then Farid and his mother heard what sounded like a burst of gunfire. They sat up and looked at each other. It was sometime after one a.m.

"Did you hear that?" Farid asked his mother in the darkness.

"Yes," she whispered. "There was a shooting. Do not go outside."

Farid ignored his mother and swung his legs down from the bed. The night was warm, and he wore only thin cotton pants, with no shirt. He stepped out onto the concrete patio outside the bedroom door. He saw a silhouetted figure in the darkness on top of the wall that encircled the property. The man shouted at him and raised a rifle. The green dot of a laser pointer danced on Farid's bare chest.

"Stop where you are! Don't move!" someone shouted in Pashto, with a Kandahari accent.

Farid darted back into his room. He grabbed his cell phone and called one of his cousins, Zalal, who told him he'd also heard gunfire. "Don't go outside or do anything stupid," Zalal warned him. Farid threw on a shirt and asked Sonia to peek through the window. She pulled the curtain aside and pressed her face close to the glass.

"It's the Americans," she said. "There are a lot of lights."

Farid could see them now, too. There appeared to be several American and Afghan soldiers standing on the mud wall and the roofs of neighboring houses. They looked to Farid like sci-fi monsters bristling with weapons and antennae. The night-vision scopes affixed to their helmets obscured their faces. The soldiers had thrown glow sticks into the yard, which cast them in an eerie green gleam. The Afghan interpreter with the soldiers continued to shout orders while the family cowered in the bedroom: *Your house has been surrounded by the National Army. Everyone must come outside, including women and children. Keep your hands in the air.*

Farid looked at his mother and sister. The room was tiny, and there was no other exit except the front door, which opened into the front yard. His mother stepped out first, and Farid and Sonia followed. Sonia carried a Koran. The soldiers ordered her to drop it to the ground. The women were not wearing shoes, and their heads were uncovered. From their position on top of the wall, the soldiers ordered the women to one side of the yard, toward a group of glow sticks. Several feet away, a circle of red light appeared in the dirt. The interpreter ordered Farid to walk toward the red. They told him to look up. And then look down. To turn around in a circle. To take off his shirt and roll up his pants. To sit down on the ground. Farid could feel his heart beating. The red light began to move. It inched over the gravel and dirt, tracing slowly across the open yard toward the locked gate, about thirty yards away. Farid could see the gray door topped with pointed spikes that Yar Mohammed checked with such diligence each night. He wondered where his father was now. The soldiers told Farid to stand up and follow the light. When he got to the door, an American soldier standing on the wall ordered, through an interpreter, that Farid open it. He said he didn't have the key and asked if he could go back into his father's room to get it. The soldier told Farid to stay where he was and ordered Sonia to get the key. She ran into Yar Mohammed's room, picked up the key, and came to the door.

"Did you see Dad?" Farid asked Sonia.

"I didn't see anybody," she replied.

The soldier ordered Farid to open the lock while keeping one hand on his head. Farid fumbled with the key, unable to do what he was asked with only one hand and a mind scrambled with fear. He asked for permission to use both hands. The American soldier agreed. Farid opened the lock and the door swung into the yard. The soldier ordered him to put his face against the door and his hands behind his back. Someone came around and cinched his wrists with plastic cuffs. Then they pulled a hood over his head and tied another blindfold over that and walked him through the door and into the alley. The path was rutted and narrow—the rough brick wall on Farid's right was separated by only a few feet from the smooth dirt wall on his left—and difficult to manage blind.

As other soldiers went inside the house, the soldier guiding Farid stopped him in the alley and started asking questions. Blindfolded and hooded, Farid could see nothing, but he heard Sonia crying. "Look, these are women. You have to have some respect for them," he told the interpreter. "Please send them to one of our neighbors' houses. You're free to go and search the house as long as you want."

An American soldier shouted at him to shut up.

Farid was asked who lived in his house. He mentioned his relatives and the two guards who slept on the roof. The American soldier told the translator to bring the guards down. They asked more questions, including one Farid remembers clearly.

"They asked me, 'Was it your brother that they killed last year?' I said, 'Yes.'"

Someone grabbed Farid's shoulder and pushed him up against a wall. He was made to sit in the dirt. He could feel the barrel of a gun on the back of his neck. It was hard for him to tell what was going on, but he could hear what sounded like the soldiers breaking the lock on a neighbor's door, then his mother and sister being led into that room. One of the soldiers grabbed his shoulder and stood him up and ordered him to walk down the muddy path. Farid tripped on a thin rut that carried a rivulet of foul-smelling water down the middle of the alley. An American soldier grabbed him by the collarbone to keep him from falling. Then he removed the hood, and Farid looked around. He could see the collapsible ladders the soldiers had used to scale the wall.

At that point, the soldiers decided to put him inside a room in the neighbor's house. They ordered the family out of the house and led Farid, his wrists still bound behind his back, into a room and sat him against a wall. They put the hood back on and cinched the blindfold over it. Khairullah and Atta Jan, the two police guards from his house, soon joined him on the floor. "I could not see anything; it was pitch-black in front of my eyes," Farid recalled. "But I could feel that they were taking my fingerprints while my hands were tied behind me. They were taking my fingerprints and they were taking pictures."

One of the guards complained that the hood had something in it and his eyes were burning. Farid was having the same problem. "I told him my eyes were burning as well and I could not control my tears," he said. As soon as he finished saying that, someone slapped him across the left side of his face.

A few minutes passed. Someone came inside and asked Farid where they'd gotten the Kalashnikovs.

"We got them from Ahmed Wali Karzai," Farid said. "We have four of them. We used to keep three in our house and one in my cousin's house." Farid added that the registration documents were in his dad's room.

"Where is my dad?" Farid asked one of the soldiers standing in the room.

"He's sitting a few yards away from you," a soldier replied.

Hours passed. Farid was unsure how many. He could see only blackness, but he knew it was dawn when he heard the village imam's call to prayer. The familiar words arose slow and mournful from the mosque loudspeaker. He couldn't remember how long it had been since he had last heard from an American soldier. He wondered if they would just leave him like this, bound and blind.

Then the interpreter returned. He wanted to know about the red Toyota Corolla parked in the yard. Farid said the car was his. The interpreter left. Farid heard other sounds he could not understand. He heard the rising thud of rotor blades as the helicopter came to life, the muffled static of radio talk, curt and coded. He heard the rustle of limbs, of disentanglement, as his fellow captives were freed of hoods and cuffs. The long night seemed to be over. A few minutes later, his hood was lifted.

"I opened my eyes and an American was right here," Farid recalled, holding his palm up to his face. The man had a red beard, white skin, blue eyes. "He was looking into my eyes. He looked into my eyes for a few seconds. Then he took out a knife. And he cut my plastic cuffs. He was the only American in the room. The last person to leave. He walked toward the door, walking backward, his gun pointed toward us. Once he stepped out of the house, they disappeared."

Farid wanted to return to his home immediately to see what had happened, but his neighbors told him to wait to be certain the Americans were gone. After a few minutes, he couldn't restrain himself and ran home. He met his cousin Zalal in the yard, and they searched the rooms. He found his bedroom in disarray, scattered with clothes and blankets. Blood and what looked like bits of flesh had spattered the white walls of his father's room. In one corner, the cousins found a bundle of blankets. They unwrapped it and saw Yar Mohammed.

"They had shot him right in the forehead," Farid recalled. "He was already dead. He was lying on his back, and the blood was streaming from his head onto the floor. Three-quarters of his head was gone, and only one of his eyes was there. The rest of his head was missing. When I saw my dad's body, I screamed."

Farid and his neighbors pulled Yar Mohammed's body out into the yard and laid him on a cot. Farid searched his pockets and found his painkillers. Many of the family's belongings were gone: Farid's car registration, driver's license, and camera; papers pertaining to their house and land; his mother's small collection of jewelry; the few thousand dollars that constituted the family's life savings. The village mullah arrived and decided that since Yar Mohammed had been martyred, they did not need to wash his entire body but could bury him in his clothes. The neighbors began digging a grave at the family cemetery, in a plot next to his son's.

That afternoon, a Thursday, Ahmed Wali Karzai came to the house during the burial preparations. Farid sat with him in one of the guest rooms. Farid recounted what had happened the previous evening. After listening to the story, Ahmed Wali shook his head.

"May God bless his soul," he said. Then he stood up and walked out.

The raid that night on Yar Mohammed Karzai's home had been conducted by a team of U.S. special operations soldiers. On the day of the killing, March 10, ISAF headquarters in Kabul released its account of the raid in its "morning operational update." These types of statements came coded in military jargon and often existed in an alternate reality. This one was no different. The U.S. military claimed to have "captured a Taliban leader, killed one armed individual and detained several suspected insurgents." The "leader" had been "responsible for the distribution of vehicle borne improvised explosive devices to fighters throughout Kandahar City. He also coordinated the receipt of weapons and materials from associates outside of Afghanistan, and distributed them to various Taliban members in the province." The security forces, ISAF claimed, "advanced to the targeted compound where they called for all occupants to exit the building peacefully before conducting searches. A member observed an armed individual with an AK-47 in an adjacent building within the same compound. The security force assessed the male as an immediate threat to the security force, and engaged him. The individual killed was the father of the targeted individual."

Nothing about the statement made sense. Karz wasn't a village known for Taliban activity. By Kandahar standards, it was almost completely peaceful. It was unclear who this captured "Taliban leader" might be. The only person killed had been Yar Mohammed. In that case, the Taliban target ISAF was referring to had to be Farid, his only living son.

If it had been any other Afghan family involved, the ISAF statement might have stood as the official and only record of the incident—an unnamed man dying in what seemed to be a legitimate and justified military operation. But this turned out to be the family of the president. Later in the day, ISAF issued an "update" to its earlier report: "Coalition forces are aware of conflicting reports about the identities of those involved, and have initiated an inquiry to determine the facts." The results of that inquiry, if indeed one took place, were never made public.

Farid and his relatives later came to the conclusion that Yar Mohammed had approached his bedroom window at the sound of the helicopter and shined his flashlight at the gate, as he did on many nights. He would have been carrying his Kalashnikov, but they believe he never took a shot, and no one in the military has alleged he did. The bullets that killed him broke through his bedroom window and struck him while he crouched inside his room.

The president kept his personal views on Yar Mohammed's killing by the Americans private. His spokesman, Waheed Omar, said that "this was the result of an irresponsible night raid and like any other case of civilian casualties, the president was very sorry to hear about it. We've called for a stop of the night raids, which often cause a loss of life and are against the culture and the Islamic values of the Afghan people."

The revenge fantasy that Hashmat Karzai had nurtured for more than a quarter century had finally been fulfilled. But was he somehow responsible? Because of his long-held grudge against Yar Mohammed, within the Karzai family suspicion immediately turned toward him. Mahmood Karzai told *The Guardian* newspaper that he smelled a "very deep conspiracy" in the killing. "If this is a deliberate setup where the US military is being given false information to settle a personal vendetta then this is very serious," he said. "Karz is our stronghold, there are absolutely no Taliban there and there never will be."

Did Hashmat, or someone close to him, have the wherewithal to plant bad intelligence with a U.S. special operations team and sit back while the target was destroyed? By that time, his brother, Hekmat, was running a think tank in Kabul that received U.S. government funding and gave occasional briefings to Centcom and the Pentagon. He would later be chosen as deputy foreign minister. Both brothers denied any involvement in Yar Mohammed's death. Several family members openly blamed them, just the same. Noor Ahmad Karzai, a cousin of Farid's who lived in Silver Spring, was convinced they were somehow involved. "Hashmat is a snake," he told me over the phone. "In Afghanistan, if you have the mighty dollar in your pocket, you can do anything. So Hashmat is the guy with a U.S. contract worth a million dollars. He could have done anything. You see a guy from welfare, and he's building a mansion in Karz. That guy was on welfare when he was here. He was part-time taking care of his grandmother and getting a check from the government." Noor Ahmad claimed to know "for a fact" that Hekmat had passed the bad intelligence. "I want the whole world to know. I know from the inside. I don't want to name the interpreter, but they told me Hekmat told the U.S. to make a raid in that house. Common sense will tell you," he said. "I want the whole world to know that their taxpayer dollars, their Marines, were there just to do a Karzai family feud. This is shameful, for a superpower.

"It's just the Afghan thing. The word in Pashtu is *turbur*. Your cousin is always your rival. *Turbur. Turbur* is the biggest rival in Afghan history."

Hashmat waved away this talk.

"We both know the Americans. Do you think I have that much power to get the Special Forces to go raid Yar Mohammed's house and do the killing?" he asked me. "The president looks at Hekmat and told Hekmat straight to his face, 'If you guys were killing the father, why did you kill the son?' Hekmat said, 'What are you talking about, Mr. President? You know the Special Forces were raiding the place.' He told Hekmat, 'I don't know who's telling me the truth, you or the Americans. Both of you are lying to me.' The president still thinks until this day that I have a hand in it.

"Fucking some people were thinking I was sitting in a helicopter. I wish I had that much power. That I was sitting in an Apache helicopter and shooting it from there. Are you crazy? God is doing his justice. Not me. I mean, maybe that was written." He chuckled. "We have a saying in our language: 'Whatever you grow, you got to cut it.' Yar Mohammed did what he did, and God gave him his punishment."

One of the top American generals in Kandahar at the time would later tell me that he did not believe that Yar Mohammed was the "legitimate target." But if he wasn't, it is not clear who was. One of the neighbors apparently sold guns, according to the cousins, but that would not seem to warrant a second look from military targeters, given the Taliban activity in Kandahar at the time.

"My recollection is, I think it was the middle of the night," the general said. "And my recollection was he went to the window with a rifle in his hand. Bad idea. When you have a lot of really good snipers covering your actions, and a guy shows up in a window with the rifle, he's voted. It doesn't matter who you are.

"It was a good operation," the general said. "Unfortunately, part of it was that it ended up killing that guy. Even when you look at why he was killed, it was the right thing to do. To be honest, it wasn't of great significance, in hindsight."

14

MAKING THE COUNTRY GREAT AGAIN

MAJOR RAHMATULLAH, a district police chief, had standards. He was proud to be a policeman. He did not abide the untrained gunmen, greedy mercenaries, tribal henchmen, the hashish-addled, bribe-demanding, arms-trafficking, drug-running little-boy-molesting Taliban sympathizers who made up a good chunk of the Kandahar police force.

On any Kandahar day, you would see them under the feeble shade of a shredded tarp, listless in the stagnant heat in their sandbag outposts, dressed in drab gray, poorly paid, cradling old AKs. They looked miserable, and you could hardly blame them. Afghan police were sacrificial, frontline cannon fodder massed in the beds of green Ford Rangers, action-movie extras dying nameless and unmourned at rates faster than any other uniformed forces in the war. Police here felt almost like a prop, a concession to the United States—who paid the salaries, bought the trucks, filled them with gas—for the sake of appearances. At least half of them, some fifty thousand, had no training. The police were so new that the institution had not yet developed its own sense of tradition or loyalty. People might wear the uniform of the Afghan police, but they often worked for someone else.

Inside the Kandahar police headquarters, a downtown base encircled by layers of razor wire and concrete walls, the chief at the turn of 2011 was a man called Khan Mohammad Mujahid. He had a placid manner, almost relaxed, but the bags under his eyes matched his black turban. He worked from an overstuffed brown armchair in a fetid second-floor office that was decorated with bouquets of pink plastic flowers and pastel yellow drapes. When I met him there in late February, he had survived three assassination attempts within the past month. A car bomb had blown up

Two Afghan police officers stand on top of a wedding hall in Kandahar City that was destroyed by the Taliban.

his house while he was out. His convoy had been ambushed on the highway while returning from the airport. Then one Saturday morning, a group of Taliban entered a wedding hall across the street from the police station, scaled five flights of stairs to the roof, and started firing rocket-propelled grenades down at his office. At the same time, three rickshaws and two Toyota Corollas exploded at different points around the perimeter of the station. Hand grenades were lobbed over the walls. Mujahid's police, and the U.S. Army advisers stationed inside, fought back, putting so many bullets into the wedding hall's façade that they shattered every window and it looked like someone had stripped the paint. Eleven of his policemen died but not him.

"There was no doubt I was the main target," he told me. This did not seem to bother or surprise him. He'd been hardened by battle while fighting the Soviets and took pride in his bravery. After he was offered the job as police chief, he told a U.S. Special Forces commander about a courtesy phone call he had taken from Mullah Omar. The Taliban's supreme leader, another veteran of many Kandahar wars, told him, "I love you like a brother, as you love me like a brother. But if you take that job, I'm going to kill you." The commander remembers Mujahid laugh-

Khan Mohammad Mujahid, the commander of the
Afghan police force in Kandahar, who would be killed not long
after this photograph was taken.

ing away the threat as he told Mullah Omar, "No, I'll kill you, you one-eyed son of a bitch."

"If I flee now, that means we have handed over all of Kandahar to the enemy," Mujahid told me. "If I leave the battlefield, people will see no reason to fight. I have thirty years of military experience, I've been a commander for thirty years; if I leave, people will lose their morale."

They killed him two months later. One of his own policemen, or a man wearing the uniform, walked up to him in the courtyard as he stepped out of his office. The man timed it so that the vest of explosives strapped under his shirt would blow up at the moment they embraced in greeting.

This was the sort of treachery that made Major Rahmatullah hold his colleagues in such low regard. He liked to say he was one of only sixteen professional police officers in all of Kandahar. Only those who had completed the four-year Soviet-run police academy, he believed, deserved to call themselves law enforcement officers. The major could speak Russian, Dari, Pashtu, and Urdu. He valued education and encouraged his daughter to study English, so that she would know more than the smattering of vocabulary he possessed. He was chief of police of Dand, one of the districts that made up Kandahar Province, commander of 120 men, and he took that responsibility to heart. For all those reasons, he had no intention of accepting Sardar Mohammad into his ranks.

"He is very, very big teef," Major Rahmatullah had told Lieutenant Colonel David Abrahams, his U.S. Army mentor.

"A teef?" Abrahams asked.

"Big thief. Very, very big thief."

On old maps of Kandahar, Dand used to encircle the downtown. When the district boundaries were redrawn, what remained was farmland south of the city: grape fields, brick-baking kilns, mud huts. It was important because of this fertile agricultural land and because the president's ancestral village, Karz, fell within its border. Two of the main north–south roads spoke to the division of power in the district. One of them ran through Barakzai tribal territory to the estate of Gul Agha Sherzai, the former governor and the Karzais' chief rival. A parallel paved road to the east passed through Karz and the Popalzai lands. Barakzai militiamen controlled the first road. The other was the responsibility of a young man with sun-darkened skin and brown eyes a bit too far apart, and slightly crossed: Sardar Mohammad.

Mohammad had spent years in service of the Karzai clan. The son of a well-known mullah, he grew up in Mashroor, a village in Dand, then moved to Zakir-e Sharif, the next village down the road from Karz. Within the Karzai brothers' trusted circle of loyalists, the guards, drivers, and servants who dedicated themselves to protecting the lives and property of the country's ruling family, many came from Zakir-e Sharif. For them, menial positions paid off over time. Mohammad Shah Kako, one of the three men who crossed over from Pakistan with Hamid Karzai on motorcycles to foment rebellion against the Taliban, was rewarded with a position of command in the palace Presidential Protective Service. Another from the village, Ruhullah, had been a Karzai bodyguard before he parlayed that access into his defense contracting fortune. Before the Karzais came to power, Sardar Mohammad farmed and sold watermelons from the roadside. When the war started, he joined Jamil Karzai, a young English-speaking cousin of the president, who was working as a fixer and translator for ABC News out of a downtown Kandahar villa. Jamil traveled across the south helping American correspondents with their stories, while Sardar was one of the guards at the house. Looking back, Jamil says he saw Sardar as a liability. "He was always smoking hashish," he recalled. "I put him on night duty and I never let him come inside."

Ahmed Wali Karzai later took Sardar on as a guard and a driver, and his stock grew within the family. He was a strong young man—lean and wiry, with ropy forearms, a thick black mustache, and a jutting jaw—who behaved toward his bosses with a deference that approached worship. When Qayum Karzai built a lavish home in Zakir-e Sharif—a triple-domed mansion elevated on a rock and surrounded by turreted walls, a house with marble floors draped in colorful carpets and fronted by seven arched windows—he put Sardar in charge of its protection. "Ahmed Wali came to me and said, 'This is the best man I have,'" Qayum recalled.

Around the Karzais, Sardar behaved like a servant. When the family gathered for meetings or meals, he refused to sit down or, if ordered to, would squat on the ground in a corner. He drove to Ahmed Wali's house daily, even on Fridays, his day off, to see if he could be of service, leaving his two daughters in the care of his wife. In the room for guests in his village home, Sardar mounted four large framed photographs, two of Ahmed Wali and two of President Karzai. "If I said a single word against these guys," his brother-in-law Abdul Malik told me, pointing to the photos, "he would have killed me."

"He was an uneducated person, but he was always serious," Hameed Wafa, one of the governor's aides, recalled. "The reason Ahmed Wali kept him was because of his loyalty to the family. He trusted him so much. Nobody could carry a gun in his house expect Sardar Mohammad."

Their bond was so sure that Ahmed Wali would bring his mother to visit Sardar. "In our culture, being a tribal elder is like being a president, or a king," Qayum Karzai said. "And he treated us that way. He grew up with us. We knew him our whole lives. He was part of our home. I had enormous respect for him. I would tell people, 'If everyone was like Sardar Mohammad, this country could be great again.'"

His loyalty won him more responsibility. He took command of more checkpoints in concentric circles around Zakir-e Sharif, encompassing the Karzai family cemetery and strategic hills and intersections. Ahmed Wali's other bodyguards estimated that Sardar oversaw three hundred to four hundred men. He built a new concrete home and a separate guesthouse with white columns and ceiling fans on the outdoor portico; standing among the other dirt hovels, it declared unequivocally his status as a man of importance. His militiamen guarded his gate all day behind dirt barriers under a canopy of dried grass. Qayum Karzai bought Sardar a motorcycle. He began to develop a reputation as a man unafraid to use violence. "He was a very good fighter, one of the Taliban's sworn enemies," Fazel Mohammed, Ahmed Wali's personal security chief, told me. "His success attracted attention, and the local government gave him more men and more outposts. He brought tight security to the area."

Sardar's hatred of the Taliban had long roots. In the late 1990s, when the Karzais were in public opposition to the Taliban regime, men such as

Sardar were considered their lackeys. If there was something he needed from the government—help dredging a canal or digging a well—the Taliban bureaucrats in Kandahar refused. Once the Karzais' political fortunes were reversed, Sardar delivered his revenge without remorse. His relatives described how he approached his enemies. "First he would go and talk to them. Tell them not to do bad things. If they didn't listen to him, he would just kill them," his brother-in-law Abdul Malik said. "He killed many people."

American soldiers valued the security Sardar provided. Dand was generally safer than other embattled districts of Kandahar. American and British commanders would visit Sardar in his home. His connection with Ahmed Wali gave his relatives entrée into jobs they might not have otherwise had. Several of them worked for the Kandahar Strike Force, the CIA-trained militia in Kandahar. "If American forces were suspicious of someone, they asked Sardar to make the arrest," a relative said. "They cooperated with each other."

On the official rolls, ninety men reported to Sardar Mohammad, and even though they technically belonged to the police, they answered only to him. Lieutenant Colonel Abrahams would see them loitering around the Dand district center. Some wore gray cotton police uniforms. Most dressed as they pleased: track pants, soccer jerseys, random camouflage. They were officially on the roster of the headquarters police reserves, collecting salaries as such. In practice, they were untouchables. At their seven privately financed checkpoints—outside the Karzai cemetery, at Qayum Karzai's palace, in front of the village school, overlooking the tomb of Jamal Baba, at the base of a cell phone tower, and at intersections in Karz and Zakir-e Sharif—they openly taxed villagers who passed by carting bundles of sticks or driving the garishly painted jingle trucks. They also moonlighted for the lucrative private security companies escorting NATO convoys overland from Pakistan. There were rumors that they ran guns and drugs. Major Rahmatullah, the district police chief, was new to Dand, so he could do little more than watch.

After Khan Mohammad Mujahid was murdered in April, General Abdul Raziq, the boyish border police commander renowned for his ruthlessness, was appointed his successor. When Raziq took over, the police force in Dand was understaffed and meagerly equipped, with just 120 men on the payroll out of an authorized roster of 536. Major Rahmatullah's men had to share about a dozen Ford Rangers. They had five machine guns and some old AK-47s. Sardar Mohammad's militia, which showed up periodically and shared the police station, had five times the weaponry: high-powered machine guns, rocket-propelled grenades, more and newer Rangers. Their checkpoints were lit through the night by generators and supplied with fresh water from independent wells.

Filling the many empty slots in the Dand police had some wider strategic significance for the U.S. military. If Major Rahmatullah could grow his force, that would allow the one thousand men from the U.S. Army battalion responsible for Dand to leave that area to the Afghans and move their fight to the far more violent battleground in Panjwayi. To accomplish this, one of Abdul Raziq's early orders as the new Kandahar police chief was for Major Rahmatullah to incorporate Sardar Mohammad and his militia into the Dand police. This order served several agendas. For the American military, it would give the appearance of relying less on warlord militias and more on the official Afghan police force. To Raziq, taking control of this Popalzai militia would strengthen his authority as police chief, while conveniently undermining a potential rival to his own Achekzai militia. Rahmatullah stood to benefit as well, because the Dand police would nearly double in size and reap a bounty of weapons and trucks. The biggest loser in the transaction would be Sardar Mohammad.

But Major Rahmatullah refused. He considered the Popalzai militia a collection of untrained thugs and wanted nothing to do with Sardar Mohammad. The major would rather keep fighting undermanned and underequipped than work alongside the Karzai family's chief henchman. He considered Ahmed Wali and his followers above the law. "He would roll his eyes when we talked about dealing with the poppy issue," said Lieutenant Colonel David Raugh, a battalion commander who worked in Dand. Rahmatullah's refusal set off weeks of negotiations with Raziq. Abrahams, who lived with his Security Force Assistance Team at the Dand district center, heard of the struggle from Rahmatullah as it unfolded each day that summer. Finally, the major budged.

"I'll take the Popalzai police," Rahmatullah told Abrahams. "But not Sardar Mohammad."

Raziq eventually agreed with this decision to incorporate the militia without Sardar Mohammad involved. Within five hours of Raziq's order, the studded tires of the Popalzai police trucks crunched into the gravel lot of the Dand district center. Abrahams watched as every machine gun, rocket-propelled grenade, and Ford Ranger from the Karz checkpoints were unloaded and submitted for inventory. Rahmatullah redistributed the weapons and men across the district. "The acquisition of all these

Popalzai police basically quadrupled the capabilities of the police force in terms of mobility," Abrahams told me. That left Ahmed Wali Karzai's most loyal and trusted lieutenant in charge of a grand total of nine policemen at two checkpoints: the first was Qayum Karzai's empty palace; the second was the family graveyard.

The following Tuesday morning, July 12, 2011, Major Rahmatullah hosted his weekly checkpoint commanders meeting in the Dand district center, a routine established by Abrahams to enforce a bit of order and military discipline. They discussed the latest security picture, relevant intelligence, plans for the week ahead—the normal tedium of the war. During the meeting, Rahmatullah's cell phone rang. He held it to his ear and listened for several seconds. He hung up and turned to Abrahams.

I have to go disarm all of Sardar Mohammad's men, he said.

Abrahams was confused. Why?

"Sardar Mohammad just killed Ahmed Wali Karzai."

15

THE FIVE FINGERS

IT HAD BEEN A NORMAL TUESDAY morning at Ahmed Wali's house. He had visitors to attend to and lunch plans with General Ken Dahl at Kandahar Airfield. By ten a.m., a couple of dozen people had already deposited their sandals in the foyer and were waiting for their audience in groups downstairs, along the wall, and up in the second-floor sitting room. Outside the temperature reached one hundred degrees and kept climbing.

Agha Lalai Dastageri, one of Ahmed Wali's colleagues on the provincial council, had dropped in for a word. Dastageri was a man-giant with a thick beard who spoke in a slow, emotionless drone that felt deeply unnerving. One U.S. diplomat told me Dastageri was the "only guy that, honestly, I was just afraid of. He's got some eyes that are really hard to hold." Dastageri seemed to be a loyal acolyte to Ahmed Wali, but there were also signs of rivalry. Not long before, Ahmed Wali had learned that tribesmen from Kandahar had traveled to Kabul to meet with the president and complain about Ahmed Wali's abuses of power. Ahmed Wali had been told that Dastageri, with an eye toward usurping him as council chief, had dispatched the tribal elders to the palace. Ahmed Wali confronted Dastageri at one of the regular weekly meetings at the governor's palace. "He was shouting and sounding crazy," recalled one of the governor's aides. "He said, 'If you ever, ever do it again.' . . . And in front of all these people."

Among the other guests that morning was the deputy head of the Mohammadzai tribe. His name was Sardar Mohammad Osman—no relation to the policeman—and he had come to discuss a disputed piece of land one of his tribesmen claimed to own. Osman did not consider himself a friend of Ahmed Wali's. In fact, he blamed him for the death of his cousin, the tribe's leader, a few years before. The cousin had gone missing after stopping by a house he had purchased inside Aino Mena. Osman often worried that his cousin had become too close to Ahmed Wali, a man not to be crossed. "Then he just disappeared. We made a lot of phone calls. We talked to his friends. But we couldn't find him. He just vanished," Osman told me. Outside the Aino Mena house, they found the cousin's white Toyota Corolla. Inside, there were a few carpets and cushions, but it was mostly unfurnished. In one room, they saw bloodstains on the carpet. "We think they were waiting for him inside. They just killed him," Osman told me. "Ahmed Wali was involved in those sorts of things. When a tribal leader or political figure was assassinated, everybody would blame him. Everybody knew that it was him." Osman begged for Ahmed Wali's help to find his cousin's body. "And Ahmed Wali's response was 'What can I do? You keep searching, and I'll keep searching.'"

Ahmed Wali had not been generous to the Mohammadzai, a small tribe but one with royal lineage. "He would always oppose the appointment of anybody from our tribe in a government post," Osman said. "Our great-grandfathers, they have ruled this country for years, and once they were removed from power, then our people had a lot of problems with other tribes. We had land disputes, we had property disputes. So he never helped us, and he would always undermine our efforts to defend our rights and to protect our property and land." And yet, here Osman was again at Ahmed Wali's door, because there was only one arbiter in Kandahar.

Friends who were enemies, enemies friends. The night before, American soldiers had raided a house occupied by bodyguards of Kandahar's governor, Toryalai Wesa. Until earlier in the year, Wesa had been guarded by Blue Hackle, a private security firm based in Washington, D.C., but that contract had expired. Half of the seventy-man force that replaced those guards was provided by Kandahar's police chief, the other half by Ahmed Wali Karzai. The governor's guards had been arrested before. This raid might have been a mistake, or maybe the guards were associated with the Taliban. Either way, it was an annoyance to Fazel Mohammed, their direct supervisor as Ahmed Wali's personal security chief. One of the guards called him that morning to complain that the American soldiers had mistreated them; he added that he planned to quit. Fazel Mohammed said he'd bring it up when he saw the boss. First he wanted to check with the police chief and the governor about the situation. As Fazel was leaving the house, Sardar Mohammad strode in carrying a sheaf of papers.

He wore civilian clothes, a brown *shalwar kameez*, with two pistols tucked into the drawstring of his pants. The weapons were not unusual. Sardar was trusted enough to be exempt from the normal procedure at the gate to search and disarm visitors. But he typically dressed in his gray police uniform. Fazel asked him why that wasn't the case today. Sardar ignored the question and proceeded up the stairs. Written on the papers he carried were the names of dozens of his policemen. For this often deadly work, the government paid these men $240 a month. Even when their wages arrived on time, they relied on Ahmed Wali for top-ups or tips, *bakhshesh*. This had lately become more important because the money flow had choked and sputtered with the arrival of the new provincial police chief, Abdul Raziq. Sardar Mohammad had complained before about his men's provisions: food, fuel, and salaries were all coming late. This was a situation Ahmed Wali should fix. It was one of the responsibilities of being a patron, how the currency of loyalty transacted.

That morning, Sardar and Ahmed Wali had other topics they might have wanted to discuss. In the preceding few months, Sardar had angered his fellow tribesmen with his treatment of village children. He had apparently violated the unwritten codes that governed when Afghan men could take boys for their sexual pleasure. "He was abusing a lot of children," Fazel Mohammed said. The villagers, according to Ahmed Wali's associates, had begun to see him as a predator.

So what was on Sardar Mohammad's mind as he walked into Ahmed Wali's sitting room? Missing police salaries? The public humiliation of losing checkpoints? His predilection for young boys? Something else? They were two comrades fighting a shadow war while running a business empire. They must have harbored many secrets known only to themselves. Sardar approached Ahmed Wali, who sat on his couch, barefoot, in discussion with his guests. Sardar asked him for a private word. They stepped into a small adjoining room. Sardar Mohammad locked the door behind himself. No one witnessed the conversation.

The sound of gunshots disoriented the other guests. Was that inside? Then there was shouting. People ran toward the adjoining room. Sardar Mohammad opened the door and yelled at everyone to stand back or he would shoot. From the hallway, Mohammed Osman, one of the house drivers, could see the lower half of Ahmed Wali's body draped over some floor cushions, one of his pant legs pushed up. Osman was a small man whose curly black locks peeked out from his skullcap. "When I saw his bare leg lying there, I lost control of my mind," Osman told me. "[Sardar] didn't fire at me. I just reached my arm inside the door and shot at him."

When Osman entered the room, Sardar was down and Ahmed Wali sprawled on pillows and cushions, his head slumped back, Sardar's papers spread out around him. He had been shot twice, in a fashion that suggested a proficient killer. A double tap: once in the chest, once in the head. "They killed Agha Mama!" someone screamed. Dastageri cradled Ahmed Wali's head while someone else lifted his legs. They wrapped a beige woolen shawl, a *patu*, around him and ferried him downstairs to an armored Land Cruiser parked in the driveway. Osman had always imagined he would be in that car, behind the wheel, when this day came. "I never thought that something like that would happen inside the house," he said. "Everybody knew Sardar Mohammad. He was Ahmed Wali's friend. He was all of our friends."

The rage reverberated across the frightened city like a shock wave. It was an unfathomable betrayal. Guards pumped more bullets into Sardar's downed body, as though seeking to inflict, through sheer physical trauma, some proportionate retribution. They hauled him outside, where policemen tied him with a rope to the bumper of a Ford Ranger and dragged his flopping corpse through the streets. When they reached Charsu, the "Four Directions" market downtown where young Farid Karzai worked, they hung Sardar by his neck, barefoot and pantless, from the second story of a sand-colored brick building, as a warning to all. In photos taken that day, a policeman can be seen standing on the roof above Sardar's dangling body, looking out over the crowded bazaar. Sardar is suspended high off the ground, next to a window with yellow shutters, his head torqued to the left by his noose, and his thin legs casting a small shadow on the building's façade. Rickshaws and vans, pedestrians and shoppers, crisscross the streets under his cocked, unseeing gaze.

When I visited Mirwais Hospital two days later, I found him in the refrigerated morgue, a converted Maersk shipping container, inside a white body bag, lying on his back on a stainless steel tray. He was thirty-five years old. His death certificate recorded eleven gunshot wounds to his neck, chest, abdomen, and face. Despite Islamic custom necessitating swift burial, his relatives were afraid to claim him, and left him lying there for days.

At the house, chaos. "Everyone was crying. Soldiers. Tribal elders. The

people who were visiting. The people who lived there," Fazel Mohammed said.

Mond Lala, a guard, screamed at Fazel Mohammed: "Motherfucker, is
this how you provide security?"

Ahmed Wali Karzai was dead by the time he reached the hospital. "No
respiration. No pulse. Nothing," one of his doctors told me. His body
would be taken home and left on blocks of ice in a small room, the air
conditioner turned to high, to await the president. According to Death
Certificate 371, the cause of death was a gunshot wound. One bullet had
entered the left side of his chest, near his heart, traveled across his body,
and exited the right side of his back. The other bullet struck under his
right eye and passed through his skull's parietal bone behind his right ear.
Before his body was taken from the hospital for burial, someone stole his
Rolex.

Shaida Mohammad Abdali was sitting in his office down a marble hallway
on the second floor of the National Security Council building when his
cell phone rang. Abdali's lifetime of service to the Karzais had earned
him the title of deputy national security adviser and special assistant
to the president. He had come a long way from the boy who washed
clothes and poured water onto guests' hands before meals at the Karzai
home in Quetta. He wore dark suits now and occupied the front row
at many important events, but other palace aides mocked him for his
humble beginnings and somewhat smarmy officiousness. He sat amid a
small shrine to his leader—photographs on desks and walls and a vase
emblazoned with Hamid Karzai's face. Abdali used to sleep in the president's residence and had then moved to a small house nearby, within the
palace walls. At night, he kept the president's cell phone in his pocket and
screened his calls. A reliable barometer of the pressure in the president's
office, he was also trusted for his discretion. That morning, he could hear
the words coming through his phone, but they wouldn't cohere in his
mind.

"Ahmed Wali Karzai's been killed," Dastageri told him.

The sentence immobilized Abdali. Ahmed Wali had been President
Karzai's political backbone in Kandahar and across the Pashtun south,
and Hamid's favorite brother. They spoke on the phone nearly every
day. "I could not move from my chair. I just sat there. Shocked," Abdali
recalled. "I just felt my head spinning. I thought, How can I move from
my chair? How can I tell the president?"

Abdali rushed downstairs and outside, into the palace courtyard. At that moment, Karzai was meeting with Haji Din Mohammed, his former campaign manager. Abdali walked through the screen door of the Gul Khana and ran into presidential spokesman Waheed Omar. "I think Ahmed Wali's been killed," Abdali told him. "Do you want to go with me to tell the president?"

Standing in front of Karzai, Abdali broke into tears. He fumbled for words, trying to explain. Karzai, who remained seated across from Haji Din Mohammed, grew frustrated.

"What happened?" he said. "Just tell me."

Ahmed Wali, Abdali told the president, had been shot.

"Is he dead or alive?" Karzai demanded.

"I think he is dead," Abdali said.

"Who did this?"

"Sardar Mohammad, from the village."

Karzai didn't say another word. He exhaled and looked away. The three men in the room watched the president. Karzai didn't move for a while. Omar had never seen him appear so shaken. The silence reminded Abdali of Karzai's reaction more than a decade earlier when he learned his father had been killed. Omar touched Abdali's arm, and the two men walked out of the office.

When they left, Haji Din Mohammed sought to comfort Karzai. He had lost his own brother, Abdul Haq, at the start of the war. Haq had been one of the most famous and outspoken mujahedeen commanders, a charismatic leader who met Ronald Reagan and Margaret Thatcher and would have been a candidate to sit in the chair Karzai now occupied, if he had not been killed in his own rebellious run into Afghanistan shortly after September 11.

"Mr. President, we have all lost brothers," Mohammed told him.

The palace staff didn't know how to proceed. Karzai had a busy day. French president Nicolas Sarkozy had arrived in Kabul that morning and was to have lunch with Karzai, followed by a joint press conference in the palace courtyard. After a few minutes, Omar returned to Karzai's office and suggested that they clear his schedule for the day. Karzai initially agreed to cancel the press conference, then changed his mind. "Afghans die every day and I don't cancel my press conferences," he told Omar.

Karzai began to make calls. He phoned his brother Shah Wali, an engineer who lived with Ahmed Wali in Kandahar. Shah Wali had not been at home when his brother was shot and could not explain fully what had happened. Karzai called the Kandahar governor, Toryalai Wesa, and the police chief, Abdul Raziq, to discuss the situation. In between calls he spoke to the small group of aides gathered in his office. "I used to worry that Afghans would wonder why they are always dying and yet the president's family is not dying," Karzai said. "Perhaps this is God's way of bringing me closer to Afghans. Because they have all lost family members."

He would go on with his day. He met with Sarkozy for lunch. Then he walked out into the dappled shade of the courtyard and stood at the podium, on a small stone patio in front of dozens of reporters. He wore his customary peaked wool hat, the karakul, and a dark blue blazer over a white *shalwar kameez*. He clasped his hands and spoke calmly into the cameras.

"This morning, my younger brother Ahmed Wali Karzai was martyred in his home. This is the life of the people of Afghanistan, and each Afghan family has suffered in such a way."

Karzai had, by this time, developed a reputation as an unusually emotional president. He cried during public speeches, to the shame and ridicule of many Afghans. In one televised address, he sobbed when he spoke about the prospect of having to send his four-year-old son, Mirwais, out of Afghanistan so he could grow up in a peaceful country. This time, in his public address, and in private back at his office, he kept his composure. "This is a personal matter," he told his staff. "Not a state matter."

Abdali wasn't so sure. The moment reminded him of an Afghan proverb: "The five fingers are brothers, not equals." For the president, Ahmed Wali had always been the most important. In the political realm, he stood as a bulwark against Pakistan in the Pashtun south, perhaps the only Afghan leader of that stature the president could trust not to succumb to ISI entreaties. Personally, his devotion to the president never flagged. During Hamid's graduate studies in India, Ahmed Wali had sent him money every month from Chicago. Ahmed Wali's logistical support from Quetta had eased Hamid's return to the country, and, since his early days with the CIA in Kandahar, he had accepted the risk of fighting for the Americans. "Ahmed Wali stayed for all those years in Afghanistan when he didn't have to. He tolerated all the accusations, he knew it was all about politics," Abdali said. "He was the president's real hand."

Despite his public image as an erratic and mercurial man, Hamid Karzai had endured losses in his personal life that he'd handled with strength and grace.

"He is a person who feels pain; it is visible on his face," his cousin Hekmat Karzai told me later. "The man knows the sacrifice he has paid: his father, his uncles, and his dearest brother, who was his right arm."

"Why would he do such a horrible thing?" Fazel Mohammed said. "I've given a lot of thought to this issue. And I still don't know."

The motive—assuming there was just one—quickly got buried under the sediment of rumor and conspiracy. In the air-conditioned corridors of Regional Command South, at Kandahar Airfield, military intelligence officers working under General James Terry received two interesting reports from the field shortly after Ahmed Wali's killing. One of them came from an Afghan police unit that responded to Ahmed Wali's house: "We found a secret room." The report wasn't very detailed. There was some type of machinery in the basement. It might be a drug lab. Or a printing press for counterfeit bills. But Terry didn't want to find out. "He ordered them to get out of there immediately," one of his subordinates told me. "This is an Afghan issue. Now that [Ahmed Wali's] dead, he felt it would affect his legacy. All of our people left immediately." If this was the smoking gun that American officials had looked for over the better part of a decade, that was the last chance to find it.

The other report the Americans picked up, from sources close to Ahmed Wali, pointed to a potential motive. Sardar Mohammad's sexual abuse of young boys had apparently gotten to the point where Ahmed Wali felt he had to take action. "AWK was trying to fire Sardar Mohammad for abusing the village boys," one senior U.S. military official told me. "He first tried to get him to stop. And took away checkpoints in areas where things were happening." Another senior American official in Kandahar at the time related the same story: "Sardar Mohammad was a pedophile, and his pedophilia had gotten way out of hand and had become an embarrassment. The Popalzai fathers had gone to AWK and said, 'You've got to rein this guy in. He's out of control.' AWK decided he was going to fire him from his security job and give him some other job. He summoned him over there that day to do it. And [Sardar Mohammad] got wind of it."

When I asked other members of Ahmed Wali's inner circle, they dismissed this theory. They claimed they had not heard until after his death about the extent of Sardar Mohammad's child abuse. There were other stories, told with equal vehemence. People talked of a police report claiming that the same gun had killed both Ahmed Wali and Sardar Mohammad, apparently shot by a servant in league with Pakistani intelligence, though I never saw such a report. Some relatives believed that Hashmat had hired or convinced Sardar to take Ahmed Wali out. Mahmood Karzai insisted the Taliban had killed his brother, after a slow process of brainwashing Sardar that had involved clandestine trips across the border to Quetta. Sardar's drug use and drinking were said to have intensified in the months prior to the killing. He had been acting erratic, on edge, demanding to see people's phones, to know whom they were calling. Another theory in circulation held that Ahmed Wali and Sardar had both had their sights on a pretty young Karzai cousin to marry. Ahmed Wali told Sardar to back off, but Sardar was burning with love. "He had no option but to kill the girl or kill AWK," as one person put it.

The death also got mixed up with the politics of the war. After the murder, Ahmad Shuja Pasha, director general of Pakistan's ISI, met with President Karzai in his palace office in Kabul and told him that the CIA had killed Ahmed Wali, according to Rahmatullah Nabil, the Afghan spy chief at the time, who was present in the meeting. That would have been an intriguing thing to hear for a president as angry at the Americans as Karzai was by that time. When I asked Nabil if Karzai believed Pasha, he lit his cigarette, then slowly exhaled. "I think to some extent he believed him."

Given the close association between the CIA, Ahmed Wali, and his circle in Kandahar, the allegation struck me as unlikely. When I visited Sardar Mohammad's home, his relatives proudly showed me their badges from the Kandahar Strike Force, the CIA-run paramilitary group that Ahmed Wali helped recruit. He was one of theirs. And Ahmed Wali's cronies unanimously rejected this notion, as did Nabil. The CIA had always been Ahmed Wali's patron and protector in the bureaucratic turf wars. "That doesn't have a basis. It doesn't make any sense," Fazel Mohammed, his security chief, told me. "Why would the CIA kill Ahmed Wali when he was acting as their eyes and ears in this region?"

Whatever the motive, the established order had been overturned. As a U.S. ambassador put it, the man who had been built into a "ten-foot giant," as much by outmaneuvering his Afghan rivals as by his cunning manipulation of American military power, had fallen. Some great structure had burned down. And once again we were all too late, left to step through its ashes, looking for something to salvage.

16

I HATE POLITICS

A LOT THAT HAD BEEN held together by Ahmed Wali Karzai fell apart when he died. Maybe the most important thing was a sense of joint purpose among the family members. There had never been unity; the worst things I ever heard about the Karzais came from other Karzais. But the notion that they were in this together, as somewhat unlikely rulers of Afghanistan, no longer felt as true. Ahmed Wali's death opened holes in the fortress wall, and people immediately started shooting through. Rivals rose to challenge Karzai business interests; the siblings turned against one another in a nastier way. President Karzai's anger at America morphed into something that now looked more like hate. At the same time, several soldiers from the 10th Mountain Division in Kandahar were devastated by the news. The military intelligence chief Ketti Davison called it "the lowest point in our tour."

Ahmed Wali wasn't soon forgotten. Kandahar became one giant shrine to him. On billboards across town, his grim, bestubbled face peered down on his former subjects. "A true servant and the leader of the Pashtun tribe," read one of them, over a photograph of Ahmed Wali giving a TV interview in a plush, thronelike chair. "Make sure you write on my forehead that I cut his throat because he refused to bow his head," another proclaimed, as Ahmed Wali gestured with yellow prayer beads in his hand. Photo after photo: Ahmed Wali receiving a reverent greeting from a police officer; talking on his cell phone; leaning into a microphone; holding his palms cupped for prayer. His face was embedded in the marble tower in the middle of the traffic roundabout at Martyrs' Square. It was pasted to car windows and all over the guard booths at the entrance to Aino Mena. "The hero martyr of beloved Afghanistan and the great leader of the Pashtun tribe," the messages went. "The one who took the desire for a green and prosperous Afghanistan to his grave."

The man left to replace him was Shah Wali Karzai, his brother. He was older, but he looked younger, and less substantial. He had a lean, angular face. Around the temples, his short hair had gone white. When I met him, not long after Ahmed Wali's death, his face was etched with strain and worry. He looked malnourished. It was a Sunday, his chosen day off, but there was still a crowd gathered in the foyer of his house in Aino Mena, and people sitting on the floor around the perimeter of a large entry room, all waiting for him. His thin shoulders slumped when he came out of a meeting and saw the acres of turban cloth and miles of beards awaiting him. People with gnarled toenails and hennaed hair reached for him. There was the musk of the not-enough washed. He pushed through the crowd, the poor and grasping with their never-ending needs and wants. *He stole my land. My brother's in prison. Help me.*

Couldn't they solve these things themselves?

Shah Wali felt unprepared for all of this. He had been trained as an engineer at the University of Maryland. He loved basketball. He wasn't a tribal leader. For several years he'd worked in happy obscurity as a project manager on the Aino Mena construction site, content to worry about solving problems like wastewater treatment and trash collection. He was quiet and self-effacing, uncomfortable as the center of attention. American military experts in the war hadn't even heard of him. But with Ahmed Wali's sudden assassination, President Karzai convened the elders and wrapped a ceremonial turban around Shah Wali's head, anointing him the leader of the most powerful tribe in Afghanistan. On top of those new responsibilities, he had to deal with his slain brother's shadowy business empire, the liaisons with the CIA and the U.S. military, and somehow keep the family hold on Pashtun politics across the south. He was fifty-two years old, and he was miserable.

"I don't want this," Shah Wali told me one day during Ramadan, his house overflowing with guests. "See, I don't have ambition. I'm just here because I have to be. I cannot fill Ahmed Wali's shoes. But I'm here. I have no choice. I don't want to be governor. I don't want to be minister. I don't want to be a district governor. I hate politics. But I'm stuck with it."

The problems placed at his feet every day seemed insurmountable: fathers begging for their Taliban sons to be released from prison; mothers demanding justice for their martyred children; a young man asking for a job on the election commission; a man who built a shop on another

Shah Wali Karzai stands inside his house in Aino Mena.

man's land. All Shah Wali could do was worry. Afghan authorities were warning him of new threats now aimed at him. A car bomb had exploded inside Aino Mena next to a picnic area one day, killing eleven people. "The scale has tipped," he said. "If they can kill Ahmed Wali, they can do anything."

Shah Wali had been born in the Panjwayi district of Kandahar, when his father served there as district governor. When the family moved to Kabul, he was still a young boy. After high school, he studied medicine for two years at Kabul University, until the Soviet invasion intervened. He and his youngest brother, Abdul Wali, were among the last of the siblings to leave Afghanistan, fleeing on buses south to the Pakistani border, past Soviet checkpoints. Because Germany wasn't requiring Afghan visas at the time, the two brothers flew from Karachi to Frankfurt. Shah Wali considered staying, and he had an opportunity to pursue his medical studies, but he ended up moving on to the Washington, D.C., suburbs, where his older brothers lived. He was twenty-two years old.

Shah Wali settled into a familiar family routine. Over four years, beginning in the fall of 1981, he took English, math, and science courses at Montgomery College, while working at the Bethesda Marriott restaurant along with Qayum and other relatives, and then at the Helmand in Baltimore when that opened. He didn't feel he could afford to go to medical school, so he enrolled in engineering courses at the University of

Maryland at College Park. He graduated with two bachelor's degrees, in civil and mechanical engineering.

He ended up occasionally traveling back to Quetta: when his father had a heart attack, then after his murder several years later. He was there attending Ahmed Wali's wedding when the twin towers fell. Shah Wali spent the first eight months of Hamid Karzai's tenure alongside his brother in the palace. When he left, there were different rumors as to why: that he had taken money from the palace slush fund, that he hadn't received a senior appointment in the interim administration, that he was too far from his mother and his new bride. In his words, he got "bored."

"You know the president. He was not allowing us to get involved in government. He says, It's going to be nepotism and all this. I said, It doesn't mean nepotism if you're qualified and educated. He said no. So I came to Kandahar to stay with Ahmed Wali."

Shah Wali dedicated himself to Aino Mena. Much of the early construction work had been organized by Hamid Helmandi, the Afghan developer who was living in San Francisco. Helmandi treated Aino Mena like his child. He'd hand-carried seeds from California and established a tree nursery in Hyderabad, Pakistan. He planted eucalyptuses, palo verdes, crepe myrtles, and when the first one hundred thousand saplings were more than a foot tall, he trucked them across the border to Kandahar so that Aino Mena would have rows of trees and dappled shade. He traveled across Texas and Arizona buying up used construction equipment—graders, pavers, front-end loaders—and had them disassembled in California and shipped by container to Afghanistan. In his designs, he chose cavity walls around the perimeter of the houses, to help with heat transfer, and double-paned windows, uncommon in Afghanistan, to preserve energy. He installed solar panels on some of the roofs. He hired and trained the construction workers. "This was nothing like back home," Helmandi told me, "how you put an ad in the paper and the next day twenty people show up. Here there was nothing. I had to pick up a guy off the street and teach him how to do credit and debit. Or with sewer lines, I had to train people how to put a pipe together. Train electricians, plumbers." Instead of cranes, they rigged up chains and motors to hoist equipment.

Helmandi's father had been in the grape business in Kandahar and had moved to Fresno, California, in the mid-1960s to open a raisin-processing facility. The family's raisins were first exported regionally, to Pakistan, India, Sri Lanka, and Nepal, before they opened an office in London and started supplying Europe with raisins. When he was older, Helmandi got involved in construction and built houses in Simi Valley and elsewhere. He considered himself an experienced, talented developer, but he had not anticipated the difficulty working in his hometown. "I didn't know that the construction was going to be so hard. It was so easy back in the U.S. If you need anything, you go online and order it and they drop it off. Here I had to walk shop to shop to find the proper nail or hinge."

But he found the work as rewarding. "We were trying to create hope, that was our goal. And provide affordable houses," Helmandi said. "We were not even making money on it. We were barely breaking even. We were trying to achieve that goal: provide shelter, create employment."

When Shah Wali joined the project, he saw things differently.

"Aino Mena was close to bankruptcy," he said. The project owed several million dollars to local contractors and still had to pay off a loan. "When I came, there was nothing, nothing," he said. "They only had one tractor. Not even one kilometer of road was paved. After the six years I worked here, there was $65 million in the bank."

Shah Wali and Helmandi disagreed about many aspects of their project. Shah Wali believed that the project was being mismanaged and that Helmandi had misspent funds. Helmandi believed that he was being pushed out just when things were getting lucrative. He felt threatened: "Shah Wali and the rest of the crooks here smelled money. I got scared. I thought maybe I was going to get killed. So I just left."

Under Shah Wali, the business strategy of Aino Mena went in a new direction. The owners shifted from selling completed houses to plots of land. There turned out to be far greater demand for empty land inside the gates, with the freedom to build houses as people saw fit, than following the American-inspired suburban design that Mahmood had first envisioned. Some of the U.S.-style houses had lower walls than Kandaharis were accustomed to, and others had no guest room, making it more difficult to sequester the women from strangers. Home owners felt exposed.

In an unexpected way, the forces contorting Kandahar's economy soon began to benefit Aino Mena. The Taliban were growing stronger, the surrounding city more dangerous. At the same time, elite Kandaharis were getting wealthier from the flood of foreign aid and military contracting. Real estate prices inside Aino Mena spiked. The bakery where Niaz Mohammed made bread had been the first in Aino Mena. Within four years, he said, there were more than ten competitors. He earned twice as much working inside Aino Mena than at his earlier shop, but the salary still wasn't sufficient for him to afford one of the houses inside the gates. The people who lived inside Aino Mena tended to have some connection to the American military. They worked as translators for soldiers or defense contractors, earning inflated salaries, or were businessmen who won logistics contracts themselves. Some were government employees with salaries topped up by NATO forces to try to entice people to take those dangerous jobs. Mohammed, who was thirty-four years old, lived in Panjwayi, a violent district the Taliban sought to control year after year, and commuted across town by motorcycle. He was careful not to let his neighbors know where he worked. "The Taliban hate Aino Mena," he told me one morning as he slid loaves of bread into an oven. "I don't even tell my brothers I work here."

Investors started buying up lots and flipping them for several times their purchase price. During his time as project manager, Shah Wali said, they paved seventy-five miles of roads and built sidewalks, sewers, and power lines. There were more than three thousand structures—houses, restaurants, bakeries, and banks. The neighborhood had a medical school for women. "We were doing all these things by ourselves," he said.

Shah Wali felt he had salvaged the project just as Helmandi had retreated to the safety of California. For a few years, they didn't see each other. As Shah Wali saw it: "Then when the company was successful, the loan was paid off, then he came back."

The intensity of the disputes between partners and the value of the property had risen in tandem. The Aino Mena partners suspected that Shah Wali was overcharging Mahmood's company, AFCO, for gravel and earning millions, something he denied. These fights over money, and the claims by the Afghan military of their rightful ownership, soured the Americans on a project they had initially championed. In the late fall of 2009, the U.S. embassy described the project as "an ostentatious Karzai property development for Afghan elites east of Kandahar City, built on land obtained from the government at rock bottom prices, with financing guaranteed by OPIC," the U.S. government agency that gave Mahmood the initial $3 million loan. One of the new partners, Haji Mohammad Jan, who had bought a 20 percent stake from Larry Doll, the Virginia developer, was the same man who'd been investigated by Kirk Meyer for his New Ansari *hawala* dealings and carting planeloads of cash out of the country. On February 18, 2011, the Treasury Department's Office of Foreign Assets Control also designated him as a narcotics trafficker under the Kingpin Act. As part of its economic sanctions program, OFAC informed the AFCO partners—those who were U.S. or dual citizens—that they could not have any association with him; if they did, they would face violations punishable by up to thirty years in prison and $10 million in fines. "I'm a U.S. citizen," Helmandi told me. "Every time I go somewhere and he's present, I run away. I don't want to break the law."

The U.S. military, by the summer of 2011, had banned AFCO from receiving government contracts (apparently the company had won a small contract at Kandahar Airfield to install plumbing fixtures). A memorandum outlining the decision argued that the AFCO had "engaged in criminal misconduct with regard to illicit real estate activities and profiteering from a major privately owned Afghan lender."

The Afghan Defense Ministry, meanwhile, was now openly accusing the Karzals of stealing government land to build their gated neighborhood; at various times, it sent soldiers to order the workers to stop building. Now riding the downslope of U.S. military presence, the wartime economy was slowing, and investors were pulling their money from Kandahar. Ahmed Wali's death had caused so much worry and uncertainty that it was affecting the economy, many Kandahar merchants insisted, and construction was one of the industries hardest hit. Home values started plummeting: prices as high as $70 per square meter fell to about $20. Partners were trying to recoup their money while they could. Investors complained to Shah Wali that AFCO was misspending its money and that promised infrastructure was not being built. "We wrote an official letter to Shah Wali asking him to freeze the money because we didn't trust these people," said Shirin Agha, one of the leaders of the investors' union. "They stopped working on the project, or most of it. They also fired a lot of people. But they were still taking out a lot of money. So we thought at one point if we don't take any decisive action, then one day all the money will be spent and there will just be a piece of brown land."

"It was my responsibility," Shah Wali told me. "They were trying to transfer money from my account to Dubai. I tried to stop it."

So without informing the other partners, Shah Wali decided to create a new company and transfer AFCO's assets to that account, even though he technically wasn't an owner of AFCO, just one of the employees. The partners whose money had suddenly vanished, including Mahmood, were not particularly pleased. "When we discovered it, we all got mad and started jumping around and saying, 'What the heck, this is illegal, why

the hell did you transfer the money to your own company account?'"
Helmandi said. Abdullah Nadi, another original partner, believed that
Shah Wali had forged his signature to transfer the money. By the partners' calculations, as much as $77 million was missing. As Mahmood Kar-
zai wrote in an e-mail to Helmandi, "This is not fare."

By the time Ahmed Wali died, many American soldiers considered him
one of their most loyal comrades in the faltering battle with the Taliban. When Major General Carter left Kandahar, he had grown genuinely
fond of him. At a farewell party hosted at the provincial council, Ahmed
Wali had given Carter a jersey, scarf, and hat from the Chelsea Football
Club, Ahmed Wali's favorite, and told him how eager he was to visit London and watch a game.

The soldiers had lost the one man they saw as powerful enough to
bend public will by gift or intimidation. He lobbied everyone, from illiterate warlords to the president, in favor of the American mission. He
kept a fractious coalition of tribal elders marching in line. Who knew
what type of chaos might emerge to fill the hole left by his murder? "He
was the ultimate Afghan, and I don't mean that negatively," said Colonel
Chris Riga, the Special Forces commander. "It brought me to tears when
he was killed." General Ken Dahl felt the same way: "I was heartbroken
when he got killed. We really were turning the corner."

In Ahmed Wali's absence, the Karzai family's grip on the Pashtuns
slipped. Qayum, who had been spending most of his time tending to the
three restaurants he now owned in Baltimore, flew back to Kandahar and
stayed for weeks to help manage the fallout. To try to retain control, the
family subdivided Ahmed Wali's responsibilities. Qayum took political
and diplomatic engagements. Shah Wali and Mahmood looked after the
business interests. They brought in Asadullah Khalid, the former governor of Kandahar and a Karzai ally, to take on a new position as security
coordinator for the province. But they couldn't hold things together the
way he had. Soon his inner circle was splintering.

It was always obvious that Ahmed Wali had been a very wealthy man.
His generosity toward his servants and guards and even strangers who
came to visit was renowned. I'd heard all sorts of stories about the kinds
of things he would underwrite. He paid for truckloads of wheat to be
handed out in Kandahar villages. He paid for young people to attend
university and for patients to fly to India for medical treatment. He paid

to house Tor Jan, a Taliban commander from the Achekzai tribe, and ten of his men when they decided to abandon the insurgency and needed protection. When the Arghandab district police chief, Haji Abdul Ahad, nearly died in a suicide bombing, Ahmed Wali gave him more than $30,000 for his doctors' bills. "Ahmed Wali Karzai was the only person who helped," he told me. Ahmed Wali had ordered one of his servants, Lajaward, to give money and food to every single person who came to the house—dozens or hundreds of people each day.

This was surely appreciated, but fear was what kept people in line. One of the few people who knew Ahmed Wali's financial details was his accountant, Haji Zmarai. The two were cousins, Zmarai a son of one of Ahmed Wali's maternal aunts. Two days after his burial, Zmarai flew to Dubai, family members said, and the relatives soon realized that Ahmed Wali's fortune had gone with him. One of Ahmed Wali's close relatives said that $300 million was missing. Others who saw Zmarai in that period reported that he spent nights out at dance clubs, dressed like an Arab shcikh, wearing diamond rings and showering money on women. The apparent brazen theft caused a panic within the family. According to relatives, one of the uncles flew to Dubai to find Zmarai. He supposedly told Zmarai that Ahmed Wali's mother missed him, and that he should come back to Kandahar to visit. When the plane landed, police trucks were waiting on the tarmac. Zmarai was arrested and locked away inside Kandahar's Sarposa prison. But the money wasn't coming back.

There were other defections from Ahmed Wali's inner circle. Mond Lala had been a loyal servant to several of the Karzai brothers. He'd joined Hamid Karzai's rebellion against the Taliban and later worked as a security guard with the brothers in Kandahar. When I met him, he had recently quit and had moved into a tiny, barely furnished town house in Aino Mena. He showed me his scrapbook of photos: standing alongside the president at the palace; his arm around Greg, the CIA officer who traveled with Hamid early in the war; shooting pool with Ahmed Wali. "Look at me: I was one of the very close people to Ahmed Wali and the family. And now I'm living in this rental house," he said. "Over the last year, nobody paid me a single penny."

The fight between Shah Wali and Mahmood over money and control of Aino Mena had disappointed him. Neither of them were the man Ahmed Wali had been, he felt. The new young sycophants at Shah Wali's house didn't pay him much respect. "I couldn't work with them anymore, so I resigned," he said.

Afterward, Mond Lala spent a couple of weeks at the palace, visiting President Karzai. "I told him what had happened and why I had resigned, and the president told me, Bravo. Good for you. You did the right thing to resign. They should be ashamed."

Since the killing, Shah Wali had relocated to a two-story yellow concrete house inside Aino Mena, surrounded by twelve-foot-high concrete blast walls. To reach it you had to pass several checkpoints and undergo pat-downs and metal-detector scans. A gray Lexus with tan leather seats (license plate 4444) was parked in the driveway. In addition to his four children, Shah Wali and his wife were now caring for Ahmed Wali's five kids as well. None of them were attending school, as that seemed too risky, given the assassination. When they weren't having sessions with their tutor, the kids watched cartoons. "They stay in the house all day," Shah Wali told me. "It's like they're in jail."

Two of the boys bounded into the room one afternoon as we were talking.

"So, do you like to play soccer?" Ahmed Wali Karzai's eldest son, Ismail, asked me.

I told him I'd enjoyed playing when I was his age.

"I was the greatest goalkeeper—now I'm the best shotter," he said. "I'm with Brazil." He looked at Adam, Shah Wali's eldest son, who was playing with his iPad. They were both eight.

"I don't know what he does," Ismail said.

"America," Adam said.

Ismail said he liked Brazil. "Any player in Brazil. 'Cause one of them, no, the specialty is to shoot very fast. And one can, when the other team gets trying to get the ball, but he doesn't miss it."

"I would say that he's a crybaby," he said of Adam. "Somebody hurt his feelings, he rush like a bull. He rush like a bull. Put his two fingers like this and controls you and they push you and then he comes up and comes to you like a bull and he doesn't stand a chance. He only stands a chance against his fat sister. His *fat* sister. I have a sister named Summa. She's very thin. She's very thin, but sometimes when we hurt her she's like a volcano. She's going to come and burst like a volcano."

"Then she's going to bite us," Adam said.

"She doesn't have teeth, but she has terrible black like teeth," Ismail said.

They talked some more about their sisters, and about soccer, naming all the Brazilian and German players they could think of.

"You're a snail," Ismail said.

"I'm not a snail," Adam said.

"Did you watch a film called *Criss Angel Mindfreak 2*?" Ismail asked me.

The plot, as he explained it, had something to do with a lamp, and a clock, and a guy who could fly and lifted a cat. They watched a lot of cartoons.

"We want to go to the United States," Ismail said.

"And President Obama," Adam said. "What's his name? B . . . A . . . R . . . S . . . A . . . C . . . K.

"Do you know President Obama? President Barsack Obama?"

"Washington, D.C. If it's so near, why don't you meet him?"

"I have heard about Washington, D.C., so much. Washington, D.C. The White House. The White House is all white, right?"

"Is that where the real king of Washington, D.C., lives?"

Sometimes it was easy to forget that the Karzais were real people. Then you met their kids

Mahmood Karzai met Abdullah Nadi and other partners at his apartment in Kabul to discuss getting their company's money back from his brother. At the meeting, they tried to reason with him. They proposed hiring a professional management company to take over the project. They drafted a letter to the Central Bank about how Shah Wali had defrauded them.

Shah Wali insisted that he was only protecting the project. One of the partners recalled, "His response was: 'Mahmood is a corrupt person, and he's trying to take the money like he took from Kabul Bank, and transfer it to Dubai. And I have a responsibility to the Kandahar people. I will not allow that to happen." Shah Wali said the others had offered him $5 million to give them access to the project's bank account again, but he had refused.

The tensions kept reaching a breaking point. Security guards for rival partners threatened each other. Relatives came to blows. The investors who had purchased land in Aino Mena were firmly behind Shah Wali. They believed Helmandi was misusing funds and that Mahmood was too engaged in politics to pay enough attention to Aino Mena. "In the U.S., they have big brands: Red Bull, Coke—people trust these brands," Mohammed Nadir, one of the investors, told me. "In Afghanistan there are no brands. People are the brands. Shah Wali Karzai is our brand."

From the palace, President Karzai tried to mediate this latest family dispute, and he even flew to Kandahar to discuss the problem. The president ordered the Afghan government to freeze the account until the problem could be resolved. Work on Aino Mena ground to a halt. Contractors streamed into Helmandi's office day after day, demanding payment. In his bedroom, he slept next to loaded guns. His son told him he should move back to California, but he couldn't let the development go. "I started this project in a tent," he told me. "There was no building here. I can't let it go. I'm so much attached to it. I wish there was a medicine or a tablet I could take to get away from this madness."

On November 28, 2012, Abdullah Nadi typed out a two-page e-mail to Mahmood Karzai and the other partners. "As we all know the project is in a very critical state; we must act now legally and responsibly to save the project from being overrun by those acting with impunity and nepotism." As Nadi saw it, the construction of Aino Mena, from its inception, had not been managed as a partnership, with input from all and group deliberations, but on the whimsical and secretive fancies of Mahmood Karzai. Or as he put it in another e-mail: "The Reality of this project: Oligopoly-dominant players, Collusion-inflated price, Patronage dependency, behave with impunity, Project Oversight non exist and inadequate, Corruption, nepotism, flow of funds to the wrong hands."

"Mr. Shawali [Shah Wali] has cheated our company by selling construction materials from his own company, to the project and made millions of dollars illegally through monopolizing the market with unfair prices," Nadi wrote. "As I understand the new scam is to give a gift to Mr. Shawali, $5 million dollars although, he has made money and has received a regular salary with benefits."

Nadi's e-mail set off more bickering among the partners. Helmandi took offense at Nadi's suggestion that all the managing partners were involved in criminal activity. "As one of the managing partners, it is insulting for me to hear that coming from someone who has done absolutely ZERO to try to make this project successful," Helmandi wrote back. "This was a hands on project, you cannot expect us to play a secretarial role for you and micromanage ourselves for you. You were welcome to come and work."

Everyone was furious at everyone else. Mahmood Karzai got upset with Helmandi for renting his own auger to AFCO to dig holes to plant trees. "You should [have] asked our company before you rented your machine to Afco this is clearly a conflict of interest," Mahmood wrote in an e-mail. "When I am here and I see the Afco's money is wasted it my duty to stop it."

In further correspondence with the group, Helmandi proposed that the partners meet in Dubai to hash out a way forward for the company. He sent out a list of questions and issues for discussion, including what the role of the partners should be, how much they should be paid, and how a partner could be terminated from the group. Abdullah Nadi chose not to attend the meeting in Dubai. His wife needed inner-ear surgery, and he wanted to remain home in Alexandria to help her through the process. Furthermore, he didn't trust the partners to treat him fairly. Some of his friends had warned him that his life could be in danger if he returned. Nadi did, however, have some last feelings he wanted to share. He wrote out six pages, listing all the things accomplished by himself and others. "As you can see no one is the champion," he wrote. "We do not need to belittle each other's contributions. There is enough credit for everyone."

He ended his appeal by saying that they should all feel proud to have been able to contribute to rebuilding Afghanistan. "Second," he added, "I don't believe we are dreadful people. Some of us couldn't handle the opportunities and found themselves like 'a kid in a candy store.'" The project, he urged, deserved better management—people who were independent and could follow basic rules.

"I conclude by saying that I can only hope that with this letter, highlighting of what seems to be our tragic historical pattern; we seem to be our own worst enemies; jealous; envious; lack of understanding; lack of fairness and obstructive to ourselves. The success of our true enemies lies in this fact. I can only hope that God will give you all the strength to take proactive measures to ensure our joined hope that one day we can work, and trust each other."

He signed off by paraphrasing Benjamin Franklin: "If we do not hang together, we shall surely hang separately."

17

EVERYBODY IN A CORNER

Honourable Citizens! Implementation of peace by America is Lame Excuse. They want to Cupture Middle Asia

—Banner hanging outside ISAF headquarters in Kabul

GENERAL JOHN R. ALLEN, an earnest Marine with a high-and-tight haircut and a riveting baritone voice, landed in Kabul in July 2011 to take over the war, with clear instructions from the White House: fix the relationship with President Karzai. Ambassador Ryan Crocker, back for his second Afghan tour, had been told the same thing by Obama. "Our president was not very happy with where we got in the relationship," Crocker recalled. "He said, 'You know him. Get us to a better place.' It was a very, very high priority."

But by then, Hamid Karzai had changed. The leader Crocker had known a decade earlier—hopeful, eager to please, optimistic—had eroded into a more jaded and distrustful man. His suspicions of America and its motives had etched themselves firmly into his political worldview. Karzai remained courtly and eloquent, but Crocker could sense a new degree of cynicism and exhaustion. "He had aged decades in a decade," he said. "He was so burned out."

Crocker and Allen wanted to present a unified American front. The previous years had frayed relations within the American mission almost as much as between the Americans and the Afghan government. Petraeus, before he'd left Kabul to run the CIA, had all but abandoned taking Eikenberry with him to the palace, wanting to avoid the bad blood with

Karzai. He wished Eikenberry had quit earlier. Allen and Crocker wanted to clear the air. They intended to meet with Karzai often, and together, so that Karzai would perceive them as a team. They also wanted Karzai to become familiar with their thinking, so that he wouldn't be surprised by American decisions. Crocker often told Karzai when he planned to meet other Afghan politicians and would ask if there was anything Karzai wanted him to mention. "Karzai had become very, very allergic to us just going off and doing things on our own," Crocker said. "His perception was that we were doing things unilaterally without consulting with him or even informing him. And clearly by that time he was extremely sensitive to the Taliban's accusation that he was nothing but an American puppet."

Allen was commanding the American withdrawal from Afghanistan. He saw his mission as shifting the burden of responsibilities to Karzai's government and shepherding the emergence of a sovereign state. He wanted, like his predecessors, for President Karzai to take ownership for the war and act as its commander in chief. But the war had gone on for so long and with so little resolution that even the most basic assumptions about what was happening were called into question. Why were the Americans even in Afghanistan? Why couldn't the world's most powerful army defeat a bunch of farmers in plastic sandals on dirt bikes? Their inability to win or leave made their motives suspect. From the palace throne to the fruit vendor's stall, nobody trusted this foreign coalition, the mysterious *kharajee* who lived behind razor wire and ballistic sunglasses, who arrested the wrong people and frightened women and killed the innocent. What did they want with Afghanistan?

That question seemed to fascinate Hamid Karzai. He had come to see foreign conspiracy everywhere he looked—or at least he found it a convenient scapegoat to account for his government's failings. He had watched as United States forces drove out the Taliban in a matter of weeks in 2001 and then added tens of thousands of troops and spent billions of dollars as they steadily lost that advantage. He seemed to think Americans did nothing by accident or by mistake. He would tell American diplomats that the only logical explanation was that the United States didn't want to win the war. This wasn't a particularly extremist view among Afghans.

When it came to the motives of foreign troops, suspicion and distrust were the default emotions. In Kandahar at one point, I heard a story that Afghans were worried about answering their cell phones, because

*General John Allen, right, shakes hands with another
American general while visiting the prison at Bagram
Airfield on April 14, 2012.*

they believed American soldiers could kill them by firing a laser from the
phone into their ears. In Helmand Province, one story went, the American bases were strategically located above uranium deposits, for clandestine mining. In the Arghandab Valley, a myth had spread about men with
white faces and blue eyes who dressed in Afghan robes and black turbans
and spoke Pashto as well as any village farmer. This ghostly band of Special Forces had a name—*Spin Taliban*, Pashto for "White Taliban"—and
their elusiveness simply seemed further proof of their unusual abilities.
"Afghanistan is a country built on legends," Habib Zahori wrote in *The
New York Times* as he described the phenomenon.

In the desert hills of Badghis Province, a forlorn and neglected corner
of the war, I once stopped by an Afghan army outpost on a berm overlooking a small American base. I found Mirwais Safai, a twenty-nine-year-old
lieutenant, sitting under a tarp, smoking a cigarette. We started chatting
about how things were going against the insurgency, and he looked hard
into my eyes. "I will tell you the truth," he said. "The Americans themselves support the Taliban."

I asked him to explain, and he sighed. Nothing would change if I published his words, he said, but he'd share them anyway. For nearly two months, Safai had commanded an Afghan army platoon alongside a U.S. special operations team. They'd fought side by side, and he had trusted his foreign comrades. But he'd begun to notice disturbing things. The Americans met inside a clinic with Afghan villagers but refused to allow the medic from Safai's platoon to listen to their conversations. "Spies were coming and going," he told me. One night, parachutes dropped from the sky, carrying military crates full of water and ammunition. The Americans gathered their boxes but left one behind in a dangerous village. Safai and his men found it the next day. They pried open the case and discovered mortars and ammunition. Safai photographed the contents, then brought the crate to his American partner.

"He was yelling at me, 'Why did you bring this here?'" Safai told me. "When he saw the ammunition, he stopped yelling. I said, 'You were giving this to the Taliban.' He said, 'It was just a big mistake.'"

When I got back to Kabul, I asked ISAF about Safai's story. Lieutenant Commander Nicole Schwegman, a U.S. military spokeswoman, confirmed the airdrop. Twelve supply crates had been delivered by parachute. Two of them collided, and one crashed into the wall of a villager's home. The soldiers apologized and offered compensation to the family. The other eleven crates were recovered. "No ammunition or explosives were left unrecovered overnight," she said. "We do not, under any circumstances, provide supplies to the Taliban."

Safai's superior, Captain Mohammad Aref, stood by his story. "He is describing things he has seen with his own eyes."

Hamid Karzai was sympathetic to these stories. His view of the war had shifted from opposition to American military operations to a conviction that the United States was in cahoots with the enemy. America's ultimate goal, as he saw it, was to weaken his government to make it unable to prevent the United States from using Afghanistan for its regional aims against Islamic militants in Pakistan and the government of Iran. This was a paranoid reading of events. But there were grains of truth to it. A large part of the U.S. motivation for keeping so many troops in the country for so long was to stop Afghanistan from reverting to a place where people could plot and train for attacks against the United States. An eight-hundred-man CIA mission was primarily focused on al-Qaeda targets across the border in Pakistan. And to find and kill those targets, they would rely on any Afghan who had information, including those warlords or corrupt mercenaries whom the other parts of the American mission wanted to move beyond. Karzai could see the contradiction in the American approach to the war and understood it for the opportunistic mess it was. When he felt well supported by the Americans, he tended to be the most responsible and decisive. But during periods of insecurity, when he was beleaguered by the foreigners, he went into a defensive crouch, refused to make decisions, blamed everyone but himself.

"People come and tell of the facts on the ground in Afghanistan," Karzai said during one of our talks. "The Taliban are actually supported by the coalition forces here. That they drop weapons to them. That they drop supplies to them. That the war is created by the U.S. in Afghanistan."

"A lot of stories emerged in Afghanistan that the international forces here, the Americans here are funding the Taliban, are equipping the Taliban. Hundreds of them. Factual stories. Of locations. Of airplanes. Of helicopters. Of how they funded the Taliban and evacuated the Taliban wounded from the battlefield, hundreds of such stories. Southern Afghanistan. Northern Afghanistan. Everywhere. All of it true. I would then verify it. All of it true."

It didn't take General Allen long to realize that he would have serious problems at the palace. In particular, he began to feel that his presence at the Sunday National Security Council meetings was unproductive. During those palace gatherings, President Karzai would enter the room with his usual ebullience, a dramatic flourish of energetic greetings, and make for his customary spot at the head of the table. He tended to disregard whatever agenda ISAF had arduously helped formulate with the Afghan staff the preceding week. Instead, he would look straight at John Allen and say, "Well, General Allen, tell me about . . ." Karzai would then raise whatever he found to be the most provocative headline from that morning's news clippings, sometimes referencing stories so recently pulled off the Internet that Allen was completely uninformed. In the midst of difficult stretches, Allen could feel the tension in the Cabinet Room the moment Karzai began talking. The palace had become a stage for Karzai's anti-American theatrics, his cabinet an attentive and wary audience.

Just three weeks into Allen's job, Karzai confronted him during a Sunday gathering about an unusual story out of Zabul Province, a sparsely populated desert along the country's southeastern border with Pakistan. The facts, as usual, were in dispute. Two days earlier, Afghan police had fired into a crowd of protesters in Qalat, the provincial capital, to quell a riot and had killed as many as four people. The protesters had convened to condemn an American raid the night before, a mission they claimed had killed civilians. To settle the confusion, the provincial police chief, Mohammad Nabi Elham, ordered that the bodies, which had been buried as soon as possible in accordance with Islamic tradition, were to be exhumed and identified. The exhumation apparently further enraged the mob, and Elham's men, under a hot August sun, resorted to spraying gunfire into their midst, a decision he justified to a Reuters reporter by saying insurgents had infiltrated the protest and had already shot one of his men, so the "police had to fire back." President Karzai, as he entered the Cabinet Room the following Sunday, lashed out at Allen. He'd heard that American troops had ordered the corpses dug up, and he angrily demanded an explanation.

There were times, Allen would later learn, when Karzai's instincts and judgment were spot-on. "When you listened to the thoughtful Karzai, you typically benefited from it," Allen told me. An example: One night, U.S. special operations troops raided the home of a man they suspected of being a "subcommander" of the Haqqani insurgent network, a group allied to the Taliban that operated in eastern Afghanistan. The man ran a pharmacy in the city of Ghazni and lived with his family outside the city. As the American soldiers scaled the wall and stormed the family's home, they killed the pharmacist's mother and wounded his father, who turned out to be a senior member of the provincial government, and shot his aunt in the eye. When he learned of the disastrous results of the raid, Allen asked the special operations commanders how they chose their targets and how they defined a "subcommander": Had he been leading fifteen Haqqani fighters? Thirty? Forty-five? Allen was told that the man had an informal relationship with just one other suspected insurgent. Knowing one insurgent was enough to be considered a "subcommander" in the military's definition. And it was enough to send a kill-or-capture team to get him, which had resulted, in this case, in killing and wounding innocent people. Allen remembered Karzai as more resigned than angry when talking about this case.

"We bagged the son, wounded the father, killed the mother, blinded the aunt, and he said to me, 'Why didn't you just arrest him on his fifteen-mile commute to the pharmacy?' I just hung my head and said, 'We should have,'" Allen recalled.

In fact, among the most important lessons Allen took from his time as commander was the need to listen, rather than dictate, to those who knew the country far better than any visiting Americans. Others had come to the same conclusion. Karzai could be overwrought and paranoid, but there was often more naked truth to what he said than most politicians shared. "So many of the problems we experienced, when they finally came to a head, were things he had raised three or four years before, and when he raised it first, it was solvable then," Allen said. "But we either didn't take him seriously or we didn't apply the resources or we weren't listening. If we were ever going to do this again, God help us, the best piece of advice I would give to that commander would be: Listen closely to the leadership of that country. Listen to them. And if you can solve their problems for them early, do it. The campaign will benefit. They'll be aggrandized for having exerted what looks like their national sovereignty. Do it. There's no downside."

Yet each day seemed to bring a new flavor of misinformation from the palace: rumor, conspiracy, conjecture, bald-faced lie. When Karzai wasn't right, he could be astonishingly wrong. On the same night Afghan police were firing at protesters in Zabul—a minor mention in the news of the war—a dual-rotor American Chinook transport helicopter was shot down in a Taliban-controlled valley in Wardak Province, and the deaths of thirty American soldiers, including twenty-two members of the country's most elite counterterrorism squad, SEAL Team Six, the same unit that killed Osama bin Laden, made it the deadliest day of the war for the United States. The next morning, the day before the cabinet meeting, Karzai called Allen to offer his condolences. The crash was a tragic loss, and Karzai expressed his sadness with genuinely solemn remarks. But that wasn't all. He was worried. He wanted Allen to come to the palace to speak further about the crash.

When Allen arrived, Karzai warned him that the war was about to change dramatically. Karzai's advisers had told him that the Taliban shot down the Chinook with shoulder-fired heat-seeking missiles, the same type of weapon that the mujahedeen had introduced onto the Afghan battlefield in the mid-1980s, thereby turning the tide against the Soviet army. History was repeating itself, Karzai warned. The Stinger missile that had decimated fleets of Soviet helicopters had made its way back. The Chinook was the first example. Karzai was convinced there would be more.

The truth, however, was that the Taliban had shot down the Chinook with a rocket-propelled grenade, a far more prosaic weapon. Allen knew that then, and a subsequent Pentagon investigation confirmed it. It had been, more than anything, a lucky shot. Allen assured Karzai that the insurgents had not obtained the Stinger. But when Karzai latched onto

*General John Allen visiting soldiers at Combat Outpost Nerkh
to celebrate Thanksgiving, November 24, 2011*

a compelling rumor from his inner circle, it could be hard to change his mind. So when Karzai launched into his accusation the next day that Americans had desecrated Muslim graves, Allen shot right back.

"Let me tell you what I know about your faith. Let me tell you how much I respect your people. Let me tell you how important a Muslim burial is to me. And how I would never do this," he recalled saying. "I didn't order the exhumation. That was done entirely at the initiative of the police chief."

Karzai, the king of snap judgments, spun toward the minister of the interior, Bismillah Khan Mohammadi, who was sitting at the conference table. "I want him fired today," Karzai ordered. The press release announcing the police chief's dismissal went out that afternoon.

Karzai's conclusions about the truth in a confusing battlefield sometimes seemed to be based solely on his own assumptions about the inferior capabilities of the insurgency. When the C-17 cargo plane carrying the visiting chairman of the Joint Chiefs of Staff, General Martin Dempsey, suffered minor damage from a rocket attack on Bagram Airfield, Karzai was again convinced that the Taliban had obtained a new lethal weapons system. An insurgent attack one night a few months later at the main coalition base in Helmand Province, Camp Bastion, left Karzai equally suspicious. A group of nearly twenty Taliban fighters had breached the perimeter fencing and begun firing grenades and setting off explosives inside aircraft hangars and refueling stations. At the end of an hours-long gun battle, two Marines had been killed, including a squadron commander, and eight Marine Harrier fighter jets had been damaged or destroyed, an attack that amounted to the largest loss of U.S. airpower since the Vietnam War. Two American generals would later lose their jobs for failing to protect the base. During Allen's briefing to Karzai to explain what had happened, the general brought out photos of the slain Taliban fighters who'd participated. Karzai eyed the corpses. They were not, he decided, Taliban. "Taliban are gangly, underfed, malnourished. Look at the muscles on these people," Karzai told him. "Those are very clearly Iranian trained men or even Iranian agents."

Allen stopped attending the Sunday security council meetings. They'd become a venue for Karzai to act presidential, to perform a sovereignty that he did not quite possess, to pronounce and have his pronouncements obeyed, to prove, as much to his own ministers as to the Americans, that he was the president. Allen was tired of playing evil foreign occupier before the royal court. The whole goal of American involvement, as he saw it, was to midwife the birth of a stable and sovereign state. Success, to him, was when the Afghan government made a decision without him around. And anyway, it was clear that Americans were no longer welcome.

The palace air was thick with paranoia. Even among his aides, Karzai acted like a man surrounded, distrustful yet demanding their fealty. He would promote those who flattered him, humiliate his oldest friends. Karzai often mocked his advisers or treated them with contempt in front of foreign guests. He'd order them to do menial tasks like fetch him tea or bring him a blanket. Karzai liked to nibble on fruit and sweets through-out the day and would sometimes reach over and swipe snacks off his cabinet ministers' plates. "Awful humiliations," one European ambassador told me. "The cabinet were all there sitting and burning with resentment against him. They were all sort of toadies. Privately they would come to us and be very rude about him."

Karzai encouraged an environment where they competed for his approval. He'd developed a reputation for undercutting his rivals before they could get too strong, but he behaved this way with his allies, too. He would appoint governors to provinces they were unfamiliar with or recall regional strongmen to Kabul, where they would not pose a political threat. In some ways, he'd mastered a politics that mirrored the tactics of the Taliban: no frontal assaults, all deception, hit and run, sabotage. His style kept even his inner circle off balance. If palace aides brought him advice he didn't like, he would say it probably came from the "yellow building," as he'd taken to calling ISAF headquarters. The finance minister, Omar Zakhilwal, complained to the U.S. embassy that Karzai was an "extremely weak man" who ignored facts but could be swayed by anyone who reported even the most bizarre plots against the palace. In his palace, his aides all knew that the gravest sin one could commit was to befriend America.

"He was suspicious of his own ministers," Rahmatullah Nabil, who led Afghanistan's spy agency, told me. "Whenever we were bringing something to him, valid points, he was thinking, 'No, this is coming from the U.S.' He mentioned it several times to the elders who came to see him: 'I don't trust my ministers. They are working for the Americans.' That put everybody in a corner."

The aides who prospered in this environment were the ones who embraced Karzai's conspiratorial inclinations about the United States. In this regard, none surpassed Abdul Karim Khoram, who took over as Karzai's chief of staff in early 2011. His predecessor in that job, Umer Daudzai, had been a cunning operative, a former ambassador in Pakistan and Iran who operated with a catlike combination of delicacy and silence (a U.S. ambassador once described him as Gandalf from *The Lord of the Rings*). Khoram, by contrast, was bearish and crude, a heavy and disheveled man who spoke indelicately and regarded others with suspicion. Khoram had suffered particularly brutal trauma during the Communist era. He had been imprisoned for years and tortured by electric shock before fleeing the country to Paris. He joined Karzai's cabinet as minister of information and culture in 2006, and developed a reputation as a hardline Pashtun conservative intent on blocking the broadcast of material he considered un-Islamic. He was famous for removing the Dari sign on the ministry building—the more common language in Kabul and of the government—and replacing it with a Pashto version. For him, the world was full of enemies: in Pakistan, Iran, America.

He believed that Afghan culture was "under assault," as he put it, from the Persians, whom he suspected of infiltrating the Afghan newspapers, books, and television programs that proliferated during Karzai's tenure. Khoram opposed, and attempted to ban, Bollywood films because of their racy content. He complained to the U.S. embassy about the Afghan station Tolo TV, which epitomized the new media freedoms, winning millions in American aid money along the way; he maintained that Tolo furthered a Persian agenda. "The Iranians are everywhere," he told an American diplomat. His purge of nearly seventy members of the government broadcaster, Radio Television Afghanistan, prompted the head of the station to resign, but Khoram defended his move by saying he was protecting the country from cultural attacks from abroad.

Khoram didn't make a lot of friends. An American general who dealt with him called him "impenetrable." Karzai's national security adviser, Rangin Dadfar Spanta, who'd been a staunch Communist in his youth, found Khoram a "stubborn ideologue." Another former colleague of Khoram's described his views as the "Afghan version of the Tea Party." Mahmood Karzai, in his colorful way, said that instead of the palace, Khoram should be "working in a slaughterhouse for sheep. He's a complete idiot."

The decision to elevate Khoram to chief of staff further divided a palace that was already balkanized into warring factions. Some people chose to quit. The president's spokesman, Waheed Omar, felt Khoram was the worst possible choice for the job. "I always told the president my job was to make sure he looks good, and this decision went against that—it would make him look ugly," he said. "The moment I heard Khoram was coming, I knew I was out."

General Allen assigned his French chief of staff, Lieutenant General Olivier de Bavinchove, as his liaison to Khoram, because of Khoram's admiration for French culture. Khoram spoke nearly unaccented French and was both intimidated by and smitten with de Bavinchove, a paratrooper with aristocratic lineage. For the United States, however, Khoram held nothing but disdain.

One day, Khoram arranged a youth conference at the palace. Teenagers stood to address the president, reading from note cards about their worries for the future. One boy said that U.S. Marines had been using biological weapons against the people, and that babies were being born with severe birth defects as a result. Palace staffers suspected that Khoram had written the note cards for the children, but the biological weapons claim piqued Karzai's interest. After the conference, he asked his staff for more information on the subject. Khoram told the president that serious research had been done on the biological weapons used by American forces. A scientist he knew could come to the palace the next day and brief the National Security Council. Over the objections of his other aides, Karzai agreed to hear the man out.

The prospect that a man with unknown medical or scientific credentials would get this type of audience with the president worried several Afghan officials, including Rahmatullah Nabil. The man coming to talk was "some crazy Afghan-American," the spy chief told me. According to Nabil, the man had relationships with Taliban leaders in Quetta. One of Afghanistan's former presidents, Burhanuddin Rabbani, had recently been blown up by a suicide bomber disguised as a Taliban negotiator, and Nabil didn't want this strange scientist briefing Karzai on anything. Nabil, like others, believed that the whole episode was just Khoram's attempt to make the Americans look bad.

The scientist came to the palace the next day. As he waited in a sitting room, Khoram asked the president if he was ready for his special briefing. Nabil interrupted. He told Karzai it was not a good idea to meet this man. He said there were recorded phone conversations of the man boasting to someone in Quetta about his appointment with the president and how it's "a great success for us." Khoram argued with Nabil, but the spy chief's intervention was enough for Karzai to cancel the briefing and send the man home. Nabil won that day, though he worried that Khoram's pro-Pashtun, anti-American agenda was shifting the direction of the palace. "Khoram changed the mentality of the president," he said.

Khoram used his newfound authority to overhaul palace messaging: both the government propaganda that went out to the world and the advice that reached the president. One of his first targets was the Government Media and Information Center, or GMIC. The office, funded by the U.S. government, had a staff of more than 130 people; they organized press conferences and pumped out news releases. Nearly every day, some cabinet minister or senior official stopped by to talk to the Afghan and foreign press. The office was organized, and its events ran on time and on schedule. A small team of five Americans, two of them soldiers in plain clothes, worked inside the GMIC. They helped schedule events and brought over information from ISAF headquarters about battlefield events from across the country. The Americans saw the office's role as refuting the claims of the Taliban, who had a thriving public relations operation of their own, tweeting and texting every day about their valiant fighters and the cowardly infidels. When the GMIC opened, in 2008, embassy officials told the Afghan palace staff they didn't want Khoram, then the information minister, involved in the project, which was partially intended as a shadow information ministry "away from Khoram's control," as a State Department official put it. Khoram was always bitter over this U.S.-funded rival, and when he became palace chief of staff, he finally had the power for revenge.

He began by suggesting that there were not enough Pashtuns in the office and that the Americans were hijacking the message of the Afghan government. He fired one of the spokesmen and replaced him with a young Pashtun. He ordered another, who had spoken positively about the partnership with the United States, to stop talking to the press. Afghans who had worked closely with Americans grew cagey; the GMIC director told an American colleague that if he showed up at the press conferences, he should act like they didn't know each other. Omar, Karzai's spokesman, and Khoram battled over the language of press releases, especially when they involved the United States or civilian casualties. Khoram always wanted to dial up the outrage. "He would argue that I was not as patriotic as he was," Omar recalled.

The problems came to a head on Christmas Eve. That day, the GMIC director was sick at home. Earlier in the week, an American air strike in Kunar Province had killed several people. Without informing the director, Khoram arranged for dozens of the victims' relatives to come to the GMIC for a news conference to denounce the Americans. One after another, the relatives blasted the United States for its brutality. In the audience, David Snepp, a State Department official on the team, sat frozen in shock. "It was a shitstorm," he said.

That night, Crocker and Allen ordered the Americans out of the GMIC. They would not be going back. The United States had spent $8.8 million on that office, had renovated the building, built a TV studio, and paid the staff's salaries; there were plans to replicate the office in three other Afghan cities. Within months, the funding would be canceled, the expansion scrapped. The staff of 130 dwindled to 22. Waheed Omar quit as Karzai's spokesman and wouldn't return. Another plank in America's relationship with Karzai's government had rotted through.

18

NOT RELIGION BUT HISTORY

A GROUP OF AMERICAN SOLDIERS at Bagram Airfield were cleaning out the prison library. The soldiers suspected that some of the inmates here—considered among the most dangerous Taliban captives—were communicating via margin notes. So they separated out about two thousand books and carted them off to a base burn pit for incineration. Torching books normally carries some troubling symbolism, no matter the titles. This case turned out to be no exception. An Afghan laborer at the burn pit started screaming when he saw what was happening: copies of the Koran, the Muslim holy book, were being tossed into the flames.

No atrocity—no killing of the young, the old, the unarmed—and no destruction of homes or razing of crops could galvanize the Afghan public like the desecration, in any form, of their religion. In 2005, riots erupted in several cities, police fired on protesters, and government buildings were ransacked following a story in *Newsweek* that included allegations that American interrogators at the prison in Guantánamo Bay had flushed a Koran down the toilet. Five years later, the Florida preacher-provocateur Terry Jones caused an uproar in Afghanistan by threatening to burn the Koran, then backed down under White House pressure. When Jones actually followed through, in March 2011, the act went mostly unnoticed in Afghanistan. Then President Karzai, in a speech and palace statement on March 24, 2011, brought the issue into public discussion, calling it a "disrespectful and abhorrent act" and demanding that the United States prosecute the perpetrators. The next week, Karzai spoke out against photographs published first in *Der Spiegel*, then in *Rolling Stone*, of U.S. soldiers posing with dead Afghans. Five Americans on the "kill team," as it became known, had been charged with murdering innocent Afghans and posing with their corpses. "They killed a young boy for entertainment, they killed an old man for entertainment, and even planned to kill children, to throw candy and then fire on them," Karzai said in a speech at a graduation ceremony for teachers. The photos would outrage the world, Karzai said, "if there is conscience left in the West."

Anti-American furor was breaking out across the country. Religious groups, leading clerics, and Afghan parliamentarians took up Karzai's call against Jones and the Koran burning, with one Muslim cleric demanding a "day of anger" in response. On April 1, the day came, and a mob left a mosque in the northern city of Mazar-e-Sharif after Friday prayers and stormed a lightly protected United Nations office, flowing past the Afghan police outside, who tried in vain to block their entry with a log. The mob torched U.N. trucks and heaved bricks at the building, then pried open the fortified door to the "safe room" where some of the foreign staff were hiding. Three European diplomats were murdered, including a female fighter pilot from Norway, along with four of their Gurkha guards.

Even on calm days, rage coursed just below the surface. At one point, I canvassed mosques in Kabul to listen to the Friday sermons and get a sense of what the general run of Kabul residents were hearing from their religious leaders. The rhetoric made Karzai's most harsh fire-and-brimstone speeches seem bland. "Let these jackals leave this country," an imam named Habibullah told the crowd at one mosque. "Let these brothers of monkeys, gorillas, and pigs leave this country." For anyone who supported a long-term American military presence, Habibullah said, "they should know that God will take revenge on them and turn their bones and flesh into dried spiderweb powder."

These were not Taliban preachers disparaging the United States but mainstream imams at government-funded mosques that received weekly talking points for their sermons from the Ministry of Hajj and Religious Affairs. Under the weathered blue dome of Kabul's largest mosque, Pul-e-Khishti, its famous mullah, Enayatullah Balegh, pledged support for "any plan that can defeat" the American forces in Afghanistan and denounced "the political power of these children of Jews." When I interviewed him later, Balegh, who was also a professor of Islamic law at Kabul University, told me, "If you see a feeling of xenophobia these days, that's understandable. I don't think even a single Afghan is happy with the presence of the foreign military forces here."

So when the phone call woke General John Allen in his quarters on the main ISAF base and he heard "American soldiers," "Bagram," "Korans," "incinerator," it was a nightmare scenario. Terry Jones burned one Koran in Florida, and an enraged mob slaughtered several people at the United Nations mission in Mazar-e-Sharif. "This was immeasurably worse," Allen recalled. "I believed this could be the end of the campaign."

Allen went public with his apology as soon as he could. Afghans woke to the news of his contrition even before they understood what had happened in the Bagram burn pit. He videotaped his statement, addressed to the "noble people of Afghanistan," for broadcast across the country. "We are thoroughly investigating the incident, and we are taking steps to ensure this does not ever happen again. I assure you—I promise you—this was *not* intentional in any way," he pleaded. By the end of the day, he had issued orders for every coalition soldier to receive new training in how to handle religious materials.

But the backlash had already begun. An angry crowd shouted outside the Bagram gates. Protests erupted in a half dozen other cities. Local authorities were already reporting a handful of deaths, and the tension showed no sign of abating. President Obama issued an apology. The Taliban whipped up fervor with their own statements calling on their followers to attack American troops, and particularly for Afghan soldiers and police to start "turning their guns on the foreign infidel invaders." Allen visited Karzai in the palace and warned him that if he chose to condemn American soldiers for these actions, as he had done with the Florida pastor, it could set in motion a series of events that could sweep him from power and cause the streets of Afghanistan to "run red with blood."

Wars seen over time seem to move like amoebas, bulging out in one direction, receding in others, growing new limbs, changing colors. The "green on blue" mutation became visible in 2011, a decade into the war. This was the term for Afghan security forces murdering their American partners: "green" meant indigenous forces, "blue" friendly ones. These types of attacks had gone on for years, but they were suddenly accelerating rapidly. Apart from the first months of the war, the whole point of the American presence was to train the Afghan troops so they could do the fighting, forestall an overthrow of their government, and allow the Americans to leave. Americans paid, almost entirely, for the Afghan security forces: their black M4 rifles, tan combat boots, forest-green Ford Rangers; for their elementary reading and writing classes, drug tests, chow halls, latrines, air conditioners, bunk beds. American and Afghan soldiers lived on the same bases. Walked the same patrols. The closer the partnership, the theory went, the faster the Afghan forces would improve, and the better their chances of defeating the Taliban. If they could become a professional army that could feed and equip itself, treat its wounded, and replenish its ranks, there seemed a chance—or at least you could argue so—that the whole Afghan government enterprise might not come crashing down the day the Americans left.

The only Afghans the Americans couldn't afford to have as their enemy were the soldiers and police. And so green on blue posed a potentially fatal risk to the mission. All the fortifications—triple coils of razor wire, V-shaped blast-resistant hulls, Kevlar helmets—would not protect against it. The attacks came from the inside. One day you patiently listened to your American adviser lecture you about marksmanship on the firing range. The next day you raised your gun and killed him. The Soviet war in Afghanistan had turned on a new weapon that a single man could carry and use to shoot down a helicopter. Green on blue acted like an autoimmune virus, sapping the host of its ability to defend itself. A strategy conceived around the idea of two groups of people working together could not completely eliminate this risk of treachery. Repeat these attacks enough and the partnership would disintegrate. Green on blue was "the greatest crisis I faced as commander," Allen said.

Allen was in Berlin when he received the phone call telling him that an Afghan soldier had shot and killed four French soldiers and mortally wounded a fifth on a base in Kapisa Province. The Afghan soldier, Allen would later learn, had heard about the YouTube video that had appeared the week prior of American Marines urinating on Taliban corpses. The Afghan soldier had not seen the video, but he had apparently dreamed about it, woken up, and decided something had to be done.

Allen made it a habit to stop in European capitals when he was traveling to or from Afghanistan, as a way to rally international support for his mission. Europeans had long since lost enthusiasm for the war in Afghanistan, and he believed it was important to explain the mission's significance whenever he could. That morning he was scheduled to fly to Paris to meet the French defense minister. From the airplane, he called Afghan Defense Minister Abdul Rahim Wardak. Days earlier, Allen had asked Wardak to allow counterintelligence agents from Afghanistan's spy agency, the National Directorate of Security, to infiltrate the Afghan army in order to learn more about the insider threat. Wardak had opposed the idea. Afghan spies had a bad reputation. During Wardak's formative years with the mujahedeen, the agency had been called the KHAD—

Khadamat-e Aetla'at-e Dawlati—and it had functioned as a brutal secret police force trained by the Soviets. Its agents had tortured and killed political opponents. The name had been changed and the intelligence agency reformed in ensuing years, but the spies were still hardly humanitarians. Interrogation remained synonymous with torture. "I'm not going to let the KHAD back in our forces," Wardak had told Allen. After the killing of the French soldiers, however, Allen demanded more. From the airplane he told Wardak, "You've got a real crisis on your hands here.

"You better get some NDS agents in your formations, and we're going to talk about it when I get back," Allen recalled saying. "I've got to have something to say to the French. And if I can't say to them that you all are gripping this problem, then we've got a very serious issue."

As Allen drove from Charles de Gaulle Airport into Paris, the military attaché at the U.S. embassy there handed him a copy of the *International Herald Tribune*. The newspaper referenced a classified study by a political and behavioral scientist named Jeffrey Bordin. Bordin had been sent to Afghanistan as part of a U.S. Army team to study the green-on-blue phenomenon. He went to a base in the eastern city of Jalalabad after an Afghan policeman murdered six American soldiers in November 2010. Bordin, who had a PhD from Claremont Graduate University, found that Afghan security forces had been responsible for 16 percent of all the killings of coalition soldiers over the five months before the report was finished, in May 2011. His interviews with some six hundred Afghan soldiers and policemen found that they viewed their American partners as "violent, reckless, intrusive, arrogant, self-serving, profane, infidel bullies hiding behind high technology." The American soldiers he interviewed considered the Afghan forces "cowardly, incompetent, obtuse, thieving, complacent, lazy, pot-smoking, treacherous and murderous radicals." The threat of green-on-blue attacks, Bordin concluded, was a "rapidly growing systemic threat" that could doom the whole American mission, and he noted that the scale of killings "may be unprecedented between 'allies' in modern history."

When *The Wall Street Journal* first found the study and published a story on it, ISAF disavowed it, branding Bordin's work poor scholarship based on lazy assumptions conveyed through bad writing. But Bordin's conclusions haunted the American efforts with each new insider killing. As Allen thought about it, driving in that morning to meet with French military officials, he decided that there were two ways to look at this problem. You could consider that Afghans and Americans were sociologically incompatible and could not exist as humans in a joint enterprise, or you could view the insider killings as a problem that could be overcome by tactical changes. "There were very strong opinions on both sides," Allen told me. "There was that element that wanted to say, 'This is a lost cause. What are we trying to do here? We can't get along with these people. They're so foreign to us. We're so foreign to them. This is ridiculous.' And then the school of thought: 'This is a military threat. Let's treat it like one and take action to stop it.' On one hand, a course of despair. On the other, it was a problem that might be solved."

Allen's European colleagues tended to view the war with more skepticism. Some indeed saw it as a lost cause. "These are savages," a French general on Allen's staff told another of his advisers. Allen, however, couldn't throw up his hands in defeat. There was no alternative but to see this as yet another manageable crisis. If it was true that Americans could not work safely with Afghans, and the entire American strategy entailed partnering with Afghans to prepare them to handle the conflict themselves, then that strategy was doomed to failure. Allen believed the answer lay in those well-worn tenets of Pashtun culture: hospitality, loyalty, righteousness, bravery, justice. The more distance between American and Afghan soldiers, the more T-walls and razor wire, the more body armor and metal plating, the more the United States sent a signal of distrust that would eviscerate any empty rhetoric about partnership he might issue from Kabul. His only hope was to look at it another way: "The closer you get to the Afghans, the safer you're going to be."

He did not want to curtail patrols the two forces conducted together or otherwise contribute to further separation. He'd faced such risky decisions before. In an earlier tour, he'd been in command in the deserts of western Iraq when insurgents began to swap sides and join the Americans in fighting the more radical members of al-Qaeda in Iraq. Enlisting thousands of former enemies, many with American blood on their hands, was a controversial decision at the time, but it proved to be the most important factor in alleviating the violence in the late years of the Iraq war. In Afghanistan, Allen recognized that the burden of this fratricidal violence was not only falling on foreigners. The killings of Afghan soldiers and policemen by their own comrades was just as common. During one tense meeting with the Afghan cabinet ministers, as Allen demanded again that they must take the insider threat seriously, an Afghan aide entered with a note for the interior minister: in Delaram, a bleak truck-stop town in the south, ten Afghan policemen had just been killed by one of their own.

The shooting of the French soldiers became a watershed moment in this phase of the war, and in the debate over green on blue, because two things resulted directly from this attack. The French, despite Allen's attempts to persuade them otherwise, decided to pull their soldiers out early. And the Taliban realized their breakthrough. Allen could read it right off the transcripts of intercepted telephone calls. By sacrificing a few of their faithful on suicide missions inside NATO bases, they could break the coalition wide open.

The second day of protests against the burning of the Koran—as crowds across Afghanistan torched effigies of President Obama, threw stones, and battled police—happened to fall, on the Afghan calendar, on the third of Hout, 1390. On that day thirty-two years earlier—February 22, 1980—thousands of Kabul residents had climbed to their rooftops and chanted into the night sky as one people, *"Allahu akbar."* God is great. That moonlit chorus marked the beginning of the national resistance to the Soviet army, whose tanks had rolled into Afghanistan just two months before. Kawun Kakar was a boy then, but he would always remember watching his father, a famous Afghan historian, shout into the darkness with all those other unseen voices. One aspect of the performance was particularly strange to the boy. His father was not a religious man. So why, Kawun asked him, was he praising God? "This is not about religion," his father replied. "This is history."

The Third of Hout became an Afghan holiday, and Kawun Kakar a foreign policy aide to President Karzai. He mentioned this story from his childhood to me one night during dinner in Kabul. The comparisons between the Soviet presence and the American one were getting harder to ignore. I had spent three years watching the slow-motion collapse of American relations with President Karzai, and Afghans more broadly. Now the unraveling was moving with startling speed. Parliament members had joined the Taliban in calling on Afghans to kill American soldiers. The U.S. embassy had gone on lockdown, preventing staffers from leaving the compound. Obama had sent a three-page letter to Karzai with his apology.

On the third day of protests, an Afghan soldier wheeled around and killed two American soldiers from a military police battalion who had been living on a remote combat outpost in eastern Afghanistan. These were the first American deaths from the Koran burnings: Corporal Timothy J. Conrad Jr., a twenty-two-year-old from Roanoke, Virginia, who had a seven-month-old baby, and Sergeant Joshua A. Born, three years older and from Niceville, Florida, a lover of *Star Wars*. When Allen heard about these killings, he flew out to the base with the Afghan army's chief of staff, General Sher Mohammad Karimi. Allen spoke to American and Afghan soldiers who'd gathered in the fluorescent glare of the base cafeteria.

"The eyes of all the ISAF countries, all fifty of them, were turned today to this FOB," he told them. "There will be moments like this when you are searching for the meaning of this loss. There will be moments like this when your emotions are governed by anger and the desire to strike back. These are the moments when you reach down inside and you grip the discipline that makes you a United States soldier, and you gut through the pain, and you gut through the anger, and you remember why we are here. We are here for our friends. We are here for our partners. We're here for the Afghan people."

Standing in front of a wall-mounted American flag, Allen shook his fists, and his voice rose until he was nearly shouting.

"Now is not the time for revenge. Now is not the time for vengeance. Now is the time to look deep inside your souls, remember your mission, remember your discipline, remember who you are, and come through this together as a unit. Now is *that* time. Now is how we show the Afghan people that as bad as that act was at Bagram, it was unintentional, and Americans and ISAF soldiers do not stand for this. We stand for something greater."

Karimi followed Allen's emotional speech with his own remarks about how the soldiers' sacrifices were not in vain and their cause was a noble one. The remarks of the generals were recorded and appeared later on YouTube. When Karzai heard about them, he dismissed Karimi as an "American dog."

Two days later, as a mob was chanting "Death to America" in the western city of Herat, an Afghan police intelligence officer walked into a small room off the National Police Coordination Center, inside the Interior Ministry in Kabul. Two American military advisers sat at their desks with their backs to the door. One was Major Robert J. Marchanti II, a forty-eight-year-old from Baltimore who was a phys ed teacher when he wasn't serving in the Army National Guard. His job, as a police mentor, was to help the Afghans run the coordination center—similar to what Kotkin or Bruha or Zellem did in Karzai's palace. It was his first tour in Afghanistan, and he had four children back home. Next to him sat John Darin Loftis, a lieutenant colonel in the Air Force from Paducah, Kentucky. He was four years younger than Marchanti but had more experience in Afghanistan, having served two years earlier on the American-run provincial reconstruction team in Zabul Province.

By chance, I had met Loftis during that first tour. He was a public information officer, which meant part of his job was to meet with reporters when they came to Zabul to work on stories. The place was a backwater: a few American troops, a contingent of Romanians, and a smattering of Afghan soldiers to look after a sparsely populated swath of desert along the Pakistani border. Poor and uneducated even by Afghan standards, and without much development money, Zabul had bad roads, bad schools, and very little hope of improvement. The Taliban used it mostly to get somewhere else.

Loftis, however, didn't seem to notice that he had a thankless job. He was both fascinated by and deeply respectful of Afghanistan, in a way that was immediately recognizable because it was so rare among Americans, soldiers or not. He was sensitive and self-effacing and about as un-macho a military man as one could imagine. He claimed to be one of three people in the Air Force who spoke Pashto, and he used that knowledge to memorize the poetry of Rahman Baba, which he recited at readings for Afghans. To his Afghan friends he called himself Ehsaan, a name that means "favor." "My reasons for going to Afghanistan include an honorable sense of duty to help others. If I had stayed home and not volunteered to go, I would have always wondered what I could have contributed," Loftis wrote to his two young daughters before his first deployment. After his tour in Zabul, he volunteered again, as part of the Afghan Hands program, this time with a desk job at the Interior Ministry.

Five days after the American soldiers had burned the Korans at Bagram, the Afghan police intelligence officer walked up behind Marchanti and Loftis as they sat at their desks and shot them both in the back of the head.

The shocking killings, inside police headquarters in Kabul by a uniformed member of the force, threatened to shred the last vestiges of the partnership Allen was trying to hold together. He drove across town from ISAF headquarters to the Interior Ministry to inspect the crime scene himself. When he got there, he was greeted by Interior Minister Bismillah Khan Mohammadi and his deputy, a four-star police general. To show his anger, Allen was wearing his body armor and helmet and carrying his 9mm handgun, something he almost never did among Afghans, as he normally wanted to express that he felt safe in their presence.

"Where are my men?" he demanded.

The Afghans showed Allen to the office, where he found the two Americans lying on the floor in pools of their own blood: one on his back, the other facedown. Allen walked around, careful not to disturb any evidence. He glanced at their desks, which faced the wall. Over one of them he saw a child's drawing. He noticed the words "Best Daddy." He took his helmet off and knelt next to each soldier, offering his prayers.

Allen went to Bismillah Khan Mohammadi's office next. He had never seen the battle-hardened Afghan general so distraught. The two American advisers had been entrusted to the care of the Interior Ministry, to the hospitality of Afghans, and he had not kept them safe. Allen told him that if they didn't solve this problem, "we will lose the campaign and Afghanistan will burn down."

The public rage from the Koran burning—built on years of frustration at the American military presence in Afghanistan—had become a risk not only to the soldiers in combat but to any American at work in the country. Allen's belief that Afghans and Americans were not fundamentally incompatible as partners, and that closeness and understanding could prevail over religious and cultural differences, had to somehow accommodate the new political reality of these two dead Americans lying in their office. He had to make changes. Allen ordered all American military advisers out of the Afghan ministries. If American advisers were going to be allowed to return to Afghan offices, he later decided, all the doors of their offices had to be equipped with push-button metal Simplex locks. Their desks must now face the door. And their guns had to be placed on their desks, within easy reach.

At the end of this brutal week, Allen and Crocker met with Karzai in the palace. The discussion quickly turned ugly. Karzai told Allen that his soldiers were worse than the Soviets, as the Soviets hadn't burned the Islamic holy book. "I wouldn't blame a lot of Afghan soldiers for wanting to kill American soldiers," Karzai said.

Allen's nerves were already raw following the crisis with the Korans and the deaths of his soldiers. Karzai's statement, which he saw as intentionally provocative, enraged him. Someone familiar with the exchange said Crocker had to hold Allen back from storming out of Karzai's office. Allen told Karzai, in effect: "You're dead wrong. And you know you're wrong."

Less than a month after the Koran burnings, a U.S. Army staff sergeant named Robert Bales walked off his base in Kandahar and murdered, in cold blood, sixteen Afghan villagers, including nine children, who had been asleep in their beds. To President Karzai, it was the "end of the rope." He flew to Kandahar to meet with the relatives of the massacre victims. That was the point when Karzai, with tears in his eyes, called the Americans demons and prayed to God that Afghanistan could be rescued from their brutalities.

When the war started, Karzai would send personal notes to a loved one of every foreign soldier who perished in Afghanistan. In one, from April 8, 2002, he wrote to the father of Sergeant Thomas Kochert, a German soldier killed in Kabul, saying that his son's untimely demise "brought profound sorrow to me. He was here on a mission of peace, a mission to bring safety and security to a beleaguered people. I can assure you that Thomas and his colleagues' presence on the streets of Kabul brought significant assurances to our people." The years and the diplomatic fights had since scrubbed away his sympathy for American lives. A massacre by the Taliban could pass without comment from the palace. His own Afghan soldiers and police dying in great numbers wouldn't merit a mention. But an American air strike that mistakenly killed an Afghan family would receive his full denunciation as president. Part of that looked like genuine frustration and anger and helplessness, but he was also wielding his most potent political weapon. "He never missed the benefit of a good crisis," Allen said.

The general grew to understand how to deal with this: "What eventually became clear to me was the way to solve the crisis was less about taking him on frontally. I remember, of course, he's a tribal leader. He comes from an ancient culture where face, honor, and shame are really important things. And when you take him on frontally in front of his people and prove him to be wrong or the nature of the conversation appears to discredit him, no matter whether you end up winning the conversation or not, you've now shamed the man. First of all, it's not right, and secondly you've got to be smart enough to know not to do that to him. I did take him on frontally a couple times, and I regret I did. It ate up a lot of the goodwill I had."

Allen wanted an end to the violence and a reconciliation with the Taliban, but Karzai's ultimate political goal was for Afghan sovereignty. He wanted to be a real president of an independent country. Karzai was terrified that his legacy would be equated with that of Shah Shuja, the nineteenth-century king who was installed by the invading British and who was murdered after their withdrawal. In a country that proudly clung to its reputation for repelling invaders, there was a special pantheon of shame for those who catered to foreigners. The Taliban would mock Karzai as a modern-day Shuja.

Karzai adopted his nation's rage for a war's worth of failures. With each new civilian casualty, he would demand the complete halt of all air strikes and night raids, and gradually he won concessions in the circumstances in which these could be carried out. He demanded full Afghan control over all prisoners and wore down the Americans in months of negotiations. He saw his most important role as wresting control from the United States: to block its military operations, to decide where its money was spent, to eliminate what he termed the foreigners' "parallel structures" to his rule, to hasten the end of their war he had long since lost any faith in them winning. He was the puppet who wouldn't dance.

19

THE PRIMARY PURPOSE OF
ITS EXISTENCE

FACED WITH WELL DOCUMENTED accusations of his complicity in a crime, Mahmood Karzai chose to rage. He never accepted the premise that he had done anything wrong in his relationship with Kabul Bank. He blamed the bank's collapse solely on the former chairman, Sherkhan Farnood, whose $4.7 million Dubai villa Mahmood had been using, and whom he described as "Genghis Khan." Mahmood insisted he had taken three legal loans from Kabul Bank: $1.2 million for his Toyota business, $2.6 million for the cement factory, and $400,000 for a steel rebar firm. He said he had paid all of them back, with 9 percent interest (albeit after the scandal broke). His argument was that what the management of Kabul Bank did with its loan portfolio was beyond his control and knowledge. He claimed he had been "fraudulently induced" to become a Kabul Bank shareholder, as he'd had no way of knowing that the bank's books were an elaborate fabrication. "Sherkhan is not only unreliable because he is trying hard to cover up his own misdeeds by shifting responsibility to others," Mahmood wrote in a letter arguing his innocence, "but he has a particular reason to lie about me since he personally dislikes me and he relishes the chance of creating problems for me."

Mahmood wrote reams of letters making his case: to Kabul Bank investigators and auditors; to the IMF; to Senate Foreign Relations Committee chairman John Kerry. He sat with journalists and bloviated for hours. He hired high-priced lawyers and held press conferences and went on TV to defend his name. As investigators and auditors finished their reports on the bank scandal, Mahmood fired off counteraccusations and second-guessed their work. In his hierarchy of blame, Mahmood reserved a special place at the top for Karl Eikenberry. The former U.S.

ambassador who had fought President Karzai, supported Central Bank governor Fitrat, and overseen Kirk Meyer's investigations was, to Mahmood's eye, the mastermind of his fall to disgrace. "It has come to my attention that in a press conference dated March 17, 2013 you accused me of taking illegal loans," Mahmood wrote to Drago Kos, the head of the Independent Joint Anti-Corruption Monitoring and Evaluation Committee, an international body that had produced a lengthy report on the Kabul Bank crisis. "I just hope that you are not influenced by a group of western individuals who I consider to be the cronies of Eikenberry, the former US Ambassador to Afghanistan. Eikenberry lost his credibility for all his unfounded allegations he heaped on me even before the Kabul Bank fiasco, such as my project in Kandahar and the Ghory Cement project." Eikenberry had by then been gone from Afghanistan for nearly two years. Mahmood could not let him go. "I know that Eikenberry and his cronies are supporting Fitrat who conspired to destroy Kabul Bank and help protect those who cooperated with the conspiracy of Eikenberry."

Mahmood argued that he had been singled out because of his last name and that other Afghan business barons had escaped with their reputations intact. He tried to have the attorney general's office prosecute Kos's team for its Kabul Bank report. "The outrage on morality that you call Anti-Corruption Monitoring is wicked enough to inflict penalties on truth," Mahmood wrote. "You accuse me of wrongdoings by your unfounded allegations but yet you are silent on major corruption cases rampant through Afghanistan. Please explain to the Afghan people how [it] is that many politicians have accumulated tens of millions of dollars, some accrued hundreds of millions of dollars, and a few have enve [*sic*] amassed over a billion dollars. Yet you are silent and for political motives you resolve to defame instead my character with smear tactics."

In his letter to Kerry, he took a more humble approach. "As you know, I am an American citizen who is the older brother of President Karzai," he began. "After 9/11, like many of my Afghan compatriots, I returned to my homeland to try and rebuild the country devastated by decades of Communist rule, the Soviet invasion, civil war, and then the Taliban. I am actively involved in business and politics." Mahmood said that his success in business and his "tendency for straight talk" had won him many enemies, who had spread rumors about his finances. "My brother, President Karzai, was very disappointed with me when you told him that I have tens of millions of dollars in bank accounts. I have no doubt that you said that to my brother because you believed it to be true. But it is false.

"I have been in business in the US since 1985," he went on. "I started in this country with double shift jobs and worked my way up to eventually owning four restaurants, some development and commercial property, and I even built my own custom home. Most of the wealth I have today is the result of my hard work over 24 years in America." He was an investor in the nation's only cement factory, he said, which, despite continuing to lose money, employed fifteen hundred Afghans. His gated town was "the first modern city in Afghanistan" and "has changed the face of Kandahar.

"Senator Kerry," he said, "I am an honest entrepreneur. I believe in transparency, something you will not find in those with something to hide. To prove my claim, I am setting forth my financial information, explaining how much money I have as well as where it came from. In my opinion, the essential question in Afghanistan after 9 years is 'Where did the money come from?'

"I certainly hope that after you and your staff has an opportunity to carefully review this information, you will find it persuasive of my good intent and conduct, and not allow others to assassinate my character by malicious innuendo and rumor. This information is current."

Over the next two pages, Mahmood told Kerry about his U.S. earnings ($305,742), the capital gains from the sale of his home in Dubai ($900,000), his deposits in his personal account at Emirates Bank in Dubai ($724,824), his payment to Georgetown University for his daughter's tuition ($202,571), and his deposit to a colleague "in anticipation of a joint venture" ($2,134,330). In an attached personal financial statement from Sandy Spring Bank, he claimed his net worth was $12,147,491. He concluded, "I hope this letter will help you realize that I am one of America's trustworthy and honest allies in this war. Knowing the friends upon whom you can rely is critical."

The closest anyone would come to the truth about what happened inside Kabul Bank was the forensic audit done by Kroll, a New York–based corporate investigations firm, in late 2012. The investigators combed over files from the bank and its affiliated *hawala* company, Shaheen Exchange, as well as Sherkhan Farnood General Trading. It was impossible to know the full picture, since there was no record for how some of the cash had been spent, or to whom it had been given. But in their confidential 277-page report, Kroll's auditors concluded that "from its very beginning, the bank was a well-concealed Ponzi scheme." Despite its optimistic annual reports, the bank had in reality been insolvent within a year of its founding, and by the time of its collapse it had a negative equity of more than $750 million. "The loan book scheme commenced from the inception of the Bank and was the primary purpose of its existence," the report read. The fraud continued "unchecked to the point where the Bank was highly insolvent and unsustainable as a going concern. Once the true nature of the loan book was revealed, the subsequent collapse of the Bank was inevitable.

"The Bank never operated as a legitimate bank: a bank that seeks to safeguard depositors' money and generate profits through successful and prudent loan book management. Instead, the Bank has been used to provide free financing to the other business interests of senior management and a group of connected persons." The auditors found that more than 92 percent of the bank's loan book, or $861 million, had gone to nineteen related people and companies, "and substantially to the benefit of 14 individuals, who were not required to make repayments."

The auditors pored over $5.2 billion of international transfers made through the bank's SWIFT server over a four-year period beginning in the spring of 2007. They found that money was zipping around the world: Dubai, Switzerland, India, Turks and Caicos, Germany, Russia, Latvia, South Korea, the United States. Kabul Bank had poured $116.4 million into trading and textile companies in China, including Farnood's Xinjiang Qitai Xilu Co. Limited, in the province of Xinjiang, bordering Afghanistan (he also ran a *hawala* in China). The bank paid $46 million to GE Commercial Aviation Funding in the United Kingdom to purchase aircraft for Pamir Airways, which Farnood partly owned and where Hashim Karzai, the president's cousin, worked as a consultant. Farnood went on shopping binges at Louis Vuitton and Versace. He spent $1.08 million on his gambling account at the Bellagio in Las Vegas, plus another $150,000 at the Commerce Casino in Los Angeles. Ferozi, the bank's chief executive, dispatched $3 million to his private HSBC account in Switzerland. Mahmood Karzai shipped more than $300,000 to accounts in his name in Dubai and $15,000 to his cousin Hashim's account in the United States. By Kroll's calculations, Mahmood owed as much as $30.5 million in total, of which he had paid off just $5.2 million. As of the day of the bank's collapse, August 31, 2010, of the five people who owed the most money in the Kabul Bank scandal, four were the most famous men involved: Farnood ($270.3 million), Ferozi ($94.3 million), the vice president's brother Haseen Fahim ($43.6 million), and Mahmood Karzai.

Kroll determined that Farnood, through 160 proxy loans provided through a collection of loans known as the Zahir Group, was responsible for $467.5 million, although since much of that money had then been redistributed to other people, the adjustment brought it down to nearly $300 million. "The main implication of these findings is that Farnood used the Zahir Group loans primarily for his own personal enrichment," Kroll found. A document given to me by one of the employees at Kabul Bank describing the Zahir Group lists the names of 229 people who apparently received money from these loans (a version used by Kroll had 227 entries). The list includes a Who's Who of the Afghan government and business elite: Vice President Mohammad Qasim Fahim, identified as Marshal Fahim ($373,928); Finance Minister Omar Zakhilwal ($233,997); former speaker of parliament Yunus Qanooni ($1.27 million); Uzbek warlord Abdul Rashid Dostum ($1.29 million); and Yama Karzai, a top intelligence official and a cousin of the president's ($346,008). However, Kroll found that the entries for these names, by themselves, could not be corroborated, as they had been provided by Farnood and existed without other documentation. "The Receivership has been unable to discern whether the allocations were correct and allocated parties are being dishonest, or whether the allocation itself was flawed. This has left the Receivership without a sound platform from which they could ultimately pursue disputed amounts," Kroll wrote. "We cannot discount the possibility that [Farnood] may be incentivized to mislead investigators and the Receivership in an attempt to conceal his own personal gains."

That finding said much about the Afghan war. You could never quite reach the bottom. Everything had deeper layers, further culprits, a society cloaked for America in a shroud of foreignness. This was the murk that the anti-corruption crusaders—Kirk Meyer, Herbert R. McMaster—submerged themselves in and were never able to emerge from. Even if you thought you knew, thought you were so achingly correct, nothing would come of it; everything slipped away. By the time of the Kroll report, more than two years after Kabul Bank collapsed, just 10 percent of the money taken had been repaid. Mahmood Karzai, in an interview with *The New York Times*, called the Kroll report "a piece of puke."

When I met Sherkhan Farnood, in the summer of 2011, he was in legal limbo following the collapse of his bank. He was not in jail but was confined to living in a dingy second-story guest room at the bank headquarters, watched by Afghan intelligence agency guards. The bank was located on a busy downtown commercial street, between two cell phone shops, in a building that had once housed the Pakistani embassy. The neighborhood, known as Shar-e-Naw, was pleasant, particularly at night, when colored lights illuminated the kebab restaurants and ice cream parlors. On the sidewalk you could buy a goldfish in a plastic bag or a peacock on a leash. Children darted in and out of traffic, swinging tin cans of smoking scented embers, a concoction said to ward off the evil eye, which they would waft over your windshield for a donation.

The bank's three-story, blue-glass façade stood out among the smaller storefronts, but it did not appear lavish, and the room where Farnood was staying, up a flight of dented metal stairs off a back courtyard, had none of the luxury of his former office. After he'd been ousted, his company had been renamed New Kabul Bank. When I met him, he was wearing a T-shirt and looked disheveled and depressed. He was working on his laptop, and I sat down on the couch next to him and waited. After an awkwardly long silence, he apologized and said he needed a little more time. He was playing online chess with a teenager in Russia, he explained, and he had to finish the game. He finally snapped shut his laptop and turned to me. "I hate to lose," he said.

His legal status was difficult to decipher. After his period of sleeping in the bank under armed guard, he was detailed to "house arrest" at a mansion, where he hosted high-stakes poker games in a pink sitting room. During this home-detention phase, I would sometimes see him on the treadmill at the Serena Hotel, in a sweaty white V-neck tee, his face red with exertion, running with bullish determination. Once when I called him, he claimed to be in prison (cell phone service apparently uninterrupted) and said that he couldn't talk but would be happy if I visited.

Just as house arrest didn't equate with staying at home, the reality of the Kabul Bank prosecutions never squared with the rhetoric of punishment and justice issuing from Karzai's palace. Under continuous pressure from the U.S. government, the IMF, and others, President Karzai had acquiesced to the forensic audit. In April 2011, he agreed to put the bank in receivership so that an independent organization could attempt to recover some of the stolen money. A year passed. In April 2012, Karzai created a special tribunal to prosecute those responsible. In his decree, Karzai ruled that anyone who paid off his debts within two months could forgo interest and would not be prosecuted. The tribunal issued indictments against twenty-one people. Mahmood Karzai, Haseen Fahim, and other shareholders who'd taken millions in loans were not among them. Farnood and Ferozi received indictments, along with rank-and-file bank staffers and the regulators at the Central Bank, including Fitrat, who by then was living in Virginia.

The case required a level of technical expertise that far surpassed the abilities of Afghan prosecutors. The country's banking system was barely a decade old and the justice ministry did not have many people trained in understanding complex financial transactions. When Farnood took the stand, he rattled off math equations, accused everyone else, insisted that he had never told a lie, waved around a water bottle, and said things like "We have studied in school that one mass cannot occupy two spaces at the same time." He announced: "My debts are zero." Then he amended this statement. In fact, he said, "the government owes me $100 million right now. But I am announcing that I won't take this money."

On March 5, 2013, the special tribunal handed down convictions of all twenty-one people charged. The Independent Joint Anti-Corruption Monitoring and Evaluation Committee, which had investigated the bank scandal, found the convictions "alarming" because of the light sentences for the perpetrators and the punishment for "others who appear to have had little or no involvement in the fraud." Farnood and Ferozi got five-year sentences and a request to return the stolen money. They were convicted of a "breach of trust," a crime they had not even been charged with. The court did not convict them of money laundering, which would have come with a court order to seize the money from their offshore accounts. Some of the staffers convicted had long since fled Afghanistan. Massoud Ghazi, the quiet accountant plunged into the whirlpool of New Kabul Bank, received a three-year sentence. Fitrat got convicted of misusing authority and intentionally failing to share information, which earned him a two-year prison term, a sentence he had no intention of serving. When I spoke to him on the phone not long after the verdict, he called it a "mockery of justice."

"The president and his clique wanted to shift the blame [onto] the Central Bank, acquit themselves and their families of wrongdoing, and find someone responsible," he said. "And those people were from the Central Bank, not the actual thieves: the president and his brother."

Fitrat's habit of following rules, and his insistence on consequences for the bank's criminals, struck some of his colleagues as naïve. "Since he'd come from the U.S., he kind of had the U.S. mentality," said Mustafa

Massoudi, who ran the Afghan government's financial intelligence unit. "We are in Afghanistan; do like Afghans do. You basically cannot always play by the rules. Relationships matter more. If you want to get things done, and you know how powerful these people are, you can't tell the president, 'All right, let's sell the bank. Let's kick these people out. Let's put them in a court of law.' That wasn't an option. That antagonized the president."

But the fact that Fitrat, and not Mahmood, ended up with a criminal conviction summed up how seriously Karzai's palace took fighting the greed among his family members and supporters. Mahmood never got indicted in the United States, either. The covert plan that was kicked around to catch him in a bribe never happened, as that investigation got swamped by the scope of the Kabul Bank scandal. For Kirk Meyer, this was another dispiriting outcome of his lost war against corruption. He believed the U.S. government had more than enough evidence to arrest Mahmood. One simple way, Meyer believed, was to use IRS rules about reporting money in foreign banks, as Mahmood held money in an account in Dubai. The Kabul Bank case offered another chance: an American citizen involved in bank fraud overseas is still subject to arrest. Although in early 2013, Mahmood announced that he had revoked his American citizenship.

Among the embassy leadership, some believed that the federal prosecutors in the Southern District of New York were under political pressure not to indict Mahmood. Others felt that the complexity, and the foreignness, of this far-off war-zone scandal may have discouraged them from pursuing it. "We had enough information to put this guy away for a long, long time," one top embassy official said.

Meyer expected an indictment, but months passed, and nothing materialized, despite his ever deeper excavations of Mahmood's behavior.

"I think the U.S. government didn't pursue it because they didn't want to irritate President Karzai," Meyer told me after he'd left Afghanistan. Even years later, talking about Afghanistan seemed to sting.

"The whole idea still bothers me," he said. "We're bankrupting ourselves on these two wars. . . . Without a strong economy, you don't have a national defense. That has to be an element in it. It can't just be guns and bullets. I can't say that we really protected that part of our national defense in these two wars."

Meyer and Calestino fulfilled their mission. They were even nominated for a federal government award, the Samuel J. Heyman Service

*Frank Calestino, left, and Kirk Meyer, right, final
ists for the Samuel J. Heyman Service to America
Medal, a federal government award, in 2010*

to America Medal, known as the "Sammies," the Oscars for the federal
bureaucracy. Their superiors praised them for discovering "extraordinarily rich information" that had "potential tentacles globally," and the
two men attended the black-tie gala in Washington, D.C. In the end they
were just finalists. They didn't win.

"We were asked: find out how bad the corruption is," Meyer once told
me. "When we found out, people didn't want to know."

20

EVIL IN HEAVEN

ONCE, AS I STEPPED OFF the airplane in Kandahar, there was a crowd gathered on the tarmac. I was familiar with the celebrity politicians and warlords who could attract such attention, the men whose photos decorated car windows and billboards, the feared and revered and hated. In Kandahar, that would mean men like Ahmed Wali Karzai or, lately, his cousin Hashmat. I hadn't noticed anyone like that on the flight.

I waited with the crowd to watch the rest of the passengers disembark. When a clean-cut elderly gentleman walked down the ramp, the crowd surged toward him, and the video cameramen jostled for position to capture his arrival. As he walked toward the terminal, people draped wreaths of colorful flowers around his neck. He was pale, with silver hair and glasses, and wore a banker's suit. I figured he was some opium lord. I asked a man next to me, and he said it was the country's most famous poet, the author of its national anthem. At that time, there was so much killing in Kandahar that people rarely left their homes without a good reason, particularly in the evening. The poet held a reading that night in the city, and more than a thousand people came to hear him.

His name was Abdul Bari Jahani, and one of his poems is called "Enmity in Heaven." It tells the story of a mullah whose words could bring people to tears, who settled their disputes with justice and fairness. One day, the mullah spoke to his followers about hell—about its scorpions, snakes, and leaping flames; about how the punishment for missing one prayer meant getting dipped seventy thousand times into the never-ending fire; where sinners spent seventy years in a smoldering pit, but each year in hell equaled seventy thousand earth years; where every snake had seventy thousand heads, and every head seventy thousand fangs. Heaven, on the other hand, was a place of fresh fruit, cool shade, tall trees, pools of milk and juice and streams of wine. The righteous would receive castles made of gems hung with golden chandeliers and be presented with seventy long-necked statuesque virgins whose bodies were whiter than marble and hands as soft as silk, and seventy nymph boys who would serve them as slaves, each one more beautiful than a necklace of pearls.

At learning this, a Pashtun man stood up in the middle of the crowd and addressed the mullah.

"Praise be to God for his virgins, nymph boys, and gem castles, and I wish that God grants me heaven and streams of milk and juice," he said. "But I want to know if there will be evil in heaven as well?

"If there will be enmity between tribes and cousins? If people will kill each other in heaven and whether men will receive women as compensation?"

The Pashtun man said that he didn't need heaven and that the mullah should sell his heaven to cowards. He said what would be the difference between a man and a goat if no one owes him the death of a relative? He said that the greatest enmity is the one that lasts for centuries and that grandfathers speak about to their grandsons. He said that life only becomes enjoyable if you harbor a boiling rage, carry a loaded gun with a hundred bullets. He said you cannot call it life if there is no fighting and enmity and if your hands are not stained with the blood of your cousin. He said you cannot call it life if there is no talk about who is superior and inferior and no spark of swords. You cannot call it life if there is no . . . difference between Ghilzai and Durrani. He said this heaven is not the place for brave men and Pashtuns, indeed it is a place for people who live on others' charity. This heaven is for mullahs, clerks, and cowards. He said God created Pashtuns for enmity. Brother is the enemy of brother. When God has created someone superior to others then how is it possible that all of them be equal in heaven. If there is no blood shed between brother and cousins then this heaven is not the place for Pashtuns.

After Ahmed Wali's death, Hashmat grew into the man he aspired to be: the *khan*, the chief, the dispenser of punishment and mercy. He won a seat on the provincial council. The former car-loan specialist at the Toyota dealership in Virginia had become a national figure in Afghanistan. Shah Wali resented his new tribal responsibilities, but Hashmat thrived on them. He made his mansion in Karz more lavish, adding a neon fountain, and brought in a pet lion, which he would stroke for the pleasure of his guests. "He thinks he's Michael Jackson," Shah Wali said.

Hashmat gave conspicuous donations to the people of his city, hosting meals for several thousand people at a time, distributing cartons of milk to the poor. He brought electricity to Karz. He fashioned his own image after his father, the fearless Pashtun fighter, often referring in public to his middle name, "Khalil." The stories that circulated showed this growing defiance. He would tell people about a visit to the president's residence in the early years, and how a big Panjshiri guard would come late at night and lock the front door from the outside, so they could not leave until morning, and how pathetic that was. He told how his Kabul neighbor Bismillah Khan Mohammadi, the famous Northern Alliance commander from the Panjshir Valley who rose to Karzai's cabinet, sent a servant to Hashmat's house to tell him to quiet his barking dog, because his sick mother was trying to sleep; Mohammadi suggested that Hashmat send his dog to Kandahar. "Tell Bismillah Khan I will not send my dog to Kandahar," Hashmat replied, as the story went. "Tell him to send his mother to Panjshir."

Before the 2014 presidential election, Hashmat ignored the entreaties of his cousins Qayum and Mahmood and signed on as a supporter for candidate Ashraf Ghani, the former finance minister. He led campaign rallies in Kandahar's stadium and hosted feasts for the masses and fully expected to be rewarded as governor of Kandahar. The choice of Ghani was significant because he came from the Ghilzai branch of the Pashtuns, the historic rivals of the Karzai Durranis. But as one relative recalled advising Hashmat, it was time to worry about uniting the Pashtuns, because "the minorities" were gaining strength in Kabul. With his rising stature, Hashmat felt free to publicly criticize the ruling Karzais.

On July 6, 2014, he posted several pictures to his Facebook page (under occupation it read, "chief executive officer at Kandahar") of a crumbling wall and piles of dun-colored debris. They showed a destroyed part of his compound near the airport, Asia Village, which he'd rented to the United Nations and other foreign contractors. The dispute over ownership of the land had gone on for a long time. The former mayor, a friend of the Karzai brothers, believed that Hashmat had stolen the land to build his hotel, allegedly forging documents to redraw the property boundaries. The mayor pressured the governor to take action, but then a suicide bomber blew up the mayor, and the issue, for a time, was forgotten. A couple of years later, the government began bulldozing part of Asia Village's wall to make room for an expansion of the highway that ran to Spin Boldak.

"Friends, you know that politics requires sacrifice and winning politics without sacrifice is not tasty," Hashmat wrote in Pashto. "I have one son, and I am ready to sacrifice to such an extent that I would sacrifice him in the name of God for the peace of the country.

"Friends, one of the sacrifices you saw yesterday is that in front of the airport [in his compound] a 620 meter long wall is being destroyed, despite all legal documents, on the order of crazy Hamid Karzai, by the incompetent governor, and the illiterate commander, [Police Chief Abdul] Raziq." The destruction was part of their "failed policy" and an attempt to anger him and "use violence against their gangster."

"Dear nation," Hashmat concluded, "I assure you that till the last drop of blood in my body I will stand against these oppressors, and will call traitor, traitor, and will ask for legal punishments for them."

The last time I saw Hashmat, we were talking about the day of Ahmed Wali Karzai's memorial. Customarily, the service, known as a *fateha*, begins the morning after the burial and runs for three days. Ahmed Wali's occurred in Kandahar's Red Mosque, a stately and colonnaded building a few blocks from his house. There were serious risks in convening such a high-profile crowd. In the three years he had been the imam at the Red Mosque, Mullah Abdul Qayum Popalzai had been shot, beaten, kidnapped, threatened, and forced to move his family. His predecessor in the mosque had been murdered in his home. The head of Kandahar's *ulema* council, the group of clerics paid by the government, was issuing fatwas on the radio against suicide bombing, a position that angered the Taliban. Young fighters would regularly turn up at his mosque to pray or attend classes at the madrassa. "I would always refuse to allow them to stay. I would tell them that the government doesn't let me and it's not only a threat for them, it would be a threat to me and my family. If they get settled here, the foreigners might raid the mosque," Popalzai said. He tried to stay neutral. "What I want is that no blood should be shed."

President Karzai had visited the mosque the year before, on his trip to consult Kandahar elders about the upcoming American military offensive in the city. The day before the visit, Popalzai stood on the concrete patio under the mosque's pink-and-white minarets and looked across the V-shaped grounds hemmed in by two city streets and low-slung walls. As he glanced around, he happened to notice a man crawling down into the concrete well at the far end of the garden. He crossed the dirt footpaths that wound through the grass and the flowering bushes and peered down at the man crouched on the straw and dirt at the bottom of the old dry well.

"What are you doing here?" he recalled asking the man.

"I was just checking it," the man replied.

The mullah kicked the man off the property and called Kandahar's intelligence office to report the intruder. Later in the afternoon, he stumbled across another man, this one hiding in one of the minarets, inside the arched windows beneath the loudspeakers used in the call to prayer. That same night, while he was busy with the evening prayers, someone from the Taliban came to his home, not far from the mosque, and threatened his wife. "He said I should not come between them and the government, that if it wasn't for me, they would have been able to kill a lot of government officials, including Karzai." The president's visit went off without incident, but the imam had been shaken by the threats. Afterward, he got in the habit of checking the mosque and its grounds thoroughly before every gathering or memorial service, poking around for hidden men or explosives.

Many of Popalzai's relatives lived in an area on the southwestern outskirts of Kandahar known as Malajat, where the Taliban had a large following. Not long after these first threats, he went to visit them. As he was preparing for dinner, there was a knock on the door. Men with weapons ordered him outside. One of the Taliban held a Kalashnikov magazine in his hand. He waved it as he accused the imam of siding with the government and the infidel Americans. Popalzai was not a small man. He had a thick chest and a trunklike neck, a black beard, and a stern demeanor. He stood in silence. The Talib tapped the magazine on his chest and stared into Popalzai's eyes, then grabbed him by the neck and led him away to a nearby home. Inside, several men took turns punching, slapping, and kicking him, then released him with another warning not to interfere with their plans.

The threats continued. The imam began receiving harassing phone calls from numbers he did not recognize. He swapped out his SIM card and changed his phone number. The calls would resume until he stopped using his cell phone altogether. His children received ominous taunts about their father from other boys in the neighborhood. Strangers would come to the house and tell his wife they should leave town. One day, while he was teaching Koranic verses in a mosque classroom, a tall man with long, dark hair walked into the room. The man sat down cross-legged in front of the imam.

"Who has appointed you as the imam of this mosque?" the man asked.

"The people have chosen me," Popalzai replied.

"Your predecessor was chosen by the government. Whoever serves this mosque serves the government and the children of America," the man insisted.

The stranger lectured the imam about his refusal to allow young followers of the Taliban to study at the mosque. He asked him how well he knew Ahmed Wali Karzai, whose house was a couple of blocks from the mosque. He did not seem to believe the answer when Popalzai told him he'd never met the man. As the stranger stood to leave, he lifted up his shirt and revealed a pistol underneath. "If you don't want to go where the imam before you went, you shouldn't support this government."

After this visit, Popalzai wrote a letter to the Kandahar office of the Afghan intelligence service. He detailed the intruders hiding in the well and in the tower, the threats and beatings, the phone calls and harassment. He asked for a police outpost to be set up at the mosque. At the very least, he wrote, he would like a gun for his own protection. He received no response.

The security for Ahmed Wali Karzai's memorial service was like nothing Popalzai had ever seen. Police and intelligence officers swept the mosque and its surroundings starting the day before. Cabinet ministers, governors, and several members of the Karzai family would be attending the ceremony, which began with a series of prayers in the morning and continued until noon, a rotating crowd of dignitaries sitting on the plush red-and-green-striped carpet to pay their respects. President Karzai decided not to attend, as it was too risky. His intelligence officers had received information from an intercepted cell phone call indicating that someone had tried to attack him at Ahmed Wali's burial the day before. The caller had been saying, "I'm close, but I can't find my way" into the cemetery, one of the president's aides told me. The man on the other end of the line told him: "Go back and see him again tomorrow." So the president returned to Kabul.

The first mourners began arriving at the Red Mosque at eight-thirty a.m., with the sun already hot and throbbing. The normal traffic around the mosque—painted rickshaws, pushcarts teetering with potted plants, flocks of dusty gray and black sheep—had thinned out that morning in deference to the police pickups and hulking armored vehicles that plugged up the lanes. After getting through the police checkpoints, mourners were frisked at the gate and again when they went into the mosque. Nine archways ran the length of the front of the mosque, each leading to a doorway, most of them closed for the event as police funneled visitors through the central entrances under the big pink dome. Security guards were everywhere on the ground, and American helicopters flew overhead. Haji Dil Jan, a border police commander from Herat whose brother was on the Kandahar provincial council, was searched three times on his way in, even though he flashed his badge.

When the service began, the Karzai brothers—Qayum, Mahmood, Shah Wali, and Abdul Ahmed—were sitting near the front of the room, off to the left of the microphones, under a slowly turning ceiling fan, with other dignitaries, including the Kandahar governor. Hashmat was not allowed to sit with them and stayed farther back, next to his brother, Hekmat. Thick concrete pillars, painted white and blue, were interspersed throughout the prayer hall. They sat next to one of the pillars, facing a series of clocks that showed the times allotted each day for Muslim prayer. Popalzai, the imam chosen by the Karzais presided, intoning passages from the Koran in a droning chant. Mourners placed their heads to the floor and held their palms to the sky, then stood to leave as others took their place near the front of the hall.

Mahmood felt uneasy about the whole spectacle. He told Qayum he was worried that something might happen. The service progressed for three hours, and when it was finished Popalzai stood in front of the gathering, at least two hundred people, and announced that a special luncheon for dignitaries had been arranged at Mandigak Palace, the hall where the provincial council met, and the rest of the visitors could eat inside the mosque. Dozens of young boys appeared at the doorways with platters of rice and lamb and plastic mats to spread on the floor. Popalzai concluded the service. He called over his two sons to help him with the microphones and speakers, opening a white wooden cabinet at the front of the room that held the sound system. When the explosion occurred, his back was to the room. He was thrown against the wall and fell to the floor. To Shah Wali, the blast sounded as if it were outside the mosque: "It was loud, but the light seemed to come from outside the windows. Then people started running." Someone shouted, "There's two more!" as smoke filled the room. The wounded screamed and writhed on the floor. Frantic guards and mourners formed a circle around the Karzai brothers and began hustling them out of the mosque. Popalzai picked himself up off the floor. He looked at the carnage.

"I saw some people were gutted. My clothes were covered in blood and small pieces of bone and pieces of brain." Windows had blown out. The curtains were tattered. Shrapnel speckled the walls and columns. He stared at a severed head on the patio.

The chief of the *ulema* council, who had waged a publicity campaign against suicide bombing, had been slain by the blast. At least two other visitors had been killed as well, and many suffered wounds from burns and shrapnel cuts. The phone intercepts the palace picked up after the attack suggested that the bomber had wanted to kill the president. He had sat patiently in the mosque for more than three hours, through the entire service, waiting for Hamid Karzai to arrive. At one point he'd made a phone call, saying, "I'm here, I'm sitting down, he's not here," an aide recalled. When the prayers concluded, and everybody rose, he realized the president would not be coming. So he blew himself up.

For the Karzai family, it was the narrowest of escapes. Investigators later determined that the bomber had hidden the explosives in his turban, which until that point were generally not unwrapped and searched. "It was a very, very, very close call," Mahmood Karzai said when I talked to him hours after the attack. "The guy didn't recognize us. It was a miracle we got out of there alive."

Hashmat, in his house in Karz, thought back to the moment of the explosion. "Boom," he said. "If you've ever been in a war, there are things like that—everything stops. That moment. It stops. It gets everything in slow motion. It gets in slow motion, and every minute is like a frickin' hour. Especially when people are yelling, screaming, running around. 'There's two more!' I sit down. I see people jumping from the windows, hitting the windows. I see people . . ." He broke off and laughed. "Unbelievable."

Hashmat looked exhausted. People kept arriving at his house, approaching him, kissing his hands, groveling, sitting and waiting silently for his attention. Once when he stood to greet a guest, I noticed that he had a black handgun under his shirt. "Eight a.m. till nine at night," he said. "I maybe get up about a thousand times. My feet at the end of the day. My God. I can barely stand.

"Sometimes, honestly, I'm not joking with you, every time I sit here when someone walks in, every individual I don't recognize, I know for a fact he's going to blow up any minute. He's going to blow up. He's going to blow up. He's going to blow up. Every minute. You can't search every individual deeply. Sometimes these new explosives are in a turban. Now they have these new things in their underwear. The old one when they put a turban under you and blow up, now they jump on you and sit on you and explode. That is basically the scariest part. I'm serious. You sit here. You watch these people. It's, like, crazy. A friend of mine once told me, 'I'm not sitting here. *Look* at these people.' That is the scariest part. That is the scariest part. That people are walking in. We're not talking about ten, twenty, fifty, a hundred. We're talking about thousands of people, and you cannot search everybody."

Popalzai, the imam from the ceremony, survived the day of the blast. But he would later be stabbed to death inside his own mosque.

On July 28, 2014, three weeks after Hashmat had posted his Facebook rant about his destroyed wall, a teenage boy walked into Hashmat's home on the first day of the Eid-al Fitr, the Muslim holiday that marks the end of Ramadan. The boy joined the crowd of guests who had come for alms. Hashmat kept a tray of five-hundred- and one-thousand-afghani notes, worth about ten and twenty dollars, respectively, and he or his guards would hand them to visitors. The boy, who carried fake identification, said that he was poor and needed money for his wedding. He was given three thousand afghanis and sent on his way. The next day, after the morning prayer, the boy returned. He wanted to thank Hashmat for his gift, to kiss the great man's hand. The guards brushed him off. But Hashmat overheard and allowed the boy to draw close. The teenager grasped Hashmat's hand and knelt into him. He also had a bomb beneath his turban. His last words before he exploded were "God is great."

Afterward, Qayum Karzai would blame the "armed opposition" and those who wanted only "chaos and disorder." Ashraf Ghani wrote on Twitter about his "immense shock," about the loss that "left a void." Hashmat's own legacy would be as divisive and disputed as all the others. Governor Wesa called him a "big wall for Kandahar." Other relatives, who would never forgive him, registered no pity. "He was one of those balloons that got too high," one of them said. "I'm glad he's gone." There wasn't much more sympathy from President Karzai's palace. "Just like all other Afghans who are the daily targets of terrorist attacks, our fam-

*Mullah Abdul Qayum Popalzai inside the
Red Mosque in Kandahar, where a suicide bomber blew
himself up at Ahmed Wali Karzai's memorial service.
Popalzai would later be killed.*

ily, too, is no exception and as every other Afghan, we, too, will have to
bear it."

When I was back in the United States, from time to time I would visit a
young Karzai relative. He walked me through the stories and legends of
Karzais living and dead. He sketched out a family tree that, with all the
intermarriage, looked more like a tangled thicket of vines. He lived in
New York and watched with interest the machinations inside his family,
but he had little interest in participating. It was all too sordid. "This is
what happens when people's only thirst is for power," he told me once.
But Hashmat's death seemed to affect him more than other tragedies had.
What died along with Hashmat, he thought, was the *khan* legacy of the
Karzai family. No one wanted to take up the mantle or be the strongest
one. As he put it: "The last temple crumbled."

"That was the light that we all tried to live up to. And we all failed," he
said. "But I would rather be a peasant here than a king in Afghanistan."

21

THE ZERO OPTION

THE CENTERPIECE OF THE AMERICAN PLAN for post-combat Afghanistan was a document known as the bilateral security agreement. It was intended to define how the United States would support Afghanistan militarily after 2014, when the combat phase ended and the bulk of the troops went home. The goal was plainly to avoid reliving the mistakes of the past. After the Soviet withdrawal from Afghanistan, American support quickly evaporated, and its geopolitical attention focused elsewhere. The Soviet foreign aid dried up, the Communist government collapsed, and the subsequent Afghan civil war and general chaos throughout the state helped spawn the Taliban and provide refuge for al-Qaeda. The Obama administration wanted to keep some level of financial support so that the Afghan security forces could fight on their own and the government wouldn't instantly crumble to the ground.

The benefits of such an agreement for the Afghan government were clear: it would get a benefactor and protector in a dangerous neighborhood. The United States would agree in principle to pay for a good chunk of the country's Army and police force years into the future, as well as providing the protection from regional rivals that a U.S. troop presence implied. The arrangement would have fewer tangible benefits for the United States. Besides access to bases for counterterrorism operations in Afghanistan or the region, what the Obama administration wanted amounted to an insurance policy that the American investment over the last decade in Afghanistan would not be completely in vain. Intelligence agencies estimated that within a year, the Taliban could recapture large portions of southern and eastern Afghanistan if the United States withdrew all its troops by the end of 2014. Nobody wanted to see that happen. But with Hamid Karzai in the palace, it would be difficult to reach any agreement. He'd developed the reputation, as Defense Secretary Robert Gates put it, as probably America's most "troublesome ally in war since Charles de Gaulle in World War II."

Negotiations about America's long-term presence in Afghanistan had been going on for most of Karzai's second term. Karzai, from the beginning, wanted something binding. If he was going to commit to entangling his country's fate with the American government into the future, he wanted to know that the United States would fight to defend Afghanistan from its rivals and pay for its survival. Karzai wanted a treaty, a mutual security agreement whereby an attack on Spin Boldak, say, was an attack on Washington, and the U.S. government would respond in kind. He wanted firm commitments on how much money would be given for how many years. The Americans considered these terms ridiculous. They told Karzai that guaranteeing billions in congressional allocations for Afghanistan from future U.S. administrations was simply unrealistic. Gates once dismissed Karzai's talk of binding arrangements by saying it had taken Congress five years just to ratify benign agreements about sharing defense technology with Canada and Australia.

Karzai had tried to confine American soldiers to their bases a full year before the end of the combat mission. At the same time, he wanted the U.S. military to commit to buying the Afghan military sophisticated weaponry such as F-22 fighter jets and Abrams tanks. Karzai complained to his advisers that the Soviets had left the Afghan military with hundreds of aircraft and thousands of tanks but the Americans weren't giving anything close. He didn't like how departing U.S. troops were taking with them all their high-tech tools or destroying things they couldn't carry out.

Karzai had demanded that any agreement be contingent on a full transfer of all detention centers to Afghan control. Regaining control of prisons had long been one of Karzai's crusades, and American soldiers regularly delayed handing over their prisoners to Afghan custody, particularly at the Bagram prison. Karzai periodically issued public ultimatums to the Americans and made angry statements about how this prison represented a "breach of sovereignty." By early 2013, American troops had authority for fewer than 20 percent of the thirty-eight hundred prisoners inside Bagram. The Americans considered a few dozen of them especially dangerous and likely to return to fight with the insurgency if released. Karzai had agreed with General Allen that he would not set these prisoners free, but then he refused to sign language to that effect when the two sides tried to finalize the deal. Allen felt Karzai had betrayed their agreement. Karzai accused Allen of holding hostages. In one meeting, Karzai ordered Allen to release all American-held detainees to Afghan custody by four o'clock that afternoon. Allen told him that this wasn't going to happen. When Karzai's demands were eventually met, he set free dozens of high-profile detainees from Bagram.

The talks stumbled through the Koran burnings and the insider attacks and Robert Bales's shooting of sixteen villagers. A milestone was reached in May 2012, when Obama flew to Kabul to sign what was known as a "strategic partnership" agreement, pledging American support for Afghanistan after 2014. But this accord was somewhat symbolic, a goodwill gesture, meant to tell the Taliban that they couldn't just wait out the war. The negotiations redoubled almost immediately after the ink was dry to hash out a bilateral security agreement with some hard numbers on dollar figures and troop counts.

The Americans and Karzai battled back and forth over the next two years, as U.S. military estimates of how many troops they would need after 2014 rose and fell. There were marathon diplomatic sessions, with Secretary of State John Kerry trying to wrangle Karzai to an agreement. The Afghan government struggled through the negotiations, partly because this was the first time it had been called upon to negotiate an agreement of this magnitude. Each night after the negotiations, the Afghan team would brief Karzai in the palace, to get his agreement on every phrase. "It was difficult because we didn't have the proper expertise," one of the main Afghan negotiators told me. "The United States has signed hundreds of such agreements around the world. We didn't want to be criticized that what we did was not in the interests of Afghanistan."

One of the main sticking points was whether the American troops who stayed after 2014 could be prosecuted for crimes in Afghan courts. The issue was a firm red line for the U.S. government. When the Iraqis had refused to give American troops immunity, the Obama administration had pulled all of them out. Karzai also held out on his adamant belief that American troops couldn't enter Afghan homes, something the United States wasn't willing to concede. But Karzai eventually agreed, heading into his last year in office, that the decision should ultimately be made by the Afghan people. The plan called for a multibillion-dollar commitment and would allow for some ten thousand troops for the decade after 2014. Any American military operations would respect Afghan sovereignty and be a complement to Afghan forces. Karzai would hold a *loya jirga*, the same type of council that had chosen him a dozen years earlier to lead Afghanistan, and let the three thousand delegates vote on the future of the American partnership.

Qayum Karzai stepped out of his black Land Cruiser in the driveway of his brother Mahmood's home in Sherpur. He entered through the front door and made his way downstairs, to where a crowd of a few dozen people had convened in a hall draped in red carpets. Iridescent pillows on the floor framed the seating area in a giant rectangle. The light fixtures were shaped like flowers. The walls were polished stone. Tribesmen from Pashtun provinces had come to hear Qayum discuss the future of Afghanistan, now that he was running for president. Seated cross-legged at one end of the room, Qayum addressed the men in Pashto. There was just one big question in this late winter of the Karzai reign, which Qayum posed to the men as he started his talk: What would happen to Afghanistan after the American troops left?

One of the bearded men called out that if Afghan soldiers could get enough weapons, they'd be fine.

"I don't think this will help," Qayum told them. In the past, the Afghan army had been powerful, but civil strife had still torn it apart. "Until our leaders are able to compromise on major national issues, it is not possible for us to become powerful."

Qayum Karzai had positioned himself against his younger brother's record. With the election coming up in 2014, and President Karzai's term soon to expire, speculation in Kabul was running wild about who would take over for the man everyone had become so accustomed to seeing in the palace. There were people willing to bet vast sums that President Karzai would finagle the rules, change the constitution, and install himself as leader for life and self-proclaimed father of the nation. Others were convinced that he'd just rubber-stamp one of his brothers as successor and start a Karzai dynasty. But from early on in Qayum's campaign, Hamid offered no help. "From day one he was against his brother," one of President Karzai's ministers told me. "He never supported him." Qayum had already told me how strongly he disliked his brother's politics, particularly his fisticuffs with the United States. Qayum felt the United States should not be judged on grievances alone; the sacrifices should also be acknowledged. He couldn't understand why his brother wasn't signing the security agreement. Hamid knew Afghanistan needed the United States, Qayum believed, so why was he being so stubborn? The one Karzai he disagreed with most was the president. "Families are not like marbles," he said. "We don't all roll the same way."

Qayum saw himself as a wise, thoughtful listener, comfortable in both Afghanistan and the West, knowledgeable about Afghan history, attuned to the traditions of negotiation and compromise. "When Hamid Karzai was facing a problem, he would always ask Qayum's advice," Shahzada Massoud, who'd known the family since their exile days, told me.

Most of Qayum's adult life had been spent in the United States. He'd made frequent visits to Afghanistan during the past decade—and even won a seat in parliament—but most of his time was devoted to running his restaurants in Baltimore. He was one of the city's prominent restaurateurs. Besides the Helmand, he and his wife had opened a Spanish tapas spot, Tapas Teatro, and a French restaurant called B Bistro. He ran the Fig Leaf Farm to supply organic produce to his restaurants. In Kandahar, he'd built up his business interests as well, although in a more discreet way than Mahmood. He owned the Hewad radio station and a television station of the same name, which had both received advertising paid by the U.S. government over the years. For the U.S. military commanders in Kandahar, he was a source of counsel on Afghan history and customs and how to handle tribal affairs without provoking outrage or violence. The role he preferred was that of a quiet, behind-the-scenes adviser. Whereas his brother in the palace was a hotheaded political improviser, he was the sober, rational, business-minded Karzai. In a time of war, he appealed for civility. "Are we going to support a Popalzai, a Tajik, a Pashtun? Or are we going there like someone preparing to pray to God, with all honesty, with a clean mind, with a mind that I am voting for the benefit of my family, village, district, province, and for the whole country?" he said at a campaign event. "If this is not the condition, then our votes will be lost and it will change nothing."

His discretion became a liability to his candidacy. Qayum was not well known, and his time abroad had made him unfamiliar to many Afghans. He was a rather dull campaigner and didn't have the charisma or following of his other brothers. His time as a parliament member—he'd been elected in 2005 to represent Kandahar—had been cut short after three years because of health troubles and sporadic attendance. Some of his critics questioned his Islamic credentials by pointing out that you could order pork and alcohol in his restaurants in Baltimore.

Qayum admitted that he wasn't a good politician. There were other men running for president who offered more moderate views than President Karzai, and they were more famous. The most prominent candidates—Ashraf Ghani, the former finance minister, and Abdullah Abdullah, the former foreign minister—planned to run independently. Even within his family, Qayum wasn't a very popular candidate. Ahmed Wali, before he died, had told an American general that Qayum was "too old" to run. (He was now sixty-six.) President Karzai led people to believe he preferred his foreign minister, Zalmai Rassoul.

The war had driven the Karzais apart in lots of ways—in their businesses and relationships, in their politics. The siblings disagreed on the conduct of American troops, on how to negotiate with the Taliban, on how to manage the nation's economy and their personal finances. Mahmood, always brash and outspoken, seemed to revel in slamming the president. He felt Hamid knew nothing about economics and failed to foster the private sector. Mahmood claimed he had no relationship with Hamid anymore. "We're not even talking right now," he told me. "I don't care about him anymore. He's a typical Middle Eastern politician."

He felt Hamid had thrown up ridiculous and unnecessary obstacles for the economy. Mahmood had given Hamid a book about the Yoshida doctrine, named for Japan's post–World War II prime minister Shigeru Yoshida, who prized economic development over military spending. But he felt the president created no incentives for the private sector. He could not understand President Karzai's decision in 2010 to add Thursday, as a government day off, to the Muslim holiday of Friday, creating a mid-week weekend out of whack with the other countries of the region and the West. He felt there needed to be higher tariffs on Pakistani goods to help the competitiveness of Afghan businesses. He believed it was "outrageous" and a "suicide mission" that President Karzai had made overtures to China to replace the United States as its main benefactor. Mahmood told the Afghan station Tolo News that he regretted having supported his brother's second-term campaign. "The guy's a dictator. He's a son of a bitch. For forty-nine years he's done nothing for this country," he told me. "To change our country, we don't have to reinvent the wheel. We can copy Dubai. We can copy Singapore. This is capitalism. I started something with four million dollars. Now everyone is making money. Under the Taliban, this was a hell on earth. Our women were treated like animals. I wanted a South Korea. He wanted another Pakistan."

Qayum's family back in Baltimore were wary about him running for president and taking on all the risks it entailed. His wife, Patricia, had lived with Qayum's relatives in Baltimore for long stretches over the years. She had grown particularly fond of his father, Abdul Ahad, who had doted on his grandchildren. She had picked up enough Pashto over the years to communicate and always tried to be respectful of Afghan customs. "My family would say, 'Why do you always wear long-sleeve blouses, this is our country? And why don't you have bacon in the refrigerator? Why do you do this?' I would just say, 'Because I honor him so much, and what he's had to give up in life.'" She had adored Hamid as a younger man, but that wore away over years of listening to him lambast America and ignore the sacrifices of the soldiers. "It's very hurtful," she said. "I know there have been a lot of innocent Afghans that have been killed, but when you know how many American soldiers have lost their lives, their limbs, their livelihoods, everything, for Afghanistan. And for him to . . ." She trailed off. "I think he has to be more mindful of what he says and how he says it. I know he means to direct it at the government, but unfortunately, if I had a brother or a son or a daughter who had lost a life or limbs there, I would take it personally. Just because I know him as being such a kind and gentle person . . . I almost wonder if what he's saying [are] really his words."

In her more than forty years of marriage, she had never visited Afghanistan. If her husband became president, she would be the first lady of a country she had never seen. It was a job she didn't want. She felt her family had already lost too much for Afghanistan. "I wasn't willing to make another sacrifice. We had sacrificed forty-some years of our lives for this."

Qayum had trouble raising money. President Karzai discouraged him from running and told others not to support him. The conversations between the brothers were civil, Qayum said, but Hamid thought that any fraud or wrongdoing in the election would be blamed on him. Others believed that jealousy was part of the issue, that he felt that another Karzai in the palace might diminish his legacy. The modern history of Afghanistan had no precedent for a peaceful transfer of power. Kings and presidents most often left office dead or deposed. President Karzai wanted to have the distinction of furthering Afghan democracy. "The worst thing that could take place would be for me to stay in office," Karzai had told Ambassador Ryan Crocker. "No, that's not the worst thing. The worst thing would be for one of my brothers to become president."

A month before the election, Qayum announced that he was pulling out of the race.

Election day dawned cold and drizzly in Kabul. In the weeks prior to the April 5 vote, a grim anxiety had gripped the capital. The Taliban were setting off bombs nearly every day, targeting Afghan officials and places frequented by foreigners. Insurgents attacked the election commission headquarters and the American charity Roots of Peace and shot up the restaurant inside the Serena Hotel. The city had a bunkered, shut-in feel. Restaurants and universities and businesses had closed, and the main roads into the city had been blocked off. Afghan police were stopping and searching cars all over the city. Election observers had fled the violence. Expats had moved away. The coalition had spent less than half as much money to organize the 2014 election as it had the previous time. The U.S. military—with far fewer troops present, and those no longer engaged in daily combat—had drifted into the background. Afghans, as they stepped out onto the desolate, rain-slicked streets and headed toward schools and mosques to cast their ballots, were far more on their own.

And yet, at the polling sites, these citizens who had lived through decades of war spoke of their hopes for peace, better schools, more jobs. Using a side entrance reserved for female voters, Zakia Raoufi, a forty-five-year-old housewife, cast her ballot at the same school where her son had graduated three years earlier, and which Hamid Karzai had attended years before that. After she had woken up, washed, and prayed, she'd said good-bye to her children and left the house for the first time in three days, a period during which she had worried about the near daily violence. "I was wondering whether I will come back home alive or not," she said. Her son had studied computer science and learned English at Habibia High School, but the family had no connections among the government elite and no money to pay bribes for employment, so he had moved to Iran and was now working as a tailor. "So this election means a lot to me," she said. "What I'm hoping for from the next president is someone to stop the bloodshed in this country, to provide us peace and stability and education and opportunities for our children."

Before the vote, polling had suggested a tight race. Karzai's inner circle had continued pushing Zalmai Rassoul, the French-educated physician and former national security adviser and foreign minister. But Abdullah Abdullah and Ashraf Ghani had been attracting large crowds at their rallies.

Early on the morning of the election, Rahmatullah, one of the bodyguards for Kabul's mayor, received a call from his brother-in-law in the central province of Sar-e-Pol. "He said, 'We have been threatened by the Taliban not to go out and vote.' I said, 'Don't worry about the Taliban, just go vote.'" Rahmatullah had proudly dipped his index finger in the blue ink at Lycée Esteqlal and had his voting card punched with a crescent moon. "Our hope is for peace and stability, for job opportunities, and to provide shelter for the homeless people," he said. "We are here to decide about the future of Afghanistan."

Ahmad Shah Hakimi, a forty-three-year-old official in the Commerce Ministry who also did business as a currency trader, was tired of working for a corrupt government. "We just want change, and we want to elect our own president," he said. "I voted in the last election, but the government turned out to be corrupted, and people are really tired of that." Qureshia Sirat Ahmadi, an eighteen-year-old high school student voting in her first election, recited verses from the Koran in her head to calm her worries as she drove to the polling station. "The enemies of Afghanistan always wants to disturb these national days, but that doesn't mean we shouldn't come and vote," she told me.

Over the past two presidential elections, voter turnout had fallen as the insurgency had gained strength. In 2009, after more than a million fraudulent votes were thrown out, election observers calculated that about 4.5 million people had voted, out of more than fifteen million registered, about half as many who had gone to the polls in 2004. By the end of Saturday's voting, with long lines of voters huddled under plastic sheeting in the rain, it began to look like turnout might have rebounded. There were estimates that six or seven million people had voted. On the night of the election, Qayum called President Karzai to congratulate him. Turnout had been far stronger than expected; the sporadic violence did not appear to have disrupted the voting. "What Truman said, 'The buck stops here.' That credit belongs to him. That the election process was so smooth," Qayum told me. The president was gracious and told Qayum that he had also performed a service to the country by agreeing to drop out of the race. It was a proud day for a lot of people. "I don't think I have, in the last thirteen years, I have not felt so satisfied, that, my goodness, things have worked so well in this one day, that might alter the destiny of Afghanistan for good," Qayum said. "It will just demoralize the armed thing, it will deliver a totally different message to the neighbors, that if this nation is so resilient, that we might as well take some different route."

Within three weeks of the election, half of the votes had been counted.

They showed that Abdullah Abdullah had a lead of more than ten points over Ashraf Ghani, but at 44 percent of the vote, he still had fallen below the 50 percent threshold that would enable him to avoid a runoff. The counting was going slowly. Ballot boxes in remote districts had to be transported along poor roads through dangerous terrain. The fraud that had eviscerated the previous election, however, seemed to be less acute. Abdullah Abdullah remained confident of his chances. Even though he claimed a mixed ethnicity—his stepfather was Pashtun, his mother Tajik—the prospect that a candidate so strongly associated with the Northern Alliance and minority Tajiks could preside over a country ruled for most of its history by Pashtuns looked as if it could become reality. The final first-round tally had Abdullah winning 45 percent of the seven million votes, followed by Ghani with 31.5 percent. Nearly all the leading Pashtun presidential candidates from the first round had lined up behind Abdullah. "The story is over—the others are 14 percent or 13.5 percent behind," Abdullah said. The runoff would be held that summer.

President Karzai's dream throughout his presidency was to find a peaceful resolution to the conflict with the Taliban. He mentioned that goal when he was sworn in for his second term, and he pursued the prospect of peace talks until he left the palace. The record of those efforts has not been written; most of it took place in the shadow worlds where spies and militants intersected. When the outreach surfaced publicly, it was normally when something went disastrously wrong. There was the "fake Mullah Mansour" episode in the fall of 2010, when a shopkeeper from Quetta purporting to be the senior Taliban leader was escorted to the palace by British intelligence and got an audience with Karzai. There was the Taliban peace emissary who came to Kabul to meet former president Burhanuddin Rabbani the next year and blew himself up during the meeting. President Karzai had dispatched Qayum on exploratory talks with the Taliban in Saudi Arabia in 2008 that hit dead ends. Ahmed Wali had also reached out to Popalzai leaders within the Taliban at various times, to little effect. In 2012, the Taliban even opened an office in Doha, Qatar, after years of behind-the-scenes work by American and German intelligence agents that many hoped was a prelude to peace talks. But that effort failed, too, because Karzai felt left out of the loop. The fact that the Taliban office had embassy-like accoutrements, with nameplates—"The Islamic Emirate of Afghanistan"—and flags flying, enraged Karzai.

"He conceived of this as an American plot, that we were colluding with Pakistan and others," U.S. Ambassador James Cunningham told me.

The Taliban had vowed that their war against the Afghan government would go on indefinitely if Karzai's administration signed any long-term agreement with the United States or troops remained in the country. Part of Karzai's distancing from America over the years always had an aspect of catering to public opinion, and the Taliban were an important part of the Afghan public. American officials believed that Karzai's provocations toward the United States were partly aimed at winning favor among insurgent leaders. Most of the American troops were leaving Afghanistan regardless of what he agreed to, and he'd become more interested in tending to the wounds of his own countrymen. "I know I have many flaws," Karzai once said. "But I do know my people."

In November 2013, standing before thousands at the *loya jirga* he'd convened for his people's decision about the future with America, Karzai balked. He decided that even if they voted for the deal, which they overwhelmingly did, he would not sign it until after the elections.

The decision shocked even his closest aides. They had spent months going over endless drafts, parsing each word. The document was littered with concessions to Karzai; you could hardly go a paragraph without finding a phrase like "with full respect for Afghan sovereignty" or "noting that the United States does not seek permanent military facilities." The United States had agreed that its troops would not enter Afghan homes except under extraordinary circumstances. They would not arrest or imprison Afghans or run prisons of any kind. There were provisions that the United States would not store chemical, biological, or nuclear weapons on the bases that Afghanistan would allow them to use in the future. The Afghans had ultimately agreed to grant U.S. troops immunity from prosecution in their country. Karzai's decision to suddenly disregard all that work and those hard-fought negotiations for the sake of some personal whim infuriated even his most loyal colleagues. Many of them had grown to loathe his capriciousness. He seemed to have become a president without any overarching vision for his country save inclusiveness for Afghans and exclusion for foreigners, a man whose energies were devoted to outfoxing his enemies. "He was a master tactician," Javed Ludin, a former chief of staff, recalled. "He would think of all scenarios, all possible moves, but he could never prepare for anything beyond a few weeks."

When asked about Karzai's greatest weakness, one cabinet minister pointed to this trait. "He was a man who was changing his mind," he said. "He was telling us he would do something, and he was not doing it. He was telling us he was consulting everybody, but at the end of the day, at the last moment, he just did what he wanted to do."

The surprise reversal meant further headaches for the Americans involved. Karzai busted the one-year timetable they'd agreed to the year prior, and the move was interpreted as his sweaty grasp at a final few months of power. By not signing the agreement, he would be a leader who would have to be reckoned with until the very end, rather than a lame duck. The palace secretly had another round of contacts going with the Taliban, with meetings in Dubai and Riyadh, and Karzai was also hoping for a breakthrough. He was releasing dozens of Taliban prisoners, to great consternation, and striking a posture about as openly hostile to America as he'd ever been.

"We want the Americans to respect our sovereignty and laws and be an honest partner," Karzai told the crowd at the *jirga*. "And bring a lot of money," he added, to laughter.

In late February 2014, after Karzai insisted that he would not sign the security agreement, President Obama talked to him over the phone. The two leaders hadn't spoken in more than seven months, and Obama had essentially washed his hands of Karzai. Obama told him that the Pentagon had begun planning for the complete withdrawal of U.S. and coalition troops by the end of the year. It was known as the "zero option." And without the troops, the warning went, there would be no money for Afghanistan. NATO secretary-general Anders Fogh Rasmussen said so plainly at a conference in Brussels: "If there is no agreement, there will be no NATO troops in Afghanistan after 2014."

But these kinds of ultimatums had failed repeatedly with Karzai. One reason they had was that the United States wouldn't follow through on its threats. Karzai knew that the Americans didn't want to withdraw all of their troops and watch the Taliban flood back into cities they had fought for years to defend. Just as they weren't prepared to cut off aid over the corruption cases, they wouldn't risk throwing everything away at the end if they could possibly avoid it.

Karzai felt that his successor, whoever that might be, should be responsible for making any pact with the United States, because he would have to live with the consequences of that decision. In speeches, he had likened the bilateral security agreement to the 1879 Treaty of Gandamak, where Afghans ceded their foreign policy to the British administration in India.

There were historical mistakes that he, too, didn't want to repeat. He insisted he would sign it only once there was peace in Afghanistan.

Karzai felt that his brinksmanship gave him leverage over the United States in the final months of his presidency, his aides recalled, but by that time there was no relationship left to manipulate.

"That was kind of the final turn of the wheel," Cunningham said.

President Karzai had remained silent during the vote-counting process, which added to suspicions. Some Afghan politicians believed he wanted the election to be a deadlock, giving him an opportunity to seize power and rule indefinitely. His aides said he was worried about Abdullah's lead and the prospect that a Tajik president could inflame the Pashtun-led insurgency. The first-round results were dramatically reversed by the runoff. Preliminary totals showed that Ghani had charged ahead, a swing of 1.9 million votes in his favor. But more disturbingly, turnout estimates were so high that many observers couldn't believe them. Abdullah, who had not challenged the first-round numbers, now screamed massive fraud. He vowed not to accept the results and demanded that all vote counting be stopped. There were soon audio recordings of election officials allegedly conspiring against him, the whole ugly replay of 2009 reemerging. Street demonstrations by both camps had become a daily occurrence. Abdullah threatened to form a Northern Alliance breakaway government based in Mazar-e-Sharif.

Nearly thirteen years after the U.S. military overthrew the Taliban, America's always fragile project appeared to be breaking under its own weight. Abdullah's followers were discussing plans to seize government buildings in at least three provinces, and potentially march on the presidential palace. The loyalty of the Afghan security forces, whose leadership was heavily represented by Tajiks, was being called into question. With both candidates declaring themselves the winner, and threats of a parallel government, they were staring at civil war. Hamid Karzai's government had been willing to forgive pretty much any sin to avoid this very scenario.

President Obama called Abdullah just after sunrise on Tuesday, July 8, to warn him not to consider seizing power and to wait until the administration's anointed crisis manager, Secretary of State Kerry, flew to Kabul. "The reason we intervened so rapidly was to urge them to stop even thinking about going down that road, which, I agree, would have been a disaster for the country," U.S. Ambassador James Cunningham told reporters in Kabul. After two days of negotiations inside the U.S. embassy and the palace, Kerry brokered an agreement in which all eight million votes would be audited. The election had failed. But they could still pick up the pieces and avoid civil war. In his talks with Abdullah's camp, Kerry had given an impassioned discourse on the sacrifices laid down for the sake of the Afghan government. As he implored the candidate's supporters not to abandon the process, he spoke of his time in Vietnam, of the soldiers who'd died in Afghanistan, of his own personal experience as a failed candidate. American officials had also warned that if the candidates resorted to violence or sought to operate outside the constitution, it would result in the end of American assistance to Afghanistan.

At the end of the second day, Abdullah and Ghani hugged in Ambassador Cunningham's living room, sealing their agreement. At the press conference afterward, flanked by Ghani and Abdullah, Kerry looked worn out. "This is unquestionably a tense and difficult moment," Mr. Kerry said, "but I am very pleased that the two candidates who stand here with me today and President Karzai have stepped up and shown a significant commitment to compromise."

One of the most important agreements they had come to, but had not admitted at the time, was to change the very structure of the government, weakening the presidential powers that had been bestowed on Karzai during his years in office and gradually establishing a quasi–prime minister position to share the authority with the president. The loser after the recount would be appointed as chief executive, with unspecified powers, followed in a couple of years by a constitutional change to a parliamentary system with a prime minister leading the government while the president remained head of state, a structure Abdullah and his fellow Northern Alliance leaders had long advocated for.

The audit itself, taking place in two roasting Kabul warehouses, overseen by teams of American and European advisers, involved counting the contents of twenty-two thousand ballot boxes, and quickly fell behind schedule and dragged on through the summer. Fights broke out at least three times inside the warehouses; people were hospitalized with scissor wounds. The agreement that the candidates had hugged upon almost fell apart several times, and Karzai was accused of plotting a coup to keep power.

It was not until Saturday night, September 20, 2014, five months after the vote, after dozens of calls from and meetings with Obama, Kerry, Cunningham, and other top American officials, that the candidates agreed that Ghani had won the election and there would be a power-sharing agreement giving Abdullah a position with authorities akin to those of a prime minister. At the last minute, Abdullah said he would agree to this only if the results of the audit were not made public, because he felt they were so marred by fraud that they should stay secret forever. Nine days later, Ashraf Ghani, with Abdullah sharing the stage as his chief executive officer, was inaugurated as the new president of Afghanistan.

A friend of mine, when I mentioned that I was starting this book, told me the worst part was that I would have to spend so much time with the Karzais. They could be slippery, greedy, histrionic, and vain. I also found them to be thoroughly alive to their times, in thrall to their moment in history. They gave everything to their work, whether building desert cities or waging political wars. They weren't the type for vacations. And making enemies, it seems, is not the worst fate.

I felt President Karzai was the most misjudged of all. He genuinely cared about his people and wanted them to stop getting killed. The war might have been exhausting, infuriating, and disillusioning, but it somehow didn't harden him. He wasn't a despot, or vengeful, or cruel. His government built him a $5 million mansion next to the palace so he could retire in luxury, but he gave it up for a house that was plainer, even though he had three children by the time he finished his presidency. He could take credit for balancing Afghan ethnic factions and perhaps preventing them from reverting to civil war. Millions of Afghans returned home during his government; millions of children, girls among them, enrolled in schools. His great political skill was compromise, and he used it to hold an improbable government together. He stood up to America and for his own people. He put the brakes on something that could have spiraled much further out of control. He didn't win the war or make peace with the Taliban. But when he left, there was still a democracy.

If you talk to the Americans who spent the most time with Karzai, who fought him the hardest, there's a surprising amount of respect. They remember his personal gestures, his private condolence calls when something happened in their families, long after they'd left Afghanistan. "I don't think there was a better choice than Karzai," Ambassador Ryan Crocker said at the end. "I didn't think so then, I don't think so now."

Captain Jason Amerine, the Special Forces commander who accompanied Karzai on the mission to liberate Afghanistan, would almost be in tears a dozen years later discussing the man he knew. He would always consider Karzai a friend—a good, idealistic man whose vision was for consensus, a *loya jirga*, and a new democratic government. "You're talking about a man who from the very start thought the U.S. was going to abandon him. We talked about that. I said, 'I can't control that, but as long as I'm on the ground I'll give you everything I've got. My life lies with my men to fight with you. That's all I can control.' He knew that. But he always assumed we'd abandon him. That was clear," Amerine said. "You see somebody just fighting for his life over there. And everybody would be defining it as if it's just him trying to maintain his power. And that was never him."

By the end of Karzai's last year in power, the U.S. Congress had appropriated more money for Afghanistan's rebuilding than America spent on sixteen European nations after World War II. In Karzai's farewell speech, he didn't mention that or America's two thousand dead. He praised minor players like India for their support. The man who began the war as arguably the most pro American Muslim leader in the world ended it with this message to the United States: thanks for nothing. "Americans did not want peace in Afghanistan," Karzai said, "because it had its own agendas and goals here." U.S. Ambassador James Cunningham's response to that was: "It makes me kind of sad." Karzai had concluded that the American presence wasn't leading the country toward peace, although he offered no other strategy to get closer. In some ways, getting pushed out of Afghanistan might be the most valuable gift Karzai could have given the United States.

Afghan politics is about men sitting around telling one another stories. There is always an enemy in them, and the bigger the enemy, the greater the tale. Karzai's successor would sign the security pact the day after being sworn in to office. But Karzai, if nothing else a patriot, could always say that he hadn't been the one to lash Afghanistan's future to the United States. That he wouldn't accept years more of the Americans' money and be forced to swallow their advice. He could tell himself the story of how Hamid Karzai became the man who finally refused.

Acknowledgments

I am indebted to the hundreds of Afghans, from President Karzai and his family to those in more humble circumstances, who shared with me their stories during a time of great upheaval in their country. I am also thankful for the time that dozens of American soldiers and diplomats devoted to explaining their tumultuous tours in Afghanistan.

Thank you to my bosses at *The Washington Post*, in particular the foreign editors David Hoffman and Douglas Jehl, who set me off on these assignments and then gave me time to turn the experience into a book. My colleagues on the Afghanistan beat—Kevin Sieff, Rajiv Chandrasekaran, Griff Witte, Karin Brulliard, Greg Miller, David Nakamura, Greg Jaffe, Karen DeYoung, Craig Whitlock, Ernesto Londoño, Pamela Constable—were my models and inspiration. The *Post*'s generous support, through the Graham and, now, Bezos eras, has been essential.

Many thanks to my agent, Rafe Sagalyn, who helped shape the book's contours and then supported it to completion. And to Jonathan Segal at Knopf, whose wisdom and insightful editing transformed an unwieldy accumulation of reporting into an actual book. Jonathan Hillman, Darya Razavi, Christina Marin, and Julie Tate helped with much-needed research along the way.

I am grateful to the Shorenstein Center on Media, Politics and Public Policy at Harvard University as well as to Woodrow Wilson International Center for Scholars in Washington, D.C. Both of those institutions generously provided financial support and a stimulating environment in which to work.

Many people in Kabul, in particular those who shared the yellow house on Street 4 in Taimany over the years, blessed me with a warm away-from-home family. Special thanks to Tamim Samee and Aryn Baker, Timur Nusratty, Victoria Longo, Asma Nassery, and John Schroder for showing me around; Lucy Martens, Golareh Kiazand, Scott Shadian, Sarah-Jean Cunningham, Amandine Roche, and Lorenzo Tugnoli for their friendship; and to Matt Rosenberg, Rich Oppel, Azam Ahmed, Maria Abi-Habib, John Dempsey, and Luke Mogelson for camaraderie throughout.

I'm especially grateful for the Afghan colleagues Javed Hamdard and Asad Haidari, who worked alongside me the longest and offered bravery, wisdom, and good humor throughout. And thanks to Habib Zahori, for his brilliant company and generous assistance.

For their unconditional hospitality, I'm indebted to friends Isham Randolph and Olivia Ellis, David Fleisher and Neilah Meyers, Macon and Emily Phillips, Michael Scherer and Yari Lorenzo, Keith Paxton and Susie Gim, and Amit Paley.

Above all, thanks to my parents, Marianne and Kenneth Partlow, and my sister, Liza, for their support and encouragement, and patience with me when I kept wandering off to faraway places. And finally to Mariana Courtney: thank you for your love and kindness as you welcomed me back to the new world.

Notes

1 A RESCUE FROM DEMONS

7 "a bleeding ulcer": Dion Nissenbaum, "General 'This Is a Bleeding Ulcer' Progress Lags as Troops Labor in Key Taliban Zone," *Houston Chronicle*, May 25, 2010, p. 8.

7 three thousand Taliban attacks: Ian S. Livingston and Michael O'Hanlon, "Afghanistan Index," *Brookings Institution*, January 10, 2014.

9 "demons": Rod Nordland, Alissa J. Rubin, and Matthew Rosenberg, "Gulf Widens Between U.S. and an Increasingly Hostile Karzai," *The New York Times*, March 18, 2012, p. 16.

2 ANY PATH WILL LEAD YOU THERE

10 nearly two per day: The August 2009 death toll for U.S. soldiers was fifty-one. Total ISAF coalition deaths for that month was seventy-seven. From the website icasualties.org.

10 "I won't say that things are all on the right track": Anand Gopal, "Afghanistan and Pakistan Take Center Stage in 2009," *The Christian Science Monitor*, January 2, 2009, p. 5.

11 "On all fronts": Rajiv Chandrasekaran, "Administration Is Keeping Ally at Arm's Length; Skepticism of Afghan Leader Shapes Policy," *The Washington Post*, May 6, 2009, p. 1.

12 forty thousand American troops: Information on U.S. troop levels in Iraq and Afghanistan by month can be found in this graphic from *The New York Times*: http://www.nytimes.com/interactive/2011/06/22/world/asia/american-forces-in-afghanistan-and-iraq.html.

12 "a crisis of confidence": Bob Woodward, "McChrystal: More Forces or 'Mission Failure'; Top U.S. Commander for Afghan War Calls Next 12 Months Decisive," *The Washington Post*, September 21, 2009, p. 1.

12 nearly six hundred attacks: Livingston and O'Hanlon, "Afghanistan Index," *Brookings Institution*, January 10, 2014.

13 four times Afghanistan's domestic revenue. "Islamic Republic of Afghanistan: Afghanistan National Development Strategy: First Annual Report (2008/09)," International Monetary Fund, country report 09/319, November 2009.

13 "The government and the public here have welcomed": U.S. Department of State cable, "Scenesetter for Visit of NSA to Afghanistan," June 21, 2009.

13 "not waste any more blood": Stanley McChrystal, *My Share of the Task* (New York: Portfolio, 2013), ePub file.

14 "I'm the Tom, Dick, and Harry": U.S. Department of State confidential cable, "Karzai Appeals to Boucher for Security in South," January 20, 2009.

16 a seven-foot-tall Afghan man: notes from *Washington Post* correspondent Kevin Sieff.

17 "I saved it": Joshua Partlow, "Karzai Faces Two Rivals in Debate; Answering Criticism of His Rule, President Says of Troubled Afghanistan: 'I Saved It,' " *The Washington Post*, August 17, 2009, p. 6.

17 "feel and resources of a sleepy": U.S. Department of State cable, "Inside Karzai Campaign Headquarters," May 10, 2009.

17 Two young Karzai nephews: U.S. Department of State cable, "Kandahar: A Snapshot of Elections Activity in an Active Province," June 22, 2009.

18 "We don't have any alternative": Joshua Partlow, " 'We Don't Have Any Alternative to Karzai'; Afghans' Low Expectations Ensure Incumbent Is Favorite in Presidential Race, Despite Poor Record," *The Washington Post*, August 19, 2009, p. 1.

19 "seriously underestimated Karzai's skill": U.S. Department of State confidential cable, "More Fractures in the United Front," March 10, 2009.

19 "As messy and convoluted": U.S. Department of State confidential cable, "IEC Publicly Reaffirms August 20 as Voting Day," March 4, 2009.

19 "We would like to know what their views are": Farah Stockman, "Amid Security Concerns, Foes of Karzai See Electoral Opening," *The Boston Globe*, June 23, 2009, p. 1.

20 "Excuses were made": Richard Holbrooke, "The Longest War," *The Washington Post*, March 31, 2008.

20 "Who would be the best": Kai Eide, *Power Struggle over Afghanistan: An Inside Look at What Went Wrong—and What We Can Do to Repair the Damage* (New York: Skyhorse, 2012), ePub file.

21 "had to go": Robert M. Gates, *Duty: Memoirs of a Secretary at War* (New York: Knopf, 2014), ePub file.

22 "We need to do everything we can": U.S. Department of State secret cable, "Afghan Elections: Challenging the Process to Deliver," June 17, 2009.

22 "using Islamic radicalism as an instrument of policy": U.S. Department of State confidential cable, "CODEL Reed's July 20 Discussions with Karzai," July 24, 2008.

22 "endemic corruption and widespread frustration": U.S. Department of State cable, "Scenesetter for Visit of Codel Biden to Afghanistan," February 19, 2008.

23 "You've already had meetings": U.S. Embassy Kabul Action Memorandum, "Meetings with Major Presidential Candidates," June 30, 2009.

23 "Karzai clearly expected": U.S. Department of State secret cable, "Karzai Dialogue on U.S.-Afghan Relations Continues," July 16, 2009.

24 "A general can lose a battle": U.S. Department of State confidential cable, "Nangarhar Governor Sherzai Ponders Presidential Run," January 6, 2009.

27 "We want very soon to stand on our own feet": Judy Shelton, "Results Oriented: More Aid? Sounds Great, but Wait . . ." *Wall Street Journal Europe*, February 18, 2002.

27 "sad black-and-white movie": U.S. Department of State cable, "Governors of Georgia, Kansas, and Mississippi Meet with President Karzai," December 14, 2005.

28 "no overt or covert": U.S. Department of State secret cable, "Karzai on the State of US-Afghan Relations," July 7, 2009.

32 $263 million: U.S. Department of State confidential cable, "GIROA Appears to Retreat on Electoral Reform," February 15, 2010.

33 "Massive, unbridled": Sandra Khadourhi, "A Review of Suspected Electoral Fraud: 2009 Afghan Presidential and Provincial Council Elections," *Democracy International*, April 2010.

34 In his domain, Karzai won: Matthew Aikins, "The Master of Spin Boldak," *Harper's Magazine*, December 2009.

34 "no reliable early returns": U.S. Department of State confidential cable, "Afghan Elections: Successful, Subdued Afghan-Led Day of Voting," August 20, 2009.

37 "rage": McChrystal, *My Share of the Task*.

40 "Afghanistan's elections have unfortunately been defamed": "Afghan President Seeks 'National Partnership' Government, or Coalition," BBC Monitoring South Asia—Political, supplied by BBC Worldwide Monitoring, October 20, 2009.

3 SO MUCH IN LOVE

42 salmon-pink house: Christina Lamb, *The Sewing Circles of Herat: A Personal Voyage Through Afghanistan* (New York: HarperCollins, 2002).

45 "charming, salon demeanor": Edward Girardet, *Killing the Cranes: A Reporter's Journey Through Three Decades of War in Afghanistan* (White River Junction, Vt.: Chelsea Green, 2011), p. 116.

45 "born diplomat": Steve Coll, *Ghost Wars: The Secret History of the CIA, Afghanistan, and bin Laden, from the Soviet Invasion to September 10, 2001* (New York: Penguin, 2004), ePub file.

45 "Hamid Karzai represented for me": Robert D. Kaplan, *Soldiers of God: With Islamic Warriors in Afghanistan and Pakistan* (New York: Vintage, 2008), ePub file.

46 "The Taliban are finished": Bette Dam, *A Man and a Motorcycle: How Hamid Karzai Came to Power* (Utrecht, Netherlands: Ipso Facto, 2014), ePub file.

47 five Black Hawk helicopters: Eric Blehm, *The Only Thing Worth Dying For: How Eleven Green Berets Forged a New Afghanistan* (New York: HarperCollins, 2010), ePub file.

49 "original sin": Mary Sack and Cyrus Samii, "An Interview with Lakhdar Brahimi," *Journal of International Affairs*, Fall 2004.

49 "dissolve their administration": James F. Dobbins, *After the Taliban: Nation-Building in Afghanistan* (Washington, D.C.: Potomac, 2008), ePub file.

49 "Someone else would like to talk": Dam, *A Man and a Motorcycle.*

50 "This meeting is a path towards salvation": Gary Berntsen and Ralph Pezzullo, *Jawbreaker: The Attack on bin Laden and al-Qaeda: A Personal Account by the CIA's Key Field Commander* (New York: Crown, 2005) ePub file.

52 "Nothing in his appearance": Dobbins, *After the Taliban.*

53 American B-52 Stratofortress bomber: Blehm, *The Only Thing Worth Dying For.*

53 "Congratulations, sir": Ibid.

53 Hamid Karzai pulled up to the palace: Berntsen, *Jawbreaker.*

54 bare radiator: Jon Lee Anderson, "The Man in the Palace," *The New Yorker,* June 6, 2005.

54 Fahim may well have been in the room: Coll, *Ghost Wars.*

54 "I saw that the roof was not there": Anderson, "The Man in the Palace."

55 The only guards: Berntsen, *Jawbreaker.*

56 "Until the time that": Mir Munshi Sultan Mahomed Khan, ed. *The Life of Abdur Rahman, Amir of Afghanistan* (London: John Murray, 1900), p. 223.

56 "There is no doubt": Ibid., p. 167.

57 Peacock Room: Lamb, *The Sewing Circles of Herat*, p. 239.

58 Rubbermaid plastic tubs: Berntsen, *Jawbreaker.*

58 "We basically need billions": Liz Sly, "New Afghan Leader Vows Unity, Peace; Afghan Leader Gets Task of Reuniting War-Torn Nation," *Chicago Tribune,* December 23, 2001, p. 3.

58 camouflage clothes and sandals: Lamb, *The Sewing Circles of Herat*, p. 236.

59 "Pictures of Ronald Reagan": Dobbins, *After the Taliban.*

59 ambitious infrastructure projects: David Rohde, "Afghan Symbol for Change Becomes a Symbol of Failure," *The New York Times,* September 5, 2006, p. 1.

59 "is not a civilian police force": Condoleezza Rice, "Campaign 2000: Promoting the National Interest," *Foreign Affairs,* January–February 2000.

60 "deft diplomatic and political touch": Joshua Partlow, "Podium Wars: President Hamid Karzai, the Foreign Press, and the Afghan War," Joan Shorenstein Center on the Press, Politics and Public Policy, Discussion Paper Series, No. D-76, January 2013.

62 "I will cut you in pieces": Chris Alexander, *The Long Way Back: Afghanistan's Quest for Peace* (New York: HarperCollins, 2011), ePub file.

65 "I had not heard that sound": Peter Tomsen, *The Wars of Afghanistan: Messianic Terrorism, Tribal Conflicts, and the Failures of Great Powers* (New York: PublicAffairs, 2011), ePub file.

65 An eighteen-year-old shopkeeper: Mujib Mashal, "After Karzai," *The Atlantic,* June 23, 2014.

66 "The stability of the Afghan Transitional Government": Henry J. Hyde and Tom Lantos letter to Secretary of State Colin L. Powell and Secretary of Defense Donald H. Rumsfeld, September 12, 2002.

4 JUMP-STARTING A COUNTRY

71 "dark cave that stretches": Phyllis C. Richman, "Turning Tables," *The Washington Post,* December 17, 1978, p. SM35.

71 "The culinary emphasis": Ibid.

78 supplicants in envelopes: Peter Maass, "Gul Agha Gets His Province Back," *The New York Times Magazine,* January 6, 2002.

79 "our country was devastated": Letter from Kandahar governor Gul Agha Sherzai to the Kandahar District Court, Correspondence No. 341, December 17, 2002.

80 "Four of the five sponsors": OPIC Small Business Center Finance Approval Memo, April 4, 2003.

81 "We have no data": Deborah Smith and Dan Horrigan, OPIC informational memorandum, "AFCO International/AFCO-Kandahar Valley," August 6, 2003.

5 BECAUSE WE SEE MORE, WE DO MORE

86 "Afghan government corruption": Sarah Chayes, *Thieves of State: Why Corruption Threatens Global Security* (New York: Norton, 2015), ePub file.

89 broken tree branch: Interview with Kirk Meyer from the Combating Terrorism Archive Project, April 2, 2014. Interview can be found at: https://global ecco.org/kirk-meyer-former-director-of-the-afghan-threat-finance-cell

91 "these arrests show a significant step": U.S. Department of State secret cable, "High Level Corruption Arrests Conducted by GIROA Major Crimes Task Force," October 27, 2009.

91 "New Ansari *hawala* network": U.S. Department of State secret cable, "Follow-up Request—Resourcing Efforts to Dismantle the New Ansari Hawala Network and Other Illicit Financing Threats," October 18, 2009.

94 involving Ahmed Wali Karzai: Tom Bowman, "Karzai's Brother Tied to Corrupt Afghan Land Deals," National Public Radio, February 1, 2010.

95 "known for being corrupt": U.S. Department of State secret cable, "Cabinet Rumors—Ten Days Before Inauguration," November 10, 2009.

96 "Sadly, the government of Afghanistan": John F. Burns and Alan Cowell, "Patience on Corruption Is Running Out, Britain Warns Afghan President," *The New York Times,* November 7, 2009, p. 10.

100 "you would not believe": U.S. Department of State secret cable, "Afghan United Bank CEO Stresses His Humanitarian Activities," February 6, 2010.

101 "These are powerful people": U.S. Department of State confidential cable, "Atmar Under Pressure for New Ansari Hawala Case," February 15, 2010.

103 an account of his arrest: Yaroslav Trofimov, "Karzai, U.S. Clash Over Corruption in Afghanistan," *The Wall Street Journal,* August 5, 2010.

105 Usually, they chose to move: Untitled U.S. embassy internal memorandum from March 2011 on rule-of-law and counter-corruption efforts in Afghanistan.

106 The female Afghan prosecutor: Ibid.

6 GOVERNMENT IN A BOX

109 didn't even have a map: Sherard Cowper-Coles, *Cables from Kabul: The Inside Story of the West's Afghanistan Campaign* (New York: HarperCollins, 2012).

110 "Pakistan wants to rule a land": Alexander, *The Long Way Back.*

111 "using Islamic radicalism": U.S. Department of State confidential cable, "Codel Reed's July 20 Discussions with Karzai," July 24, 2008.

111 "If these people": Carlotta Gall, "Karzai Threatens to Send Soldiers into Pakistan to Fight Extremists," *The New York Times,* June 16, 2008, p. 6.

111 "meant every word": U.S. Department of State confidential cable, "Karzai Threatens Pakistan and Means It," June 16, 2008.

112 donating $50,000: Dam, *A Man and a Motorcycle*.

113 "Popalzai show": U.S. Department of State cable, "Governing Herat: Not an Easy Task for the Taliban," October 19, 1995.

113 "Taliban-designated UN rep": U.S. Department of State cable, "Afghanistan: Response to the Taliban Letter to the Secretary," December 10, 1996.

114 "little clarity": U.S. Department of State cable, "Afghanistan: Popalzai Leader Hamid Karzai Expresses Concern About Radical Islamists," January 14, 1997.

114 "on the move": U.S. Department of State cable, "Taliban Angry, Their Opponents Support US," August 21, 1998.

115 "I would go every week": Coll, *Ghost Wars*.

115 "Our economy is in ruins": Hamid Karzai, in *The Taliban: Engagement or Confrontation? Hearing Before the Committee on Foreign Relations*, United States Senate, 106th Cong., July 20, 2000.

116 "nothing undermined the legitimacy": Thomas Barfield, *Afghanistan: A Cultural and Political History* (Princeton, N.J.: Princeton University Press, 2010), ePub file.

117 "not an adequate strategic partner": U.S. Department of State cable, "COIN Strategy: Civilian Concerns," November 6, 2009.

120 green army dress uniform: McChrystal, *My Share of the Task*.

120 "What is it that we don't understand": Ibid.

121 forty-five minutes on the elliptical trainer: Mashal, "After Karzai," *The Atlantic*.

121 "prosperous but not wealthy": Ibid.

121 "graceless": Anderson, "The Man in the Palace."

121 floral print furniture: Ibid.

122 "We're a go": Rajiv Chandrasekaran, "U.S. Launches Afghan Surge; Troops Move on Taliban; Coalition Stages Largest Offensive Since 2001," *The Washington Post*, February 13, 2010, p. 1.

122 "Ever the agile tactician": U.S. Department of State confidential cable, "GIROA Appears to Retreat on Electoral Reform," February 15, 2010.

7 AN ORDINARY AFGHAN

125 "a head without a nose": Mir Munshi Sultan Mahomed Khan, ed., *The Life of Abdur Rahman Amir of Afghanistan*, p. 208.

125 "a kaleidoscope of competing tribal principalities": William Dalrymple, *Return of a King: The Battle for Afghanistan, 1839–42* (New York: Knopf, 2013), p. 25.

127 "The seventh bomb": Miles Amoore, "CIA Adds to Web of Riddles Over Killing of 'King of Kandahar,'" *The Sunday Times* (London), July 17, 2011.

128 "an ordinary Afghan": Joshua Partlow, "The Brother Karzai: Powerbroker with Grip on Kandahar Is Both an Ally and Obstacle to U.S. Strategy," *The Washington Post*, June 13, 2010.

131 Kandahar had 110 local water representatives: Interview in Kandahar with Engineer Sher Mohammed Attai, director of the Arghandab River Sub-Basin Authority, July 23, 2012.

135 education in wine: Alison Arnett, "A Taste for Adventure: Once, egg foo yong was the Boston diner's idea of exotic food. No more. Three restaurants illustrate the new upscale look of ethnic cuisine," *The Boston Globe*, July 6, 1997.

136 "gentle spokesmen": Margaret Sheridan, "Exotic Food from Afghanistan Has Found a Home in Chicago," *Chicago Tribune,* January 30, 1986.

136 pumpkin dish, *kaddo bourani*: Maria Cianci, "Humdrum Pumpkin Does a Cinderella Act," *The San Francisco Chronicle,* October 28, 1998.

136 "In capitalism, you invest": Arnett, "A Taste for Adventure," *The Boston Globe.*

139 "As the kingpin of Kandahar": U.S. Department of State confidential cable, "Kandahar Politics Complicates U.S. Objectives in Afghanistan," December 6, 2009.

140 "You can easily bribe": U.S. Department of State confidential cable, "Ahmed Wali Karzai and Governor Wesa on Governance in Kandahar," October 3, 2009.

143 "should use his authority to": U.S. Department of State secret cable, "Scenesetter II: US-Afghan Strategic Partnership Bilateral Meetings March 13–14," March 8, 2007.

143 "Both have well-known reputations": U.S. Department of State secret cable, "The Day After, Meetings with the Candidates," October 21, 2009.

143 "Given his suspected ties to narco-trafficking": U.S. Department of State cable, "Scenesetter for November 2–3 Visit to Washington of Canadian Ambassador to Afghanistan William R. Crosbie," October 29, 2009.

144 "are widely believed to profit": Carlotta Gall, "Afghan Poppy Growing Reaches Record Level, U.N. Says," *The New York Times,* November 19, 2004, p. 3.

145 "British hand": Notes of Afghan cabinet meeting from November 22, 2004.

145 "leads the whole trafficking structure": Ron Moreau and Sami Yousafzai, "A Harvest of Treachery: Afghanistan's Drug Trade Is Threatening the Stability of a Nation America Went to War to Stabilize. What Can Be Done?" *Newsweek,* January 9, 2006, p. 32.

145 "flailing": U.S. Department of State confidential cable, "Karzai Dissatisfied; Worried About *Newsweek*; Plans War Against Narcotics," January 10, 2006.

146 "One of the most symbolically important things": U.S. Department of State secret cable, "Scenesetter for President Karzai's Upcoming Visit to Washington," September 19, 2006.

149 "Nobody is that stupid": U.S. Department of State secret cable, "Ahmed Wali Karzai: Seeking to Define Himself as a U.S. Partner?," February 25, 2010.

8 SMASHING THE CHINA SHOP

152 "pre-eminent warrior-thinker": Dave Barno, "Major General Herbert Raymond McMaster," *Time,* April 23, 2014.

158 "to warn against hubris": McChrystal, *My Share of the Task.*

164 "enormously soft heart": Anderson, "The Man in the Palace."

164 "Afghan families tend": Hamid Karzai and Nick Mills, *Letter from Kabul* (Hoboken, N.J.: John Wiley & Sons, 2006), uncorrected proofs, p. 25.

165 six state-owned banks: Jelena Pavlovic and Joshua Charap, "Development of the Commercial Banking System in Afghanistan: Risks and Rewards," IMF Working Paper, July 2009.

165 "It soon became clear": Ake Lonnberg, "Building a Financial System in Afghanistan," International Monetary Fund, May 29, 2003.

168 "required to remain politically neutral": Memo from Central Bank governor

Abdul Qadir Fitrat, "Chief Executive Officers of Licensed Commercial Banks General Managers of Permitted Branches of Foreign Banks," January 4, 2009.

169 "collusion with drug smugglers": Afghan intelligence report from the chief of Department 74 of the National Directorate of Security, "Supervision and Financial Risk Management," October 20, 2009.

170 "want to remind you": Letter from Central Bank governor Abdul Qadir Fitrat to President Hamid Karzai, February 24, 2010.

171 "several opportunities to learn about fraudulent activities": "Review of USAID/Afghanistan's Bank Supervision Assistance Activities and the Kabul Bank Crisis," Report No. F-306-11-003-S, USAID Office of the Inspector General.

174 "a mere smoke screen": From findings of fact in the case Juan Carlos Yeh Gutierrez V. Helmand Boston, Inc., before the Labor Commissioner of the State of California, signed by hearing officer Thomas J. Nagle, August 1, 2000.

175 "I've asked him constantly": Application for state of charges from Robie Allen Thomas, District Court of Maryland, September 8, 2003.

175 "He grabbed me by my right arm": Ibid.

175 "At the beginning I was impressed": Mahmood Karzai's testimony in Baltimore City Circuit Court on September 23, 2007.

176 "a complete disaster": Ibid.

177 "clearly has great expectations for the AIC": U.S. Department of State cable, "Afghanistan Investment Company Closing In on First Project," February 20, 2006.

9   CLOSE COUSINS

183 "Each contender waited for an opportunity": Barfield, *Afghanistan: A Cultural and Political History.*

187 large Georgian cottage in Summer Hill: Hamid Karzai and Nick Mills, *Letter from Kabul* (Hoboken, N.J.: John Wiley & Sons, 2006), uncorrected proofs, p. 23.

187 "expressions such as 'turning turtle'": Lamb, *The Sewing Circles of Herat*, p. 42.

187 "there was a lovely cinema": William Dalrymple, "How Is Hamid Karzai Still Standing?" *The New York Times Magazine*, November 20, 2013.

187 "eat salad or boiled eggs": Roland Watson, "Restaurant View of New Leaders," *The Gazette* (Montreal, Quebec), December 8, 2001.

191 "high moral standards": Karzai and Mills, *Letter from Kabul*, p. 14.

191 "never really bonded": Dam, *A Man and a Motorcycle.*

194 spacious house downtown: Karzai and Mills, *Letter from Kabul*, p. 17.

195 "laid the foundation": Nick B. Mills, *Karzai: The Failing American Intervention and the Struggle for Afghanistan* (Hoboken, N.J.: John Wiley & Sons, 2007), ePub file.

195 "glowed in the evening": Rodric Braithwaite, *Afgantsy: The Russians in Afghanistan 1979–89* (New York: Oxford University Press, 2011), ePub file.

196 between twelve and fifteen thousand: U.S. Department of State confidential cable, "Meeting with Soviet Diplomat: Part III of III—Human Rights," June 25, 1979.

196 "3,000 political prisoners": Ibid.

196 "frequent use of electric shocks": "Afghanistan: Torture of Political Prisoners,"

Amnesty International (New York: Amnesty International Publications, 1986), p. 2.

199 "I suddenly realized": Kaplan, *Soldiers of God.*

10   WHO'S RUNNING THIS PLACE?

214 "lonely and alone man": U.S. Department of State confidential cable, "Negative Influence of Certain Karzai Advisors," March 2, 2009.

219 ten-minute break: Notes from Afghan cabinet meeting on April 21, 2003.

219 eight-hour Afghan government workday: Notes from Afghan cabinet meeting on March 25, 2002.

219 steering wheels: Notes from Afghan cabinet meeting on March 19, 2004.

220 age limit for mayors: Notes from Afghan cabinet meeting on January 20, 2003.

220 animal husbandry: Notes from Afghan cabinet meeting on September 30, 2003.

220 too few trees: Notes from Afghan cabinet meeting on November 29, 2004.

222 "diagnosed as a manic-depressive": Bob Woodward, *Obama's Wars* (New York: Simon & Schuster, 2010), ePub file.

225 "I would not kill an ant": Lamb, *The Sewing Circles of Herat,* p. 239.

225 carried a gun: Anderson, "The Man in the Palace."

228 "The sun cannot be hidden": Edward Zellem, *Zarbul Masalha: 151 Afghan Dari Proverbs* (Kabul: Karwan Press, 2011), ePub file.

228 "tremendous civilian casualties": Joshua Partlow and Habib Zahori, "65 Civilian Villagers Were Killed in U.S. Military Operation, Afghan Officials Say," *The Washington Post,* February 21, 2011.

229 "I have reviewed the footage": Joshua Partlow, "Karzai Aides Decry Petraeus Remarks," *The Washington Post,* February 22, 2011.

231 "With great honor and with great respect": Rod Nordland, "Afghan Leader Questions U.S. Military Operations," *The New York Times,* March 13, 2011.

232 "You do for me": Zellem, *Zarbul Masalha.*

11   WHERE EVERYONE GETS ACCUSED

235 He tried Citibank: Interview with Abdul Qadir Fitrat, April 19, 2013.

237 "Reports by certain media": "Reports on Collapsing of Kabul Bank Baseless: Central Bank Governor," Xinhua General News Service, September 1, 2010.

239 "respectfully would like to apprise you": Letter from Central Bank governor Abdul Qadir Fitrat to President Hamid Karzai, September 21, 2010.

240 "I'm not a dictator": Interview with Abdul Qadir Fitrat, April 19, 2013.

241 "the prevailing culture of impunity": Miloon Kothari, "Adequate Housing as a Component of the Right to an Adequate Standard of Living," Report by the Special Rapporteur, United Nations Mission to Afghanistan, August 31–September 13, 2003.

241 "This cabinet has lost its credibility": Notes from Afghan cabinet meeting on September 15, 2003.

243 forty-seven bedrooms: Karin Brulliard, "Garish 'Poppy Palaces' Lure Affluent Afghans," *The Washington Post,* June 6, 2010, p. 1.

244 "The problem is with foreign relatives": U.S. Department of State secret cable, "Karzai Looks Forward," December 3, 2009.

251 Members of the Afghan air force: Maria Abi-Habib, "Afghan Air Force Probed in Drug Running," *The Wall Street Journal*, March 10, 2012.

252 The Dawood National Military Hospital: Maria Abi-Habib, "Graft, Deadly Neglect Sting Afghan Military Hospital—Injured Soldiers Routinely Died of Simple Infections at U.S.-Funded Institution Amid Corruption Allegations," *The Wall Street Journal*, September 6, 2011.

252 Of the roughly 2,000 corruption cases: Adam Goldman and Heidi Vogt, "Afghanistan Obstructs Graft Probes," Associated Press, October 11, 2011.

253 After input from various agencies: Portions of the draft cable were read to and reviewed by the author.

12   COULDN'T BE MORE HELPFUL

256 "nobody brought us any evidence": "Afghan Leader Says US Visit Cements Washington-Kabul Ties," BBC Monitoring South Asia—Political, supplied by BBC Worldwide Monitoring, May 18, 2010.

261 "Afghanistan will be fixed": Joshua Partlow, "Karzai's Defiant Stance Concerns U.S., Afghan Officials; Some Colleagues Fear His Recent Remarks May Affect Funding, Support," *The Washington Post*, April 5, 2010, p. 6.

263 "I don't want to be piling up": Joshua Partlow, "In Southern Afghanistan, Even the Small Gains Get Noticed," *The Washington Post*, February 9, 2010.

264 spent nearly a decade: Aram Roston, "How the US Funds the Taliban," *The Nation*, November 11, 2009.

265 guarding thirty-five hundred U.S. supply trucks: figure from "Warlord, Inc.: Extortion and Corruption Along the U.S. Supply Chain in Afghanistan," a report by the Majority staff of the Subcomittee on National Security and Foreign Affairs of the Committee on Oversight and Government Reform of the U.S. House of Representatives, June 2010.

268 "What is the focus": Joshua Partlow, "Afghan Corruption Is the Enemy. Unless It Helps Us," *The Washington Post*, January 31, 2010.

272 $100 million worth of damage: "Troops Caused 100 Million Dollars' Damage: Afghan Officials," Agence France-Presse, January 11, 2011.

273 Loy Kandahar: Rajiv Chandrasekaran, *Little America: The War Within the War for Afghanistan* (New York: Knopf, 2012).

13   A MOVIE STORY

278 "At the Kakraka Clinic": From a September 12, 2002, memorandum for the commander in chief, United States Sepcial Operations Command. Subject: Investigation of Civilian Casualties, Oruzgan Province; Operation FULL THROTTLE, June 30, 2002, p. 58.

288 "What a motherfucker": Interview with a Karzai relative in attendance at the tribal gathering, October 17, 2014.

296 "very deep conspiracy": Jon Boone, "Claim of 'Deep Conspiracy' After US Troops Kill Afghan President's Cousin in Botched Raid: Karzai's Brother Fears ISAF Acted on False Information; 30-Year-Old Family Blood Feud at Centre of Allegation," *The Guardian*, March 11, 2011, p. 19.

15 THE FIVE FINGERS

312 "This morning, my younger brother": Joshua Partlow and Kevin Sieff, "Karzai Brother Killed by Gunman," *The Washington Post*, July 13, 2011, p. 1.

16 I HATE POLITICS

320 "an ostentatious Karzai property": U.S. Department of State confidential cable, "Kandahar Politics Complicate U.S. Objectives in Afghanistan," December 6, 2009.

17 EVERYBODY IN A CORNER

330 "Afghanistan is a country built on legends": Habib Zahori, "Tales of 'White Taliban' Sketch a New Legend," *At War* (*New York Times* blog), July 23, 2013.

333 "police had to fire back": Hamid Shalizi, "Four Killed in Anti-NATO Protests," Reuters, in the Montreal *Gazette*, August 6, 2011.

337 "under assault": U.S. Department of State confidential cable, "Iran and Former Soviet States Vie for Influence in Afghan Media," April 10, 2009.

338 "stubborn ideologue": U.S. Department of State confidential cable, "Pressing Afghans on VOA Medium-Wave Transmitting Station in Khost," October 27, 2009.

18 NOT RELIGION BUT HISTORY

341 riots erupted in several cities: Carlotta Gall, "Demonstration by Afghans Turns Violent," *The New York Times*, May 12, 2005.

342 "They killed a young boy": Laura King, "Karzai Denounces Alleged 'Kill Team'; Afghan President Says Photos of U.S. Soldiers Posing with Bodies of Civilians Should Stir Global Indignation," *Los Angeles Times*, March 31, 2011, p. 3.

342 "Let these jackals leave this country": Joshua Partlow, "With Sermons Often Decrying U.S., Afghan Clerics Wage Political Battle," *The Washington Post*, February 18, 2011.

343 "turning their guns": Alissa J. Rubin, "2 G.I.'s Killed Amid Protests Over Burning of Holy Book," *The New York Times*, February 24, 2012.

345 first found the study: Dion Nissenbaum, "The Afghan War: Report Sees Danger in Local Allies—Study Says Killings of Americans by Afghan Security Forces Represent a 'Systemic Threat' to the U.S. War Effort," *The Wall Street Journal*, June 17, 2011.

349 "My reasons for going to Afghanistan": Micah Garen, "Call Me Ehsaan," documentary movie, *The New York Times*, Op-Docs, March 23, 2012.

19 THE PRIMARY PURPOSE OF ITS EXISTENCE

353 "Sherkhan is not only unreliable": Letter from Mahmood Karzai to Drago Kos, March 24, 2013.

354 "It has come to my attention": Ibid.

355 The closest anyone would come to the truth: "Final Audit Report for Kabul Bank," Kroll, March 14, 2012.

356 $5.2 billion of international transfers: Kroll asset tracing report for Kabul Bank, November 22, 2012.

357 "a piece of puke": Matthew Rosenberg, "Audit Says Kabul Bank Began as 'Ponzi Scheme,'" *The New York Times*, November 27, 2012, p. 9.

358 In his decree: Hamid Karzai, Presidential Decree No. 281, April 4, 2012.

20 EVIL IN HEAVEN

362 "Enmity in Heaven": Abdul Bari Jahani, *Pand Aw Ebrat* (Lessons and Advice) (Kandahar: Alama Reshad Publishing Association, 2011), pp. 376–381. Translation of the poem by Habib Zahori.

370 "Just like all other Afghans": Amir Shah, "Suicide Bomber Kills Afghan President's Cousin," Associated Press Online, July 29, 2014.

21 THE ZERO OPTION

373 "troublesome ally in war": Gates, *Duty*.

379 "So this election means a lot": Joshua Partlow and Kevin Sieff, "Defying Taliban, Afghans Go to the Polls," *The Washington Post*, April 6, 2014.

381 "The story is over": Alissa J. Rubin, "Afghan Contenders Accept Results and Move On," *The New York Times*, May 16, 2014, p. 14.

383 "We want the Americans to respect our sovereignty": Azam Ahmed, "Karzai Says He'll Wait to Sign Security Pact with U.S. Until Next Year," *The New York Times*, November 22, 2013, p. 4.

383 "If there is no agreement": Helene Cooper, "Hard Talk Aside, Little Desire by the West to Leave Afghanistan," *The New York Times*, February 27, 2014, p. 10.

384 "The reason we intervened": Carlotta Gall and Matthew Rosenberg, "Anxious Moments for an Afghanistan on the Brink," *The New York Times*, July 15, 2014, p. 10.

Index

ILLUSTRATION CREDITS

A NOTE ABOUT THE AUTHOR

Joshua Partlow is a foreign correspondent for *The Washington Post*. Since 2006, he has covered the wars in Afghanistan and Iraq; he has also been the paper's bureau chief in Rio de Janeiro and Mexico City. His reporting from Afghanistan won an Overseas Press Club award. He is from Olympia, Washington, and lives in Mexico City.

A NOTE ON THE TYPE

This book was set in Janson, a typeface long thought to have been made by the Dutchman Anton Janson. However, it has been conclusively demonstrated that these types are actually the work of Nicholas Kis (1650–1702), a Hungarian, who most probably learned his trade from the master Dutch typefounder Dirk Voskens.

Composed by North Market Street Graphics,
Lancaster, Pennsylvania

Printed and bound by Berryville Graphics,
Berryville, Virginia

Designed by M. Kristen Bearse